Best Plants for New Mexico Gardens and Landscapes

Best Plants

FOR NEW MEXICO GARDENS AND LANDSCAPES

KEYED TO CITIES AND REGIONS
IN NEW MEXICO AND ADJACENT AREAS

Baker H. Morrow

University of New Mexico Press ❦ Albuquerque

LIBRARY OF CONGRESS
CATALOGING-IN-PUBLICATION DATA

Morrow, Baker H., 1946–
Best plants for New Mexico gardens and
landscapes : keyed to cities and regions /
Baker H. Morrow.

    p. cm.

Includes bibliographical references
and index.

ISBN 0-8263-1595-X

1. Plants, Ornamental—New Mexico.
2. Landscape gardening—New Mexico.
3. Plants, Ornamental—Southwest, New.
4. Landscape gardening—Southwest, New.
I. Title.

SB407.M875 1995
635.9'09789—dc20
95-4331
    CIP

All photographs by author unless otherwise noted.
Printed and bound in Hong Kong.

DISCLAIMER

Although great care has been taken to suggest good
plant selections for general locations throughout
New Mexico and in surrounding states, it is not
possible to present or consider such factors as
specific soil conditions, varying weathers, irrigation
availability, microclimates, the health or handling
of plant stock, individual planting approaches, or
maintenance once planting operations are complete.
Therefore, neither the author nor the publisher can
assume any responsibility whatsoever for the selection
or installation of any of the plant species described in
this book.

"GO AND SEEK ANOTHER PARADISE,
. . . A PROMISED LAND, ALL FLOWERS
AND BLESSINGS."
Joseph Conrad, *Tales of Unrest*

"FROM THESE TWO, ART AND NATURE,
IT IS FITTING, IF YOU RECALL HOW
Genesis BEGINS, FOR MEN TO MAKE
THEIR WAY, TO GAIN THEIR LIVING."
Dante, *The Inferno*
Allen Mandelbaum, translator

For JoAnn and Susan,
with much love

CONTENTS

SECTION THREE

SECTION FOUR

ACKNOWLEDGMENTS

I must thank one cheerful group of students after another who quizzed me endlessly about the nature of landscape plants in my landscape architecture classes at the University of New Mexico. Their impatience and my disgust with so many books concerned with "southwestern plants suitable for all states except New Mexico" have led to *Best Plants*.

Mr. David Johnson, Mr. Jon Childers, Mr. Dick Hobson, Ms. Shirley Staehlin, Ms. Roz Menton, and several other friends were most helpful in the early years of research for this book. They commented on the wide range of species to be found in many New Mexico towns, let me photograph and study the plants in their nurseries and parks, and allowed me to review the general lists of suitable species for New Mexico that they had drafted.

From the offices of Morrow and Company, Ltd., Landscape Architects, Ms. Elizabeth Reardon, my associate and an extraordinarily accomplished landscape architect, provided years of support and encouragement. Ms. Dolores Pizzola, Ms. Suzanne Mortier, Mr. Robert Torres, Ms. Kathy Esquivel, Ms. Elizabeth Calhoon, Mr. Randell Smith and Mr. Anthony Ulibarrí assisted with many parts of this long labor, and I am most grateful. But the writing of this book would never have come to an end without the steadfast help of Ms. Susan Lowell and Ms. Rosine Stodgell who struggled tirelessly with very long manuscript components and endless illustrations and made them all work together harmoniously.

Ms. Beth Hadas, the director of UNM Press, and Ms. Dana Asbury, my editor believed in this book from the first and waited most patiently for it to take shape. Ms. Emmy Ezzell and Ms. Sue Niewiarowski did their usual superb job of design. I owe them all a very large debt of gratitude.

My tolerant and wonderful friends, Mr. V. B. Price, Mr. Craig Sowers, and Mr. Ray Trujillo, provided encouragement and a lot of coffee through the years as *Best Plants* took shape. As always, I appreciate everything they do.

My wife, JoAnn Strathman, and my daughter, Susan Elizabeth Morrow, withstood a phenomenal number of plant tours and species counts with humor and enthusiasm. They allowed me time in my garret to work up an unruly stream of notes into some notion of order and sense. I will always appreciate their graciousness and their affection.

BHM
Albuquerque
February 1994

PREFACE

These are plants that I am very fond of, as they have helped to complete my landscape design schemes for over two decades. They are, for the most part, great popular favorites as well. I like them for their toughness, adaptability, and sturdy beauty in a difficult climate. I also admire their cheerfulness and their ability to grace our lives with shade, helpful protection from the wind, and an endless series of wonderful colors.

Although a careful study of the trees, shrubs, ground covers, and smaller plants used throughout the state turns up a number of species that seem to thrive everywhere, we must be cautious. New Mexico ranges in altitude from a bit over 3000 feet (915 m) near Carlsbad to just over 13,000 feet (3965 m) at Mount Wheeler near Taos. In precipitation, the range is from 7 inches (175 mm) a year in the White Sands to over 30 inches (750 mm) a year in the Sangre de Cristo Mountains. Soils in the state can be loose and gravelly, thick and hard with clay or lime, or dark and rich along moist river bottoms and in the plains counties. It's no wonder that each city or town and its surrounding area displays horticultural peculiarities. That is why each species described in the plant file section is followed by a note on where it grows best.

I have carefully selected a wide range of plants for everyday use in home, commercial, and public landscape plantings, but there are also numerous species that can be planted for special conditions. The top hundred-plus species for each location are listed, and these plants are tried and true: they'll grow quite well under local conditions. For more adventurous souls, I have also indicated a number of species that may not be common in a particular locale in New Mexico but that will nonetheless thrive with a little extra effort.

New Mexico is blessed with historic landscapes—old gardens, parks, plazas, streetscapes, and the like—that have contributed to the cultural development of their times. Where practical, I have listed local examples of these. They're usually found just out the door and down the block, and they're well worth a visit. Anyone interested in the historic plant favorites of New Mexico will also enjoy Chapter 4 in Section 1 of the book. It's quite possible under most circumstances to design a modern landscape made up of many of the authentic plants of New Mexico's past.

In addition, there is usually in each community a favorite garden or other landscape that has been well planned and well maintained and that is open to the public for a visit. I have tried to list these wherever they occur; they are frequently worth seeing because of their high plant quality, good design development, or the general effect they create with nearby buildings.

Native Southwestern and Rocky Mountain plants increase in popularity every year, and most gardens and larger landscapes throughout the state contain at least a few of these hardy and colorful trees, shrubs, and smaller plants. *Best Plants* includes a large number of these valuable plants and discusses their general availability, often the single limiting factor in their usefulness.

By and large, I haven't listed plants that are not consistently available for home, commercial, or public landscape use. Most of the trees and shrubs in the plant file can be had in a number of different sizes to fit most pocketbooks, and many of the ground covers, flowers, and vines can be found not only in a container of some sort but also as seed.

I have included a series of design tips in Section 2. It is not difficult to select trees, shrubs, and smaller plants that will handily satisfy most New Mexican landscape situations, and fundamental information on growth habits, general form and color, and interesting peculiarities is also listed for each plant.

With over 4400 native species and many hundreds of exotic species, New Mexico is surprisingly blessed with one of the largest and most diverse assortments of plant types to be found in any temperate climate. Pick one or several of these for use in your own garden or landscape; you'll be surprised, delighted, shaded, and perhaps even fed by the results for many years to come.

QUICK REFERENCE

HOW TO USE THIS BOOK

1. To find a *specific plant,* listed by type (such as deciduous tree, bulb, evergreen shrub, and so forth), turn to the *New Mexico Plant File.*

2. To find the plant recommendations for a *specific town* or *city,* turn to the *City and Town Plant Recommendations and Notes.*

3. To find the best plants for *special landscape situations,* turn to the *Tips for New Mexico Gardening and Landscaping* section.

4. To find out about *New Mexican planting conditions,* turn to Section One, *Background to Landscape Plantings for New Mexico, Southern Colorado, and El Paso.*

5. For the names of local and governmental organizations that can furnish *additional information and help* regarding plants, horticulture, and landscape design, see the *Appendices.*

6. To find *quick,* immediately useful *information on plant choices,* see the *Gist List* at the end of Section Two, *Tips for New Mexico Gardening and Landscaping.*

Section One

BACKGROUND TO LANDSCAPE PLANTINGS FOR NEW MEXICO, SOUTHERN COLORADO, AND EL PASO

THE NATURE OF THE NEW MEXICAN LANDSCAPE

Believe it or not, there are remnant palm jungles at the mouth of the Rio Grande in far southern Texas

Lower Sonoran grassland

A knowledge of exotic and native plants is critical in the design of modern landscapes of all kinds in New Mexico. Cultivated food plants of the Southwest, both Indian and European, have made a great imprint on human life throughout the West. But very little civilized life is possible without ornamental plants. Their friendly, useful, and often colorful forms have graced human habitations and helped to create highly practical outdoor space since villages began to appear at the end of the last Ice Age.

Many if not most of the native plants of New Mexico are not unique to the state. In the larger view, they form part of the flora of the Rocky Mountains, the Great Plains, the Mexican deserts and cordilleras, and the Colorado Plateau. They are simply segments of a great continuous (and sometimes discontinuous) pattern that enters the state from all directions. Some of our trees, such as the aspen and the bigtooth maple, have continental ranges. Others, such as the ponderosa pine and white fir, show our strong connections with the Rockies and the Mexican Sierra Madre.

New Mexico's buffalo, grama, and wheat grasses are found throughout the central continental plains. Particularly tough and durable, they historically have been able to withstand the constant grazing of the bison and the gnawing of the smaller prairie mammals and have in many instances adapted well to the endless munching and trampling of domestic livestock.

The lyrically beautiful oak woodlands of the southwestern New Mexico foothills are visible reminders of the state's proximity to Old Mexico. In the canyons and swales of

Lower Sonoran zone

this sun-swept ranching and mining country, cottonwoods, soapberries, ashes, hackberries, and the stark, giant Arizona sycamores mark the slow fall of the land to the Pacific Basin. The hills here are now harder pressed than they were before the coming of men with cattle. In Arizona, Sonora, Chihuahua, and elsewhere in New Mexico, the story is much the same: cows and people and sometimes sheep working hard—sometimes too hard— to wring a living out of a rolling, dry, reluctant, and now legendary landscape.

The uplands of the Colorado Plateau are scrub juniper and piñon country, with a mixture of unusually sparse brush and intermittent grasses. On the high ridges and in the isolated mountain ranges of the plateau, ponderosa pines and Gambel oak, skunkbush, greasewood, and tall stands of narrowleaf cottonwood lend their character and color to the landscape.

Transition zone

Canadian zone

The dry lowlands in the southern part of the state constitute the northernmost extension of the Chihuahuan Desert. Mesquite, creosote, broom baccharis, and littleleaf sumac are found here in tremendous stands, with tough desert grasses in isolated pockets scattered among them. The desert willow and screwbean—and sometimes the ash—are the classic arroyo trees in this desert. Along permanent streams and near springs, various willows and hulking mountain and valley cottonwoods (*Populus fremontii* varieties) add a great deal of welcome green life to the tawny desert hills.

In the Rockies and their offshoot ranges, evergreens predominate. Ponderosa and limber pines, Douglas fir, white fir, and Engelmann spruce are the standards of these relatively wet mountains. Aspens, maples, New Mexico locust, box elder, serviceberry, chokecherry, elderberry, and a host of other appealing trees, shrubs, and lesser plants make these true forests rich in concentrated plant life.

All in all, it's a most attractive mixture of natural conditions and plants. But this diversity raises a few nettlesome questions about the nature of a good *designed* landscape in New Mexico.

First, the native plants of the Southwestern mountains have not naturally occurred in the lowlands for thousands of years, since the last Ice Age. Though very appealing in their natural habitat, they often do not adapt well to city life on the plains or along the river valleys. The soils may be too thin, the drainage too poor, or the air too dry. The reverse is also true. Plants now adapted to the hot deserts and plains, or to low valleys, generally do not thrive in the higher, wetter, cooler mountains.

To complicate matters, many plant species in New Mexico, whether in the lowlands or the highlands, are found only along watercourses. These riverine or riparian species are genuine water-guzzlers, even though they are as thoroughly native to the Southwest as are the drought-resisting ocotillos, junipers, piñons, and prickly pears of the hillsides. Some species grow only on north-facing canyon slopes; others thrive in sunny south- or west-facing locales.

These complications point to one good generalization about the native plant communities of the New Mexico countryside: Most landscapes in New Mexico are *transitional* in nature—mountain into desert, arroyo into river, plain into foothill, forest into mesa. The native landscape seems always to be on the verge of changing into something else—whatever is just around the corner.

The same is true of the *cultivated* landscape developed by the people of New Mexico over the past thousand years. An ancient Indian influence (an Anasazi plaza or terrace, a Mimbres irrigation sluice) can combine almost effortlessly in a backyard or along a storefront with a Spanish patio or Mexican *plazuela* of the last three and a half centuries. An Anglo-American picket fence can surround a green lawn that features as its pride and joy a classic Mexican *glorieta*, or gazebo. New Mexico's gardens and other man-made landscapes always seem eager to reflect the long, rich history of the state. More often than not, they, too, have an appealing quality of transition. The capacity for change and integration seems to be built into them as strongly as it is built into the state itself. They add a great deal to the character of modern New Mexico.

New Mexico's best plants, then, can be natives, exotics, or naturalized selections—outside species that came in with settlers, later escaped, and have done well on their own. We need not be too troubled by questions of origin. What should concern us is whether we have chosen the right plant for the situation—the best plant to produce shade, block the wind, provide a little winter greenery, add color, or hold the soil in place.

The right plant also should be available with little or no trouble. It should not be too susceptible to disease or insects. It should do well in our unconsolidated, young, often thin soils. It should gulp little sips of water wherever possible. And, more frequently than not, it should not take a lot of maintenance.

Add up all these qualities and you will find the best plant for a New Mexican garden or landscape.

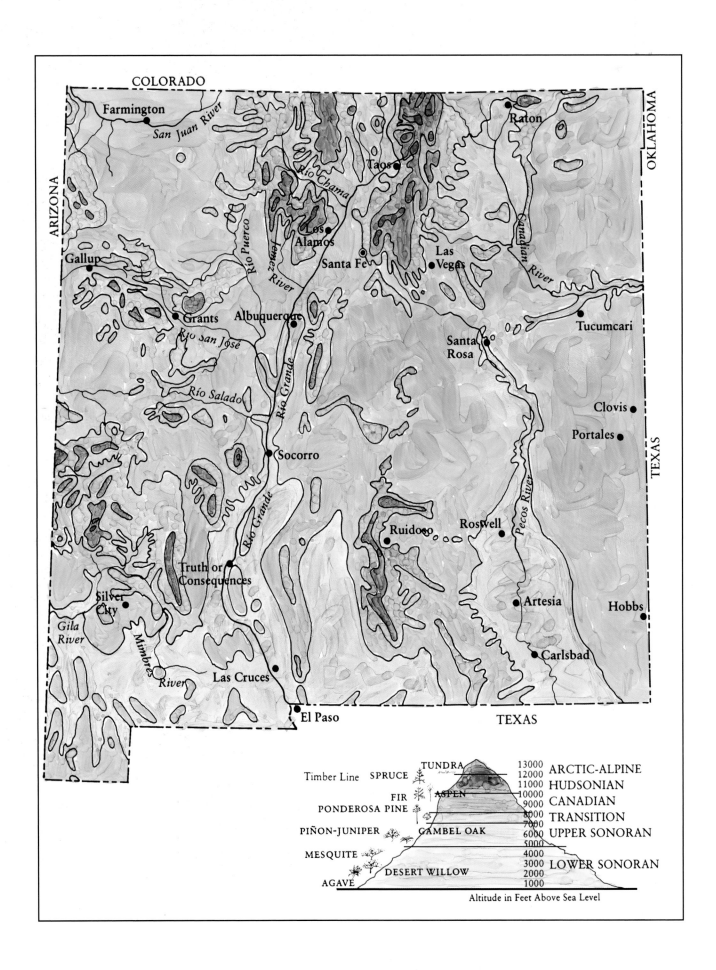

COLORADO

ARIZONA

OKLAHOMA

TEXAS

TEXAS

Farmington
San Juan River
Raton
Taos
Rio Chama
Rio Puerco
Los Alamos
Jemez River
Las Vegas
Santa Fe
Canadian River
Gallup
Grants
Albuquerque
Rio San José
Tucumcari
Santa Rosa
Rio Salado
Río Grande
Clovis
Portales
Socorro
Pecos River
Ruidoso
Roswell
Truth or Consequences
Silver City
Gila River
Artesia
Hobbs
Mimbres River
Carlsbad
Las Cruces
El Paso

TUNDRA — 13000 — ARCTIC-ALPINE
Timber Line SPRUCE — 12000 — 11000 — HUDSONIAN
FIR ASPEN — 10000 — CANADIAN
PONDEROSA PINE — 9000 — 8000 — TRANSITION — 7000
PIÑON-JUNIPER GAMBEL OAK — 6000 — 5000 — UPPER SONORAN
MESQUITE — 4000 — 3000 — LOWER SONORAN
DESERT WILLOW — 2000
AGAVE — 1000

Altitude in Feet Above Sea Level

Lower Sonoran zone

Upper Sonoran zone

LIFE ZONES

C. A. Merriam conducted a ground-breaking study of typical Southwestern plant distribution in 1889 on the slopes of the San Francisco Peaks near Flagstaff, Arizona. He devised a listing of six basic life zones of native vegetation that corresponded well to northern and southern exposure and to altitude in Arizona and New Mexico. From lowest to highest, these included the Lower Sonoran, Upper Sonoran, Transition, Canadian, Hudsonian, and Arctic-Alpine zones.

Merriam found that typical trees, shrubs, and ground covers would tend to occur together in predictable patterns given certain geographical conditions. A simplified version of his premises follows:

1. The lowest-altitude life zones (Lower Sonoran, Upper Sonoran) cover the largest areas. Each successive life zone occupies a smaller geographical area.

2. Southwestern life zones are tied to altitude and are related to latitude. A trip of 1000 feet (305 m) up a mountainside is equal to a trip north of several hundred miles.

3. Life zones in mountainous terrain are much like the fingers of two folded hands, with one hand held higher than the other. They extend up and down canyons, valleys, and hillsides because of northern or southern exposure, soil conditions, water availability, and related geographic factors.

4. Typical overstory (tree), understory (shrub, small tree), and ground-cover plant species occur in all life zones but the Lower Sonoran. In the Lower Sonoran zone, this sequence is found only at streamside locations.

5. Riparian (water's edge) vegetation is almost always the exception, not the rule, in all zones.

Merriam's work has been overtaken in the twentieth century by much more precise systems of soil, plant, and animal classification. Yet his essential life zone classifications remain very useful in grasping the essence of a botanically complex region.

Hudsonian and Arctic Alpine zones

Canadian zone

Transition zone

A FEW ESSENTIAL CULTIVATION REQUIREMENTS

Human societies in the Americas have been cultivating plants for many thousands of years, so it would be logical to assume that most plant-rearing practices would be more or less standard by now. After all, the Anasazi built a very successful (and spectacular) civilization in the Southwest on the basis of a few well-cultivated species—corn, amaranth, several kinds of squash, beans, and cotton. Their neighbors, the Hohokam of modern-day Arizona, were masters of constructed irrigation works, which they used for centuries to supply their well-planned fields. And the Europeans brought their time-tested, centuries-old agricultural practices and tools with them when they came to the New World.

However, there continue to be many competing schools of thought when it comes to preparing the soil for virtually any kind of ornamental planting.

In agriculture, there is very little quibbling about soil preparation: A farmer traditionally will modify his soil as extensively as his budget allows to ensure a good crop. Traditional gardening practices also make good use of compost, manure, and local mulches to ensure success with ornamental plantings. However, many ornamental species that are planted in thin Southwestern soils will live but never thrive. Their growth may be stunted and their appearance anemic. Where lawns are planted, many will soon be chlorotic or awash in weeds.

Agricultural chemicals, largely derived from petroleum, have helped to make it possible in the twentieth century to feed many billions of people. These same chemicals, when used in ornamental landscapes, often will give quick results in terms of growth, flowers, seeds, and fruit. Their essential flaw is that they do nothing to build topsoil; worse, they cause hard lenses to form in lower soil horizons that prevent water and air from getting down where they should be, and they sometimes contaminate water supplies.

In New Mexican landscapes, the soils are frequently typical of deserts: young, generally unconsolidated, and still in the process of very slow formation. Because they are developing under dry conditions, they often contain very little organic material and are alkaline, or basic, as a result. Their pH rating may be high.

Disking recycled organic amendments such as manure or bark into the soil can control erosion and create a very healthy planting base

Topsoil develops over a period of centuries in New Mexico (below)

They may not fit classifications based on soil studies made in wetter climates. They will support native plants, exotic plants (those that come from outside the region), and naturalized plants (exotic species that now thrive on their own in the Southwest) with varying degrees of success.

The thoughtful gardener or landscaper will want to promote the health of his or her plant stock by considering the nature and health of the soil first.

SOIL BUILDING

You can only improve the quality of the soil in relatively small areas. A garden, an office landscape, or a city park can benefit from soil amendments. Animal manures, sawdust, bark, pecan hulls, leaves, shredded newspapers, and compost can be mixed in, preferably to a depth of 1 foot (300 mm) or more, where they will be broken down by soil bacteria, fungi, and other microorganisms. This process will help to create a healthy topsoil, and most landscape plantings will thrive in it.

However, in areas larger than a few acres, soil building can become very expensive indeed. At this scale, green manure may be the best answer. A cover crop such as winter wheat can be planted. Once it matures, it is disked into the soil to help make the area better suited for ornamental or other landscape use.

However you improve the soil for landscape planting, remember that soil building is an ongoing process. It's a good idea to add a half-inch or so of manure to tree and shrub planters, vegetable gardens, flower beds, and lawns every year to contribute to the long-term health of the soil and the landscape.

RECYCLING

Construction of new buildings in Southwestern cities or towns invariably means destruction of local soils. Topsoil is often stripped away and wasted, and subsoils are compacted severely by heavy construction equipment. Construction debris can be scattered about the building site or even buried in new planting areas. Worse, many existing

Disturbed soils next to new construction can benefit from the application of organic amendments to restore their productivity. Compare the intact natural landscape to the right

plants are destroyed by construction. Their ability to allow water and air to infiltrate the local soil and produce oxygen for humans and animals is squandered.

To make up for this loss, it is a very good idea to recycle local human wastes (sewage sludge) and animal wastes (manures and other food processing by-products) by using them to build soil in city landscapes. These materials are quite rich in nitrogen, phosphorus, potassium, carbon, and other minerals that contribute to healthy soils. Their addition to local subsoils or unconsolidated soils allows the development of useful topsoil *in situ*.

Topsoil is anything but "just dirt." It is an active, changing, living community of microorganisms, mineral particles, air, and water that makes it possible for plants protruding from its surface to thrive. It prospers on waste products. Plants will flourish in newly constituted manmade soils, furnishing oxygen, shade, excellent air (smog) filtration, and general amenity for many generations to come. Improved soil tilth and fertility also contribute to an improved environment for many animal species, so new generations of animals struggling to adjust to life with humans have a better chance to survive.

At the residential level, homeowners can easily recycle leaves, newspapers, clippings, and wet kitchen garbage through composting to build topsoil and relieve increasing demand for landfill space.

WATER IN THE SOIL

The addition of substantial amendments to a planting site also improves the water-retaining characteristics of the soil. Even shredded newspaper (a material so thoroughly processed for its primary use that it has almost forgotten it is organic) mixed in with the soil decomposes with moisture into an excellent soil builder. It holds water exceptionally well.

Many Southwestern soils are sandy (sand particles are the largest of all soil particles), and water drains quickly away from plant roots. Clay soils often contain substantial quantities of lime, or caliche, and their very tight structure (clay particles are the smallest soil particles) keeps water from draining

away from plant roots and cramps growth. Silty soils have a structure that is in between those of sandy and clay soils.

Most landscape plants grow best in loam —a genuine topsoil containing a base of about 50 percent sand, 25 percent clay, and 25 percent silt, with as much decomposing plant and animal debris as possible. Loam allows both excellent water penetration *and* excellent retention, as well as good uptake of soil minerals by plant roots.

The essential alkalinity or acidity of a soil is measured by the pH (hydrogen ion) scale. When organics (recycled local wastes) are added to soil, its pH will go down, and consequently its fertility will go up. In most cases, the amount of water necessary to keep the landscape in good condition will also decrease as organics are mixed in.

WATER DEEPLY

When you water, water slowly and deeply. Deep watering washes harmful salts far into the ground and away from plant roots. It also encourages many plant species to root more deeply, thus providing for improved health.

Without decent soil preparation, water does not soak in—it runs off the surface of the planting area and is very often wasted. Thorough incorporation of plant amendments will help to prevent this problem.

WATER AT NIGHT

If you're sprinkling lawns, it pays to water when the air is most still—perhaps after midnight. Wind drift can draw off much of the water tossed into the air by sprinklers and deposit it in the street or gutter. Even a "sharp" breeze of 5 mph can blow airborne moisture completely away from your plants.

Another advantage of watering at night is that very few people will be bothered by it. During the day, people use landscapes for all kinds of activities, and they'll be annoyed if you get them, their dogs, or their cars wet. Water pressure is often better at night, too, because the demand for water decreases as people retire.

Conventional irrigation at work near a Spanish Pueblo Revival house

The grounds of older landscapes, such as Old Town Plaza Park in Las Vegas, often have well-developed, healthy "pocket" topsoils that hold water adequately and support long-term plant growth

Although many gardeners and landscape professionals worry about plant diseases induced by nighttime watering, these very rarely seem to be a problem in the arid Southwest.

THE NATURE OF IRRIGATION

In the wild, plants naturally grow with each other in communities or associations. Each species has an eco-niche to fill, growing as an integral part of the overstory (trees, or large shrubs in the desert), the understory (shrubs or smaller trees), or the ground cover (grasses, flowers, vines, and similar species). No wild plant grows out of context.

In virtually any man-made landscape, however, species are forced to grow out of context, in an artificial situation—even when native species are grown in a "native" landscape. No tree ever evolved in an asphalt parking lot, and no flower ever began its existence as a species in a windowbox. *All* plants in cultivated landscapes need a bit of extra care to flourish.

After good soil preparation, irrigation is the foremost priority. First the soil should be mulched in planter areas with shredded bark, compost, pecan hulls, manure, cottonseed hulls, or (in limited areas) crushed rock to hold in any moisture that is applied. Then the landscape area should be irrigated regularly.

Conventional irrigation (bubblers, spray heads, rotaries, impacts, and the like) is a good choice for commercial or public landscapes, where tender loving care may not be the rule. Anyone can observe the sprinkler or bubbler heads in action with this sort of system and make adjustments if something isn't working correctly.

Drip or subsurface irrigation is a good bet in smaller landscapes (especially home gardens) in which the owner is out on the grounds every day and can keep a close eye on the emitters. These are the "spaghetti tube" microspray heads that concentrate water only around the base of a plant. They tend to clog from the hard water of the Southwest and may begin to malfunction. Repairs are easy, but plugged lines must be replaced quickly. A section of drip emitters will usually operate for many hours to deliver the proper supply of water to the plants in a landscape, but none of it will run off and weed growth between plants will be kept to a minimum. Furthermore, only a third or so of the water that would be used for the same purpose by a conventional irrigation system will be required by the drip system.

Conventional irrigation is necessary for both traditional bluegrass mixtures and native grass lawns. Since bluegrass, fescue, rye, and Bermuda need comparatively heavy watering and mowing, these grasses seem to be slowly heading out of style in the Southwest. In the future, traditional green lawns will probably become the exception rather than the rule. They seem to work best in small, private spaces or in athletic fields. Elsewhere, buffalo grass, blue grama, and even galleta are taking their place. These grasses are now widely available, use much less water than traditional species, have good color and pleasant texture, and tolerate thin topsoils. Unfortunately, they often "green up" later than bluegrass and the other exotics, sometimes take years to establish, and cannot withstand a great deal of foot traffic. So, with the fundamental shift in lawn types and sizes there comes a distinct difference in usefulness.

Both conventional and drip irrigation systems should be equipped with automatic controllers. These regulate water flow exactly and also time water application nearly perfectly. They are excellent water-saving devices.

Good irrigation systems provide the "edge" or insurance that a new landscape needs to flourish in the Southwest. Whether installed casually or formally executed, landscape improvements represent a considerable investment to cities, businesspeople, and homeowners. A well-thought-out irrigation system simply protects the investment and helps turn even a modest garden into a formidable oxygen and air conditioning machine—something that is good for all of us.

NATIVE PLANTS

Mountaintop native species often do not flourish in New Mexico's cities and towns, which frequently are located in foothills, on benches above rivers, or alongside streams or springs. Likewise, many Lower Sonoran (desert) natives do not thrive in higher-elevation gardens and landscapes. Plants from the far south do not feel at home in the far north, and northern species dislike many hot southern locales. Species from the eastern New Mexico plains may not flourish on the Colorado Plateau, and Mexican woodland (cordilleran) plants from southwestern New Mexico are not necessarily adapted to the Rocky Mountain environment of Taos or Raton. In short, it is well to remember that a place as geographically varied as New Mexico has many differing kinds of "natives."

That said, the fact remains that anyone wanting to plan a native landscape will have a lot of company. More growers and sellers than ever before are offering regional species for sale, and native plant and garden clubs are filled with enthusiasts eager to share their knowledge of local plants with each other and with newcomers to the Southwest. Here are a few useful guidelines to keep in mind regarding gardening with regional species:

1. The modern fascination with native plants is healthy. It signals a growing acceptance by the public of the local landscape, topography, climate, and flora.
2. The best native landscape is simply an intensification of wild plants and natural features, that have been left intact on a site during construction. It is not a re-creation of an ideal "wild" landscape brought into being on a site that has already been destroyed.
3. Patience is a virtue. Many native species take time to germinate and develop. They may come into their own only after several seasons. Other natives are only available as tiny specimens. But the natives are generally hardy and gratifyingly forgiving of poor soils, planting mistakes, and lapses in care. Many seem to flourish with a small to medium level of attention.

4. Desert soils tend to degenerate under cultivation, and a disturbing amount of compaction may occur in subsurface soil horizons if organic matter declines in the top ("A") soil horizon. Scratch in a little manure before you plant and add more as the years go by. Let leaf litter accumulate. But don't disturb the soil any more than necessary.
5. Be prepared to explain your plants to the neighbors and to visitors. They may not be used to the look of the natives and often will wonder when you're going to replace the "weeds" with a real landscape. You may wish to point out the very real beauty and quality of your plants.
6. Expect to water the natives from time to time throughout their lives. It won't kill you. No cultivated landscape, including one planted in local species, can thrive without care—especially in the generally appalling planting conditions of the Southwestern city. Pick up the papers and wind debris, do a little pruning, fertilize with a bit of aged manure from time to time. A "natural" landscape is not a carefree landscape. It will need your attention.
7. Mix native with exotic species to create new landscape effects. Or create "regional" and exotic areas within your overall landscape.

Many natives and other trees and shrubs are sold in plastic or metal containers. One-, two-, five-, seven-, and fifteen-gallon sizes are very common (top left)

Some native trees and shrubs may be "heeled in" in sawdust or bark over the winter (bottom left)

8. Don't expect low-maintenance, small-scale landscape design approaches to work particularly well at the scale of the large park or commercial center. Large-scale, purely native plantings require a great deal of specialized maintenance and considerable time to establish. Landscape contractors and maintenance firms are developing and refining their plant-care approaches as the native plant industry grows and more species become available. However, it is still difficult to keep up a native landscape of many acres in size without mowing it or plucking it. And there are exotics that just plain do better at some jobs: football is never going to be played on fields of sideoats grama, no matter how much we may like this beautiful species.

9. Many New Mexico towns (as well as El Paso) have sprung up in areas that have no natural trees and even relatively few shrubs. Local trees from nearby mountain ranges are strangers (exotics, if you will) in these areas and should be given as much care as their exotic cousins when first transplanted.

10. Use only seed, cuttings, or field-grown native stock to create your landscape. Do not buy or install collected plants unless they come from reliable sources and have been replaced with equal or greater quantities of the same species in the same place they were dug.

11. Plant in layers: Tall, medium, and small plant species can all help each other to grow. Don't leave bare, disturbed ground unplanted or unmulched; it will surely blow or wash away.

12. Native species, carefully arranged, will give your landscape a powerful sense of place. Both owner and visitor will know that they're somewhere in the Southwest.

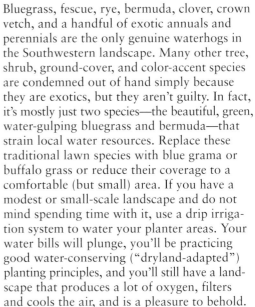

Bluegrass, fescue, rye, bermuda, clover, crown vetch, and a handful of exotic annuals and perennials are the only genuine waterhogs in the Southwestern landscape. Many other tree, shrub, ground-cover, and color-accent species are condemned out of hand simply because they are exotics, but they aren't guilty. In fact, it's mostly just two species—the beautiful, green, water-gulping bluegrass and bermuda—that strain local water resources. Replace these traditional lawn species with blue grama or buffalo grass or reduce their coverage to a comfortable (but small) area. If you have a modest or small-scale landscape and do not mind spending time with it, use a drip irrigation system to water your planter areas. Your water bills will plunge, you'll be practicing good water-conserving ("dryland-adapted") planting principles, and you'll still have a landscape that produces a lot of oxygen, filters and cools the air, and is a pleasure to behold.

TOPOGRAPHY DETERMINES

New Mexico's topography has a profound influence on the landscapes of the state. As you prepare to install a landscape or garden of any scale, here are a few unusual design conditions to keep in mind.

HIGH ELEVATION

Ultraviolet radiation can stymie plant growth, particularly in young plants, and it intensifies as altitude increases. Shade-loving and ground-cover species are particularly vulnerable. Enriched soil and extra water as plants are established can help.

ARIDITY

In this quite dry climate, never count on the weather to bring the water your plants may need. Aridity also means very low levels of soil organics. New Mexicans have been irrigating their gardens for well over a thousand years. Modern technology can irrigate gardens and landscapes extremely well with only a fraction of the water that would have been necessary just a few years ago.

Winds, high elevation, and aridity often combine to produce the distinctive ground-hugging native plant palette of New Mexico's countryside

SPRING WINDS

These are invariably southwesterlies, and they come along just in time to pull all the late-winter moisture out of the top layers of soil. They work with the warmth of the sun and capillary action to rob plants of the water they need just as the spring growth cycle begins.

The solution? Good, thick mulches (3 to 4 inches) that will not blow away and adequate moisture supplied to your plants (especially the youngest plants) so that they can resist the tremendous drying effects of the wind.

Spring winds frequently bring dust as well. Perhaps more comprehensive and thoughtful grazing and plowing policies throughout the state will reduce the wind's ability to lift soil off the range and carry it away.

WINTERBURN AND DIURNAL VARIATION

Vertical cracks on the south and west sides of tree trunks can cause serious injury or death to young plants. This condition is called "winterburn," and it is created when the sap in a tree begins to rise during warm winter days. As the temperature plummets at night, the sap freezes, expands, and ruptures the tree's trunk tissue.

Winterburn most often occurs in very young exotic tree specimens. Wrapping a tree's trunk with tree-wrapping tape from the ground to the first or second branch seems to help, though many people believe otherwise.

Diurnal variation refers to the great fluctuation of temperature (sometimes over 50 degrees F) that can occur at high altitudes in a 24-hour period. It is amplified by New Mexico's powerful continental climate; there are no moderating large bodies of water in the Southwest to keep air temperatures from changing quickly. In addition to causing winterburn, diurnal variation frequently ruins the flowering and subsequent fruiting of apple, cherry, peach, pear, apricot, and plum trees in New Mexico. However, our extremes of temperature can just as often be responsible for much of the great flavor to be found in New Mexican fruit.

CHANGING CULTIVATION TECHNIQUES

American agriculture is changing rapidly. The days of the old moldboard plow turning over the earth every spring with a regular, businesslike firmness now seem to be numbered. More and more farmers across the country are practicing new "residue management" farming, in which plant seed is drilled into a field amid the stubble of last season's crops. No earth is exposed to be blown away by the wind or rain, and the soil remains intact and allows its microcommunity of plants and animals to flourish. As a result, high crop yields can be produced at savings of 25 percent or more.

The equivalent trend in horticulture, of course, is the growing movement in the Southwest toward using native and drought-tolerant plants and limiting the sprawl of bluegrass and bermuda lawns.

We still need our landscape grasses, trees, and shrubs for oxygen production, air filtration, and general amenity, but we are discovering that these benefits can be produced with very little waste of water and with an actual net improvement in soil quality—and therefore in the quality of our lives.

This hilly residential landscape combines very little ongoing disturbance of the soil with an attractive massing of native shrubs, trees, and boulders

A SOUTHWEST LEGACY OF TREES AND STONE

A NOTE ON NEW MEXICO'S HISTORIC MAN-MADE LANDSCAPES

New Mexico has several truly ancient landscapes, still intact, that extend the history of American landscape architecture back to the tenth century A.D. The great Anasazi plazas at Chetro Ketl, Hungo Pavi, and Pueblo Bonito, all part of a single sprawling urban community at Chaco Canyon, are now beginning to rewrite our ideas of the distant origins of American landscape architecture.

The Anasazi, predecessors of today's Pueblo Indians, also designed and executed an extraordinary series of terraces, patios, arcades, berms, grid gardens, and roads in northwestern and north central New Mexico for a period of some four to five centuries before the arrival of Columbus. Among the local plant species used by the Anasazi were ponderosa and piñon pine, ricegrass, cottonwood, New Mexico olive, hackberry, and singleseed and Utah juniper. Anasazi influence on the distinct regional architecture and landscape architecture of the Southwest has been profound, but it has never been well understood.

New Mexico's Registry of Historic Landscapes, a long-term study by Morrow and Company, Landscape Architects, is finally attempting to make sense of Anasazi design as a fundamental part of the history of landscape architecture in New Mexico for the past thousand years. The registry has played a very active role in identifying and cataloging the cultural landscapes of the state's past. It began as an attempt to sort out and record for further study what many people imagined to be a few dozen old parks, plazas, and private gardens. These, of course, would be taken from all the long centuries of New Mexico's history—not just the remote heyday of the Anasazi. After more than a decade, the registry has grown to include more than 400 sites, and the job of interpreting the raw information collected in the field research will undoubtedly take many more years of analysis and comparison.

Certain questions are asked about all of New Mexico's historic cultural landscapes. Did the site contribute in some way to the cultural history of its time? Was it important to the social, political, military, horticultural, or artistic history of its era? If the answer is yes, the landscape must be considered for inclusion in the registry.

Although there are many ways to evaluate and classify an old landscape, assigning it to an historic era is often the simplest and best way to review it in context. Five basic periods of New Mexican history are typically considered.

Pre-Columbian Era, c. A.D. 850–1540: The best examples of this period are found in the Anasazi sites of Chaco Canyon, Bandelier and Aztec National Monuments, the Galisteo Basin, and the tributary valleys of the Rio Grande in far northern New Mexico. Tyuonyi at Bandelier and Pueblo Bonito and Chetro Ketl at Chaco are perhaps the best-known sites. These settlements feature well-designed plazas, terraces, mounds, and roads or paths in abundance. There is evidence that the Anasazi may even have developed some extraordinary ornamental plantings at Chaco Canyon. Excellent Anasazi sites are also found in Colorado and Utah (Mesa Verde, Yellowjacket, Hovenweep) and in Arizona.

Chaco, edge of plaza at Pueblo Bonito

Plaza (with blue grama) at Gran Quivira

Plaza and church atrio at Quarai

Arthur Park, Estancia

Territorial ranch house, near Cimarron

Spanish Colonial Era, 1540–1821: Early Spanish colonial times saw the creation of several haciendas with enclosed courts, peristyle walkways, gardens, and orchards, all based on Spanish (Mediterranean) and Mexican models. But the greatest landscapes of the period are found in town plazas and *plazuelas* (Santa Fe, Chimayó, Socorro, Albuquerque, Taos), and particularly in the church grounds of the day. These included starkly beautiful enclosed entry courts (*atrios*) and the patios of the friaries (*conventos*) built next to the great mission churches. The Franciscan priests also introduced orchards, vineyards, and gardens stocked with cuttings and seeds of exotic European and Mexican plant species hauled laboriously north from New Spain across the immense distances of the Camino Real. Chiles, peaches, apples, grapevines, and wheat were widespread introductions.

The earliest hybrid Euro-Indian towns in what is now the United States came into being during the early Spanish colonial period (1540 to 1680). The classic small towns of Abó and Quarai in the Manzano Range and the prairie-edge emporium of Gran Quivira near Chupadera Mesa in central New Mexico are now preserved almost exactly as they were as components of the modern Salinas National Monument. They show how the first Europeans in the Southwest re-created the architecture and landscape architecture of the Mediterranean in the midst of late Anasazi settlements.

Open space design of the late Spanish colonial period (1692 to 1821) incorporated plaza and patio refinements and such impressive courtyard, orchard, and field landscapes as those of the hacienda of Don Antonio Severino Martínez in Taos.

Mexican Era, 1821–1846: Many of the vignette courtyards of Santa Fe, tucked away behind long building fronts, were developed during this short interlude in New Mexico's history. The wonderful Sena Plaza on East Palace Avenue in the state capital is surrounded by one- and two-story structures and heavily planted in native tree and shrub species (box elders, white firs, cottonwoods) and new plants brought over the Santa Fe Trail by enterprising American merchants.

The plaza of La Mesilla in far southern New Mexico was the most important new square created during the Mexican period. It is probably more famous for being a hang-out of Pat Garrett and Billy the Kid than for its cottonwood-shaded (now ash-shaded) center. It was an important stop on the Butterfield Trail and the site of the signing of the Gadsden Purchase.

U.S. Territorial Era, 1846–1912: Kit Carson's house at Rayado near Cimarron has been restored by the Boy Scouts and is now a good model of how the pre-railroad, early territorial compound would have appeared. An open

Butte Gardens, Elephant Butte

14

Carnegie Library Park, Las Vegas

Federal Oval, Santa Fe

Vignette courtyard, Santa Fe

central courtyard is surrounded on three sides by the house itself and on the fourth by a low wall that looks out on nearby orchards and fields. The courtyard has many plantings, a well, and a protected area in which poultry can forage, as well as a shady three-sided veranda, or *portal* accented with woodbine, that provides cover from the hot glare of the summer sun.

Late Territorial landscapes (dating from after the coming of the railroad in 1879) are much more "mechanized," reflecting Anglo-American commerce and new ideals of open-space design. The Hotel Alvarado in Albuquerque, now pointlessly demolished, was a lavish railroad stopover with fountain courts, tree-lined approaches, and romantic, California mission –style architecture. Its counterpart in Las Vegas was the Hotel Castañeda, with its many connections to an Americanized plaza, a new Carnegie Library park, and the stately Lincoln Park, with its prim green gazebo (often used in later years for the reunions of Teddy Roosevelt's Rough Riders).

Courthouse squares had also become highly influential town landscapes by the turn of the century. The Federal Oval in Santa Fe is both the best developed and best preserved of these. Perhaps not surprising is the fact that American elms, lilacs, and bluegrass are the familiar plants in these landscapes.

Statehood, 1912–present: The great New Deal landscapes of the 1930s are perhaps New Mexico's most visible (and useful) historic landscapes of the statehood era. Constructed mostly by the Civilian Conservation Corps (CCC) in streamside or lakeside locations around the state, these projects now form the backbone of New Mexico's state park system. The Butte Gardens at Elephant Butte, Albuquerque's Roosevelt Park, tiny Estancia's Arthur Park, and Clovis's Hillcrest Park are among the finest examples of these painstakingly handmade public gardens. New Deal landscapes also feature the best stonework since the days of the Anasazi. Siberian elms, native cottonwoods, stately native Arizona ashes, silver poplars, native soapberries, and arborvitae are very common in these landscapes.

In the near future, a state historic landscape garden system, modeled on the British National Trust, might be set up to allow visitors to enjoy New Mexico's more spectacular sites on a regular basis. It would also be gratifying if more cities and towns around the state were to preserve, restore, or even expand their rich legacy of outdoor spaces and maintain in good condition, wherever possible, the many historic trees, shrubs, and other plants that contribute to these historic landscapes.

New Mexico's old landscapes and the plants they contain have certainly produced a new perspective on the way the West really developed. As W. G. Hoskins, the eminent English landscape historian, put it, "The landscape itself, to those who know how to read it aright, is the richest historical record we possess."

This rich legacy now can be studied and used to produce modern landscapes of great character and regional integrity.

Sena Plaza, Santa Fe

Section Two

TIPS FOR
NEW MEXICO
GARDENING
AND LANDSCAPING

Perennials instead of lawn (right)

PLANT SELECTION

Daffodils

The species on the "Best Plants" lists that follow are among my personal favorites. I have selected them for their hardiness, their adaptability, their consistent performance and rate of growth, their interest and beauty—and their availability. No matter how desirable or striking a species may be, I won't recommend it if it cannot be found and used with little trouble.

Although everyone knows that direct work with plants or gardening is fundamentally good for people, no one wants to be chained to an ill-conceived landscape that raises endless problems in its management. People seem to be extraordinarily busy as the twentieth century winds down, and landscape maintenance, though healthy for us, can be reduced in many instances to only an hour or two a week (or even less) during the growing season. During the off-season, a moderate monthly watering and clean-up generally will suffice.

Mature Mexican elders (above)

Herb garden (right)

ULTIMATE HEIGHT AND WIDTH

Look at the New Mexico Plant File (Section 3) for ultimate sizes. Then space your plants as though the tree or shrub were already fully grown. Never assume that you can prune back a tree that will be too big for its area. Don't plant a large tree under or near an overhead utility line or too close to a building foundation or landscape wall.

COLOR

Everyone has a favorite color or colors. Plants selected because they have leaves, bark, limbs, flowers, fruit, or seeds that meet your color wishes are likely to make you happy. Feel free to use them as much as you wish.

TEXTURE AND FORM

Leaf canopies or leaves themselves often have pleasing textures. So do trunks and visible roots. People frequently select plants because they like certain forms. Remember that juvenile and adult plant forms may differ.

SCENT

Certain plants simply smell terrific. Who can forget a rose? Old ponderosa pine trunks smell like vanilla. Russian olive in bloom has the aroma of a candy factory. Nothing smells fresher than a droplet-spattered, newly emerged daffodil after an early spring rain.

WHIMSY AND NOSTALGIA

Some people will pick a certain tree for the landscape because it reminds them of their beloved Uncle Ernie, or Iowa, or the shaded gazebo they played in as children. Others dislike certain plants because they are associated with childhood unpleasantness of some kind (willows and switches come to mind, or castor oil). Almost all of us are capable of becoming emotionally attached to various plants in the landscape, given the right circumstances.

Texture and Form:
Chinese windmill
palms, with their
striking fans, contrast
pleasantly with brush-
finish concrete in a
radiating pattern.
The flower accent
to the right is
annual vinca

POLITICAL CORRECTNESS

People sometimes can't tell the difference between plants and themselves. We mix up plants and human morality. We may select certain species because they only need a little water, flourish naturally just around the corner, or never complain about poor growing conditions and general neglect, disguised as a profound "need" for low maintenance. And people may make this sort of plant selection with a certain sense of righteousness.

But plants are neither moral nor immoral—they're just plants. A honey locust or white fir is no more evil or good than a bee or a badger. Not even tumbleweeds or elms, I'm sorry to say, are "bad;" like the rest of us, they're just trying to eke out a living under sometimes trying conditions.

It's probably best to select plants for the landscape for simple, functional reasons (please see the Gist List later in this section), and because we humans plainly have an ancient, abiding affinity for them, whatever their origin.

LOCAL CHARACTER

Plant selections that fit in well with the local neighborhood, office or commercial complex, general streetscape, or cityscape will help to create a good "fit" when a new landscape or garden is constructed. There is often a native species available that is a close relative of older, exotic trees, shrubs, or other plants that have been in place for decades. Use the native if it can save water or grow with less care while providing much of the same amenity and character as the older, exotic species.

Aging plants (especially trees) in the community always have a graceful tale of toughness and adaptability to tell. Consider them carefully, and don't cut them down.

As a general approach, it's good to try to let deserts be deserts, plains plains, and mountains mountains. But there is nothing in the rule book against creating small, enclosed, intensely planted green oases, or colorful patios and terraces screened from the wind and tucked into their sites snugly and with a bit of a flourish.

Local Character:
Desert meets riverside
in the Mesilla Valey
(left)

A spring park in Farmington
(above), and a hotel garden
with traditional palms and
fountain in Las Cruces (left)

Arizona or New Mexico alder, in leaf or out of leaf, is spectacular (left)

The Anasazi, early pioneers of the south-west, frequently raised corn, beans, squash, and amaranth in their gardens (right)

Deodar cedar has a dramatic presence

EVERGREEN AND DECIDUOUS

Contrary to popular belief, evergreens (both needled and broadleafed varieties) shed their leaves year-round, with the largest drop occurring in the fall. They are, nevertheless, generally green all year long. Deciduous trees and shrubs shed their leaves in the fall.

For best results, design a mixture for your landscape of about two-thirds deciduous and/ or flowering ornamental species and one-third evergreen species. Many areas of New Mexico are out of leaf (deciduous leaf, that is) for four to five months of the year, and you'll need the slow-growing, sometimes dull, but basically reliable evergreens for their winter color. The balance of the landscape will be gray, brown, and beige against the vivid blue of the sky.

If you plant your evergreen or deciduous specimen in a lawn, be sure to create a bark ring around the tree about 3 feet in diameter and about 3 inches deep. The bark ring will protect the tree from passing mowers and from weedeaters used for close-in clipping.

A NOTE ON VEGETABLES

Most vegetables grow quite happily and well in New Mexico. Our long hours of sun-light and often generous growing season make this form of edible gardening very productive. Remember to mix abundant quantities of manure or compost into the soil. Vegetables do best at low (acidic or neutral) pHs, and these can be achieved with repeated soil amendments. If you wish, you can mix kitchen waste and a limited quantity of newspaper directly into the ground instead of composting them. Simply dig a hole in the vegetable bed, fill it with water, put in the wet garbage, and cover with dirt. Decomposition (and soil improvement) will proceed with amazing speed.

To avoid potential salt damage (from salty water or ground) to your growing plants, seed on the sides—not the tops or the bottoms—of the furrows. Straw, shredded bark, or compost spread along your vegetable rows as mulch can cut down substantially on water loss through evaporation.

Keep in mind that a small, well-planned vegetable garden is so productive that it can feed a family of three or four all year—and it will easily do so at a cost of $25 or less.

Most landscape plants are field-grown or raised in a nursery before transplanting.

Balled and burlaped tree (above)

Tender plants may be raised or sold in a lath house (right)

Typical staking

BACKFILL

If you shovel about one-third shredded bark into the backfill of tree and shrub pits in your landscape, the plant roots will benefit from the soil's increased ability to hold moisture and from the improvement in its aggregate structure or general soil architecture. There is no question that the organic material raises the quality of the soil, and it's quite easy to mix it in. Just add one shovelful of bark to every two shovelfuls of native earth that go back into the planting hole. If you're adventurous, you can substitute manure for the bark *with deciduous plants only.* Some landscape contractors get good results by using bark and a concentrated fertilizer tablet or two in the planting pit.

Remember to soak the planting pit thoroughly as you plant—it's nearly impossible to overwater during transplanting. It is also a good idea to create a water-conserving earth basin (a "saucer") around the base of each tree or shrub in planter areas, but not in lawns.

Many tree growers, landscape contractors, and gardeners do not modify backfill at all. They believe that the landscape plants will have to get used to our sometimes-harsh Southwestern soils quickly and either thrive or die in them.

I would argue that transplanting is the single most unnatural process that humans can inflict on plants. Whether they're natives or exotics, it's something they never undergo of their own accord or in the wild. Anything we can do to reduce the trauma associated with transplanting and give domestic trees and shrubs a little early assistance in their new settings will work to their long-term benefit. One helpful technique is to free up the roots around the plant's rootball (especially if it has just come out of a container) with a knife before it goes into the ground. Always plant the tree or shrub no higher or lower in the ground than it was in the nursery. And be sure not to cover up the root crown or expose the roots in any way.

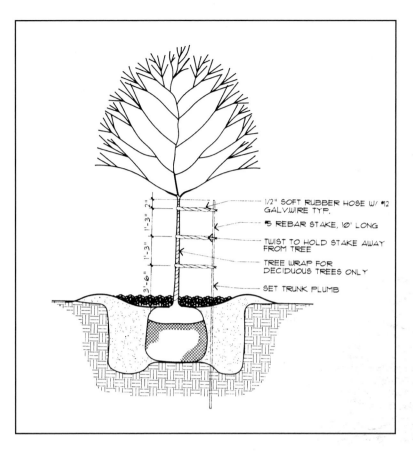

1/2" SOFT RUBBER HOSE W/ #12 GALV.WIRE TYP.

#5 REBAR STAKE, 10' LONG

TWIST TO HOLD STAKE AWAY FROM TREE

TREE WRAP FOR DECIDUOUS TREES ONLY

SET TRUNK PLUMB

STAKING OR GUYING

In general, staking or guying a young tree is like giving a pair of crutches to a child whose leg isn't broken. The motion of the wind is what gives strength to the tree, just as running does to a child's limbs. It's something that needs to be encouraged. Staking may make *you* feel better, but it will do little for the tree.

If you absolutely must stake, don't strap the trees so rigidly that they can't move in the wind. They'll always be spindly. Rig up a simple stake with plastic expansion tape that won't chafe or bind and remember to take it off after a single growing season.

Beware of tall trees with undersized trunks and heavy crowns that cause them to lean or flop. They may have been grown too closely together in the nursery, and they will have great trouble maturing upright and true to form. A fifteen-gallon (container) or 1.25-inch-caliper tree is ideal for many landscape situations. The tree will be about 6–8 feet (about 2–2.5 m) tall and will grow rapidly once established. It will not be prohibitively expensive.

PRUNING

TREES

Don't prune a tree unless it is absolutely imperative to do so. Generally, the simplest and best course is to leave the tree alone. However, you can always take off crossover branches or thin the underside of a tree crown carefully so that limbs will not scratch people's faces or otherwise interfere with foot traffic. "Downer" branches are usually a nuisance and should be lopped off. Suckers or water sprouts emerging at the root crown should be clipped.

It's useful to remember that nature has endowed each tree with a wonderful genetic code that tells it how, when, and in what form to grow. The tree does indeed know best. When in doubt, don't prune. In a troublesome case, call a member of the American Society of Consulting Arborists (see the Yellow Pages) for an opinion or a consultation; landscape architects can also be quite helpful.

The best form of pruning is disbudding, and you can do it in the spring with your thumbnail. Just rub off any buds that may lead to a limb, leaf, flower, or fruit that you don't want. Resist any other urges in the spring that would have you take up the clippers and maul the trees. If you must take off a branch, do it cleanly. Don't leave an unsightly stub that will only cause bacterial or viral infection in the tree.

Anyone who offers to "flat-top" or massively cut back a tree for you is a tree butcher and a fraud. Pay no attention to these people; they are responsible for thousands of needless tree maimings and deaths each year, and they create great ugliness through their grim work.

SHRUBS

There is no pressing need to clip shrubs unless you are shaping lines of them into a hedge. It *is* a good idea, however, to prune back older shrubs here and there to keep them tidy or encourage new growth. You may also wish to remove flowers after their prime to get ready for next year's blooming.

Remember that most shrubs only live a fraction as long as a tree, so they generally need to be replaced much more often.

A mangled tree. The form is ruined by completely unnecessary pruning (above)

A lightly-pruned tree with excellent form (below)

CHLOROSIS

Chlorosis is an iron deficiency in plants that shows itself as yellowing leaves with green veins. It frequently occurs in very alkaline soils with high pH ratings (generally 8.3 or above) and can affect native, naturalized, or exotic species.

The necessary iron may indeed be present in the soil, but it is locked up in chemical compounds that make it unavailable to plants. The long-term solution is to lower the pH of the soil through substantial organic amendments, such as manure, bark, leaves, and compost. In the short term, sulphur, iron sulphate, or iron chelate (the fastest-acting of these) may be added to the soil to improve plant health. Results should be noticeable within a week or two after application.

NATURAL PLANT SUCCESSION

You'll notice a considerable crop of weeds (actually, pioneer plants) sprouting after you have seeded an area with native or exotic plants as part of a landscape or revegetation program. It's best to leave these, as their role in the scheme of things is to provide shade and cover for the more desirable plants that will germinate hard on their heels. You can certainly mow them if they begin to get out of hand, but mow high—at 4–6 inches (about 140 mm). Even if you do not mow, the weeds will recede after a year or two, and the desirable plants will emerge strongly.

Hoeing up the plants and raking them across the ground to be burned in a pile is the surest way to reseed your weeds. They'll thank you for your efforts on their behalf by happily resprouting the next spring.

Normal plant associations found in an undisturbed area constitute a "climax" vegetation. In forests, woodlands, and some rangelands, the succession of plants from weeds to climax vegetation may take ten, twenty, or a hundred years—sometimes longer. In deserts, natural succession happens irregularly, if at all. The soil in many desert grasslands is filled with many thousands or even tens of thousands of seeds per cubic foot; given the proper conditions, plant succession may take only two to three years.

Allowing natural succession to take place is largely a matter of setting up the proper reseeding or revegetation sequence, executing properly and at the right time of year (generally, during the summer monsoons in July and August), and then standing back to let nature take her ancient course with as little interference as possible.

Climax vegetation in a typically dry New Mexico canyon

I find landscapes and gardens so pleasant that I work on them—well, at least on their design—every day. As J. B. Jackson says, they are an "archetype," or primary feature, of Western civilization, and we generally expect a great deal from them. They show up in our literature, our movies, and our paintings. They appear in our music. Gardens and landscapes can serve as romantic retreats, spots for picnics, and places where we can grow a delicious tomato or an aromatic rose with the right water and sunshine and a little care. Businesspeople expect them to generate money when they are constructed around office complexes and shopping centers, and city fathers (and mothers) think they should be intensely green, easily maintained, and always ready for both a casual stroll and a hard game of soccer. Native plant enthusiasts are sure that landscapes should be furnished with local species, although no two experts will agree on precisely what qualifies as a "native" or "local" plant. Landscape architects like to design with natives for the sheer delight of their color, texture, or form.

So there continues to be much to learn and discuss about the plants we use in landscape design; our studies never seem to be finished. No single plant is reliable under all conditions, and careful consideration must be given to varying planting circumstances in this part of the Southwest if we are to use the best plant in a given garden or landscape situation. However, a few rules or precepts apply throughout New Mexico. Briefly stated, here they are:

11 PRECEPTS OF LANDSCAPE DESIGN

WITH AN EMPHASIS ON NEW MEXICAN CONDITIONS

1. The design should be site-specific. Don't try to apply old, clichéd design ideas to a brand-new locale that should be planned on its own terms.

2. Reductionism
   a. Attempt, where possible, to study local landforms and other geographic features for possible inclusion or abstraction in the designed landscape.

   b. Develop intense—not sprawling—green landscape features.

3. Use 12 to 15 plant species (or fewer) to avoid clutter in the finished landscape. Make each species perform a number of design tasks, if possible. In general, the simpler the landscape plan, the greater its chances of succeeding and lasting.

4. Use the appropriate plant for the task at hand, whether it be exotic, native, or naturalized. Pick the right species for shade, spring or fall color, wind protection, winter greenery, screening, or other use. Select plants that will live as long as possible.

5. Know the historic landscape precedents in the area and include these, if applicable, in the design at hand.

Reductionism: Stylized local streambed (top)

Private house, Clovis (above)

Photograph by Suzanne Mortier

Formal design, St. Petersburg, Russia (top left)
Informal Japanese design (top right)
Formal design, Alhambra, Spain (above)

The wall serves as an excellent foil for lilacs and flowering crabs in a Santa Fe garden (above)

Pavement treatment outside a private home in Albuquerque (right)

6. Formal design was the European and Middle Eastern norm until the eighteenth century. Informal design is the traditional Oriental pattern. Either of these approaches, or a combination of them, may be used in contemporary design. For greater clarity of line and feeling, use only one style in an individual design. Practice will make it easier to combine both formal and informal approaches. The best patterns of design make it possible for all design elements to fit together seamlessly and gracefully and yet retain their dynamism.

7. Study the soil. It is a good indicator of the optimum landscape solution for a site. For example, old farmland will support an intense planting with modest maintenance; thin, stony, desert soil will support a sparser design with a medium maintenance effort.

8. Pick one or two pavement materials and stick with them. Don't clutter a landscape or garden with competing textures or forms.

9. Use the concept of feature and foil to help determine the relationship of the landscape to nearby buildings or other structures. Use good landscape line or form (in the appearance of an eye-catching, multi-stemmed tree, for instance) to add to, contrast with, screen, or highlight building features. Or use a plain building to accent a good landscape.

10. Take advantage of existing local specimen plants (especially trees) or plant communities whenever possible. As is true with soil, outstanding local plant masses or specimens may well determine the character and line of the landscape.

11. Always expect to support the cultural landscape with irrigation. It's kind to the plants, and it will protect your investment.

SUMMARY NOTE

The thoughtful and consistent application of these guidelines, singly or jointly, will likely lead to a landscape or garden of great integrity and good regional quality. The best of these, in turn, will contribute to the refinement of our distinctly local New Mexican landscape architecture.

BEST STREET TREES

Street trees are reappearing along New Mexico's lanes and roads in greater quantity than at any time since Territorial days. Their qualities of civility, beauty, and general amenity improve the overall appearance and livability of cities throughout the state. The following species grow consistently well and are tough and colorful.

1. American sycamore—*Platanus occidentalis*
2. Arizona ash—*Fraxinus velutina*
3. Aspen—*Populus tremuloides* (above 6200 feet/1900 m only)
4. Black locust—*Robinia pseudoacacia*
5. Bradford pear—*Pyrus calleryana* ('Bradford')
6. California fan palm—*Washingtonia filifera* (southern New Mexico and El Paso only)
7. Chinaberry—*Melia azedarach*
8. Chinese pistache—*Pistacia chinensis*
9. Fruitless mulberry—*Morus alba* (best in rural areas)
10. Golden rain tree—*Koelreuteria paniculata*
11. Green ash—*Fraxinus pennsylvanica*
12. Horsechestnut—*Aesculus hippocastanum*
13. Japanese pagoda—*Sophora japonica*
14. London plane tree—*Platanus acerifolia*
15. Marshall's seedless ash—*Fraxinus pennsylvanica* ('Marshall's seedless')
16. Modesto ash—*Fraxinus velutina* ('Modesto')
17. Moraine honey locust—*Gleditsia triacanthos inermis* ('Moraine')
18. Oriental plane tree—*Platanus orientalis*
19. Pecan—*Carya illinoiensis*
20. Purpleleaf plum—*Prunus cerasifera* and varieties
21. Raywood ash—*Fraxinus oxycarpa* ('Raywood')
22. Shademaster honey locust—*Gleditsia triacanthos inermis* ('Shademaster')
23. Silver maple—*Acer saccharinum*
24. Sunburst honey locust—*Gleditsia triacanthos inermis* ('Sunburst')
25. Sycamore-leaf maple—*Acer pseudoplatanus*
26. Western catalpa—*Catalpa speciosa*
27. Common (western) hackberry—*Celtis occidentalis*
28. White ash—*Fraxinus americana*

Bradford pear, Park Square, Albuquerque

BEST PATIO TREES

Patios are quite popular outdoor entertaining and general utility "rooms" in New Mexico. The selection of a good patio tree or trees will add immensely to the overall enjoyment and usefulness of these traditionally important outdoor spaces.

1. Aspen—*Populus tremuloides* (above 6200 feet/1900 m only)
2. Bradford pear—*Pyrus calleryana* ('Bradford')
3. Chinaberry—*Melia azedarach*
4. Desert willow—*Chilopsis linearis*
5. Eastern redbud—*Cercis canadensis*
6. English hawthorn—*Crataegus laevigata*, and Washington hawthorn—*Crataegus phaenopyrum*
7. Flowering crabapple—*Malus* species
8. Golden rain tree—*Koelreuteria paniculata*
9. Honey locust, Sunburst variety—*Gleditsia triacanthos inermis* 'Sunburst'
10. Mesquite—*Prosopis glandulosa* (below 4500 feet/1400 m)
11. Mexican elder—*Sambucus caerulea neomexicana* (below 4500 feet/1400 m; above 4500 feet this tree is shrub-like)
12. Russian olive—*Elaeagnus angustifolia*
13. Salt cedar—*Tamarix chinensis*
14. Silk tree—*Albizia julibrissin*

These trees generally grow at a moderate or fast pace, form substantial crowns, create intimacy and seasonal color, need only moderate amounts of water, and do not have disruptive root systems. For specific descriptions, please see the New Mexico Plant File.

Honey locust, Barelas pedestrian walkway, Albuquerque

Modesto ash, street scene, Albuquerque

BEST HEDGE PLANTS

A number of hedge-producing species, including a surprising quantity of natives, will perform quite well in New Mexico.

DECIDUOUS

1. Althea (rose of Sharon)—*Hibiscus syriacus*
   Terrific late summer–early fall color; excellent as a tall, strong-stemmed hedge. Somewhat formal.
2. Apache plume—*Fallugia paradoxa*
   Plant anywhere. Medium-sized native, needs almost no water or care. Good, continuing white and pink bloom and seed color. Informal.
3. Golden bamboo—*Phyllostachys aurea*
   Fast-growing, semi-evergreen. Strong screening plant, but can sucker out of control. Informal.
4. Spanish broom—*Spartium junceum*
   Thick, tall, rounded, with good yellow spring color. Quite drought-tolerant. Informal.
5. Rockspray cotoneaster—*Cotoneaster microphyllus*
   Attractive, tiny gray leaves. Takes well to shearing. Formal, medium-sized.
6. Forsythia—*Forsythia* spp.
   Brilliant yellow spring color, attractive green foliage for the rest of the growing season. Formal.
7. Common lilac—*Syringa vulgaris*
   Unbeatable in the spring for aroma and lavender color. Excellent informal hedge. Tall.
8. New Mexico olive—*Forestiera neomexicana*
   Most versatile of native small trees. Good in informal lines, or formally shorn. Both stems and foliage are very attractive.
9. Privet—*Ligustrum* spp.
   The classic exotic hedge plant. Excellent in all situations and locales, but it likes water. Almost always shorn formally.
10. Bridal wreath spirea—*Spiraea prunifolia*
    Excellent informal hedge plant. Spring-blooming, with a heady scent and small, attractive leaves. Grows in pleasant, billowing rows.
11. Coyote willow—*Salix exigua*
    Attractive gray-green foliage. Red twigs. Usually informal, but clipping thickens it into a striking, formal appearance. Native.

EVERGREEN

1. Arborvitae—*Thuja* and *Platycladus* spp.
   Good, exotic intermediate or tall hedge plant. Generally takes shearing well. Taller species make fine windbreaks. Formal.
2. Japanese barberry—*Berberis thunbergii*
   Extraordinarily beautiful, with small, attractive, brilliant green leaves. Thorny. Generally deciduous in New Mexico, with tiny red berries that last for winter color. Formal.
3. Prickly pear—*Opuntia* spp.
   Can be planted in rows for spectacular effect. Red, orange, and yellow flowers, wide "leaf" (pear) pads. Very thorny native. Informal.
4. Parney cotoneaster—*Cotoneaster lacteus*
   Tall broadleaf evergreen with attractive berries. May get leggy with age. Informal.
5. Pfitzer juniper—*Juniperus chinensis* 'Pfitzerana'
   Sprawling character, but adapts well to shearing. Tough. Blue or green varieties available. Long-lived.
6. India hawthorn—*Rhaphiolepis indica*
   Low-growing broadleafed evergreen. Forms a good, compact hedge with shearing. Often tender.
7. Heavenly bamboo (nandina)—*Nandina domestica*
   Delicate-looking but quite hardy. Multi-colored. Accepts shearing readily. Frequently slow-growing.
8. Rubber rabbitbrush (chamisa)—*Chrysothamnus nauseosus*
   Hardy, adaptable, silver-green native shrub. Fast-growing. An excellent hedge plant, either shorn or left to its own devices, watered or unwatered.
9. Sand (threadleaf) sage—*Artemisia filifolia*
   Especially good in hot, sandy places. Very fine, lace-leafed specimen plant. Best unshorn. Little water or care needed. Fast-growing.
10. Texas ranger (purple sage)—*Leucophyllum frutescens*
    Attractive gray foliage. Startling purple flowers. Should be left informal and watered only occasionally.

Apache Plume

Prickly pear

Blue spruce

Salt cedar

BEST WINDBREAK PLANTS

Windbreaks from 8 feet (2.5 m) to more than 30 feet (9 m) in width and height are widely used in New Mexico. Most are not clipped. Southwesterly (summer) and northerly (winter) winds can be controlled or deflected by a well-planned, consistently maintained windbreak.

DECIDUOUS

1. Siberian elm—*Ulmus pumila*
2. Black locust—*Robinia pseudoacacia*
3. New Mexico locust—*Robinia neomexicana*
4. Russian olive—*Elaeagnus augustifolia*
5. Lombardy poplar -*Populus nigra 'Italica'*
6. Coyote willow—*Salix exigua*
7. River cane—*Arundo donax*
8. Golden bamboo—*Phyllostachys aurea*
9. Spanish broom—*Spartium junceum*
10. Common lilac—*Syringa vulgaris*
11. New Mexico olive (New Mexico privet, desert olive)—*Forestiera neomexicana*
12. Sand plum—*Prunus americana*
13. Bridal wreath spirea—*Spiraea prunifolia*

EVERGREEN

1. Leyland false cypress—*Cupressocyparis leylandii*
2. Arizona cypress—*Cupressus arizonica*
3. Blue spruce—*Picea pungens*
4. Engelmann spruce—*Picea engelmanni*
5. Eastern red cedar—*Juniperus virginiana*
6. Rocky Mountain juniper—*Juniperus scopulorun* and its varieties
7. Afghan pine—*Pinus eldarica*
8. Arborvitae—*Thuja* spp.and *Platycladus* spp.
9. Parney cotoneaster—*Cotoneaster lacteus*
10. Oregon grape—*Mahonia aquifolium*
11. Fraser's photinia—*Photinia fraseri*
12. Chinese photinia—*Photinia serrulata*
13. Pyracantha—*Pyracantha coccinea* spp.
14. Silverberry—*Elaeagnus pungens*
15. Pampas grass—*Cortaderia selloana*

Generally, windbreaks are most effective when planted in double, parallel rows of the same or complementary species.

BEST SPECIMEN PLANTS

Most landscape plants can be developed to serve as accents or specimens under the right circumstances. However, a very few species in common use are unusually appealing as "eye-catchers" wherever they are found. Among these are:

DECIDUOUS TREES

1. London plane tree—*Platanus acerifolia* Excellent as a multi-trunk specimen. Whitish-green and yellow-gray bark is smooth, branch structure is extraordinary, upper and lower leaf surfaces differ in color and texture.
2. Russian olive—*Elaeagnus angustifolia* Excellent multi-trunk specimen with gray foliage, sweet smell.
3. Paper birch—*Betula papyrifera* White bark is striking. Extraordinary as a multi-stem tree.
4. Aspen—*Populus tremuloides* Wonderful bark, slim, streamlined form, dazzling green leaves (above 6000 feet/ 1830 m only).
5. Umbrella catalpa—*Catalpa bignonioides 'Nana'* Thick lollipop form. Produces total shade.
6. White (silver) poplar—*Populus alba* Maple-like, two-tone leaves. Whitish, mottled bark. Roots may be a problem.
7. Chinese (evergreen) elm—*Ulmus parvifolia* Extraordinary, multi-hued, speckled, pastel bark; delicate leaves. (Does *not* produce the obnoxious seeds of its cousin, the Siberian elm.)
8. Maidenhair tree (ginkgo)—*Ginkgo biloba* The fan-shaped leaves and cheerful fall color of this "fossil" tree make it a remarkable accent.
9. Sunburst honey locust—*Gleditsia triacanthos inermis 'Sunburst'* Yellow new growth in spring gives this tree the appearance of a flowering ornamental. Very tough and fast-growing.
10. Purple robe locust—*Robinia ambigua 'Purple Robe'* Striking compound leaves, unbelievably purple spring flowers.
11. Japanese maple—*Acer palmatum* Miniature tree of exceptional quality and structure. Leaves especially fine, almost filigreed. Grows only in shade.
12. Texas oak—*Quercus texana* Multi-trunked, well-developed, tough feature tree.

Lilacs as screens (top)
Hedge (above)

London Plane tree (above)
Aspen (below)

California fan palm

26

13. Arizona sycamore—*Platanus wrightii*
    Bark, trunk, leaves all unusual. Very large. Usually multi-stemmed in the wild. Rangy; looks like a "Western" tree.
14. Arizona walnut—*Juglans major*
    Black trunk (good as a "multi"), striking pinnate leaves.

Desert willow bloom

FLOWERING ORNAMENTAL

1. Desert willow—*Chilopsis linearis*
   Twisted trunk, willow-like leaves, orchid-like flowers are all exceptional.
2. Mexican elder—*Sambucus caerulea neomexicana*
   Picturesque, gnarled trunk(s) forms quickly; umbelliferous, yellow flowers.
3. Hawthorn—*Crataegus* spp.
   Multiple trunks, refined leaves, bright spring color.
4. Bradford pear—*Pyrus calleryana* 'Bradford'
   Formal shape, striking spring color, red leaves in fall.
5. Smoke tree—*Cotinus coggygria*
   Sprawling, haphazard form, and lavender-pastel flowers that look like puffs of smoke.

DECIDUOUS SHRUBS

1. Bird of paradise—*Caesalpinia gilliesii*
   Baroque, whiskered, red and yellow flowers, refined limb and compound leaf structure. Looks like a native, too (it isn't).
2. Red osier dogwood—*Cornus stolonifera*
   Grown for its striking red winter branch structure.
3. New Mexico olive—*Forestiera neomexicana*
   Multiple small trunks, wonderful lime-green leaves. Often tree-like.
4. Sand plum—*Prunus americana*
   Native wild plum. Stunning spring bloom, good edible fruit by September.

Hawthorn

BEST EVERGREEN TREE ACCENTS

A surprisingly large number of native and exotic evergreen tree species grow quite well in New Mexico. In general, they are drought-resistant and long-lived, with slow to moderate growth rates. Several species are eye-catching and make fine accents.

1. All the true cedars have striking forms and foliage. Most are hardy as far north as Albuquerque, but they grow especially well in southern New Mexico and El Paso.
   a. Atlas cedar—*Cedrus atlantica*
      Use the ice-blue form.
   b. Cedar of Lebanon—*Cedrus libani*
      Very slow to start, but an immense character tree when mature.
   c. Deodar cedar—*Cedrus deodara*
      Kelly green foliage, fine-textured, weeping branch tips.
2. Italian cypress—*Cupressus sempervirens*
   Pencil-like; good skyline tree in southern New Mexico, El Paso.
3. White fir—*Abies concolor*
   Gray-white trunk, lofty form, wonderful soft-green new needle growth in spring. Best in Santa Fe, elsewhere in the north.
4. Alligator juniper—*Juniperus deppeana*
   Blue-gray foliage, cherry-colored trunk when young. Bark looks like an alligator's hide with age.
5. Texas madrone—*Arbutus texana*
   Peeling, cherry-colored bark; multiple trunks; pointed leaves.
6. California fan palm—*Washingtonia filifera*
   So rare in New Mexico, where it actually grows quite happily, that it is always a conversation piece. Usually looks best with a closely trimmed trunk. May brown a little in winter, but it recovers.
7. Chinese windmill palm—*Trachycarpus fortunei*
   Trunk looks upside down—thicker at the top, tapering at the bottom. Wonderful courtyard palm. Plant in manure-enriched soil and water very well.
8. Japanese black pine—*Pinus thunbergiana*
   Twisting trunk, spreading form. Try to neutralize and enrich the soil before planting. Very hardy and slow-growing.

Pinon pine and big sage

9. Piñon pine—*Pinus edulis*
   "Character" piñons can set the mood for a courtyard. Don't buy a piñon if it doesn't come from a tree farm; tree thieves siphon a continuous supply of these beautiful trees from national forests and BLM (Bureau of Land Management) land for resale.
10. Dawn redwood—*Metasequoia glyptostroboides*
    A living fossil. Handsome, hardy, quick-growing, and bright red in fall (it's actually deciduous).
11. Western red cedar—*Thuja plicata*
    Actually an immense arborvitae, but so handsome that it makes an excellent specimen plant.
12. Joshua tree—*Yucca brevifolia*
    Grows extremely well in Albuquerque and throughout southern New Mexico. A branching tree that also happens to be a genuine yucca.
13. Palm yucca—*Yucca torreyi*
    Formal, single-stemmed tree, always eye-catching as an accent. Do not plant in lawns; palm yucca needs a dry planter and little water.

BEST LARGE-AREA GROUND COVERS

Intense sunlight, with its accompanying ultraviolet (UV) radiation, damages many ground covers in New Mexico's high altitudes. Drying spring winds and generally thin soils add to the woes of most ground-cover plants.

Generally, almost all ground covers perform best if planted in small areas (about 100–150 square feet) with filtered shade and some shrubs present. (Please see the Ground Cover section of the New Mexico Plant List.) The soil should be prepared by the addition of a great deal of manure or other organic, humus-producing material and sulfur.

A very few species may be used in lieu of bluegrass or other turf grasses or mulches to cover large areas. To qualify as a turf replacement, the ground cover must be tough, resistant to foot traffic, and unusually adaptable. Recommended plants include:

EVERGREEN

1. Honeysuckle—*Lonicera japonica* varieties
   Hardy, tenacious, flowering, and fast-spreading. Low to moderate watering needed. Evergreen.
2. Creeping euonymus—*Euonymus fortunei*
   Rich green. Fast-spreading. Low to moderate watering. Evergreen. Tough and recommended in medians and parkways.
3. Horizontalis and sabina junipers—*Juniperus horizontalis* and *Juniperus sabina* varieties
   Tough, hardy, moderate-to-fast growers. These junipers withstand heat. Little watering needed.

DECIDUOUS

1. Clover—*Trifolium* spp.
   Ultra-fast from seed. Short-lived (3–4 years). Gulps water but builds soil as an important legume. Flowers are abundant and cheerful. Can replace turf.
2. Crown vetch—*Coronilla varia*
   Best ground cover for steep, hot slopes. Likes water but, like clover, fixes nitrogen in the soil. Lush, twining growth, many flowers. Crown vetch will consume small shrubs placed within its grasp.

BUNCH GRASSES

Low water-use native bunch grasses make fine ground covers. They are attractive, relatively quick to spread, and easy to maintain. Among the best of these for general use are:

1. Galleta—*Hilaria jamesii*
2. Indian ricegrass—*Oryzopsis hymenoides*
3. Blue grama—*Bouteloua gracilis*
4. Buffalo grass—*Buchlöe dactyloides*

All can withstand terrible heat, neglect, and drought, although a bit of attention and care will certainly produce better results. Grama, galleta, and buffalo grass will withstand a considerable amount of foot traffic.

Joshua tree

Bluegrama

Bigtooth maple

28

BEST SHADE-LOVING PLANTS

It is always difficult to plan for shade-loving species in New Mexico. Unless the plant is to be installed on the north or east side of a building or a sheltering cliff, you must wait until new saplings or young shrubs grow large enough to cast the proper shadows for these plants.

Nevertheless, a few species always seem to be reliable in their habits and performance.

TREES

1. California buckeye—*Aesculus californica*
   A good, small horsechestnut that tolerates northern exposures well.
2. New Mexico locust—*Robinia neomexicana*
   Prefers sun, but grows in any combination of sun and shade.
3. Bigtooth maple—*Acer grandidentatum*
   Very colorful native understory tree. Neutral or acidic soil.
4. Japanese maple—*Acer palmatum*
   Classic, delicate exotic. Good as an understory or by itself in light or deep shade. Will burn badly in the high-altitude sun.
5. Rocky Mountain maple—*Acer glabrum*
   Striking, often mottled gray trunk, good fall color. Sun or partial shade. Neutral or acidic soil.
6. Gambel oak—*Quercus gambelii*
   Good understory to pine plantings. Sun or shade.

SHRUBS

1. Cranberry cotoneaster—*Cotoneaster apiculatus*
   Colorful, low-growing deciduous shrub with red berries in the fall.
2. Currant, gooseberry—*Ribes* spp.
   Partial shade. Good spring color and tasty fruit in summer. Thorny.
3. Shrub honeysuckle—*Lonicera tatarica*
   Colorful red berries; partial shade.
4. Skunkbush—*Rhus trilobata*
   Highly adaptable native—will take much sun or much shade. Grows rapidly with very little water.
5. Aucuba—*Aucuba japonica*
   Superb exotic for full shade. Highly adaptable. Neutral or acidic soil is best.

6. Barberry—*Berberis* spp.
   The native *Berberis fendleri*, Colorado barberry, tolerates deep shade very well.
7. Parney cotoneaster—*Cotoneaster lacteus*
   Gets a little leggy in deep shade, but Parney cotoneaster is hardy and will grow quite tall to reach the sun.
8. India hawthorn—*Rhaphiolepis indica*
   Likes partial shade. Evergreen with good pink spring flowers. Sometimes delicate.
9. Oregon grape—*Mahonia aquifolium*
   Large broadleafed shrub with yellow spring flowers, blue berries, and crimson-tinged leaves in fall.
10. Nandina—*Nandina domestica*
    Handsome, small exotic with cane-like stems.

GROUND COVERS

1. Spring cinquefoil—*Potentilla tabernaemontanii*
   Cheerful, small-scale ground cover with yellow flowers.
2. Mint—*Mentha* spp.
   Fresh-smelling, rampant, small-scale plant.
3. Ajuga—*Ajuga reptans*
   Blue flowers, highly geometric leaves.
4. Common juniper—*Juniperus communis*
   Good low-growing native juniper. Usually cultivated as a small shrub under trees.
5. Kinnickinnick—*Arctostaphylos uva-ursi*
   Colorful, sprawling, tiny, native ground cover.
6. Creeping mahonia—*Mahonia repens*
   Looks like a miniature Oregon grape. Very hardy native.
7. Periwinkle—*Vinca major* and *Vinca minor*
   Viney exotic with pleasant, arching stems and little violet flowers.
8. Japanese spurge—*Pachysandra terminalis*
   Small rosettes that grow abundantly in shade.
9. Strawberry—*Fragaria* spp.
   Fast grower in partial shade. Will only last a few seasons without good cultivation and/or replanting.

Japanese maple

Cranberry cotoneaster

Creeping mahonia

Ajuga

Purple threeawn

GRASSES

Only the fescues (*Festuca* spp.) among the grasses are widely available and especially useful in the shade.

VINES

1. Canyon grape—*Vitis arizonica*
   Hardy, bright green native.
2. Virginia creeper—*Parthenocissus quinquefolia* and *P. inserta*
   Grows strongly in sun or shade. Native/naturalized.
3. English ivy—*Hedera helix*
   Tenacious, hardy, ultra–drought-tolerant, handsome.

FLOWERS

1. Impatiens—*Impatiens* spp.
   All-time champion of shade annuals. Unbelievable continuous bloom.
2. Pansy—*Viola x wittrockiana*
   Tremendously colorful. Partial shade only.
3. Bear's breech—*Acanthus mollis*
   Rhubarb-like leaf, enormous flower. Resembles a broadleaf shrub. Great curiosity plant.
4. Columbine—*Aquilegia* spp.
   These colorful natives have amazingly complicated flowers. Dappled shade is best.
5. Violet—*Viola odorata*
   Native and exotic species both like damp soil. Striking leaves; pleasant, understated flowers.

Impatiens

NATIVE PLANT ALL-STARS

The creative application of native plants can lead to a spectacular landscape. A well-designed outdoor space furnished largely or entirely from a native plant palette will also generate a strong sense of place.

However, the use of native plants alone does not guarantee low maintenance or an "instant" landscape. Generally, the gardener or landscaper needs to have a little extra patience, be willing to learn about a new approach toward caring for plants, and have an eye for unexpected forms of beauty. Most native-plant users will also need to explain their ideas to the neighbors. This is generally a happy problem, as the use of these species generates its own sort of infectious enthusiasm.

More native species than ever before are now available for use in New Mexican gardens and landscapes. Here are a few of my tried-and-true favorites.

TREES

Deciduous

1. Aspen—*Populus tremuloides*
2. Arizona (New Mexico) alder—*Alnus tenuifolia*
3. Arizona ash—*Fraxinus velutina* (also its variety, Modesto ash)
4. Native cottonwoods—*Populus species.* Fremont, Rio Grande, lanceleaf, and narrowleaf are good choices.
5. Netleaf hackberry—*Celtis reticulata*
6. New Mexico locust—*Robinia neomexicana*
7. Bigtooth maple—*Acer grandidentatum*
8. Rocky Mountain maple—*Acer glabrum*
9. Mesquite—*Prosopis glandulosa*
10. Gambel oak—*Quercus gambelii*
11. Arizona sycamore—*Platanus wrightii*
12. Arizona walnut—*Juglans major*
13. Peachleaf willow—*Salix amygdaloides*

Flowering ornamental

1. Desert willow—*Chilopsis linearis*
2. Mexican elder—*Sambucus caerulea neomexicana*

Mormon tea

Modesto ash

Soaptree yucca

Agave

30

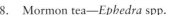

Evergreen

1. Arizona cypress—*Cupressus arizonica*
2. White fir—*Abies concolor*
3. Alligator juniper—*Juniperus deppeana*
4. Rocky Mountain juniper—*Juniperus scopulorum* and varieties
5. Madrone—*Arbutus texana*
6. Bristlecone pine—*Pinus aristata*
7. Limber pine—*Pinus flexilis*
8. Blue spruce—*Picea pungens*
9. Engelmann spruce—*Picea engelmannii*
10. Palm yucca—*Yucca torreyi*
11. Soaptree yucca—*Yucca elata*

SHRUBS

Deciduous

1. Apache plume—*Fallugia paradoxa*
2. Shrubby cinquefoil—*Potentilla fruticosa*
3. Cliff fendlerbush—*Fendlera rupicola*
4. Currant—*Ribes species*
5. Red osier dogwood—*Cornus stolonifera*
6. Fernbush—*Chamaebatiaria millefolium*
7. Hop tree -*Ptelea trifoliolata*
8. Mountain mahogany—*Cercocarpus montanus*
9. New Mexico olive (New Mexico privet)—*Forestiera neomexicana*
10. Sand plum—*Prunus americana*
11. Smooth sumac—*Rhus glabra*
12. Skunkbush—*Rhus trilobata*
13. Coyote willow—*Salix exigua*
14. Winterfat—*Ceratoides lanata*

Evergreen

1. Agave (century plant, mescal)—*Agave* spp.
2. Beargrass—*Nolina microcarpa*
3. Common cholla cactus—*Opuntia imbricata*
4. Prickly pear—*Opuntia chlorotica* or *Opuntia engelmannii*
5. Common juniper—*Juniperus communis*
6. Algerita—*Mahonia haematocarpa*
7. Agritos—*Mahonia trifoliolata* (also frequently called algerita)

8. Mormon tea—*Ephedra* spp.
9. Ocotillo—*Fouquieria splendens*
10. Rubber rabbitbrush—*Chrysothamnus nauseosus*
11. Big sage—*Artemisia tridentata*
12. Threadleaf sage—*Artemisia filifolia*
13. Fourwing saltbush—*Atriplex canescens*
14. Sotol—*Dasylirion wheeleri*
15. Texas ranger—*Leucophyllum frutescens*
16. Narrowleaf yucca—*Yucca glauca*
17. Spanish bayonet—*Yucca baccata*

GROUND COVERS

Deciduous

1. Prairie sage—*Artemisia ludoviciana*

Evergreen

1. Kinnickinnick (mountain bearberry)—*Arctostaphylos uva-ursi*
2. Creeping mahonia—*Mahonia repens*
3. Pussytoes—*Antennaria parviflora*
4. Sedum—*Sedum* spp.
5. Strawberry—*Fragaria* spp.

GRASSES

Native Turf and General-Use Species

1. Buffalo grass—*Buchlöe dactyloides*
2. Galleta—*Hilaria jamesii*
3. Gramas—*Bouteloua* spp.

Ornamental Species

1. Alkali sacaton—*Sporobolus airoides*
2. Sand dropseed—*Sporobolus cryptandrus*
3. Indian ricegrass—*Oryzopsis hymenoides*
4. Purple threeawn—*Aristida longiseta*

Limber pine

Shrubby cinquefoil

Indian ricegrass

Native sedum

Gaillardia

VINES

Deciduous

1. Canyon grape—*Vitis arizonica*
2. Virginia creeper (woodbine)—
   Parthenocissus inserta
3. Clematis (Western virginsbower)—
   Clematis ligusticifolia

FLOWERS

Annuals

1. Purple aster—*Aster bigelovii*
2. Firewheel (gaillardia)—*Gaillardia pulchella*
3. Sunflower—*Helianthus annuus*
4. Wallflower—*Erysimum capitatum*

Perennials

1. Desert baileya—*Baileya multiradiata*
2. California poppy—*Eschscholzia californica*
3. Mexican poppy—*Eschscholzia mexicana*
4. Columbine—*Aquilegia* spp.
5. Coneflower—*Ratibida columnifera*
6. Fendler's sundrops—*Calylophus hartwegii fendleri*
7. Blue flax -*Linum perenne*
8. Indian paintbrush—*Castilleja integra*
9. Jimsonweed (sacred datura)—*Datura meteloides*
10. Wooly yarrow—*Achillea* spp.

Bulbs

1. Rocky Mountain iris (blue flag)—
   Iris missouriensis

Colombine

If you find an appealing plant, be sure to look it up in the New Mexico Plant File (Section 3) or in the appropriate town or city summary (Section 4). Not every native species will grow in all landscape situations. Don't neglect natives or forget to give them a little care; the domestic garden or city landscape is usually as foreign a place for them as Antarctica would be for you. They are out of their element and away from their support systems. They will reward your kind attention.

A good general rule of thumb to remember with native plants is this: As altitude increases, survivability is determined by a plant's resistance to cold. As altitude decreases, it is determined by drought resistance.

Coneflower

Jimsonweed

Green ash

THE GIST LIST
A SHORTHAND GUIDE TO QUICK PLANT SELECTION

Do you need a shorthand list to help you make your landscape plant selections?

Think of your garden or landscape as an outdoor "room" or series of rooms. Then review the Gist List for good basic selections to help create the outdoor space you want. Remember to use no more than twelve to fifteen species if you want to avoid clutter or "busyness" in the landscape.

The Gist List introduces significant plants in a simple, new way: by **clearly defined function.**

"OUTDOOR ROOM" ELEMENT	SUGGESTED SPECIES AND PLANT TYPE
Bearing walls, Ceilings	*Shade trees:* ashes, honey locusts, sycamores, elms, cottonwoods/poplars, locusts, nut trees, catalpas/desert willows.
Winter color, Solids: Walls	*Evergreen trees for winter color, solid backgrounds:* pines, spruces, cypresses, arborvitae, junipers, cedars, firs, false cypresses, false hemlocks.
Spring notes	*Flowering color accent trees:* crabs, plums, pears, golden rain trees, peaches, salt cedars, Sunburst honey locust.
Hardy Intermediates	*Foundation deciduous shrubs:* lilacs, forsythias, spireas, rabbitbrush, Apache plume, privet, roses, abelias, potentillas, cotoneasters, rose of Sharon, fourwing saltbush.
Hardy Intermediates	*Foundation evergreen shrubs:* junipers, India hawthorn, yuccas, barberries, mahonias, photinias, hollies, pyracanthas, oleanders.
Walls between rooms	*Hedges:* privets, New Mexico olive, pampas grass, silverberry, arborvitae, elm, photinias, rabbitbrush, Apache plume, river cane, golden bamboo.
Ground accents	*Bulbs:* tulips, daffodils, crocuses, narcissus, cannas, gladiolus, irises.
	Perennials: carnations, penstemons, mums, geraniums, Shasta daisy.
	Annuals: marigolds, gaillardias, petunias, pansies, impatiens, ageratum, lobelias, coleus (foliage), begonias, snapdragons.
Drapes	*Vines:* ivy, honeysuckle, clematis, morning glory, woodbine, trumpet vine, silverlace vine.
Floors	*Ground covers:* clover, honeysuckle, crown vetch, ajuga, potentilla, creeping euonymus.
Floors and ground-level "seats"	*Lawns:* Bluegrass, fescue, rye, buffalo grass, blue grama, bermuda.
Accent furnishings	*General accents:* Russian olive, birch, New Mexico olive, hawthorn, crape myrtle, cacti, smoke trees, desert willows.

Apache plume

Plants and hard landscape materials can create and define entire outdoor spaces (rooms), including walls, floors, and ceilings, in amazing combinations of color, form, and texture. Incidentally, 80 to 90 percent of the plants that grow well in New Mexico grow well elsewhere, too. New Mexico has a huge natural flora of over 4,400 species *plus* several hundred exotics, so there is no real limit to the exciting plant mixtures available to both amateur and professional gardeners.

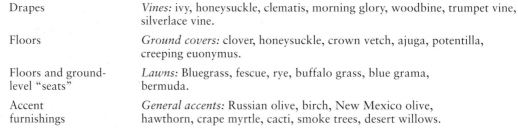

Petunias

Section Three

THE NEW MEXICO PLANT FILE

The following list contains notes on native, naturalized, and exotic plant species that grow well in New Mexico. The origin of each plant is clearly indicated.

Not every species grows in every corner of the state, so this selection of plants is best used in conjunction with the town-by-town plant lists in Section Four, "City and Town Plant Recommendations and Notes."

This collection of useful species is not final. But the trees, shrubs, vines, grasses, ground covers, flowers, and other plants found here are generally hardy, relatively easy to obtain, and highly useful in a wide variety of New Mexican planting situations.

TREES
DECIDUOUS SHADE, STREET, AND SPECIALTY TREES

ALL PLANTS IN THIS SECTION ARE IDENTIFIED AS NATIVE, EXOTIC, OR NATURALIZED.

ASHES

All things considered, these wonderful shade, street, and park trees must rank, along with the honey locusts, as the very best in their class for New Mexican gardens and landscapes. They are generally hardy, easily available in both native and exotic species and varieties, and not demanding in terms of their care. They grow well and usually quickly in thin soils, provide good shade, and are long-lived. Most species do not surface-root badly, if at all, and there is a species of ash that will perform well in virtually any location in New Mexico.

Arizona alder (New Mexico alder)

Alnus oblongifolia
Spanish: *Aliso.*

Unusual, statuesque native tree, common in and about the Gila country of New Mexico. Also occurs in mountain ranges in central New Mexico and as far north as Los Alamos. Alternating, scaffold branches, very straight trunk, and cheerful, bright green leaves. Pyramidal shape when young, with crown rounded and well developed as the tree ages. Quick-growing; now propagated from root cuttings. Often grows in linear clumps along streams and on hillsides above 5000 feet (1525 m). Very hardy. May reach 40 feet (about 12 m), spreading to 20–25 feet (about 6–8 m). Prefers gravelly soil, moderate moisture, full or partial sun. Fine lawn, shade, or specimen tree.
Grows Best: Statewide, up to 8000 feet/ 2440 m.

Arizona ash

Arizona ash (velvet ash)

Fraxinus velutina
Spanish: *Fresno.*

Native tree found in hot southern valleys and foothills. Deciduous, 20–30 feet (6–9 m) tall, spreading equally wide. Good yellow fall color. Medium growth rate. Highly adaptable and useful in the landscape for shade, street tree plantings, or as a feature. Full sun, moderate water, any soil.
Grows Best: Statewide, up to 6000 feet/1830 m.

Modesto ash

Fraxinus velutina 'Modesto'
Spanish: *Fresno.*

Variety of the New Mexico native Arizona ash, but entirely seedless. May grow 5–10 feet (about 2–3 m) taller and wider than Arizona ash. An extremely desirable street, shade, and fall color tree, planted in masses or as a specimen. Its compound leaves are shinier than those of *Fraxinus velutina*, its crown is rounder, and as a juvenile its trunk is smoother. Generally hardy in the southern two-thirds of New Mexico—wherever Arizona ash is hardy. Not a tree for the north. Full sun, fast growth, any soil.
Grows Best: Statewide, up to 6000 feet/1830 m.

Modesto ash

Arizona alder

Green ash

Fraxinus pennsylvanica
Spanish: *Fresno.*

Exotic tree with many varieties, originally from the eastern United States. Deciduous, 30–40 feet (9–12 m) tall, spreading equally wide. Brilliant but short-lived fall color. Trunk has interesting, regular, vertical fissures. Horizontal branching, slow or medium growth rate. Widely used as a street and shade tree. Very hardy; adapts well to cold. Full sun, moderate water, any soil.

Popular varieties include Marshall seedless green ash (*Fraxinus pennsylvanica* 'Marshall'), which has an attractive diagonal branching pattern and a fast growth rate; summit ash (*Fraxinus pennsylvanica* 'Summit'), very similar to Marshall ash in hardiness, shape, and color; and Patmore ash (*Fraxinus pennsylvanica* 'Patmore'), an oval-crowned tree that can withstand the coldest of growing conditions.
Grows Best: Statewide, literally anywhere.

Green ash

White ash

Raywood ash

Fraxinus oxycarpa 'Raywood'
Spanish: *Fresno.*

Exotic tree (actually from Australia) with five leaflets arranged in a more compact form than those of Arizona or green ash. Hardy, often grown for its deep purple or red autumn color. Good specimen or shade tree; heavy shade. About 25 feet (8 m) tall and 20 feet (6 m) wide at maturity. Contrasts well with other ashes and is distinct enough to be planted with them in a complementary composition. Quick growth rate. Full sun, moderate water. Appreciates well-manured soil.
Grows Best: Statewide, up to 6000 feet/1830 m.

White ash

Fraxinus americana
Spanish: *Fresno.*

Very like the Arizona ash (*Fraxinus velutina* and its varieties) in form, color, and growth habits, white or American ash is characteristically a bit more roundheaded and larger, reaching 50 feet (15 m) or more in height and spread. Exotic, fast-growing, with attractive, well-formed, compact leaflets. Hardy; makes a good median and street tree. Full sun, any soil, moderate watering.

The variety *Fraxinus americana* 'Autumn Purple' has striking purple fall foliage, is seedless, and is widely available. Other varieties are commonly planted as well.
Grows Best: Statewide.

Raywood ash

Paper birch (white birch)

Betula papyrifera
Spanish: *Abedul.*

Exotic tree from northern Europe, much prized for its white bark. Grows 25–30 feet (8–9 m) tall, about 15–20 feet (5–6 m) wide. Prefers acidic soils but grows well in New Mexico, especially in colder areas. For best results, add peat moss, shredded bark, or other organic soil amendments to backfill in large quantities to help condition the soil. Medium to fast grower. Full sun or sun and shade, moderate amounts of water.

Other birch species also grow well in New Mexico and, like the paper birch, are showy and short-lived. Birches are out of place in the desert but do well in high mountain towns.
Grows Best: Statewide, above 5000 feet/1525 m.

White birch

Western catalpa

Chinaberry

Western catalpa (also northern catalpa)

Catalpa speciosa
Spanish: *Catalpa.*
Enormous exotic tree, usually found growing in thick soils in New Mexico's great river valleys. Deciduous, with large heart-shaped leaves and impressive late-spring flowers. Good shade tree but sometimes chlorotic and frequently very slow to mature. Used as a feature tree on school and college campuses and in parks. May reach 70–80 feet (21–25 m) tall, with a crown spread of 25–35 feet (8–11 m). Not for a small garden. Hardy. Full sun, some water, adapts to most soils.
Grows Best: Statewide.

Umbrella catalpa

Catalpa bignonioides 'Nana'
Spanish: *Catalpa "paraguas."*
Exotic small tree with large leaves and characteristically dense shade. Planted as a curiosity. Deciduous, 15–20 feet (5–6 m) tall, spreading equally wide. Short-lived. Full sun, medium quantities of water, medium growth rate. Not fussy about soils. Typically crowns very low. Variety of the southern catalpa, *Catalpa bignonioides.*
Grows Best: Statewide, up to 6000 feet/1830 m.

Catalpas

Chinaberry

Melia azedarach
Spanish: *Acederaque, jabonero de las Antillas.*
Usually no taller than 25 feet (8 m) nor wider in crown spread than 20 feet (6 m), chinaberry is a symmetrical, dependable, spring-flowering shade tree much used in southern New Mexico and as far north as Albuquerque. Delicate compound leaves are reminiscent of locusts; lavender flowers are star-shaped and very aromatic. Produces yellow berries in late summer. Tolerates the poorest soils but responds to well-manured backfill. A good street, shade, and parking lot tree. Grows at a moderate rate. Variety 'Umbraculiformis' is widely planted. Drought-tolerant.
Grows Best: Generally, southern New Mexico; full size as far north as Albuquerque.

Western chokecherry

Prunus virginiana
Spanish: *Capulín.*
Multi-trunked, bushy, small tree, a native of cool hillsides and streamsides above 7000 feet (2135 m) throughout New Mexico. Creamy white spring flowers, astringent cherries in midsummer (you can eat them, but they'll make your mouth pucker). May grow to 15 feet (5 m) or taller and equally wide. Deep green leaves. Well-manured soil and moderate water will contribute to blooms and chokecherry production. Needs selective pruning if raised as a tree; is more typically planted as a tall shrub mass. Very hardy. Cultivated varieties are available. Virtually always suckers.
Grows Best: Statewide.

Chokecherry

Aspens

COTTONWOODS, ASPEN, AND POPLARS
Trees of the genus Populus

Aspen, quaking aspen

Populus tremuloides
Spanish: *Álamo temblón.*
    Native of mountainous New Mexico, generally found at elevations of 7000 feet (2135 m) and higher. Spongy pale green or white bark with a rich, pungent smell. Grows to 70 feet (about 21 m) tall, spreading to 10 feet (3 m). Likes moist, rich soils, cool temperatures, lots of water. Excellent accent, shade, or street tree in northern New Mexico, Ruidoso area. Moderate rate of growth. Most delicate of poplars and cottonwoods; spectacular fall color. Leaves "dance" in the slightest breeze. Good patio tree.
Grows Best: High altitudes (above 6500 feet/ 2000 m) statewide.

Carolina poplar

Populus canadensis
Spanish: *Álamo.*
    An exotic, the Carolina poplar is widely planted in the Southwest for its unbelievably fast growth, generous shade, and uncomplaining nature. An enormous tree, it can reach 70 feet (21 m) in height, with a crown spread of perhaps 40 feet (12 m). Short-lived, with very invasive roots. Any soil; prefers a lot of water. Stocky form, but strongly resembles the native cottonwoods of the state. Deciduous.
Grows Best: Anywhere.

Fremont cottonwood

Populus fremontii
Spanish: *Álamo.*
    This is the native, deciduous "mountain" cottonwood of New Mexico. Holds its white, mottled bark into young maturity and typically has a slightly diagonal branching pattern. The bark and leaves have a fresh, somewhat astringent smell. Its variety 'Wislizeni,' or "valley" cottonwood, is quite similar but weaker in its branching patterns. Fremont cottonwood is tall (up to 70 feet/21 m), wide (40 feet/12 m or more), and yellow-orange in the fall. Any soil; drought-resistant, but likes water. Surface-rooting, but a good shade and specimen tree in parks or other large landscapes.
Grows Best: Statewide.

Carolina poplars

Lanceleaf cottonwood

Lanceleaf cottonwood

Populus acuminata
Spanish: *Álamo.*
    Immense native cottonwood reaching 70 feet (21 m) or more and about 40–50 feet (12–15 m) in crown spread. Glossy, deep green, arrowhead- or spearpoint-shaped leaves. Closely resembles the native Fremont or mountain cottonwood and the narrowleaf cottonwood. It is frequently confused with these species. Fast-growing, any soil, full sun. Very few insect pests. Moderate watering. A good but very large shade tree, with the usual annoying cottonwood habit of shallow or surface rooting. Smooth, shiny, very pale green bark matures to a fissured gray.
Grows Best: Statewide.

Mountain cottonwood

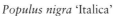

Lombardy poplar

Plains cottonwood

Lombardy poplar

Populus nigra 'Italica'
Spanish: *Álamo de Italia* or *chopo lombardo*.

Handsome, popular, thin, very tall exotic used frequently as a windscreen, border, or sky-line tree. Fast-growing, water-loving, indifferent to soils. Likes full sun. May reach 60 feet (18 m) or taller. Good yellow fall color. Not for small yards—has invasive roots that may extend horizontally for 40 feet (12 m) or more. Fades after 15–20 years. Not subject to disease. Good shade when planted in rows.
Grows Best: Statewide.

Narrowleaf cottonwood

Narrowleaf cottonwood

Populus angustifolia
Spanish: *Álamo mimbreño*.

This strong- and fast-growing native tree with willow-like leaves and an aggressive root system reaches 60–70 feet (18–21 m) in height with a crown spread of about 30 feet (9 m). Typically found above 7000 feet (2135 m). White bark in youth, quite reminiscent of aspen. Good fall color. Full sun, plenty of water, most soils. Very cold-hardy.
Grows Best: Statewide.

Plains cottonwood (prairie cottonwood)

Populus sargenti
Spanish: *Álamo*.

A truly enormous native tree of the plains and foothills of eastern New Mexico. May exceed 80 feet (25 m) in height and spread. Striking, triangular leaves, deeply fissured bark, extensive root system. Fast-growing, but relatively long-lived. Full sun; likes water but is drought-resistant. Similar to *Populus fremontii* but larger. Good for parks, rural roadsides, or shade in any large open space. Most soils. Very cold-hardy.
Grows Best: Anywhere.

Rio Grande cottonwood (valley cottonwood)

Populus fremontii 'Wislizeni'
Spanish: *Álamo*.

The classic native river-forest tree of New Mexico. Often called "valley" cottonwood. Extremely hardy and large—will grow anywhere. Not particular about soils, but surface roots may make it a nuisance. Withstands drought but likes water. Grows to 60 feet (18 m) tall or taller and is wide-crowned—60 feet or more. Broad, triangular leaves, deeply fissured bark, interesting (often grotesque) shape at maturity. Useful for fast, heavy shade but is not particularly long-lived. Weak branches snap in wind. Remarkable fall color. Leaves may turn bronze and stay on tree all winter. Not for small yards.
Grows Best: Statewide.

Rio Grande cottonwood

White poplar

American elm

Chinese elm

White poplar (silver poplar)

Populus alba
Spanish: *Álamo, Álamo blanco.*

An exotic that has naturalized well in New Mexico. Striking, maple-like leaves are teal-green on top and downy gray underneath. Very tall, up to 70 feet (21 m) in height with a spread of 40 feet (12 m) or so White or pale green bark, often mottled. Any soil, fast-growing, full sun. Impressive along roadsides. Inhabits disturbed streambeds, usually in mountainous areas. Often found above 5000 feet (1525 m). Invasive roots.
Grows Best: Statewide.

American elm

Ulmus americana
Spanish: *Olmo.*

Perhaps the most beautiful of elm trees. Very large, black-trunked and -limbed. American elm is an exotic, reaching up to 50 feet (15 m) in height, almost equal in spread. More solid in form than the similar (Asian) Siberian elm. Does not produce obnoxious seeds in spring. Strong grower at a medium rate. 'Wisconsin' variety is nearly immune to Dutch elm disease; good street tree, but should not be placed in grates. Full sun, moderate water, any soil. Very hardy.
Grows Best: Statewide.

Chinese (evergreen) elm

Ulmus parvifolia
Spanish: *Olmo.*

Evergreen in Southern California and similar climes, deciduous in New Mexico. An exotic tree, easily the most misidentified plant (it is always confused with its cousin *Ulmus pumila*, the Siberian elm) in the mountain West. Well-behaved (no excessive seeding), slow-growing to 20–30 feet (6–9 m), bigger in eastern New Mexico. Chinese elm is small-leaved, with striking, exfoliating bark. Likes full sun, is not particular about soil, prefers modest amounts of water. An excellent shade tree.
Grows Best: Southern New Mexico as far north as Albuquerque; eastern New Mexico.

Siberian elm

Ulmus pumila
Spanish: *Olmo.*

Naturalized tree from the vast North Asian interior. Probably the most widespread shade and windbreak tree in New Mexico. Often considered a pest, and much maligned; ironically, it was a favorite feature of the great CCC (Civilian Conservation Corps) parks of the 1930s. Almost supernaturally hardy; thrives in any soil with little or no water and is not affected by heat or cold. Can grow to 80 feet (25 m) in height, with a 50-foot (15 m) crown. Reseeds itself profusely in early spring. Too large for the small garden, it can serve as a good hedge plant or as a tough park or lawn tree under conditions of little to no maintenance. Often makes people sneeze. Frequently called "Chinese" elm, which it is not. Good windbreak tree. Prefers full sun but will grow in complete shade. Suffers from Dutch elm disease and elm beetles, but these pests only tend to slow it down somewhat and make it unsightly. A common roadside tree. Spectacular winter profile.
Grows Best: Statewide.

Siberian elm

Ginkgo

Common hackberry

Honey locust

Maidenhair tree (ginkgo)

Ginkgo biloba
Spanish: *Ginkgo.*

Among the most ancient of trees, the ginkgo, a native of China, is now a common exotic street, shade, and curiosity tree across the United States. Extremely adaptable, with unique, fan-shaped leaves. Full sun or partial shade, moderate water, not particular about soils. Modest growth to about 30 feet (9 m) in New Mexico. Excellent deep yellow fall color. Select males for planting, as females produce malodorous, messy fruits. Several varieties.
Grows Best: Anywhere.

Hackberry

Common hackberry

Celtis occidentalis
Spanish: *Palo blanco.*

Exotic shade tree used in streetside and park plantings. Much resembles elm, to which it is closely related. May reach 40 feet (12 m) or more, spreading as wide, with a moderate growth rate. Likes well-manured soil and adequate water, must have full sun. Resistant to trying urban conditions but may be slow to establish (and sometimes chlorotic) in alkaline soils. It is sometimes erratic in sidewalk plantings but very beautiful as it matures. Hardy and deep-rooting.
Grows Best: Statewide.

Netleaf hackberry

Celtis laevigata var. *reticulata*
Spanish: *Palo blanco.*

Rangy native tree, often sparse but interesting in form. In New Mexico it grows to about 18 feet (5.5 m) in both height and width. Likes stony or gravelly soil, full sun, regular water. Occurs in small groves naturally in watercourses in southern and southwestern New Mexico. Has small, edible berries that attract birds in the domestic landscape. Good as an accent, especially in masses. Slow to moderate growth rate.
Grows Best: Statewide.

Honey locust

Gleditsia triacanthos inermis and varieties
Spanish: *Acacia de tres espinas.*

This is a native American tree from the Midwest, prized in cultivation for its lithe form, feathery shade, and intriguing compound leaves. Grows in most soils but prefers rich loam. Modest watering needed. Moderate growth rate, often fast when young. A very common lawn and street tree, may grow up to 40 feet (12 m) tall, with an equal spread. Non-invasive roots. Full sun or partial shade. The native tree is savagely thorny, so cultivated thornless varieties should be used. Some varieties also produce no seed pods. Inconspicuous, green flowers, rusty-orange foliage in fall.

Among the most commonly planted varieties of honey locust are these:

'Shademaster.' Tall, well-formed, substantial crown.

'Moraine.' Tall, more densely branching than 'Shademaster.'

'Sunburst.' Strongly horizontal in branching habit. Modest size. Yellow early leaves give it the appearance of a flowering ornamental, but these turn deep green in summer. Grows well and fast in caliche (lime) soils.
Grows Best: Statewide.

Horsechestnut

Western (common) hackberry growing at an Anasazi hamlet (Hovenweep National Monument)

Japanese pagoda

Horsechestnut

Aesculus hippocastanum
Spanish: *Castaño de Indias.*

Common in Santa Fe, this striking exotic shade tree has distinctive, six-fingered leaves and waxy, white, upright spring flowers. Grows to 35–40 feet (11–12 m) tall, with a spread that is equally wide. Moderate growth rate. Prefers full sun in any soil. Likes water but can survive with little irrigation once established. An excellent street tree, with a characteristic teardrop shape. (Also infrequently found is red horsechestnut, *Aesculus carnea.*)
Grows Best: Albuquerque and northern New Mexico.

California buckeye

Aesculus californica
Spanish: *Castaño de Indias.*

A small shade tree with whitish-yellow spring flowers, comfortable in sun and shade or heavy shade. Grows well even in poor caliche (lime) soils. In New Mexico, may reach 15 feet (5 m) in height, with an equal spread. Good small patio tree. Likes a moderate amount of water. Relatively slow grower. Sometimes hard to obtain.
Grows Best: Albuquerque and southern New Mexico.

Japanese pagoda

Sophora japonica
Spanish: *Sófora.*

This compound-leafed shade tree also produces abundant yellow flowers in spring. Feathery shade. Grows in tough conditions, including caliche (lime) soils, to a height of 60-plus feet (18 m), with a spread of about 30 feet (9 m). Moderate rate of growth. As the tree ages, its limbs and trunk twist and develop great character. This green-trunked tree somewhat resembles black locust when young. Moderate to heavy water.
Grows Best: Anywhere.

Jujube (Chinese jujube)

Zizyphus jujuba
Spanish: *Azufaifo.*

Exotic tree that, despite its name, probably comes from the Middle East. Should be more widely cultivated in New Mexico, as it serves as an excellent, drought-resistant patio tree. Trunk and branches become gnarled and blackened, acquiring character with age. Interesting bright green, alternate leaves. Slight yellow flowers in spring. Grows to about 20 feet (6 m) tall and as wide. Not fussy about soils, but produces better shade with good manuring. Drought-resistant but likes periodic deep watering. Full sun. Long-lived. Slow to medium growth rate.
Grows Best: Albuquerque and southern New Mexico. Fond of deserts.

Jujube

California buckeye

Black locust

Linden

Idaho locust

Littleleaf linden

Tilia cordata
Spanish: *Tilo* or *Teja.*

Very hardy exotic lawn and park tree with deep green, heart-shaped leaves. Needs full sun, well-manured soil, plenty of water. Wonderful shade, sweet-smelling whitish flowers in summer. Grows slowly to about 40 feet (12 m) in New Mexico, and spreads as wide or wider. Symmetrical in shape. Relatively rare. Several cultivars are available.
Grows Best: Albuquerque and northern New Mexico.

Black locust

Robinia pseudoacacia
Spanish: *Acacia falsa.*

Naturalized shade, street, and specimen tree. A very tough legume; hardy throughout New Mexico and the West. Covered with white flowers in May and June, followed by pods. Usually spiny. Reaches 40 to (rarely) 50 feet (about 12–15 m) in height, spreading to 25–30 feet (8–9 m). Light to medium watering, full sun, any soil; in fact, black locust does very well in New Mexico's thin soils. Fast grower. Charcoal-colored, ridged trunk develops good character over time.

Excellent choice for difficult planting conditions. Strong root system is good for erosion control but may also lead to objectionable suckering.
Grows Best: Anywhere.

Hybrid locusts

Robinia amibigua and varieties
Spanish: *Acacia falsa.*

These are the pink flowering locusts frequently used as accents or for spring color throughout New Mexico. Exotics. Generally good growers and cold-hardy, but not as tough or adaptable as black locust. These trees generally reach 25 feet (8 m) in height, spreading to approximately 20 feet (6 m). Moderate to fast growth rate. They take heat and drought well and are not particular about soils. Full sun and moderate watering after planting will speed growth. As a rule, hybrid locusts are not long-lived, and they do not sucker as badly as black or New Mexico locust.

Varieties include:

Idaho locust, *Robinia ambigua* 'Idahoensis.' Brilliant deep pink or reddish-purple spring bloom, light gray bark. Spectacular when it grows, Idaho locust is fussy: don't overwater. It seems to perform better in planters and tree grates than in lawns.

Purple robe locust, *Robinia ambigua* 'Purple Robe.' Beautiful, shining new foliage, deep purple blossoms. Very attractive and seemingly more dependable than Idaho locust.

Decaisneana locust, *Robinia ambigua* 'Decaisneana.' Light pink bloom, reliable growth pattern, nearly as hardy as black locust and with handsomer flowers. Not found as commonly as Idaho and purple robe varieties.
Grows Best: Statewide.

New Mexico locust

Robinia neomexicana
Spanish: *Acacia falsa.*

Surprisingly hardy and thorny small tree covered with attractive pinkish blossoms in late spring and summer. Native legume. Very fast-growing up to 20 feet (6 m) or more and thicket-forming. Older specimens have black, ridged trunks much like the black locust. Largest specimens are found in the Sandia and Manzano ranges, where pure, tall stands or small forests occur with some frequency in canyons. Excellent patio tree, massed background plant, or windbreak. Likes full sun or partial shade, any soil, little or moderate water. Very good for erosion control. Drought-resistant.
Grows Best: Statewide.

New Mexico locust

Bigtooth maple

Bigtooth maple

Acer grandidentatum (Acer saccharum grandidentatum)
Spanish: *Arce.*

All the maples like good drainage, and this brightly colored (in fall) understory tree of the New Mexico mountains is no exception. Many botanists consider it a subspecies or form of the eastern sugar maple, *Acer saccharum.* Usually rare in its forest habitat. Its delicate leaves are a good contrast to the conifers it usually accompanies. It is often shrubby and as a tree rarely exceeds 20–25 feet (about 7 m) in height. Its spread is extremely variable. Prefers shade, limestone soils, light to moderate water. Slow to moderate growth rate.

Bigtooth maple is very useful as a shade-area garden accent. Along with Rocky Mountain maple, it may be grown in any garden locale in which you would plant a Japanese maple.
Grows Best: In shade, above 6000 feet (1830 m).

Box elder

Acer negundo
Spanish: *Arce.*

This tousled, shaggy native tree can grow to a surprising 40 feet (12 m) when cultivated, spreading to about 30 feet (9 m). It has curious simple *and* compound leaves, frequently on the same tree; prominent, warty galls covering trunks and branches; and sugary sap, much like that of the sugar maple, *Acer saccharum.* You can tap a box elder for syrup. The tree is often plagued by box elder beetles, which cause little harm but buzz noisily around the heads of unsuspecting visitors. Transplants well and easily, lives a relatively short life, and adapts well to any planting soil or situation. Likes water but takes drought; in the mountains, it invariably prefers streamsides. Shade or full sun. Generally messy.

This sturdy but uncouth tree has a niche in the countryside as a shade tree for outbuildings or massed in groupings for windbreaks. Box elder is perhaps not a prime maple, but it certainly has personality, character, and a rough-edged charm. Birds like it. A little judicious pruning (sometimes performed by windstorms) can turn it into a surprisingly interesting curiosity or accent.
Grows Best: Anywhere.

Box elder

Japanese maple

Acer palmatum
Spanish: *Arce.*

* In lg. Raised Bed. Look in western Garden book under Acer palmatum.

Delicate, slow-growing, shade-loving exotic tree or shrub. Fond of rich, moist soils but will grow in almost any New Mexican soil. Usually reaches 12–15 feet (about 4 m) in height, spreading as wide. Very fine branching structure. Japanese maple is one of the few true shade-loving plants available for New Mexican landscapes. Quite drought-tolerant once established. Usually employed as an accent for a small space but also effective in mass plantings. Many varieties available, including a popular one with red leaves that grows extremely slowly. Never plant in full sun in New Mexico.
Grows Best: Statewide in shade.

Norway maple

Acer platanoides
Spanish: *Arce.*

Highly adaptable exotic shade tree growing to about 30 feet (9 m) tall in New Mexico, and nearly as wide. Has broad, thick, deep green leaves (bright yellow in fall), and fissured, well-formed gray trunk. Grows at a moderate rate. Needs full sun, medium watering, and well-manured soil for best performance. Roots may surface somewhat, and the tree is sometimes affected by aphids. Nevertheless, it is a good, long-lived shade tree for lawns and gardens. Purple-leafed variety is sometimes difficult to start and/or stunted as it matures.
Grows Best: Albuquerque and similar elevations (5000–6000 feet/1525–1830 m).

Japanese maple

Norway (Schwedler) maple

Rocky Mountain maple

Silver maple (reticulated, or deep-lobed, form)

Sycamore-leaf maple

Rocky Mountain maple

Acer glabrum
Spanish: *Arce.*

Small, colorful native maple of mountainsides and canyons in New Mexico. Grows to about 20–25 feet (6–8 m) tall but is typically 10–15 feet (about 4 m) wide, with an irregular crown. Never common, it usually occurs as an accent in high spruce and fir forests. Often multi-trunked. Slow-growing, fond of sun or partial shade and moist soils, and develops an interesting mottled gray trunk. Like bigtooth maple, Rocky Mountain maple may be used as a small accent or beautiful curiosity tree or as a good native substitute for Japanese maple.
Grows Best: In shade, above 6000 feet (1830 m).

Silver maple

Acer saccharinum
Spanish: *Arce.*

Fast-growing, very large, exotic shade tree with attractive, silvery bark and purple branch tips. Good mature form (up to 50 feet/15 m, spreading to 40 feet/12 m), pleasant leaf texture (green on top, silver on bottom). Often suffers from chlorosis in alkaline soils (i.e., throughout New Mexico), and branches frequently snap off in the wind. Highly invasive roots often surface to disrupt sidewalks, patios, and foundations. Good fall color—usually yellow tinged with red.

Silver maple grows in full sun, likes moderate watering, and prefers rich soils. Nevertheless, it will grow in partial shade (when young) with very little water and in extremely poor soils. It is useful as a shade or park tree under difficult conditions. Most frequently a second-choice tree, it does seem to thrive in the Southwest in great open lawn spaces, where the extensive grass can keep its root zone cool. In these situations, it may form remarkable buttress roots.
Grows Best: Statewide, but not fond of deserts.

Sycamore-leaf maple

Acer pseudoplatanus
Spanish: *Arce.*

With a leaf that closely resembles that of the American sycamore or London plane tree, the exotic sycamore-leaf maple grows very well in a wide variety of landscape settings in New Mexico. It prefers well-manured soil, full sun, moderate water. Slow to moderate growth rate, forms a good crown and provides dense shade. A good parkway, lawn, and park tree. Long-lived. Gray, fissured trunk, generally attractive. Strong-branching. May reach 35 feet (11 m) tall, about 25 feet (8 m) wide. Probably the best of the maple shade trees for New Mexico.
Grows Best: Statewide, 4500–6000 feet (1400–1830 m).

Honey mesquite

Prosopis glandulosa
Spanish: *Mesquite, tornillo.*

A sizable tree (up to 25 feet/8 m in height and width) or thorny shrub occurring naturally in the Rio Grande Valley, the Pecos Valley, and the eastern plains of New Mexico. A common medium-sized park tree in El Paso and Las Cruces. Compound leaves produce light, filtered shade. Attractive yellow flowers. Moderate growth rate. Very drought-resistant. Prefers full sun, is indifferent to soils. Grows quickly with water and produces an unbelievable taproot—40 feet (12 m) long or longer. Close relative screwbean (*Prosopis pubescens*) is much less dense, usually grown as a shrub. (Please see section on deciduous shrubs.)
Grows Best: El Paso and southern New Mexico, as far north as Isleta.

Mountain ash (rowan)

Sorbus aucuparia
Spanish: *Mostajo* or *serbal (de los cazadores).*

A beautifully formed small tree with an excellent diagonal branching habit and clusters of red berries in late summer and fall. Compound, delicate leaves; bronze autumn color. Trunk is orange or bronze. Moderate water. Well-behaved, slow-growing up to 25 feet (8 m) in Santa Fe and northern New Mexico. Does not mind alkaline soil but dislikes hot deserts. Exotic. Good for accent or modest patio shade.
Grows Best: 5000 feet (1525 m) and above.

Fruitless mulberry grove

Mountain ash

Paper mulberry

Fruitless (white) mulberry

Morus alba
Spanish: *Morera*.

This fast-growing exotic is a much-prized provider of shade in southern New Mexico and the El Paso area. Gives very dense shade very quickly (grows up to 6 feet/2 m per year); may reach 40 feet (12 m) in both height and width. Broad, serrated, heart-shaped, kelly-green leaves; the same tree may display deeply lobed leaves. Drought-resistant but likes water and loves heat. Any soil, full sun. Branches awkwardly. Fruiting mulberry has a much better shape but creates a terrible mess in summer. Mulberry typically produces invasive surface roots and multiple, suckering branches after pruning. Extremely hardy. Many people are allergic to its pollen.

The weeping varieties, *Morus alba* 'Pendula' and *M. a.* 'Teas' Weeping,' only grow to 15 feet (5 m) and are compelling garden curiosities. *Grows Best:* Statewide, below 7500 feet (2300 m). Grows exceptionally well in El Paso, Ciudad Juárez, and the Mesilla Valley.

Paper mulberry

Broussonetia papyrifera
Spanish: *Papelero*.

Exotic curiosity tree, very hardy, and closely related to true mulberries (*Morus* species). Paper mulberry grows to about 20–25 feet (6–8 m) in New Mexico, spreading to 18 feet (about 6 m) or more in width. Heart-shaped leaves may also be lobed. Moderate growth rate in any soil. Full sun or partial shade. Takes drought once established. A more refined tree than true mulberry. *Grows Best:* Albuquerque and southern New Mexico.

Mesquite

46

Cork oak

OAKS

This genus of sturdy, legendary hardwood trees and shrubs has many dozens of flourishing native representatives throughout New Mexico. However, oaks are generally so difficult to propagate and so slow-growing that almost none of the native species has been brought into common cultivation. Of the five species recommended here for New Mexico gardens and landscapes, three are exotics from nearby states and one is the classic, semi-evergreen cork oak of the Mediterranean.

Oaks are so strikingly handsome and so widely characteristic of New Mexico, the Rockies, and the Southwest that we can certainly expect them to be much more widely used in the region in the near future. They can be grown successfully from wild, collected acorns. (Please do not dig individual trees or clumps of trees in the wild —they transplant poorly, and their removal may violate state and federal law and cause erosion and general environmental degradation.) But don't expect quick results: oaks have always been trees that you plant for your children or grandchildren.

Gambel oak

Cork oak

Quercus suber
Spanish: *Alcornoque, encina.*

An attractive and surprisingly robust exotic, well suited to lawns in warm southern New Mexico. Tolerates thin, alkaline soils. Moderate growth rate, full sun, semi-evergreen. In New Mexico, may reach 30 feet (9 m) in height and about 20–25 feet (6–8 m) in crown spread. Leaves are green on top, gray underneath. Very drought-tolerant. The thick, peelable bark is a striking curiosity.
Grows Best: Las Cruces, Deming, Alamogordo, El Paso, as far north as Truth or Consequences.

Gambel oak

Quercus gambelii
Spanish: *Roble.*
(Other small scrub oaks are called *encina* [live oak] and *carrasco* [live oak].)

Characteristic oak of the foothills and mountains of central and northern New Mexico. Generally shrubby and thicket-forming, with attractive bark, limb and trunk structure, leaves, and acorns. Slow-growing, tough, completely cold-hardy, best in richer soils. Needs moderate watering. Can reach 25 feet (8 m) or more and is highly variable in spread. Often associated with ponderosa pine. Yellow, tan, or reddish-brown fall color. Shade or sun. Frequently difficult to find domestically, but quite striking when used in higher-altitude landscapes.
Grows Best: Albuquerque and northern New Mexico, western New Mexico, Ruidoso area.

Pin oak

Quercus palustris
Spanish: *Roble.*

Extraordinarily appealing exotic shade tree, relatively fast-growing, and well adapted to most New Mexican soil conditions—especially on the eastern plains. Tall (may reach 60 feet/18 m or more) and spreading widely with maturity. Wonderful, many-lobed leaves with pointed tips. Needs full sun, well-manured soil, moderate to heavy water. Good in lawns. Grows relatively quickly. Often develops chlorosis, which can be easily treated with iron sulphate or chelate.
Grows Best: Statewide.

Southern live oak

Quercus virginiana
Spanish: *Encina, carrasco.*

Semi-evergreen in New Mexico, the exotic southern live oak is an enormous tree in its native Texas and elsewhere in the South, where it is used for street, park, and large lawn plantings. Long-lived. Likes well-manured, deep soils and heavy watering. Not fond of alkaline soils. May reach 30–40 feet (9–12 m) in height in New Mexico, spreading to about 45 feet (14 m). Slow to moderate growth. Needs full sun and plenty of room. Semi-hardy.
Grows Best: Hobbs, Lovington, Carlsbad. Also Las Cruces, El Paso. Elsewhere in southern New Mexico, but quite rare. Two specimens as far north as Albuquerque.

Texas oak

Quercus texana
Spanish: *Roble.*

Slightly exotic, the Texas oak grows to about 30 feet (9 m) in New Mexico, with a crown spread of about 20 feet (6 m). It is an extraordinary accent or lawn specimen for the plains of eastern New Mexico, a region of very few native trees, where it seems to adapt readily. It has beautifully deep-lobed leaves and a habit of growing with appealing multiple trunks. Moderate growth rate. Highly wind-resistant. Prefers full sun and moderate water, and tolerates heavy soils and alkalinity. Few pests or objectionable growth habits.Widely and easily available. Closely related to Shumard oak, *Quercus shumardii.*
Grows Best: Eastern New Mexico.

Osage orange (bois d'arc)

Maclura pomifera
Spanish: *Maclura.*

Osage orange is a remarkable member of the mulberry family with a fruit that resembles a heavy, warty grapefruit. Slightly exotic, native to Oklahoma and Texas. In New Mexico it grows to about 30 feet (9 m) or taller, spreading equally wide. Tough, hardy, and thorny. The enormous, heavy fruits (several pounds each) form only on female trees, but they limit the use of osage oranges to hedges, fencelines, and backdrop plantings, where no one will be surprised by a thump on the head. Fast-growing, any soil, full sun, any amount of water. Very little maintenance required.

Bois d'arcs (pronounced "bow-darks") are classic nineteenth-century trees in New Mexico, where they are often found growing happily in old mining and ghost towns. They have naturalized themselves in some mountain locations.
Grows Best: Statewide. Anywhere.

Osage orange

Pecan

Carya illinoiensis
Spanish: *Pacana.*

Very tough, long-lived shade and nut tree. Especially well adapted in the valleys of southern and eastern New Mexico, where it is an important agricultural tree. Exotic. Requires full sun, deep, rich (manured) soil, and a good deal of water. Actually a relatively quick-growing hickory. May reach 60 feet (18 m) or taller, spreading to about 50 feet (15 m). Beautiful compound leaves; savory, pleasantly scented nuts. Excellent shade or orchard tree. Sometimes available only in bareroot because of its deep taproot. Many varieties.
Grows Best: Southern New Mexico, as far north as Albuquerque.

Pecans

Texas oak

Southern live oak

Chinese pistache

Chinese pistache

Pistacia chinensis
Spanish: *Pistacho, alfóncigo.*

Exotic shade and specimen tree reaching 30–40 feet (about 12 m) tall and nearly as wide. Impressive compound leaf structure. Leaves turn a brilliant red in fall. Fruit (inedible) is also red early in the season, later turning blue. Moderately fast grower. Likes well-manured, deeper soils but will tolerate both alkaline New Mexican soils and drought once established. Full sun, moderate water for best growth. Chinese pistache also makes a reliable, hardy street tree.
Grows Best: As far north as Albuquerque; primarily southern New Mexico.

Pistachio

Pistacia vera
Spanish: *Pistacho, alfóncigo.*

Nut-bearing, exotic tree grown in southern New Mexico as a valuable orchard crop producer. May reach 25 feet (8 m) in height and spread as wide. Prefers full sun, well-manured soil, and deep, periodic waterings, but can take drought handily. Not as showy as Chinese pistache, but an excellent bearing tree. Both males and females must be planted to insure successful nut production. May need to be staked when young for best form.
Grows Best: Southern New Mexico.

Russian olive

Elaeagnus angustifolia
Spanish: *Cinamomo, olivo, aceituno (ruso).*

Naturalized, gray-leafed deciduous tree or very large shrub, fast-growing, tough, and widely adapted throughout New Mexico. Likes water but can withstand drought with few problems. Yellow, sweet-smelling flowers in summer, followed by "olives" that are palatable to wildlife. Excellent park, shade, windbreak, or specimen tree. Very hardy. Sun or partial shade. Any soil. May be thorny and is sometimes short-lived. Grows to 30 feet (9 m) tall or more, equally wide. Closely resembles its relative the European (true) olive, *Olea europaea.* Can be trained as a hedge, as it takes pruning well. May become a noxious pest in stream courses.
Grows Best: Statewide.

Russian olive

Silk tree (mimosa)

Albizia julibrissin
Spanish: *Mimosa.*

Remarkable exotic, noted for its fine, compound leaves that curl up at sundown, its parasol-like canopy, and its pink, pompon-like flowers. Medium growth rate to 25 feet (8 m), with very wide crown (up to 40 feet/12 m). Likes rich soils but will grow almost anywhere. Full sun, moderate watering. Good as a lawn tree; good shade tree for patios, but it is messy. Little or no fall color. May die back in center from cold or other causes.
Grows Best: Southern New Mexico as far north as Albuquerque; eastern New Mexico.

Silk tree

American sycamore

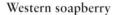
Soapberry

Arizona sycamore

Western soapberry

Sapindus drummondii
Spanish: *Sapindo.*

Native tree of extraordinary character, usually occurring along arroyos and streams in the lower Rio Grande drainage of New Mexico but widespread in the Southwest and central plains and in Mexico. May reach 50 feet (15 m) or more in both height and width. Fast-growing and attractive, with pinnate leaves and many attractive fruits (berries). The bark is scaly and gray-orange. Soapberries need full sun but will grow in any soil. Moderate watering preferred, but highly drought-resistant. Very good shade and parking lot tree. The berries will lather up into soap and are poisonous; however, they are bitterly inedible at all stages.
Grows Best: Statewide.

Sweet gum

Liquidambar styraciflua
Spanish: *Liquidámbar.*

Exotic tree, infrequently grown as a curiosity in New Mexico for its red fall color. Slow-growing, sometimes chlorotic in alkaline soils. Likes good drainage and does not flourish in New Mexican soils. Likes water, full sun. May reach 20–25 feet (6–8 m) in height, with an equal spread. Leaves have attractive, pointed lobes.
Grows Best: Southern New Mexico as far north as Albuquerque.

American sycamore

Platanus occidentalis
Spanish: *Plátano.*

Tall, wide-branching, sturdy exotic, grown in several varieties. Noted for its striking, exfoliating bark. May reach 60 feet (18 m) or taller, with an equal spread. Moderate growth rate. Premium shade tree, useful in large lawns, as a park street tree, for plaza shade, or as a feature. Any soil, but subject to chlorosis. Medium to heavy watering. Full sun. Cultivated in several varieties. Hardy.
Grows Best: Statewide.

Arizona sycamore

Platanus wrightii
Spanish: *Plátano.*

Tallest of native deciduous trees, found in the Gila River drainage of southwestern New Mexico and along one tributary of the Rio Grande in south central New Mexico. Immense, multi-trunked, stunning tree with creamy-white bark and, in older specimens, branches like the arms of ghosts. Leaves deep-lobed. Moderate growth rate. Found along watercourses; prefers sandy or stony soil, good drainage. Full sun. Excellent park or street tree, or may be grown as a curiosity. Up to 90 feet (28 m) tall, 50 feet (15 m) wide.
Grows Best: Southern New Mexico, as far north as Albuquerque.

Sweet gum

California sycamore

California sycamore

Platanus recemosa
Spanish: *Plátano.*
Very similar to Arizona sycamore in appearance, growth habits, and detail, the exotic California sycamore is not as widely planted in New Mexico. Informal in appearance, typically used in naturalistic landscapes. Not as hardy as Arizona sycamore in the high desert. May suffer from spider mites. Quick growth rate.
Grows Best: As far north as Albuquerque. Best in southern part of state, but it may perform erratically.

London plane tree (sycamore)

Platanus acerifolia
Spanish: *Plátano.*
An immense, hybrid exotic, possibly New Mexico's most popular shade tree. Classic vase shape up to 50 feet (15 m) or higher, spreading to 40 feet (12 m) or more. Dense shade, with attractive, wide, three-lobed leaves. Hanging, late fruits in spiny balls. Fast growth rate. Any soil, full sun, moderate water. Very hardy. Excellent park and street tree, especially in formal plantings, but not for small gardens. Wonderful, exfoliating bark. May suffer from chlorosis. Parent species are likely *Platanus occidentalis* and *Platanus orientalis.*
Grows Best: Statewide except at highest altitudes.

London plane tree

Oriental plane tree (oriental sycamore)

Platanus orientalis
Spanish: *Plátano.*
Stately shade tree, and the fabled *chenar* of Persian, Arab, and Spanish gardens. This is the plane tree of the water gardens of Kashmir, Samarqand, Isfahan, and the Caucasus, especially Georgia. Very tall (up to 70 feet/21 m), spreading to 40–50 feet (12–15 m). Three-lobed leaves with filigreed (interestingly serrated) margins. Likes moderate water and full sun, does not mind New Mexico's indifferent soils. Excellent shade, street, and curiosity tree. Moderate growth rate. It is one of the parents of the London plane tree (*Platanus acerifolia*), which is much more frequently planted.
Grows Best: Albuquerque and southeastern New Mexico.

Oriental plane tree

Ailanthus (tree of heaven)

Arizona walnut

English walnut

Tree of heaven

Ailanthus altissima
Spanish: *Zumaque del Japón, árbol del cielo, ailanto,* or *barniz del Japón.*

Naturalized deciduous tree found statewide. With salt cedar and Siberian elm, the most maligned tree in New Mexico. Grows anywhere, in any soil, with any amount of water and care. Profuse suckers, or water roots. Often found in ruined gardens and on the sites of abandoned towns. Up to 30 feet (about 9 m) tall, spreading to 20 feet (6 m). Profuse flowers and seeds; the male is reputed to produce a disagreeable odor. Despite its difficulties, ailanthus can make a very pleasant shade or street tree in the right setting, and its fast growth generates much-needed shade. Curiously, it does not transplant well.
Grows Best: Statewide, positively anywhere.

Arizona walnut

Juglans major
Spanish: *Nogal.*

Spreading, usually multi-trunked native tree with a wonderful, fresh scent. Attractive, compound leaves, handsome black bark. Grows along sunny arroyos and streams in southern and south central New Mexico. Likes full sun, moderate water, will tolerate most soils. Usually reaches 30 feet (9 m) or more, in both height and width. Fast-growing. Nuts are a delicious by-product of this fine shade tree. May be grown easily in place from nuts themselves if plant stock is not available. Tough-natured; can withstand drought.
Grows Best: Southwestern New Mexico, eastern Plains, Rio Grande Valley as far north as Albuquerque.

English (Carpathian) walnut

Juglans regia
Spanish: *Nogal.*

Pleasant-smelling, tall, sturdy, nut-producing, exotic hardwood. Grows to about 30–40 feet (9–12 m) in height and width. The walnuts themselves are borne in attractive, ball-like clusters among the rounded, lime-green leaflets. Leaves and nut casings release their aroma when damaged or crushed. Slow-growing, except when young, and very long-lived. Messy. Although English walnut prefers rich soil and abundant, deep water, it adapts generally well throughout central New Mexico. Full sun. Bark is a rich, silvery gray that develops prominent ridges as the tree grows older. Better in planters than lawns. Many varieties; 'Mesa' is hardiest of all (to -50° F).
Grows Best: Albuquerque and central New Mexico up to about 6000 feet (1830 m); eastern New Mexico.

Corkscrew willow

Salix matsudana 'Tortuosa'
Spanish: *Sauce, mimbre.*

Curious exotic tree with twisted branches. Very attractive in winter profile or in leaf. Upright branching pattern to about 25 feet (8 m), spreading to 20 feet (6 m). Hardy. Likes water, but can resist drought well. Any soil. Fast rate of growth. Needs full sun. More delicate than many tree willows, including the very closely related globe Navajo willow. Adapts virtually anywhere.
Grows Best: Statewide.

Corkscrew willow

Globe willow

Peachleaf willow

Salix amygdaloides
Spanish: *Mimbre, sauce.*

Common, tall, native willow (up to 30 feet/9 m tall, about 25 feet/8 m wide) with an attractive, dark-colored trunk and leaves very like those of peach trees. Fast-growing, phenomenally hardy. Grows as high as 8000 feet (2440 m) in the northern mountains and down watercourses to the plains of eastern New Mexico. Likes moisture but is not fussy about soils. Good, sometimes short-lived shade tree. A good choice for a rural allee, or double row of trees shading a road. Disruptive roots near buildings.
Grows Best: Statewide.

Globe Navajo willow

Salix matsudana 'Navajo'
Spanish: *Mimbre, sauce.*

An enormous exotic, but very much at home in the San Juan Valley, where it can reach 60–70 feet (18–21 m) in height, spreading to 50 feet (15 m) or more. Rich greenish-yellow dolor, and one of the first trees to bud out in the spring. Fast-growing, formally shaped. Grows in any soil but likes water. Full sun. May be short-lived, often dying in the center, but it will be generally trouble-free throughout its life span. Not for small areas. Very tough. Intense shade. Striking landscape effect.

A quite similar but smaller tree is the common globe willow, *Salix matsudana* 'Umbraculifera.'
Grows Best: Statewide.

Weeping willow

Salix babylonica (also *Salix alba tristis,* golden weeping willow, and occasionally *Salix blanda,* Wisconsin weeping willow.)
Spanish: *Mimbre, sauce llorón.*

A remarkably beautiful exotic, looks best beside a pond or on a stream bank. Very fast-growing, with sweeping, hanging branches. Generally climbs to about 40 feet (12 m) and spreads as wide. Graceful, pleasant-smelling leaves. Hardy, likes moisture, but tolerates most soils. Short-lived. A switch cut off and placed in moist soil will produce a new tree. Stake or train it a bit to make it crown high. Close relative of the cottonwoods and poplars.
Grows Best: Statewide.

Peachleaf willow

Weeping willow

TREES
FLOWERING ORNAMENTALS

ALL PLANTS IN THIS SECTION ARE IDENTIFIED AS NATIVE, EXOTIC, OR NATURALIZED.

Desert willow bloom

Apricot

Prunus armeniaca varieties
Spanish: *Chabacano* or *albaricoque.*

    An exotic tree of multiple uses. Grown for its strong flowering color, shade, and fruit. Frequently reaches 20 feet (6 m) in both height and width. Shiny, rounded triangular leaves. Modest growth rate, full sun. Prefers good soil, good drainage, and adequate watering but is not fussy. As a stone fruit, may be subject to borers, but not to the degree suffered by its relatives the plums. Hardy. May bloom early and be nipped by frost.
Grows Best: Statewide.

Flowering cherry

Prunus serrulata and varieties
Spanish: *Cerezo.*

    This exotic and the closely related *Prunus serrula* are frequently found in New Mexico gardens. Quite tall for a flowering fruit tree (up to 20–30 feet/6–9 m). Flowering cherry is actually the tallest of the stone fruits. May be equally wide. Moderate growth; needs full sun and good drainage, modest watering. Hates pruning. Sometimes planted for brilliant bark alone (*P. serrula*). Attractive, saw-edged leaves. Often successful in New Mexico in gravelly or sandy but fertile soils.
Grows Best: Statewide.

Flowering crab

Malus 'Hopa' et al.
Spanish: *Manzano silvestre (manzano de conservas).*

    Very hardy, showy, sturdy, exotic flowering ornamental. Planted for its spring blossoms, which may range in color from white to pink to cheerful red. Produces a light to heavy crop of crab or small apples, often used in jellies. A small tree, 12–16 feet (4–5 m) tall, sometimes taller, with a crown of equal width, it has a better form than the true apple. Slow-growing, but tolerant of virtually any soil and elevation. Full sun, moderate water. Can be planted anywhere in New Mexico.
Grows Best: Statewide.

Desert willow

Chilopsis linearis
Spanish: *Mimbre.*

    Widespread native tree or large shrub, up to 30 feet (9 m) tall with a crown spread of 20–30 feet (6–9 m). Remarkable gnarled trunk and small size make it an ideal patio tree as far north as Bernalillo. Occurs in Rio Grande, Pecos, and Gila drainages (dry washes) throughout the southern two-thirds of New Mexico. Fast growth; light to heavy watering acceptable. Desert willow is at home in a lawn or on a dry, sunwashed hillside. Colorful, orchid-like flowers cover the tree from late spring to early fall. Any soil. New cultivars available; *C. l.* 'Hope' is very tall and hardy.
Grows Best: Southern two-thirds of the state, as far north as Bernallillo or Algodones.

Apricot

Flowering cherry

Flowering crab

Desert willow

Hawthorn

Mexican elder

Flowering peach

Mexican elder

*Sambucus caerulea neomexicana
(Sambucus mexicana)*
Spanish: *Saúco.*

Very large native elder, grown as a substantial shrub or small tree as far north as Bernalillo. Grows in the cool seasons—spring and fall. Winter deciduous in the north, often summer-dormant or deciduous in the south. Evergreen during mild winters. Phenomenally fast growth—4 feet (1.2 m) or more in a season. May reach 20 feet (6 m) or more in height, equally wide. Drought-resistant, but grows faster with water and in well-manured soil. Excellent patio tree in south. Light yellow flowers, often strong-smelling, very profuse; fruit (elderberry) is bluish-black, round, delicious.

Trees usually need hard pruning for form to develop proper parasol shape. Reaches full size from a scraggly five-gallon plant in two to three years.
Grows Best: Southern New Mexico as far north as Bernalillo.

Hawthorn

Crataegus spp.
Spanish: *Majuelo* or *espino.*

Hawthorns are tough exotics from Europe and the southern United States that are often used in New Mexico as multi-trunk accents. English hawthorn, *Crataegus laevigata*, grows to about 20 feet (6 m), spreading approximately as wide. Attractive three-lobed leaves, spring flowers, reddish fruit. Likes moderate water, most soils, full sun or some shade. Appreciates well-manured soil. Modest to fast growth rate. Very spiny. May be grown as tall hedge. Washington hawthorn, *Crataegus phaenopyrum*, is as tall as English hawthorn, with shiny leaves and good standard tree form. All hawthorns hybridize freely.
Grows Best: Statewide.

Flowering peach

Prunus persica
Spanish: *Durazno.*

Extremely colorful, spring-flowering version of the fruit-bearing peach. Striking pink blossoms. An exotic, it is a modest grower (12–15 feet/4–5 m). Full sun, considerable water, sometimes fitful growth. Prefers rich soils. Subject to borers and chlorosis (it usually needs iron), and generally a delicate tree.
Grows Best: Statewide, but somewhat fitfully.

Bradford pear

Pyrus calleryana 'Bradford'
Spanish: *Peral.*

Shapely exotic flowering tree, uniquely attractive in four seasons because of its branching structure, blossoms, shade-tree height, and red fall color. Bradford pear is useful not only as a flowering ornamental but also as a shade and street tree. Likes full sun, well-manured soil, light to moderate watering. Tough and adaptable. May reach 30–35 feet (10–11 m) in height, 25 feet (8 m) or more in width. Grows quickly, with no fruits (or inconsequential ones). Bright, shining leaves.

Pyrus calleryana 'Redspire,' *P. c.* 'Chanticleer,' *P. c.* 'Aristocrat,' and other varieties are good growers that are also frequently used in New Mexico plantings.
Grows Best: Statewide.

Bradford pear

Purpleleaf plum

Purpleleaf plum (flowering plum)

Prunus cerasifera varieties
Spanish: *Ciruelo.*

Small, colorful, spring-flowering tree with purple, red, or dark green leaves. Exotic. Grows up to 20 feet (6 m) and spreads about as wide. Sometimes taller under very favorable circumstances. Very tough, but does not often flourish in wet, green lawns. Give it full sun and a place in a planting bed for best results. Good in masses. Crown is low and dense, so selective pruning as the tree "heads out" is important. Not a good street tree. Unusual leaf color makes it a summer and fall accent even after it flowers in the spring. Responds to well-manured soils but will grow anywhere. Prefers light watering. Modest rate of growth. May be subject to borers. Often not long-lived.

Prunus cerasifera has many cultivars in landscape use. Most set little if any fruit. *Prunus cerasifera* 'Atropurpurea' is the classic purpleleaf plum; its leaves are reddish, then purple, then deep green as the seasons pass, and it sets small fruits. *Prunus cerasifera* 'Newport,' *Prunus cerasifera* 'Thundercloud,' and *Prunus cerasifera* 'Krauter Vesuvius' are also very popular in New Mexico landscapes and are widely available.
Grows Best: Statewide.

Golden rain tree

Koelreuteria paniculata
A first-rate, exotic, small-scale shade and flowering ornamental species. Tough, very hardy, fast-growing, long-lived. Yellow blossoms in late spring, colorful pink seed pods in late summer and early fall. Attractive compound leaves. Grows up to 20 feet (6 m) tall, with a spread of 15 feet (5 m). Needs moderate watering but grows well in lawns. Not fussy about soils or exposure, grows well in full sun. Not bothered by pests. This and desert willow are easily the best small patio trees for most parts of New Mexico.
Grows Best: Statewide.

Eastern redbud (Judas tree)

Cercis canadensis
Spanish: *Botón encarnado, árbol de Judas, algarrobo loco.*

Exotic spring-flowering tree noted for its pinkish-lavender show in April or early May and its distinctive heart-shaped leaves. Deciduous. Redbud is small (10–20 feet, 3–6 m) and slow-growing, spreading to about 15 feet (5 m). Develops into a good patio shade tree. Water-loving, tender when young. Not particular as to soil. Prefers full sun or partial shade. Extremely hard wood, wounds slow to heal. Sets small seed pods in late summer.
Grows Best: Statewide.

Salt cedar (tamarisk, tamarack)

Tamarix chinensis (formerly *Tamarix pentandra*)
Spanish: *Tamarisco.*

Like the snakeweed (*Gutierrezia sarothrae*), this naturalized tree or small shrub is a plague in the New Mexican countryside yet a handsome landscape ornamental. Salt cedar may be trained into an interesting specimen tree up to about 20 feet (6 m) tall with an equal crown spread. Long, narrow, greenish-blue leaves. Wonderful spring flowering color, very gnarled trunk and character with age. Grows fast anywhere, in virtually any soil. Slower growth in lawns. Best use is as flowering ornamental under tough conditions; do not plant as hedge or where it might escape.
Grows Best: Statewide, probably unfortunately so.

Redbud

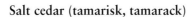

Salt cedar

Golden rain tree

Smoke tree

Vitex

Smoke tree

Cotinus coggygria
Spanish: *Fustete.*

Exotic, highly unusual accent tree. Rounded, green, handsome leaves. Puffy, pastel flowers are notable in spring, early summer. Very tough. Likes full sun and adapts well to poor or thin soils. Smoke tree likes only occasional watering. Characteristic form is wide, sometimes amorphous. Slow-growing, up to 20 feet (about 6 m) high and 15 feet (5 m) wide. Excellent as a garden curiosity. Varieties *Cotinus coggygria* 'Purpureus' and *C. c.* 'Royal Purple' have purple leaves.
Grows Best: Statewide, up to 8000 feet/2440 m.

Vitex (chaste tree)

Vitex agnus-castus
Spanish: *Agnocasto, sauzgatillo.*

Excellent small exotic tree or large shrub for late summer and fall color. Spiky lavender or light purple flowers are profuse, even splashy, in the summer months. Loves heat; tolerates terrible soils, in which it blooms well, and low winter temperatures. Full sun, moderate watering. Usually slow-growing in New Mexico but eventually makes a good small shade tree. Normally multi-stemmed; will reach about 15 feet (5 m) in height and grow as wide. Attractive, pale green, pointed leaves. Several varieties are commonly available. Resembles the smaller and more aromatic butterfly bush, *Buddleia davidii.*
Grows Best: Southern New Mexico as far north as Albuquerque.

TREES
EVERGREEN

ALL PLANTS
IN THIS SECTION
ARE IDENTIFIED
AS NATIVE,
EXOTIC, OR
NATURALIZED.

Atlas cedar

Atlas cedar

Cedrus atlantica
Spanish: *Cedro* or *tuya*.

This exotic tree and the related deodar and Lebanon species have a great deal of character. The Atlas cedar can get quite tall (up to 60 feet/ 18 m) and broad (up to 40 feet/12 m), but it grows slowly. Atlas cedar grows well in stony or alkaline soil as far north as Albuquerque, though the best specimens are found in southern New Mexico. Intense blue and weeping varieties are available. Moderate water. Best as accent or background evergreen tree.
Grows Best: Southern New Mexico, sometimes as far north as Albuquerque.

Cedar of Lebanon

Cedrus libani
Spanish: *Cedro* or *tuya*.

Slow-growing, stately exotic that lends a great presence to a landscape. Very tall (up to 75 feet/23 m) and spreading to almost an equal measurement. Used as an accent in New Mexico. Likes moist, well-draining soil, prepared with a good deal of humus-producing material. Deeper green and with finer needles than Atlas cedar. Good curiosity piece in a landscape as a genuine "biblical" tree. Very hardy.
Grows Best: Southern New Mexico; some good specimens in Albuquerque.

Deodar cedar

Cedrus deodara
Spanish: *Cedro* or *tuya*.

With its characteristic weeping form, this exotic cedar from the Himalayas has a cool, greenish-blue color and stately quality that make it an extraordinary skyline tree. Wonderful for winter interest against New Mexico's blue skies. Although hardy once established, the deodar cedar is subject to winter dieback in its early years. Likes good drainage, well-manured soils, full sun, and moderate watering. Can reach 40–50 feet (12–15 m) in height, about 30 feet (9 m) wide. Most commonly planted cedar in New Mexico; does especially well in the south. Moderate growth rate.
Grows Best: Southern New Mexico; many prime specimens in Albuquerque.

Arizona cypress

Cupressus arizonica
Spanish: *Ciprés*.

Typically a pale greenish-blue, this very handsome native evergreen is widely planted in New Mexico as a windbreak or specimen tree. Produces distinctive small cones. Grows well in any soil, faster with adequate water. A tree of the hillsides in the wild. May reach 35–40 feet (11–12 m) or more in height, with a crown spread of about 20–30 feet (6–9 m). Rich, cherry red bark with exfoliating scales. Likes full sun. Delicate when first planted, then quick-growing. Comes in many natural varieties found in California, Nevada, Baja California, Arizona, Chihuahua, New Mexico, and Texas; also in cultivated varieties. *Cupressus arizonica* var. *arizonica* has red-rough bark. *Cupressus arizonica* var. *glabra*, or smooth (Arizona) cypress, has satiny, exposed-red bark. Both are widely available.
Grows Best: Grows well almost everywhere; best examples are at Fort Bayard, near Silver City. Not for extremely high altitudes.

Cedar of Lebanon

Deodar cedar

Arizona cypress

Italian cypress

Italian cypress

Cupressus sempervirens
Spanish: *Ciprés.*

Stately exotic tree, very typical of landscape plantings in southern New Mexico and West Texas. Semi-hardy, moderate growth rate to 40 feet (12 m) or taller, fastigiate form. Is winter-damaged at about 5° F. Likes full sun, any soil, very little water once established. Skyline tree, good winter accent. Italian cypress in Albuquerque rarely exceeds 20 feet (6 m) in height, often needs extra care. Deep, rather dull green; usually grown as an accent because of its striking form.
Grows Best: Southern New Mexico, as far north as Albuquerque.

Douglas fir

Eucalyptus

Douglas fir

Pseudotsuga menziesii
Spanish: *Pino real, abeto.*

An immense native conifer (100 feet/30 m or more) frequently used as an accent in landscape plantings. Often smaller in domestic situations, Douglas fir has soft, finely wrought needles and a tall, narrow form. Attractive orange-flecked, textured bark. Not for most residential plantings. Full sun, well-manured soil, moderate water. Slow growth rate. Stately tree for parks, large open spaces. Highly adaptable. Prefers good drainage.
Grows Best: Statewide, above 5000 feet/1525 m.

Cider gum (eucalyptus)

Eucalyptus gunnii
Spanish: *Eucalipto.*

Fast-growing, exotic, broadleaf evergreen from the Snowy Mountains of southeastern Australia. Vertical form, long, delicate leaves, attractive trunk with two-tone green and white bark. Cold-hardy and drought-resistant. May reach 25–30 feet (8–9 m) tall, about 10–15 feet (3–5 m) in crown spread. Attractive small flowers in June. Likes full sun, very little water once established. Good curiosity tree, winter-color selection, or accent.
Grows Best: Albuquerque and southern New Mexico.

White fir

Abies concolor
Spanish: *Abeto, pino real.*

Showy native evergreen, often used as a Christmas tree and a hardy ornamental in northern New Mexico. Naturally occurs in mountains throughout the state at approximately 6500 feet (2000 m) and higher. Prefers moist, well-drained soils and exposures from full sun to partial shade. Softly curling, upright, blue-green needles on greenish-white limbs and trunk. Can grow up to 90 feet (28 m) tall and 20 feet (6 m) wide, usually at a moderate rate. Good background evergreen and accent tree in Santa Fe, Taos, Las Vegas, and elsewhere in the north. Generates a fresh, balsam scent in landscape and garden settings. Handsome cones.
Grows Best: Above 6000 feet/1830 m.

White fir

Alligator juniper

Juniperus deppeana
Spanish: *Enebro.*

Hardy, enormous native juniper tree (up to 50 feet/15 m), spreading to 35 feet/11 m or more. In its fast-growing juvenile form, alligator juniper features luminous, blue-green foliage and cherry bark and is virtually indistinguishable from Arizona cypress except by its berries. In mature form it develops its famous "alligator-hide" bark and grows at a moderate pace to become a large evergreen tree. And in "old" form it becomes gnarled, often half-dead, and picturesque. Full sun, modest water, and gravelly soil are preferences. Excellent accent or windbreak tree. Can live for 500 years or more. Tolerates heat and drought extraordinarily well.
Grows Best: Statewide, below 8000 feet/2440 m.

Chinese juniper

Juniperus chinensis varieties
Spanish: *Enebro.*

Moderately large exotic tree juniper, also found as a shrub in some varieties (see "Evergreen Shrubs"). Will generally grow to 15–20 feet (5–6 m). Likes sun, very little water, and is not particular about soils. Hardy, tough, slow to moderate growth rate. Always sold as one of its varieties, the most popular of which follow:

Hollywood twister juniper, *Juniperus chinensis* 'Torulosa.' Irregular, clumping, upright growth. Branches may rise up like the splayed arms of a candelabrum from the central tree mass. Bright green. Grows to about 15 feet (5 m).

Keteleer juniper, *Juniperus chinensis* 'Keteleeri.' Has a regular pattern of growth up to about 20 feet (6 m) and looks like a slightly smaller, somewhat diagonally branched version of the Canaerti juniper (see Eastern red cedar). Good as a curiosity or tall windbreak evergreen.

Irish juniper, *Juniperus chinensis* 'Stricta.' Closely resembles the Italian cypress in its tall, columnar form but is much hardier. Can reach 20 feet (6 m) or more and is handsome, tightly branched, and bright green. Good choice for narrow spaces in need of pointedly upright evergreen plantings.
Grows Best: Statewide.

Chinese juniper

Eastern red cedar

Juniperus virginiana
Spanish: *Cedro de Virginia, enebro.*

Tall (30 feet/9 m or more, 20 feet/6 m wide), deep green, vigorous tree juniper. Exotic. Not fussy about soils, likes little water and full sun. Good winter color and windbreak tree. Moderate growth rate. Few natural enemies; flourishes virtually anywhere. Well-known varieties include the hillspire juniper (*Juniperus virginiana* 'Cupressifolia'), which is much more compact, reaching a height of about 15 feet (5 m), and the Canaerti juniper (*Juniperus virginiana* 'Canaerti'), a tall, slender, wonderfully "scatter-branching" cultivar that may reach 20 feet (6 m) or more. All the eastern red cedars are hardy and long-lived.
Grows Best: Statewide.

Rocky Mountain juniper

Juniperus scopulorum
Spanish: *Enebro.*

Essentially shaped like a 30-foot-tall (9 m) equilateral triangle, this hardy Western native is grown most commonly in cultivars. Highly cold-resistant, not particular about soils, and happy with an occasional watering. Resembles Arizona cypress but is often darker green in color, with finer-leaved foliage. Sun or partial shade. Attractive berries; generally slow-growing. Long-lived and miraculously tolerant of city conditions. Good as specimen, windbreak, or winter-color tree. Popular varieties, many of which have distinct forms or colors, include, among others: Welch's juniper, *Juniperus scopulorum* 'Welchii'—tall, shiny green, and narrow—and Pathfinder juniper, *Juniperus scopulorum* 'Pathfinder'—blue-gray, quite tall, strongly triangular in shape.

The list of good additional nursery varieties of Rocky Mountain juniper is impressively extensive, and all are sturdy, hardy, and quite dependable under New Mexican growing conditions.
Grows Best: Statewide.

Alligator juniper

Hillspire juniper (eastern red cedar)

Rocky Mountain juniper

Madrone

60

Singleseed juniper

Singleseed (one-seed) juniper

Juniperus monosperma
Spanish: *Enebro, sabino.*

Essentially an overgrown shrub, this classic native New Mexican juniper is the common evergreen of the state's foothills. Often associated with piñon pine at the upper end (about 6000 feet/1830 m) of its range. Pleasant lime-green in color, about 10–16 feet (3–5 m) tall and just as wide. Very drought-resistant, but also very slow-growing. Likes hillsides, full sun, any soil. Fragrant, frequently covered with attractive blue berries. Good wildlife cover. Tolerates intense cold, is long-lived and scruffy.
Grows Best: Statewide.

Utah juniper

Utah juniper

Juniperus osteosperma
Spanish: *Enebro.*

At first glance quite similar to its close relative the singleseed juniper. However, Utah juniper is taller (20 feet/6 m or more, about 15 feet/5 m in crown spread), more tree-like, and generally handsomer. Extremely hardy and drought-resistant. Prefers full sun, very modest water. Native. Trunk, bark, foliage, and berries are picturesque. Not fussy about soils but seems to prefer good drainage. Wind-resistant. As slow-growing as singleseed juniper, and long-lived (hundreds of years). Classic tree of the Mesa Verde–Four Corners country.
Grows Best: Statewide.

Leyland false cypress

Leyland false cypress

Cupressocyparis leylandii
Spanish: *Ciprés falso.*

This wonderful but odd exotic tree is actually an intergeneric hybrid—a cross between Alaska yellow cedar *(Chamaecyparis nootkatensis)* and Monterey cypress *(Cupressus macrocarpa).* It performs well in New Mexico, usually as a quick-growing windscreen. Is not fussy about soil, prefers moderate amounts of water. Reaches 20 feet (6 m) or more in southern New Mexico, with a canopy of about 15 feet (5 m) or wider. Likes full sun but will take shade. Individuals look best in small groves or as members of a tall hedge. However, one tree can stand alone as a specimen. Non-invasive roots.
Grows Best: Statewide.

Texas madrone

Arbutus texana
Spanish: *Madroño.*

This rather amazing native tree from the Guadalupe Mountains of Eddy County often remains shrubby or multi-trunked and rarely exceeds 25 feet (8 m) in height. It may spread to about 15 feet (5 m). It has striking pinkish or cherry-colored bark (it peels), thick, pointed, deep green leaves, and soft white flowers very early in spring, followed by reddish fruits in the fall. Moderate growth rate. Sun or part shade, any soil. Moderate water. *Arbutus texana* is commercially available and closely related to the Arizona madrone, *Arbutus arizonica* (also a New Mexico native), and the Pacific madrone, *Arbutus menziesii.* All the madrones attract wildlife very well.
Grows Best: Statewide, up to 6000 feet/1830 m.

California fan palm

Chinese windmill palm

Southern magnolia

Magnolia grandiflora
Spanish: *Magnolia.*

Enormous, exotic, broadleafed evergreen, sometimes reaching 40–50 feet (12–15 m) in height and about 35–40 feet (11–12 m) in width. This most ancient of all flowering trees produces very large, aromatic, white or pinkish flowers. Likes well-manured, wet soil and full sun. Slow to moderate growth rate. Grows best in southeastern New Mexico, especially Hobbs. Also at its best in lawns, with consistent watering. Common in the American South, but a great accent or curiosity in New Mexico plantings. Leaves and blooms can be messy. Its smaller relative, *Magnolia soulangiana,* is also a favorite spring-flowering accent.
Grows Best: Southeastern New Mexico; found as far north as Albuquerque, where it generally will not thrive.

California fan palm

Washingtonia filifera
Spanish: *Palma, palmera.*

This hardy and spectacular exotic, a native of the Arizona and California deserts, grows well in southern New Mexico, especially in the cities of Las Cruces and Alamogordo, but also in Deming, Lordsburg, Carlsbad, and as far north as Truth or Consequences. Very commonly cultivated in El Paso and Ciudad Juárez, where there are superb specimens. Moderate to quick growth pattern, sometimes reaching 30 feet or more, with a crown spread of 10–12 feet (3–4 m) and a massive trunk. Beautifully shaped, fan-like leaves; the stalks have sawtooth edges. Needs a bit of room, full sun, and regular but not excessive water. Gathered seed sprouts easily, but because of New Mexico's relatively low winter temperatures, California fan palm should be planted from container sizes of 15 gallons or larger.

Leaves may brown in winter cold snaps, but the tree almost always recovers. Will grow in most soils but responds very well to manured backfill. Extraordinary accent as a single tree or in groups; may be used as a patio or street tree as well. Takes cultivation readily. Quite drought-resistant once established.
Grows Best: Southern New Mexico; excellent in El Paso and Ciudad Juárez.

Chinese windmill palm

Trachycarpus fortunei
Spanish: *Palma.*

The hardiest of palms, Chinese windmill palm thrives as far north as Albuquerque. An extremely ornamental exotic, it can grow to more than 15 feet (5 m) in height in New Mexico with a spread of about 5–6 feet (2 m). Best when planted as a 15-gallon or larger specimen. Showy fan-shaped leaves, with interesting seed clusters and a remarkable trunk that is wider at the top than the bottom. Seed sprouts readily, creating a small circlet of miniature palms around the parent. Prefers full sun but will tolerate some shade. Slow to medium growth rate. Any soil will do, but rich, well-manured topsoil with moderate watering is best. Chinese windmills imitate the form and growth pattern of the native Rio Grande palm, *Sabal mexicana,* found at the mouth of the river near Brownsville, Texas.
Grows Best: Southern New Mexico; sometimes marginal in Albuquerque.

A row of southern magnolias

Mediterranean fan palm

Chamaerops humilis
Spanish: *Palma, palmera.*

Bushy, exotic palm with several trunks and pleasing, luxuriant foliage. Tends to remain shrubby for a long time, finally growing into a short tree of about 12-15 feet (3–4 m), spreading equally wide. Likes sun or partial shade, well-manured soil, moderate water. Takes drought very well once established. Hardy, but not as tough as Chinese windmill palm in New Mexico. Likes deserts. Excellent accent or garden curiosity, and when planted in masses.
Grows Best: El Paso, Las Cruces, Alamogordo, Truth or Consequences, Deming, Carlsbad, Lordsburg, and elsewhere in southern New Mexico.

Mediterranean fan palm

Afghan pine

Mexican fan palm

Bristlecone pine

Aleppo pine

Mexican fan palm

Washingtonia robusta
Spanish: *Palmera, palma.*
Very similar to the California fan palm (its close relative) in appearance, growth habits, and distribution, this remarkable exotic grows well in El Paso and Ciudad Juárez and is sometimes cultivated in Las Cruces and Alamogordo. Tall (reaching 90 feet/28 m or more in Southern California, about 25 feet/8 m in New Mexico) with long, slender trunk, compact crown, medium growth rate. Same cultivation requirements as California fan palm, but the Mexican fan palm is not as hardy.
Grows Best: El Paso, Ciudad Juárez, Alamogordo, Las Cruces.

Afghan pine

Pinus eldarica
Spanish: *Pino.*
Very handsome exotic, and the fastest-growing of any pine in New Mexico. Kelly green. May grow up to 3 feet (1 m) a year, reaching 30 feet (9 m) or more and 15 feet (about 5 m) in crown width. Loves heat, adequate watering; grows well in alkaline, desert soils. Tolerates poor drainage. Prefers full sun. Available in a wide variety of sizes. Somewhat cold-sensitive when young; not for high altitudes or areas with extremely cold winters. Use as specimen or massed as a windbreak.
Grows Best: Southern New Mexico as far north as Albuquerque.

Aleppo pine

Pinus halepensis
Spanish: *Pino.*
A massive, irregularly shaped, exotic pine that grows well in El Paso and southern New Mexico. A little cold-sensitive when young, it tolerates hard-packed, alkaline soils. Moderate to fast growth; up to 80 feet (25 m) tall, 50 feet (15 m) wide. Dusty and sprawling in appearance as it ages. Likes water. Good park or specimen evergreen and, at times, curiosity tree. Good shade producer. Not for small gardens. With the Afghan pine, *Pinus eldarica,* the best pine for hot, intermediate desert areas.
Grows Best: Carlsbad; Mesilla Valley; El Paso–Ciudad Juárez.

Austrian pine

Pinus nigra
Spanish: *Pino.*
Large exotic pine from central Europe, widely used in New Mexican landscapes for groves, winter color, and accent plantings. Very hardy, likes cold, indifferent to soils. Takes moderate watering, full or partial sun, and grows at a consistent but modest rate. Does best in soils with good drainage. Reaches 30–40 feet (9–12 m), with a crown of equal or slightly smaller dimensions. A cheerful, sparkling tree, a bit rounded in form, and quite reliable.
Grows Best: Statewide. An excellent tree for all locales.

Austrian pine

Italian stone pine

Japanese black pine

Limber pine

Bristlecone (foxtail) pine

Pinus aristata
Spanish: *Pino.*
 Beautiful native evergreen tree, found in small numbers over a wide range of mountains at high altitude in northern New Mexico and throughout the West. Its soft, full, long-needled branch tips resemble a fox's tail—hence "foxtail" pine, its other common name. Up to 25 feet (8 m) tall, 15 feet (5 m) wide. Prefers rich, neutral or somewhat acidic soil, good drainage, copious water. Does not like lower altitudes. Grown as a garden and landscape curiosity. Matures very slowly. Elderly specimens in California and Nevada are thousands of years old.
Grows Best: Above 7000 feet/2135 m in moist locations.

Italian stone pine

Pinus pinea
Spanish: *Pino.*
 A sturdy, very attractive exotic pine from the Mediterranean. Sometimes cold-sensitive in its early years, it grows slowly to 40–50 feet (12–15 m) with a crown spread of 30 feet (9 m). Orange-gray bark, long, lime-green candles in spring. Likes good drainage, moderate watering; will grow in alkaline soils but prefers a neutral or acidic pH. Classic parasol shape in the Mediterranean results from pruning of lower branches for firewood; normal crown form is globular. Good accent pine.
Grows Best: Albuquerque and southern New Mexico.

Japanese black pine

Pinus thunbergiana
Spanish: *Pino japonés.*
 Moderately fast-growing exotic that reaches 25–30 feet (8–9 m) in height, 20 feet (6 m) in width. Irregular shape; good as a specimen tree. Prefers full sun and good, well-drained soils but adapts to alkaline conditions. Not at its best in hot deserts. Moderate watering needed. Will grow in extremely narrow planters. Good substitute for native irregular piñon. Widely available.
Grows Best: Statewide.

Limber pine

Pinus flexilis
Spanish: *Pino.*
 An aristocratic native pine, it is found mixed with ponderosas in the upper elevations of the transition zone but is smaller, more densely needled, and rarer. A good specimen landscape tree, very cold-hardy, and a sturdy though slow grower at lower elevations. Prefers moderate watering, neutral soils, full sun or partial shade. Up to 30 feet (9 m) tall, 15–20 feet (5–6 m) wide. Pale green, loose-limbed in the wind.
Grows Best: Statewide, above 4500 feet/1400 m.

Piñon and big sage

Ponderosa pine

Scotch pine

Dawn redwood

Ponderosa pine (western yellow pine)

Pinus ponderosa
Spanish: *Pino.*

Majestic native pine, may reach 100 feet (30 m) or taller, about 20 feet (6 m) in crown width. Moderately fast grower but subject to many pests and diseases at lower altitudes, where it does not flourish. Bark of older trees smells like vanilla. Needs full sun, rocky or gravelly soil, regular watering, and very good drainage. Full, rounded form, lime-green or darker needles. Beautiful specimen tree or winter color plant. Long-lived when it lives. Only nursery-grown stock should be used.
Grows Best: Statewide, above 6000 feet/1830 m.

Scotch pine

Pinus sylvestris
Spanish: *Pino escocés.*

Exotic pine from Scotland, surprisingly well adapted to New Mexico. Very tall tree (may reach 75 feet/23 m or taller, spreading to 20–25 feet (6–8 m). Striking orange bark; deep green, small needles. Moderate rate of growth; likes moderate watering, well-drained neutral or acidic soil. Good substitute for ponderosa pine. Hardy.
Grows Best: Statewide.

Dawn redwood

Metasequoia glyptostroboides
Spanish: *Metasecoya.*

Remarkable deciduous evergreen from China —an exotic "living fossil." Resembles coast redwood, *Sequoia sempervirens.* Pyramidal shape, bright red foliage in fall. May reach 60 feet (about 18 m) or taller, spreading to 20 feet (6 m). Moderate to fast grower. Needs room to flourish. Likes well-manured soil, moderate water, average drainage. Very cold-hardy, but can suffer from dryness. Good in masses or as an accent.
Grows Best: Statewide, somewhat moist sites.

Piñon pine

Pinus edulis
Spanish: *Piñón.*

Native tree, very common in foothills and low mountain areas throughout New Mexico. Very slow-growing, irregular or tall and well-branched, up to 35 feet (11 m) tall, 25 feet (8 m) wide. The piñon likes good drainage, full sun, very moderate water. Not at its best in lawns. Landscape specimens may be 150 years old or older. Small needles, edible seeds in cones. Extremely aromatic. Only nursery-grown (not collected) specimens should be used. New Mexico state tree.
Grows Best: Statewide.

Giant sequoia (big tree, redwood)

Sequoiadendron giganteum
Spanish: *Secoya.*

This wonderfully symmetrical exotic from the Sierra Nevada grows surprisingly well under special conditions in New Mexico. It likes good soil, moderate watering, and lawns best; it must have the extra humidity of turf grass or massed shrubs to perform well. May grow up to 3 feet (1 m) a year. New Mexico's largest specimens (about 30–40 feet/9–12 m, and still growing) are in Santa Fe, but individuals may also be found in Albuquerque. Full sun, plenty of room.
Grows Best: Moist sites above 7000 feet/2300 m.

Blue spruce

Picea pungens
Spanish: *Pinabete* or *pruche.*

Very symmetrical, handsome native evergreen of the high mountain forests of northern New Mexico. Used as lawn tree, evergreen accent statewide. May grow to 70 feet (23 m) or more in height; crown spread is 15–20 feet (5–6 m). Crown becomes rounded at lower elevations. Moderate water, sun or partial shade, slow growth. Prefers slightly acidic soil but will adapt to other soil conditions. Regenerates cut branches; sharp, strong, bristly needles. Many shades of green or blue. Long-lived. *Grows Best:* Anywhere.

Engelmann spruce

Picea engelmanni
Spanish: *Pinabete* or *pruche.*

Tall native evergreen tree of high mountain forests throughout New Mexico. Very similar to blue spruce but generally thinner in form and branching to ground. Usually deep green. Up to 80 feet (25 m) tall, 15 feet (5 m) wide. Prefers adequate water, enriched soil. Very widely planted as an ornamental; good winter background or specimen tree. Slow-growing, attractive cones, shorter than those of blue spruce. Hardy. *Grows Best:* Statewide.

Redwood

Black Hills spruce

Blue spruce

Black Hills spruce

Picea glauca densata
Spanish: *Pinabete* or *pruche.*

Very slow-growing Western evergreen (an exotic in New Mexico), common in northern Rockies and South Dakota. Prefers neutral or somewhat acidic soil, good watering, full or partial sun. A good container plant, small-scale garden evergreen. May attain 20 feet (6 m) of height in New Mexico, with a 15-foot (about 5 m) spread. Quite tough, unaffected by cold. Rare. *Grows Best:* Northern New Mexico.

Western red cedar

Thuja plicata
Spanish: *Tuya.*

This sturdy West Coast exotic, by far the handsomest of the arborvitae, is underused in New Mexico. It is a strong-growing evergreen that can reach 50–60 feet (15–18 m) in height, with a crown spread of perhaps 20 feet (6 m). Excellent accent or windbreak tree; resembles redwood. Not particular about soils, moderate growth rate; likes water but is drought-resistant and very cold-hardy. Full sun. Best specimens are found on the grounds of the Grant County Courthouse in Silver City, but this tree is widely, if rarely, grown in many towns around the state. *Grows Best:* Statewide.

Engelmann spruce

Western red cedar

Joshua tree

Torrey yucca

Soaptree yucca

Joshua tree

Yucca brevifolia
Spanish: *Amole, yuca.*
    The classic tree of the Mojave Desert.
Does very well in New Mexico as a specimen
as far north as Albuquerque. May reach 15 feet
(5 m) or taller with a spread of 10 feet (3 m)
Pale green blades. Full sun, dry, gravelly soils,
light watering. Slow growth rate, with creamy,
greenish flowers in spring. Withstands cold.
Excellent curiosity tree. Exotic, but looks
like a native.
Grows Best: Southern New Mexico; particularly
striking and large in Albuquerque.

Palm yucca

Yucca torreyi
Spanish: *Amole, yuca.*
    This unusual native tree found in the foothills
of southern New Mexico and elsewhere in the
Southwest can reach a height of 15 feet (5 m) or
higher, with a crown spread of about 4 feet (1.2 m)
or greater. Fond of dry soils, full sun. Very little
water or care needed. New, creamy-white flowers
in the spring rarely set fertile seed in transplanted
specimens because of the lack of a fertilizing
moth. Striking formal form. Moderate growth
rate. Evergreen. Best in stony or gravelly soils.
Often rots if planted in lawns.
Grows Best: Southern and eastern New Mexico;
Albuquerque.

Soaptree yucca

Yucca elata
Spanish: *Amole, yuca.*
    Small, thin-bladed native tree of New
Mexico's southern deserts, 3–15 feet (1–5 m)
or taller. The crown is modest, usually 3–5 feet
(1–1.5 m) wide. Gravelly, sandy, or rocky soils.
Full sun. Occasional watering only. Modest
growth rate, but spectacular yellow-white
flowers each summer. Excellent, tough accent
plant. *Yucca thompsoniana* is similar.
Grows Best: Southern New Mexico;
grows very well in Albuquerque.

Abelia

Althea

SHRUBS
DECIDUOUS

ALL PLANTS IN THIS SECTION ARE IDENTIFIED AS NATIVE, EXOTIC, OR NATURALIZED.

Glossy abelia

Abelia grandiflora
Spanish: *Abelia.*

This semi-evergreen exotic displays its attractive, abundant, pinkish flowers from early summer (June) to mid-fall. Likes well-manured soil, full sun, copious watering. May reach 8–9 feet (about 3 m) in height, about the same in width. May be cold-sensitive when young.

Abelia grandiflora 'Edward Goucher' is a common, popular, lower-growing variety (up to about 4 feet/1.2 m).
Grows Best: Statewide.

Flowering almond (dwarf)

Prunus glandulosa
Spanish: *Almendro florido (arbusto).*

This small, unassuming shrub, an exotic that is usually no taller or wider than 3–4 feet (about 1 m), bursts into color for a couple of weeks in the spring with a bright white or pink show. A relative of the plums, cherries, and other stone fruits, it prefers sun, moderate water, and manured soil. Medium grower; generally does not fruit.
Grows Best: Statewide.

Althea (rose of Sharon)

Hibiscus syriacus
Spanish: *Rosa de Siria* or *hipericón.*

A coarse, broad, tall, sturdy, exotic, old-fashioned garden shrub prized for its show of white, pink, or purple flowers in late summer and early fall. Other colors are common as well. In form, much like a small, multi-stemmed tree with interesting, deeply lobed leaves. Can grow up to 15 feet (about 5 m) tall, 10 feet (3 m) wide. Modest growth rate; needs medium amounts of water. Will grow in most New Mexico soils but tends to get chlorosis in heavily alkaline areas. Full sun to light shade. Not for tiny gardens or tight spaces.
Grows Best: Statewide.

Apache plume

Fallugia paradoxa
Spanish: *Pluma de Apache, chamiso.*

The classic arroyo shrub of the central Rio Grande Valley, often found in massed clumps on sand or gravel islands. Prefers gravelly or sandy soils in landscape situations as well. Extremely hardy and drought-tolerant, although it prefers periodic deep watering. Full sun. Fast-growing to about 6 feet (2 m), equally wide. Continuous small white flowers and fluffy pinkish seed heads cover Apache plume all summer. Adapts well to cultivation as a massed shrub, hedge, or accent. Grows up to 8500 feet (2600 m) or higher.
Grows Best: Statewide.

Apache plume

Flowering almond

68

Golden bamboo

Bird of paradise

Spanish broom

Common butterfly bush

Golden bamboo

Phyllostachys aurea
Spanish: *Bambú* or *bamboa.*
This almost-naturalized grass may grow to small-tree size (15 feet/5 m) or taller. Spreads by underground runners and does so very readily. Excellent tall screen. Really semi-deciduous. Will grow in most soils well, looks its best with moderate watering. Needs to be controlled in most gardens or larger landscapes. Grows well in containers. Sun or partial shade. Fast growth rate. Very hardy.
Grows Best: Southern New Mexico, Albuquerque.

Bird of paradise

Caesalpinia gilliesii
Spanish: *Ave de paraíso.*
This leguminous exotic from Argentina has naturalized well in New Mexico. Interesting compound leaves, absolutely spectacular red and yellow flowers. Shrub or small tree, up to 12 feet (4 m) tall and wide. Very drought-resistant. Prefers full sun, little water. Any soil. Resembles other local desert species such as catclaw acacia (*Acacia greggii*), honey mesquite (*Prosopis glandulosa*), and similar shrubby trees. Quick growth under normal conditions.
Grows Best: Albuquerque; eastern and southern New Mexico.

Spanish broom

Spartium junceum
Spanish: *Retama española.*
Unusual exotic with green branches, tiny leaves, yellow aromatic flowers in spring or summer. May grow 8 feet tall (2.5 m) or taller, equally wide. Looks like a tall version of the native Mormon tea (*Ephedra* spp.). Adapts very well to thin soils and little water. Grows fast, but may suffer frost damage. Full sun.
Grows Best: Albuquerque and southern New Mexico.

Common butterfly bush

Buddleia davidii
Spanish: *Buddleia.*
Hardy exotic with attractive, lavender flowers, up to 9 feet (3 m) in both height and width. Grows very quickly. Usually deciduous, performs well in New Mexico's thin soils. Full sun, moderate watering. Responds well to pruning. Does attract large butterflies, including tiger swallowtails and monarchs. Fountain butterfly bush, *Buddleia alternifolia,* is taller. Often resembles *Vitex agnus-castus,* and is common in New Mexico and West Texas.
Grows Best: Statewide.

Shrubby cinquefoil

Shrubby cinquefoil

Potentilla fruticosa
Spanish: *Cincoenrama.*

Extremely popular native, low-growing (up to 2.5 feet/0.75 m tall, equally wide), long-blooming shrub found in high, wet, sunny mountains throughout New Mexico. Many cultivated varieties and colors, but the original native plant has pale green foliage and yellow flowers. Likes water and neutral or somewhat acidic soil but is very adaptable. Generally hardy, but dislikes shade. Grows quickly.
Grows Best: Statewide.

Cranberry cotoneaster

Cotoneaster apiculatus
Spanish: *Cotoneastre* (colloquial).

Deciduous, exotic shrub with large, cranberry-like berries. Grows to about 3 feet (1 m) tall, 4 feet (1.2 m) wide. Bright red in fall. Fast-growing. Likes sun or partial shade, adequate water, manured soil. Tiny, round leaves. Good ground cover. Can be shorn into low hedge. Attractive in borders or as an accompaniment to a tree or shrub with a more vertical form.
Grows Best: Statewide.

Rock cotoneaster

Cotoneaster horizontalis
Spanish: *Cotoneastre* (colloquial).

Very hardy, showy exotic. Red-berried, deciduous, gracefully branching. Excellent tall ground cover. Grows to 2–3 feet (up to 1 m) tall, 4–5 feet (about 1.5 m) wide. Likes full sun, but will take shade. Moderate watering, mulching insure good growth rate. Barely out of leaf in winter. May be trained as low hedge. Particularly good in medians, parkways.
Grows Best: Statewide.

Rockspray cotoneaster

Cotoneaster microphyllus
Spanish: *Cotoneastre* (colloquial).

Grayish, somewhat stiff-branching exotic shrub, festooned like its relatives with appealing red berries. Evergreen or nearly so in southern New Mexico. Fast-growing to 3–4 feet (about 1 m) in height, 5–6 feet (about 2 m) in width. Not picky about soils. Sun or partial shade. Makes a good low hedge or tall ground cover.
Grows Best: Statewide.

Crape myrtle

Lagerstroemia indica
Spanish: *Mirto crespón.*

Very showy tall exotic shrub or small tree, grown for its remarkable branching habit, bronze bark, and deep pink or red summer flowers. May reach 10–15 feet (3–5 m) in New Mexico. Likes full sun, moderate water, improved soil. May spread to 8 feet (2.5 m). Leaves are deep green, glossy, small, and round. Deciduous. Slow to moderate growth habit. Frequently dies back in winter.
Grows Best: Southern New Mexico. Shrubby in Albuquerque.

Cranberry cotoneaster

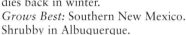

Rock cotoneaster

Crape myrtle

Rockspray cotoneaster

Currant

Red osier dogwood

Winged euonymus

Currant, gooseberry

Ribes spp.
Spanish: *Grosellero.*
    Ribes odoratum, the clove currant, grows in sunny and partially shady spots throughout New Mexico. Likes highlands. Exotic; likes water, good soil. Has showy, aromatic, yellow flowers. Excellent fruit plant. Good fall color. About 3–5 feet (1–2 m) tall, just as wide. *Ribes sanguineum,* the flowering currant (an exotic), and *Ribes aureum,* golden currant, are equally popular. Native species include *Ribes pinetorum* (orange gooseberry), *Ribes inerme* (whitestem gooseberry), and others, but these are rarely cultivated.
Grows Best: Statewide.

Tiger swallowtail on cliff fendlerbush in the spring

Red osier dogwood

Cornus stolonifera
Spanish: *Cornejo.*
    Striking native plant of mountain stream banks, noted for its red stems in wintertime. In summer, an attractive green-leafed shrub. Prefers wet, somewhat acidic soil and full or partial sun. Grows about 3–7 feet (1–2 m) tall, equally wide. Will sucker in moist soil. White flowers in summer, red leaf color in fall are pluses. Very hardy. The yellowtwig dogwood (*Cornus stolonifera* 'Flaviramea'), an exotic, is also popular.
Grows Best: Statewide, wet places.

Winged euonymus

Euonymus alata
Spanish: *Bonetero.*
    This tall (about 12 feet/4 m in height and width), handsome exotic shrub is cultivated for its brilliant red fall foliage, which is the source of its other common name: "burning bush." Pale yellow flowers in spring. Moderate growth rate. Grows well in most soils, likes full sun and occasional watering. Good accent plant. Hardy. Attractive, pointed leaves.
Grows Best: Statewide.

Cliff fendlerbush

Fendlera rupicola
    Extraordinarily beautiful spring-blooming native shrub, common in hot canyons and on hillsides. Grows to about 6 feet (2 m) tall and nearly as wide. Creamy-white flowers occur all over the plant in April or May. Very drought-resistant, any soil, full sun. Leaves are a dull green. Moderate to fast growth. Long-lived, a magnet for butterflies. Quite hardy.
Grows Best: Statewide.

Fernbush

Chamaebatiaria millefolium
Spanish: *Helechero.*
    This fast-growing, fresh-smelling native shrub looks like a fern that has taken its vitamins. Candle-like, off-white flowers and ferny leaves are attractive. This shrub is fast-growing; usually deciduous, but may be evergreen in southern New Mexico. Indifferent to soils. Grows to 6 feet (2 m) or taller, equally wide. Likes sun and water, but tolerates dry soil after it has become established. Good curiosity plant.
Grows Best: Statewide.

Fernbush

Edible fig

Forsythia

Edible fig

Ficus carica
Spanish: *Higuera.*
   This unusual large shrub, an exotic, becomes tree-like in southern New Mexico. Good curiosity plant. Likes sun, water, good soil, but will adapt to almost any soil conditions. Rich green, deeply lobed leaves, moderate growth to 20 feet (6 m) or more; delicious fruits in early fall, sometimes bears a first crop in early summer. May need careful pruning when winter-damaged. Spectacular and amazing feature tree throughout the Otero County village of La Luz.
Grows Best: Southern New Mexico; Albuquerque (shrub-like).

Forsythia

Forsythia spp.
Spanish: *Forsitia.*
   Tall, exotic shrub, lush green and very striking in appearance, covered with pleasant, bright yellow flowers in spring. Up to 10 feet (about 3 m) tall, equally wide. Fast-growing, hardy; likes sun, manured soil, moderate water. Good hedge or specimen plant. *Forsythia x intermedia,* or border forsythia, and its varieties are widely grown.
Grows Best: Statewide.

Shrub or tatarian honeysuckle

Lonicera tatarica
Spanish: *Madreselva.*
   Very old-fashioned, exotic garden shrub, up to 10 feet (about 3 m) tall and as wide. Likes rich soil, partial sun, moderate water; withstands drought when established. Good against adobe walls and as an informal hedge or windbreak. Pinkish spring flowers, crisp red fruits. Hardy and tough; medium rate of growth.
Grows Best: Statewide.

Hop tree or wafer ash

* good for part shade

Ptelea trifoliata
Spanish: *Ptelea.*
   Charming native shrub, up to about 10 feet (about 3 m) high, spreading to 3–4 feet (about 1 m) wide. Looks uncannily like an ash, but the genera are not related. Yellow in fall. Grows well with moderate watering in alkaline soils, partial shade. Slow-growing; generally shrubby, but may become tree-like as it ages. Attractive, lemony aroma, circular seeds.
Grows Best: Statewide, partial shade. Best at altitudes above 5000 feet/1525 m.

Shrub or tatarian honeysuckle

Hop tree or wafer ash

Sweet mock-orange

Flowering jasmine

Lilac

Flowering jasmine

Jasminum nudiflorum
Spanish: *Jazmín.*

Cheerful, yellow-blooming, exotic shrub, among the very first to flower in the spring. May be seen in blossom in chill February snowstorms. Stiffly arching branches, growing to about 5 feet (1.5 m) tall and as wide. Very tough; survives on little water, indifferent fertilizing. May be used as a rather tall and somewhat unkempt ground cover. Good in parking lots. Likes full sun or shade. Moderate growth. Tiny green leaves. Long-lived.
Grows Best: Hardy north to Albuquerque; southern and eastern New Mexico.

Lilac

Syringa vulgaris
Spanish: *Lila.*

Exotic, almost naturalized shrub, very widely planted in Santa Fe and Taos. Grown for its superb lavender or white flowers in mid-spring. Extremely drought-resistant but grows moderately quickly in rich soil with adequate watering. Can grow to 15 feet (5 m) by 15 feet. Often used as hedge, screen, or feature. Among the longest-lived of shrubs, it is often cultivated for the scent of its flowers. Thrives with very little care.
Widely available.

The Persian lilac, *Syringa persica,* is also much cultivated in New Mexico. It reaches about 6 feet (2 m) in height and width and produces light lavender or violet flowers over daintier leaves than those of its cousin, *S. vulgaris.*
Also tough, but slow-growing.
Grows Best: Anywhere. Greatest color and bloom above 6000 feet/1830 m.

Screwbean mesquite

Prosopis pubescens
Spanish: *Tornillo.*

Tall, wispy native shrub (up to 9 feet/3 m) useful as an accent or small-scale feature in landscape plantings. Prefers rocky or gravelly soils and is generally indifferent to moisture. Moderate growth rate. Needs full sun. Leaves, which are very light in form and bipinnately compound, are rivaled in interest in late summer and fall by the curious seeds, which resemble thick, long screws—hence the name. Close relative honey mesquite (*Prosopis glandulosa*) is generally grown as a tree. (Please see "Deciduous Trees.")
Grows Best: Socorro and south.

Sweet mock-orange

Philadelphus coronarius
Spanish: *Jeringuilla, celinda.*

Also known as common mock-orange, this rather old-fashioned shrub is cultivated for its foliage and its sweet-smelling flowers. Branches typically droop and need pruning to stay handsome. Late spring flowers are white with gold stamens in the center. Surprisingly hardy; likes well-manured soil, but will tolerate almost anything. A bit leggy in substantial shade. Survives and even thrives with little or no water. Moderate growth rate. About 6–8 feet (2–3 m) tall, just as wide. Exotic.

The native species *Philadelphus microphyllus,* littleleaf mock-orange, grows on rocky hillsides, is small-leaved, and features large masses of fragrant white flowers that continue to bloom all summer.
Grows Best: Statewide (both varieties).

Screwbean mesquite

Screwbean mesquite

Mountain mahogany

 New Mexico olive

Mountain mahogany

Cercocarpus montanus
Spanish: *Caoba de la sierra* (colloquial).

Very handsome tall native shrub, known for its attractive foliage and the feathery, persistent "tails" of its fruits. Semi-deciduous, drought-resistant, may reach 10 feet (about 3 m) by 10 feet or larger in size. Grows well in landscape plantings at a moderate rate. Likes stony or gravelly soils and a bit of water. Sun-loving. Very hardy. *Cercocarpus ledifolius,* closely related, is evergreen.
Grows Best: Statewide.

? planted behind well

New Mexico olive (New Mexico privet)

Forestiera neomexicana
Spanish: *Ligustro nuevomexicano.*

Small tree or large shrub. *Forestiera* is a true member of the olive family. Extremely graceful in cultivation, used as accent, small patio tree, or in masses as a hedge. Grows in any soil up to 7500 feet (2300 m). Little to moderate water, prefers full sun. Found in deserts, along river courses, and in foothills. Hardy, fast-growing. Can sucker profusely. When pruned as a multi-stemmed tree, resembles its relative, Arizona (velvet) ash. Stems are greenish-white with bronze undertones. Unusually adaptable. May grow up to 18 feet (6 m) tall, spread to 15 feet (5 m).
Grows Best: Statewide; adapts well virtually anywhere.

Cistena plum

Prunus cistena
Spanish: *Ciruela.*

An exotic red-leafed plum in shrub form. Spring-blooming, somewhat tall (up to 5 feet/1.5 m or taller, equally wide). Likes full sun, richer soils. Grows best in south central New Mexico. Moderate rate of growth. Good spring flower color. Moderate watering needed. Forms good hedges in southern New Mexico.
Grows Best: Statewide, but excellent in south.

Sand plum (wild plum)

Prunus americana
Spanish: *Ciruela cimarrona.*

Spectacular spring-flowering shrub, often reaching 10 feet (about 3 m) in height, perhaps twice that in width. High mountain native, particularly striking in Taos. Soft white flowers, good plums in late summer. Likes well-manured soil, full sun, ample water. Completely cold-hardy, adapts well in New Mexico's lowlands. Thicket-forming. Good wildlife attractor. In landscapes, especially good along walls, fences, watercourses.
Grows Best: Statewide.

Pomegranate

Punica granatum
Spanish: *Granado.*

Tall, exotic, deciduous shrub (up to 10 feet/3 m, equally wide) with very shiny leaves, reddish-orange flowers, and fruit in fall. Bears alkaline soil conditions well, likes warm walls and hot, full sun. Can withstand drought after a year or two of life. Moderate growth. May be used for informal hedges. Several varieties.
Grows Best: Southern New Mexico, as far north as Albuquerque; eastern New Mexico.

Cistena plum

Sand plum

Pomegranate

73

Pussywillow

Privet

Pussywillow

Salix discolor
Spanish: *Sauce pequeño (de amento sedoso).*

Elegant, large, exotic shrub, much planted for its silky spring catkins. These are an inch or so long, glistening gray or silver, and frequently cut for table arrangements. Pussywillow may reach small tree size (20 feet/6 m) but usually stays shrubby. Shiny reddish stems and bright green leaves are also attractive. Sun or partial shade, any moist soil. Trouble-free, fast-growing, short-lived.
Grows Best: Statewide.

Flowering quince

Chaenomeles speciosa
Spanish: *Membrillo floreciente.*

Exotic shrub with attractive, salmon-colored, early spring flowers. Usually about 3 feet (1 m) high at maturity and as wide, but some varieties are taller. Handsome structure when out of leaf. Grows easily under virtually any soil conditions and is hardy. Light to medium water, full sun for best bloom. Large number of cultivars available.
Grows Best: Virtually anywhere in New Mexico.

Raspberry

Rubus spp.
Spanish: *Frambueso.*

Extremely attractive native and exotic shrubs, berry-producing and thorny. The native thimble-berry, *Rubus deliciosus,* typically colonizes stony mountain roadsides in New Mexico, Colorado, and elsewhere in the West. Grows to a height of 3–5 feet (1–2 m), spreading to 5–6 feet (about 2 m). Useful for erosion control. Attractive flowers, wonderful fruit. Raspberries like full sun, good drainage; respond well to adequate manure and water. Stake on horizontally strung wires for good control and fruit production. Raspberries sucker readily.
Grows Best: Statewide.

Privet

Ligustrum spp.
Spanish: *Alheña* or *ligustro.*

The classic hedge plant of the Western world, privet is a tough exotic that is generally used to produce formal, shorn "living fences" in the landscape. Grows quickly to 12 feet (about 4 m) or more in New Mexico, spreading to about half that height. Planted very tightly—at 12–18 inches (300–450 mm)—for thick growth. Likes full sun or partial shade, well-manured soil (though privet will withstand any soil), and a lot of water. Few pests. Evergreen form, *Ligustrum japonicum* (see "Evergreen Shrubs"), has similar characteristics.

Most commonly used deciduous privet species are *Ligustrum ovalifolium,* California privet; *Ligustrum vulgare,* common privet; and *Ligustrum amurense,* Amur privet, used in very cold areas. All are well adapted to New Mexico but more labor-intensive to maintain and perhaps not as easily adapted to garden conditions as native rabbitbrush, saltbush, sage, Apache plume, and forestiera.
Grows Best: Statewide.

Raspberry

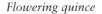

Flowering quince

Memorial rose

Rose

Rosa spp.
Spanish: *Rosa*.

Legendary shrubs, vines, climbers, and small standard trees, with both exotic and native forms. Generally hardy, very receptive to cultivation. Roses prefer well-manured soil and plentiful water applied to the roots, not the leaves. Fast-growing; like full sun. Mounding around base in winter with manure or rich soil is a good cultivation practice, as is "dead-heading" on a regular basis during bloom. Singles and doubles are both widely grown in great profusion.

Two large classes of roses are generally used. *Old roses* include such favorites as the white (York) rose, *Rosa alba*; the Austrian copper, *Rosa foetida*, a deep orange-red, bushy rose; the memorial rose, *Rosa wichuriana*, a white flowering ground cover vine (see "Vines"); and others. *Modern roses* have been developed from old roses and include many new varieties each year. Among the most famous of this class are the hybrid teas, floribundas, grandifloras, miniatures, climbers, polyanthas, and their infinite varieties. Of these, the hybrid teas, large and vigorous, have been the perennial best-sellers since the 1860s.

Rosa woodsii, the woods rose, is the native New Mexico species. It features handsome pink single flowers and grows along mountain streams to a height of 3–4 feet (about 1 m) and as wide.
Grows Best: Statewide, with some cultivation restrictions.

Snakeweed

Gutierrezia sarothrae or *Xanthocephalum sarothrae*
Spanish: *Bistorta, serpentaria de Virginia*.

A short (1–2 feet/0.5 m tall, equally wide), persistent, shrubby native perennial, deciduous or semi-deciduous. Yellow flowers in fall on a bright green base. Extremely widely distributed, sun-loving, drought-proof. Any soil and any amount of watering, even no watering, will suffice. A noxious pest in the countryside and a sign of a ruined range, snakeweed is nonetheless beautiful and a good landscape plant for low-maintenance gardens.
Grows Best: Statewide.

Snowball

Viburnum opulus 'Roseum'
Spanish: *Viburno, mundillo*.

A large (7–10 feet/2–3 m tall and wide), exotic, vigorous shrub, noted for its deep green, maple-like foliage and especially its round "snowball" flowers in spring. Common snowball viburnums produce attractive red fruit, but *V. o.* 'Roseum' is totally sterile. Likes well-manured soil, adequate water, sun. Grows relatively fast. A very attractive specimen or eye-catcher plant. Hardy, likes cities.
Grows Best: Albuquerque and northern New Mexico, eastern plains.

Spirea

Spiraea spp.
Spanish: *Espirea*.

Graceful, low-maintenance, exotic flowering shrubs, widely planted for good spring color and excellent summer foliage. Not picky about soils, but prefers well-manured earth in sun or semi-sun. Moderate water.

Popular species within this genus include bridal wreath spirea (*Spiraea prunifolia*), a very old-fashioned, profuse bloomer (tiny white flowers) in mid-spring with good red autumn color (about 6 feet/2 m tall, and as wide); and Anthony Waterer spirea (*Spiraea bumalda* 'Anthony Waterer'), a short (2 feet/0.6 m tall), brilliant red shrub used as a low accent. Van Houtte spirea (*Spiraea vanhouttei*) is a popular hybrid commonly found in gardens filled with traditional exotic species. Usually reaches 6 feet (2 m) tall and grows equally wide.
Grows Best: Statewide.

Snowball

Spirea

Snakeweed

Rose

76

Littleleaf sumac

Skunkbush

Littleleaf sumac

Rhus microphylla
Spanish: *Zumaque.*

Mounding, native desert shrub, extraordinarily hardy, very good for wildlife habitat and informal hedge plantings. Likes full sun and sandy, well-drained soils. Moderate growth rate. Long-lived. May reach 6 feet (2 m) or more in height, 6–8 feet (2–3 m) or more in breadth. Not yet as popular as its cousins the skunkbush and smooth sumac, but it deserves broad use. Deep green and gray.
Grows Best: From Socorro south, in deserts and foothills.

Smooth sumac

Skunkbush

Rhus trilobata
Spanish: *Zumaque.*

Skunkbush, or threeleaf sumac, is a widespread mountain native of New Mexico. Typically 3-4 feet (about 1 m) tall and as wide, it grows well in semi-shaded locations, although it will take full sun. Prefers well-manured soil, light to moderate watering. Fast-growing, resists drought. Attractive features include three-lobed leaves with reddish or bright yellow fall color and comparatively fast growth rate. Good in masses. Red berries.
Grows Best: Statewide.

Smooth sumac

Rhus glabra
Spanish: *Zumaque.*

Strikingly beautiful native of the New Mexican foothills and lower mountain slopes of about 6000–8000 feet (1830–2440 m). Generally grows in masses; may be a pioneer species in some locales. Useful in erosion control. Excellent accent. Prefers full sun, or shade and sun, drier soils, modest watering. Up to 4–5 feet (about 1.5 m) tall, 2-3 feet (1 m) wide. Berries and rich red leaves in fall. Very similar in appearance to staghorn sumac, but not as tall.
Grows Best: Statewide.

Staghorn sumac

Rhus typhina
Spanish: *Zumaque.*

Exotic. The single fastest-growing shrub in the temperate United States—can reach 12–15 feet (4–5 m) in a single season. Hardy, with showy red leaf color in the fall. Compound leaves are often mistaken for *Ailanthus*. May become a small, many-branched or multi-trunked tree. Little to moderate water, full or partial sun, any soil. Responds to good manuring of soil in spring. Accent, mass, or hedge. May sucker.
Grows Best: Statewide.

Staghorn sumac

Weigela

Weigela ✳

Weigela florida
Spanish: *Weigelia* or *Diervilla rosea*.

Frequently called "old-fashioned" weigela, this hardy exotic is usually planted in one of its varieties—*W. f.* 'Bristol Red' is particularly popular. Grown for its wonderful late-spring flowers, which are usually pink or red. Likes full or partial sun. Infrequently grows taller or wider than 5–6 feet (about 2 m) in New Mexico. Moderate growth rate; likes manured soil and modest watering. Light pruning after bloom improves the next year's flowers.

Despite the spelling, this shrub's name is pronounced "wy-jeel-ya."
Grows Best: Statewide.

Coyote willow (basket willow, sandbar willow)

Salix exigua
Spanish: *Mimbre, sauce.*

Small native willow often found along stream and ditch banks. Gray-green, modest, feathery foliage. Red twigs. Rounded small shrub up to 10 feet (about 3 m) tall. Sun or shade; typically grows in sandy soil but adapts virtually anywhere. Moderate watering needed. Good as an accent or a mass; may be clipped into a handsome hedge. Fast growth rate; spreads to about 4–5 feet (1.5 m). Extraordinarily hardy and easy to grow.
Grows Best: Statewide.

Winterfat

Ceratoides lanata (Eurotea lanata)
Spanish: *Eurotia.*

Gray-leaved, small, native shrub with handsome pastel-white tips that take on an unusual "glow." Much valued by livestock. Particularly attractive in landscape applications next to adobe walls. About 2–3 feet (roughly 1 m) tall and wide. Fast-growing, indifferent to soils, demands very little water, likes full sun. Works best in small masses as an intense accent.
Grows Best: Statewide.

Winterfat

SHRUBS
EVERGREEN

ALL PLANTS
IN THIS SECTION
ARE IDENTIFIED
AS NATIVE,
EXOTIC, OR
NATURALIZED.

Arborvitae (arborvita)

Agave

Aucuba

Agave

Agave spp.
Spanish: *Agave, mescal.*

A spectacular native succulent, agave is grown as a curiosity plant or specimen and is highly useful in desert garden compositions. Very widespread in the foothills of the Southwest. With most species, a tall, flowering stalk resembling a candelabrum is produced after several years, and it can mature in a few short weeks. The flowers are very showy. Agaves require little care, preferring scant watering, rocky or gravelly soil, and full sun. They may sucker after blooming. Three species are commonly used in New Mexico landscapes:

Century plant, *Agave americana.* Classic Mexican agave with long, succulent, spiny, curving leaves up to 6 feet (2 m) long or longer. Tall flower (reaching 30 feet/9 m or more) produced after several years. Grows best in southern New Mexico, where it flourishes virtually anywhere. Variegated forms are available.

Parry agave, *Agave parryi.* A perfectly symmetrical agave with chunky leaves radiating from the plant center in rosette form. About 2–3 feet (up to 1 m) tall and equally wide, this modest-sized plant can produce a flower 15 feet/5 m tall in two weeks. Flower color is a rich, glowing, dusky yellow. Found on rocky hillsides throughout southern New Mexico and hardy in gardens as far north as Albuquerque. Slow growth, but well worth the wait. Many varieties.

Lechugilla, *Agave lechugilla.* More like a clustering, ground-cover yucca in form than an agave, the lechugilla is a common feature in dry-land rock gardens. Native to extreme southeastern New Mexico (sometimes as far north as Carrizozo), lechugilla reaches a foot (300 mm) or so in height, 16 inches (375 mm) in width. Likes heat and very dry, stony settings. Hardy. Produces a flower 12 feet (4 m) high, tends to sucker freely. Often grown as a curiosity or accent. Very common in El Paso.
Grows Best: As noted above.

Arborvitae (arborvita)

Thuja spp. *and Platycladus* spp.
Spanish: *Tuja.*

Arborvitae are reliable, very hardy, very symmetrical evergreen shrubs and trees. Easy to establish; generally a bright lime-green in color, with small blue cones. Drought-resistant and tough. Will grow in any soil. Prefer sun but tolerate some shade. These evergreens typically look like topiary specimens, even when left unshorn. Best as windbreaks and hedges; most arborvitae respond well to shearing. Too formal and old-fashioned for many modern gardens. Long-lived.

Thuja occidentalis includes the American arborvitae varieties. Some can grow to 40 feet (12 m), spreading to 20 feet (6 m) or more. *Platycladus orientalis* includes the Oriental arborvitae varieties, widely planted as shrubs and trees. Some types reach 15 feet (5 m) in height, about 8 feet (2.5 m) in width. *Thuja plicata* (western red cedar) is an excellent choice for evergreen tree plantings in New Mexico (see "Evergreen Trees").
Grows Best: Statewide.

Aucuba (gold dust plant)

Aucuba japonica
Spanish: *Oro en polvo, aucuba.*

Grown for its remarkable leaf structure, aucuba is an excellent broadleafed evergreen for shaded planting situations in New Mexico. Male and female flowers are on separate plants, so plant both if you want large red berries. Slow-growing and somewhat stunted (about 4 feet/1.2 m tall and wide) in the Southwest, and needs deep shade. Likes richly manured soil and adequate water. Exotic. Good choice for exterior-stairwell planters, narrow service-area "slot" planters, and as a viewing plant in isolated, self-contained courtyards. Variety *A. j.* 'Variegata,' the gold-dust plant, has speckled leaves and is more frequently used than the species.
Grows Best: As far north as Albuquerque.

Barberry

(handwritten: But takes moderate water)

Berberis spp.
Spanish: *Berberís*.

The barberries are a fascinating group of spiny, mostly exotic shrubs that are used extensively in New Mexico landscaping. Closely related to the mahonias, which are themselves sometimes classified wholesale as barberries. Good hedge, color, and curiosity plants. Mostly evergreen. Yellow spring flowers; attractive, small, generally ovate or elliptical leaves; red fall berries. Barberries prefer sun or partial shade, moderate water, and well-manured soil, although any soil will do. Quick growth rate. Excellent choice for parks and other exposed, public landscapes because they defend themselves well. The most popular species are:

Colorado barberry, *Berberis fendleri*. This small but very attractive native shrub tends to grow in masses of straight, unbranched stalks under ponderosa pines throughout the state. Up to 3 feet (1 m) tall, but only 4 inches (100 mm) wide. Small yellow flowers, spines, deep red fall berries. Good curiosity plant.

Japanese barberry, *Berberis thunbergii*. Grows to 5 feet (1.5 m) or taller, equally wide. Exotic. Lustrous, small, round, green leaves, underset with many spines. Deciduous, but with attractive red berries that last the winter. Good in hedges or as specimens. Japanese barberry has a number of varieties, the most-used of which is probably *Berberis thunbergii* 'Atropurpurea,' redleaf barberry, grown for its raspberry-shaded foliage. It is smaller than its parent plant. Tiny *Berberis japonica* 'Crimson Pygmy,' dwarf redleaf barberry, is also common.

Three-spine barberry, *Berberis wisleyensis* (*Berberis triacanthophora*). Distinguished by pale green, narrow leaves and groups of three spines radiating from branches. Evergreen and rounded in form. Tough, very hardy. Grows to about 3–4 feet (1 m) tall and as wide. Excellent in parks and small hedges. Drought-resistant.

Wintergreen barberry, *Berberis julianae*. Evergreen, very tall (6 feet/2 m or more and as wide), deep green, formidably spined. Exotic. Leaves are thick and somewhat coarse. Used for tall hedges, takes shearing well. Variety *Berberis julianae* 'Mentorensis,' mentor barberry, is exceptionally drought-tolerant. Widely planted, it is a cross between wintergreen and Japanese barberries.
Grows Best: Statewide.

Beargrass

(handwritten: w/R'd for good for front area?)

Nolina microcarpa
Spanish: *Sacahuiste, sacahuista*.

A spectacular native, beargrass prefers stony foothills in full sun throughout the Rio Grande and Gila drainages in New Mexico. Very hardy; not particular about soils; needs little water. Can grow 5 feet (1.5 m) tall, spreading to as much as 7–8 feet (2.5 m). Attractive, large flowers on stalks, similar to yucca or sotol blooms. In landscapes, composes very well with granite boulders, upright junipers, cacti. Grows quickly. Very widely adapted. Harvested in southern New Mexico to make brooms.
Grows Best: Statewide, below 8000 feet (2440 m).

Japanese boxwood (box)

Buxus microphylla and varieties
Spanish: *Boj*.

Exotic, small-leaved, evergreen shrub, grown as low hedge plant. Mostly hardy; takes shade or sun. Slow-growing. Often no higher than 2–3 feet (up to 1 m) in New Mexico, where the ultraviolet radiation seems to restrain its growth. Usually clipped and shaped formally. Attractive lime-green foliage. Varieties *B. m.* 'Green Beauty' and *B. m.* 'Winter Gem' are hardier than the species. Moderate water needed; tolerates most soils but responds to well-manured garden earth. Often burned by frost.
Grows Best: From Socorro south.

Japanese boxwood

Redleaf barberry

Beargrass

Claret cup cactus

Echinocereus triglochidiatus
Spanish: *Cacto vino tinto.*
   This small cluster cactus is native to the deserts of southern New Mexico. About 1–2 feet (0.5 m) tall and as wide, it makes a spectacular accent with its striking red flowers in the spring. Likes sandy or gravelly soils, full sun, very little water. Slow-growing, usually planted from seed.
Grows Best: From Albuquerque south.

Claret cup cactus

Common cholla (cane cholla)

Opuntia spp.
Spanish: *Cholla.*
   This ubiquitous native is a symbol of New Mexico's vast rangelands, where it often appears in colonies if overgrazing has occurred. Beautiful, glistening flowers (generally yellow), followed by delicious edible fruits in fall that resemble pomegranates in flavor. Grows up to 5 feet (1.5 m) tall and as wide. Spiny; should not be planted near paths, seats, or close to patios. Needs full sun, well-drained gravelly soil, and only occasional water. Succulent. The plant is easily propagated from seed or by inserting a small, broken-off stem segment into the soil. Very hardy. *Opuntia imbricata* is commonly planted.
Grows Best: Statewide, but totally out of context away from deserts and desert grasslands.

Common cholla

Prickly pear

Opuntia spp.
Spanish: *Nopal* (the fruit is *tuna*).
   Prickly pear or flat-ear cactus is a very hardy native shrub that occurs throughout the deserts, plains, and foothills of New Mexico. A well-armored evergreen, it reproduces by means of seeds and vegetative cuttings. Prefers full sun, light to medium water, good drainage. Fruits are pomegranate-like, edible, and delicious. Grows slowly up to 5–6 feet (about 2 m) tall and 6–10 feet (2–3 m) wide. Good spring-flowering species. Excellent accent, but should be planted well away from foot traffic. *O. chlorotica* and *O. engelmannii* are commonly found in gardens.
Grows Best: Anywhere. Best in deserts and foothills.

Parney cotoneaster

Cotoneaster lacteus
Spanish: *Cotoneastre* (colloquial).
   Very sturdy, evergreen exotic, tall-growing (up to 8 feet/2.5 m or higher, equally wide), with attractive red berries. Widely used throughout New Mexico. Indifferent to soils; drought-resistant once established, although it likes water. One of the largest of the cotoneasters, it may reach small tree size with age. Full sun or partial shade. Good hedge specimen.
Grows Best: Statewide.

Creosotebush

Larrea tridentata
Spanish: *Creosota.*
   Native shrub of the southern New Mexican deserts, growing as far north as Isleta Pueblo. Creosote possesses an uncanny hardiness and can reach 10 feet (3 m) or more in height, spreading as wide. Needs full sun. Will grow in any soil with no water or care but assumes a remarkable round form with thick green foliage if given a little water. Many-stemmed. Frequently a range pest but a good choice for rugged desert landscapes or gardens. Spring flowers are an attractive yellow, and the odor of creosote after a rain is surprisingly pleasant. Moderate growth rate. Very long life span—perhaps centuries.
Grows Best: From Albuquerque south.

Parney cotoneaster

Holly

Creosotebush

Holly

Ilex spp.
Spanish: *Acebo.*

Classic exotic, broadleafed shrub, not often grown in tree form in New Mexico. Shiny (almost waxy) green, sawtoothed leaves, bright red berries. (Be sure to plant both male and female shrubs to insure good berry production.) Most hollies like well-manured soil, will take some shade, and do well with good watering. Modestly fast growers. Generally used for hedges, foundation plantings. Popular species include:

Burford holly, *Ilex cornuta* 'Burfordii.' Leaves are smooth with almost no sharp points. May reach 9 feet (3 m) or more in height and as wide. Grows statewide.

English holly, *Ilex aquifolium.* Very large shrub (more than 12 feet/4 m tall, equally wide) that does best in the 7000-feet-plus (2300 m–plus) altitudes of northern New Mexico. Spiny leaves—very pointed, with red, clumpy fruit. Usually grown as a tall evergreen background plant.

Wilson holly, *Ilex altaclarensis* 'Wilsonii.' Best general shrub holly selection. Hybrid; likes sun or shade, heat, most soils. Usually reaches about 6 feet (2 m), but as a standard will turn into an evergreen tree. About 6 feet (2 m) wide as a shrub. Spring leaves, red berries. Makes a good hedge. Grows statewide.

Yaupon holly, *Ilex vomitoria.* Native of Texas, very resistant to alkaline soils. Grown as an attractive, small, multi-stemmed tree in southeastern New Mexico. Evergreen, smooth-edged leaves. Reaches about 15 feet (5 m) in height, 10 feet (3 m) in width. Dwarf variety (*Ilex vomitoria* 'Nana') frequently employed as low hedge plant. Other varieties of yaupon have also been developed. Grows best in southeastern New Mexico.

Though well-proven as garden plants elsewhere in the world, hollies have traditionally been replaced in most New Mexico landscapes by Oregon grape (*Mahonia aquifolium*) or its native relatives (*algerita* or *Mahonia haematocarpa,* and *agritos* or *Mahonia trifoliolata*), all of which closely resemble the true hollies in size, shape, leaf form, growth habit, and other characteristics.
Grows Best: As noted above.

India hawthorn

Rhaphiolepis indica
Spanish: *Acerolo de India.*

An exotic evergreen shrub with many varieties grown for its winter color and late spring (pink) bloom, or as a low hedge. Likes half-sun, rich soil, adequate water. Not completely winter-hardy; can be damaged by bad frosts when young. Slow to moderate growth rate, up to 3–4 feet tall (about 1 m) and as wide.
Grows Best: Southern New Mexico, as far north as Albuquerque.

India hawthorn

Prickly pear

82

Armstrong juniper

Chinese junipers

Juniperus chinensis and varieties
Spanish: *Enebro.*

These useful exotic shrubs are a mainstay of public and private landscapes throughout the West. Drought-resistant; good in sunny or partially shaded locations. Flourish in most soils with little care. Very hardy. Grow moderately fast. Often used in "backbone" or foundation plantings. The following varieties are commonly used:

Armstrong juniper, *Juniperus chinensis* 'Armstrong.' Staccato diagonal branching pattern; up to 3–4 feet (about 1 m) tall, equally wide. Unimposing basic green color. Fast to assume its final size. Looks like a smaller version of green Pfitzer juniper.

Pfitzer juniper, *Juniperus chinensis* 'Pfitzerana.' Sharp, tall (may reach 6 feet/2 m or more), many-branching juniper, often sprawling to 16 feet (5 m) or more. This hardy juniper is frequently grown for its striking silhouette, as its remarkable shape distinguishes it from its less assuming close relatives. Although a great number of Pfitzer types are available, the two most commonly planted are *Juniperus chinensis* 'Pfitzerana' itself—the green Pfitzer, reliable and fast-growing—and *Juniperus chinensis* 'Pfitzerana Glauca'—the blue Pfitzer, with shining blue foliage. They are virtually identical in habit and appearance except for color. Compact, gold-tipped, and other Pfitzers are also widely used in New Mexico.

Sea green juniper, *Juniperus chinensis* 'Sea Green.' More compact than the Pfitzer juniper, the sea green juniper has a rich color and more formal habit of growth. About 4 feet (1.2 m) tall and wide. Good specimen juniper.

Chinese junipers may also be found in tree and ground-cover varieties. See "Evergreen Trees" and "Evergreen Ground Covers."
Grows Best: Statewide, virtually anywhere. For additional ground-cover junipers, please see "Evergreen Ground Covers."

Common juniper

Juniperus communis
Spanish: *Enebro.*

The only native New Mexican shrub juniper, common juniper grows under evergreen forest canopies in New Mexico's ponderosa and spruce-fir forests. Very hardy and shade-tolerant. May reach 4 feet (1.2 m) in height, spreading to about 6 feet (2 m). Likes a moderate amount of water. Prefers well-drained soils but will adapt. Soft branching pattern; often rounded in form. Slow-growing. Striking contrast to more popular exotic species. Variety Hornibrook *(Juniperus communis* 'Hornibrookii') is low-spreading, widely available.
Grows Best: In semi-shade, statewide.

*Oregon grape (*Mahonia aquifolium)

pt. shade

Mahonia

Mahonia spp.
Spanish: *Algerita, agritos.*

Attractive broadleaf evergreen, holly-like shrubs, robust and hardy, grown for their sunny yellow flowers, substantial presence, and fall berries. Very closely related to the barberries. Two native and one exotic species are found in New Mexico gardens, as well as an attractive ground-cover species. Mahonia is not particular about soils, is drought-resistant, and will be happy in sun or sun-and-shade situations. Moderate to quick growth rate. Frequently spread by birds. Mahonias include:

Algerita, *Mahonia haematocarpa (Berberis haematocarpa).* Common, leathery-leafed native shrub in the foothills. Pointed, sawtoothed leaf margins, red berries; long-lived, tough, and cold-resistant. Spectacular yellow flowers in May. May reach 10–12 feet (3–4 m) in height and width. Draws wildlife, composes well with boulders, beargrass, and oaks in landscape situations. Grows best up to 8000 feet/2440 m.

Agritos (algerita, desert mahonia, desert barberry), *Mahonia trifoliolata (Berberis trifoliolata).* Also called algerita. Very closely resembles its more northerly cousin. Native. Occurs naturally in West Texas, southeastern New Mexico, southwestern New Mexico. Somewhat smaller than *Mahonia haematocarpa,* reaching 8 feet (2.5 m) in both height and width. Also a very tough foothills species with yellow spring flowers and red fall berries. Grows best below 8000 feet/2440 m.

Oregon grape, *Mahonia aquifolium (Berberis aquifolium).* Grown for its bristly, holly-like evergreen foliage, pleasant-smelling yellow flowers in spring, and blue berries in fall. Among the best broadleaf evergreens for New Mexico landscapes. Exotic. Likes well-manured soil, moderate watering. Fast-growing to 8–9 feet (about 3 m) and as wide. Tolerates shade and full sun equally well. New plants appear in odd garden spots, spread by the birds. Grows anywhere.

Creeping mahonia, *Mahonia repens (Berberis repens).* For a description of this native evergreen ground cover, please see "Evergreen Ground Covers."
Grows Best: As noted above.

Nandina

Mormon tea (desert joint fir)

Ephedra spp.
Spanish: *Canutillo.*

Very tough native desert shrub, found in many species across the Southwest in open deserts and foothills. Green, jointed stems with minute leaves. Roughly resembles Spanish broom at smaller scale. Any soil, full sun, little water. Grows moderately to 2–3 feet (up to 1 m) tall, spreading to 5–6 feet (about 2 m). Used in landscaping primarily as a curiosity. *Ephedra nevadensis,* Nevada ephedra, is commercially available. *Ephedra torreyana,* true Mormon tea, is very widespread along river drainages throughout New Mexico.
Grows Best: Statewide, under 7000 feet/2300 m.

Mormon tea

Nandina (heavenly bamboo)

Nandina domestica
Spanish: *Bambú celestial.*

A cheerful, easy-to-care-for, multi-hued exotic shrub, grows in sun or shade in any soil. Likes water and manure but survives without much of either. Tall (up to 6 feet/2 m) and as wide, often producing handsome canes. Slow to moderate growth rate; responds well to pruning. Lime-green, evergreen foliage; very delicate structure belies the plant's toughness. Modest white spring flowers. Turns red and orange in fall or winter, with good-looking red berries. Extraordinary in compositions with granite boulders and tam junipers. Compact varieties *Nandina domestica* 'Nana' and *N. d.* 'Harbor Dwarf' are rounded, small (about 1 foot/300 mm high), and useful as ground covers. Leaves are wider than the parent species.
Grows Best: Southern New Mexico, as far north as Albuquerque.

— have in back triangle Bed in W.R.

Oleander

Ocotillo

Photinia

Ocotillo

Fouquieria splendens
Spanish: *Ocotillo.*

Spectacular foothills plant of the southern New Mexico deserts. The native ocotillo can be as tall as a tree (up to 15 feet/5 m, about 6 feet/2 m wide) but is usually grown as a shrub. Ocotillo is fast-growing, thorny, and fond of full sun and stony soils. It is drought-deciduous, greening up and producing attractive, bright red flowers when water is available. Hardy as far north as Albuquerque and native as far north as Socorro. Useful as a curiosity plant and, when planted in a line, as a tall, living fence.
Grows Best: As far north as Albuquerque (up to 5500 feet/1675 m).

Oleander

Nerium oleander
Spanish: *Adelfa, baladre.*

Round-formed, glossy-leafed, exotic evergreen shrub, fast-growing in southern New Mexico. May reach 7–8 feet (about 2.5 m) in height, spreading as wide. Flourishes in desert heat and can withstand highly alkaline, limey soils. Leaves are shiny and willow-like; flowers in most common varieties are red, white, or shades thereof. Oleander blooms continually and spectacularly during the warmer months. Highly drought-resistant but grows fast with moderate watering. May winter-kill, but will resprout quickly from base. Oleander is a good hedge, windbreak, and background or screen plant; however, it is highly poisonous. Do not plant near children's play areas.
Grows Best: Southern New Mexico, as far north as Truth or Consequences.

Photinia

Photinia spp.
Spanish: *Fotinia* (colloquial).

An appealing, hardy, exotic evergreen, commonly grown in the United States in about four species. Broadleaved, tall (up to 15 feet/5 m or more), wide (10–12 feet/3–4 m), fast-growing, and usually formal in development. Attractive pink new foliage at branch tips in spring, turning lime-green or Kelly green in summer. Likes sun, gets leggy in shade. Prefers well-manured soil and considerable water.

Japanese photinia *(Photinia glabra)* and Oriental photinia *(Photinia villosa)*, though hardy, are not commonly grown in New Mexico. The most popular and widespread species in the Southwest are:

Chinese photinia, *Photinia serrulata.* This is an enormous shrub, and it can be pruned to become a small, multi-trunked, broadleafed evergreen tree. Chinese photinia has sawtooth-edged leaves, showy white flowers, and reddish fruit in the fall. Fast-growing; may be used as a foundation, accent, or hedge plant.

Fraser's photinia, *Photinia fraseri.* Lime-green leaves with markedly pink or orange new growth in spring, white spring flowers. Good hedge plant. Not as large as Chinese photinia, but more popular. Fraser's photinia is a hybrid of the Chinese and Japanese photinias.
Grows Best: Statewide.

Mugo pine

Pinus mugo
Spanish: *Pino de mugo.*

A terrifically hardy and attractive exotic from the Alps. Generally rounded in form, with dense branching and clusters of needles producing a compact juvenile and adult form. Up to 4 feet (1.2 m) tall and wide in New Mexico, occasionally taller. Likes full sun but withstands some shade. Prefers good drainage, modest water. Slow-growing; at its best on a slope or in a rock garden. Variety *Pinus mugo mugo* is very symmetrical, reliable. Grow near other shrubs, next to cool lawns, or amid ground covers in hot desert.
Grows Best: Statewide.

But moderate water.

Mugo pine

Pittosporum (tobira)

Pittosporum tobira
Spanish: *Tobira* (colloquial).

Growing up to 3–4 feet (about 1 m) tall and 6 feet (2 m) wide in New Mexico, pittosporum is a brilliant, light green shrub raised for its handsome foliage. Exotic. Fragrant whitish flowers in spring. Useful as a sprawling foundation plant or for mounding and draping over walls. Likes sun or some shade, very well-manured soil, moderate watering. Slow to moderate growth rate. Several varieties are available.
Grows Best: Far southern New Mexico— Carlsbad, Alamogordo, Las Cruces. Does well in El Paso and Ciudad Juárez.

Waxleaf privet (waxleaf ligustrum)

Ligustrum japonicum
Spanish: *Ligustro.*

Glossy-leaved, hardy, evergreen exotic, widely used as a hedge plant. Very dense. Fast-growing, can reach 10 feet (3 m) or more in height, 6–8 feet (2–2.5 m) in width. Takes shearing extremely well, but unshorn it produces white spring flowers and small black "berries." Attractive to birds. Privet prefers full or partial sun, well-manured soil, moderate water. Variety *Ligustrum japonicum* 'Texanum' is very common. See "Deciduous Shrubs" for deciduous privet species.
Grows Best: Statewide, but not fond of hot deserts.

Pyracantha (firethorn)

Pyracantha spp.
Spanish: *Piracanta.*

Rangy, tall, evergreen exotic grown for its sweet-smelling white flowers, orange berries, and ability to form thick screens. Terrifically thorny. Fast grower. Used for hedges and showy, background massed plantings. Likes moderate watering, full sun, any soil, but may become chlorotic in severely alkaline conditions. Give pyracantha enough room, as generally large (up to 10 feet/3 m in height and width), hardy species are grown in New Mexico. *Pyracantha coccinea* varieties are very popular and are usually good choices. 'Lalandei' and 'Government Red' are among these. Other pyracantha species are widely cultivated as well.
Grows Best: Southern New Mexico, as far north as Albuquerque.

Pittosporum

Rubber rabbitbrush (chamisa)

Chrysothamnus nauseosus
Spanish: *Chamisa.*

Very popular, easy-to-grow native shrub, generally 4–5 feet (1.5 m) tall and as wide. Often semi-evergreen, covered with very bright yellow flowers in fall. Fast-growing, gray-green foliage (actually, often a cool blue). Full sun, little water, any soil. Quite adaptable. An excellent erosion-control plant, flourishes in disturbed ground anywhere, especially along roadsides. Takes shearing well; may be used as a formal or informal hedge. Quite beautiful against adobe walls. Pungent scent. A green variety of this plant is also commonly cultivated.
Grows Best: Statewide.

Big sage

Artemisia tridentata
Spanish: *Artemisia.*

This widespread New Mexico native is perhaps *the* classic shrub of the Western landscape. It is common in the higher elevations of northern New Mexico and found in particular abundance in the wide flats and rolling hills around Taos. Very hardy. Prefers alkaline soils. Grows at a moderate rate to 3 feet (1 m) tall; spreads to 3-4 feet (about 1 m) or so. Prefers full sun and light watering. Produces a very satisfying effect against adobe or stucco walls. Its aroma after a rain is unequalled.
Grows Best: Statewide.

Waxleaf privet

Pyracantha

Big sage

Rubber rabbitbrush

Threadleaf sage

Fourwing saltbush

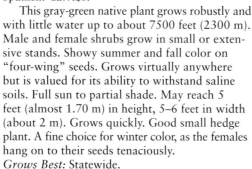

Seepwillow

Sand sage (threadleaf sage)

Artemisia filifolia
Spanish: *Artemisia.*

Very common, feathery native shrub, extraordinarily hardy, and frequently found on sandy benches along the central and lower Rio Grande drainage. Very little maintenance needed. Fast growth, full sun, very little water. Blue-gray color and light texture make it an attractive landscape plant. Grows to 3–4 feet (about 1 m) wide. Roots bind soil well, and the plant is a good erosion control. Looks good in compositions with desert baileya, desert willow, purple aster.
Grows Best: Statewide.

Fourwing saltbush

Atriplex canescens
Spanish: *Carrizo.*

This gray-green native plant grows robustly and with little water up to about 7500 feet (2300 m). Male and female shrubs grow in small or extensive stands. Showy summer and fall color on "four-wing" seeds. Grows virtually anywhere but is valued for its ability to withstand saline soils. Full sun to partial shade. May reach 5 feet (almost 1.70 m) in height, 5–6 feet in width (about 2 m). Grows quickly. Good small hedge plant. A fine choice for winter color, as the females hang on to their seeds tenaciously.
Grows Best: Statewide.

Seepwillow (desert broom, broom baccharis)

Baccharis sarothroides
Spanish: *Sauce colador* (colloquial).

Seepwillow is an impressive native screen or curiosity shrub. The green stems give it its rich color, as the plant is nearly leafless. Produces white flowers (tiny but massed) in autumn. Fast grower to about 7–8 feet (2.5 m), equally wide, assuming a pleasant, rounded form when mature. Often found along watercourses but takes drought well. Likes gravelly soils but will grow anywhere in sun or partial shade. Grows faster with water. Good in revegetation, erosion control, or as a very low-maintenance accent.
Grows Best: Statewide.

Silverberry

Elaeagnus pungens
Spanish: *Eleágno.*

Among the coarsest of shrubs, this enormous exotic (up to 10 feet/3 m tall and wide) is often grown as a hedge or used as a foundation plant for large buildings. Leaves are typically dark green on top, silver beneath, and rough to the touch. Plant grows at a moderate rate, tolerates alkaline soil (although it may become chlorotic), prefers sun. Moderate watering. Hardy. Closely related to the Russian olive, *Elaeagnus angustifolia.*
Grows Best: Statewide.

Sotol (desert spoon)

Dasylirion wheeleri
Spanish: *Sotol (amole).*

Sotol, a native succulent, is frequently mistaken for broadleaf yucca. It is found in the wild in hot southern locales up to 6000 feet (1830 m). Its leaves differ from the yucca's in their longitudinal twist (they rotate on their axes along the entire length of the leaf) and sharply serrated edges. Grows up to 9 feet (3 m) tall, with a strong, single flower stem that may be taller. A striking and impressively formal Southwestern shrub, good as a landscape feature. Hardy as far north as Bernalillo. Prefers full sun, stony or gravelly soil, little water. Fast grower.
Grows Best: Southern and eastern New Mexico; north as far as Bernalillo, Tucumcari.

Silverberry

Sotol

Alberta spruce

Alberta spruce

Picea glauca 'Conica' *(Picea albertiana)*
Spanish: *Pinabete, pruche de Alberta.*

This handsome, small, exotic evergreen is an excellent garden accent. It is a perfectly conical garden shrub—a miniature version of the common Engelmann and blue spruces of the New Mexican mountains. Grows slowly to 5–6 feet (about 2 m), likes a good deal of water, and produces a very fine surface texture. Prefers a richer soil and full or partial sun. Alberta spruce creates a set effect in the garden that will last for many years. Hardy.
Grows Best: Statewide, protected gardens.

Texas ranger (purple sage)

Leucophyllum frutescens
Spanish: *Cenizo.*

Gray-leafed native or near-native shrub with showy purple flowers, very handsome, and widely used in southern New Mexico dry-land landscapes. Likes full sun, any soil that drains well, and very little water. Hardy as far north as Socorro. Grows rapidly to about 6–8 feet (about 2 m) tall, and as wide. Good in hedges (formal or informal), as low windbreaks, and as a specimen. Very little maintenance required. Like ocotillo, it blooms after a rain. Many varieties available.
Grows Best: Southern New Mexico as far north as Socorro.

Texas ranger

Yucca

Yucca spp.
Spanish: *Yuca, amole, palmilla.*

As one of the two or three most characteristic native plants of the Southwest, yuccas in landscape and garden settings are tough, moderately quick to grow, showy, and—oddly enough—usually very formal in appearance. They like full sun, little water, and most soils. Creamy-white flowers in summer. They are very neat as garden plants, producing virtually no debris. Cut back dead flower stalks to improve appearance. Exotic yuccas also grow well in New Mexico. The following species are most commonly cultivated:

Narrowleaf yucca, *Yucca glauca.* A modest native plains yucca, low-growing (up to 1.5 feet/450 mm, and as wide), with a 3-foot (1 m) flower stalk. Possibly the hardiest of yuccas, growing as far north as Montana. Stays low, and typically spreads its leaves in a sparse half-radial rosette. Useful in naturalistic compositions; underutilized as a formal landscape element. Grows statewide.

Softblade yucca, *Yucca recurvifolia.* This spectacular exotic is the only common yucca in New Mexico from the *southeastern* United States. Very hardy and drought-resistant. Will grow in any soil but prefers rich loam. Showy, waxy white flowers. May grow into low tree form (up to 10 feet/3 m) with several branches. Leaves characteristically droop at midpoint, hence the name. Slow-growing; likes full sun, but will tolerate shade. Excellent as accent or in mass plantings. Prefers moderate watering, and may sucker. Grows best in southern New Mexico, as far north as Bernalillo.

Spanish bayonet (banana yucca), *Yucca baccata.* A wideleaf native yucca with creamy flowers and pulpy fruits, growing in foothills and rocky outcrops throughout New Mexico. An excellent character plant. Reaches 3 feet (1 m) in height, often spreading to 4–5 feet (1.5 m). Very little care required. Usually slow-growing. Sharp, very sturdy leaves. Grows anywhere.

Coral-flower yucca, *Hesperaloe parviflora.* A yucca-like plant originally from northern Mexico, grown as an exotic in New Mexico. Coral-flower yucca belongs to the Agavaceae (agave) family. Reaches about 3–4 feet (about 1 m) in height and width. Tall, waving flower stalks with pale, reddish ("coral") flowers give the plant its name. Hardy, quick-growing, and showy. Excellent feature plant, especially when set out in masses. Best conditions south of Albuquerque.
Grows Best: As noted above.

Spanish bayonet

Coral flower yucca

Narrowleaf yucca

Clover

GROUND COVERS
DECIExxOUS

PLEASE NOTE THAT THE ABBREVIATION "O.C." STANDS FOR "ON CENTER," THE DISTANCE FROM THE MIDDLE OF ONE PLANT TO THE MIDDLE OF THE NEXT. ALL PLANTS IN THIS SECTION ARE IDENTIFIED AS NATIVE, EXOTIC, OR NATURALIZED.

Spring cinquefoil

Spring cinquefoil (potentilla)

Potentilla tabernaemontanii
Spanish: *Cincoenrama.*

An exotic, low-growing ground cover, hardy, with yellow flowers in late spring and through the summer. Semi-evergreen, fast-spreading; should be planted at 1 foot (300 mm) o.c. Prefers rich, moist soil and will grow across a shallow mulch. Spreads best under sheltering shrubs or trees. Very low, rarely exceeding 3–4 inches (100 mm) in height. Planted from pots or flats. Grows best in partial shade and in planting areas of modest size (less than 100 square feet/3 m2).
Grows Best: Statewide, partially shady spots.

Clover

Trifolium spp.
Spanish: *Trébol.*

The clovers, both native and introduced species, are important ground covers and soil conditioners. Clover responds well to moist soils with a substantial phosphorus—not nitrogen—content. Full sun to partial shade. All the clovers are legumes and "fix" atmospheric nitrogen in the soil. They generally improve any soil in which they are present. Species include:

White (Dutch) clover, *Trifolium repens,* naturalized. This is the species used most often. Formerly common in lawn mixes, now utilized as a ground cover in large areas. Grows profusely up to 18 inches (450 mm) tall from seed in a single season. Deep-rooting. Medium to heavy watering. Attractive white or pink flowers draw bees. Lush, full, brilliant green effect.

Strawberry clover, *Trifolium fragiferum,* naturalized. Cultivated from seed, its growth characteristics are similar to those of *Trifolium repens.* However, it roots more deeply (to 6 feet/ 2 m or deeper), will grow under some saline soil conditions, has generally pink or "strawberry" flower heads, and tolerates drought better than white clover. Seems to flourish with less water than *Trifolium repens.* A new variety, *Trifolium fragiferum* 'Fresa,' or Fresa strawberry clover, has just been developed by New Mexico State University.

Mountain clovers—*Trifolium subacaulescens, Trifolium lacerum, Trifolium fendleri.* These native clovers may occur up to 10,000 feet (3100 m) and are frequently found on forest floors or in meadows. They are attractive and quite similar to domestic clover species but not widely cultivated.
Grows Best: Statewide.

Cranberry cotoneaster

Cotoneaster apiculatus

Compact, low-growing, exotic cotoneaster often planted as a ground cover (typically at 3–4 feet/about 1 m o.c.) in well-manured soil. For a description, please see Cranberry cotoneaster under "Deciduous Shrubs."

Crown vetch

Crown vetch

Coronilla varia
Spanish: *Arveja de coronilla.*

This rough but wildly beautiful exotic member of the pea family is a close relative of clover and alfalfa. An invaluable ground cover, it is at its best controlling erosion on steep slopes. Rank-growing, deciduous, deep-rooting; flowers all summer long. Invasive. May be planted from pots or seed. Grows to 3 feet (1 m) tall but may cover shrubs and short trees through its vining habit. Prefers full sun but can withstand partial shade. Water-loving, fond of well-prepared soil. Intensely green. Not for the small garden or delicate planter.
Grows Best: Statewide.

Mint

Prairie sage

Mint

Mentha spp.
Spanish: *Menta* or *hierbabuena (yerbabuena).*

Very tough herbaceous plants that regenerate from year to year from a tenacious root system. Mints are naturalized, very common "folk" ground covers in shady or semi-shady areas. Likes moist soil but will grow virtually anywhere. Common spearmint, *Mentha spicata*, is an old garden favorite and may reach 2 feet (600 mm) in height. Highly invasive—one or two plants will spread throughout a small planter in a season. Best as an accent, well-contained in a grade-level bed or in a pot or planter, and as a garnish for iced tea.
Grows Best: Statewide.

Prairie sage

Artemisia ludoviciana
Spanish: *Artemisia.*

Handsome, low-growing native that can reach 2–3 feet (about 1 m) tall. Grows easily and fast in virtually any soil with full sun and little to no watering. Grayish-green foliage, very aromatic, typically upright. Variety *Artemisa ludoviciana albula*, Silver King artemisia, is bushy, silvery, somewhat larger. Prairie sage is highly useful as a backdrop for red-, yellow-, and purple-flowered annuals and perennials.
Good pathway accent.
Grows Best: Statewide.

Memorial rose

Rosa wichuriana
Spanish: *Rosa.*

Please see description under Roses in "Deciduous Shrubs."

Snow-in-summer
(white mouse-ear chickweed)

Cerastium tomentosum
Spanish: *Cerastio de Granada.*

An excellent exotic ground cover, remaining small (about 8 inches/200 mm) and compact as it matures. Profuse white flowers. Does well in sun and sandy or gravelly soil. Good rock garden plant. Light to moderate water. Plant at about 18 inches (450 mm) on center. Fast-growing, but best in New Mexico in small to medium planter areas.
Grows Best: Statewide.

Prairie sage

Snow-in-summer

Ajuga

GROUND COVERS
EVERGREEN

Dwarf coyotebrush

Ajuga (bugleweed)

Ajuga reptans
Spanish: *Brígula rastrera*.

Excellent, exotic, evergreen ground cover for small areas. Green-and-copper-leaved varieties are available. Ajuga prefers partially sunny or shady areas and moderate water. May grow 4–6 inches (about 150 mm) high. Should be planted in well-prepared soil at approximately 6–8 inches (180 mm) o.c. Colorful tiny blue flowers. Grows well under or near shrubs or small trees.
Grows Best: Statewide, in partially shaded areas.

Bearberry cotoneaster

Cotoneaster dammeri
Spanish: *Cotoneastre* (colloquial).

Evergreen exotic, very low-growing (to 1 foot/300 mm), spreading to 3 feet (1 m) or more. White flowers in late spring, bright red berries in autumn. Attractive and hardy, quick to cover an area. May become untidy, but generally attractive spilling over container edges and the tops of walls. Many varieties available. Full sun or partial shade. Likes any soil but only light or modest watering. Best in New Mexico near trees. Not for huge areas. Like *Cotoneaster apiculatus* (please see "Deciduous Shrubs"), good for erosion control.
Grows Best: Statewide.

[handwritten: good for front end.]

Dwarf coyotebrush

Baccharis pilularis
Spanish: *Bácara, bacaris*.

Small-leaved, mounding, pale green ground cover. Semi-evergreen exotic. Responds to enriched soil and regular watering but is tough and adaptable. Likes full sun. May reach 6 inches (150 mm) in height and spread 3 feet (1 m) or more. Looks good on banks and slopes, but often freezes in the winter. Trim back in late winter or spring to encourage new growth. Needs little care once established. Several varieties available.
Grows Best: Southern New Mexico; sheltered locales in Albuquerque.

Dichondra

Dichondra micrantha
Spanish: *Dicondra* (colloquial).

Broadleafed, exotic, evergreen ground cover, similar in appearance to violets. Likes sun or shade, but grows tallest (about 3 inches/75 mm) in shade. Thrives in heat. Used as a substitute for lawn in small areas or as a highly ornamental, ground-hugging curiosity planting in shrub beds. Needs water, well-manured soil. Likes good drainage. Not as hardy as grass, but has survived in sunny locales as far north as Albuquerque. At its best in El Paso, Las Cruces, Alamogordo, Carlsbad. Can be planted as seed or from flats. Takes some foot traffic and occasional mowing.
Grows Best: El Paso, extreme southern New Mexico.

Creeping euonymus

Euonymus fortunei
Spanish: *Bonetero*.

Sturdy, exotic evergreen in most circumstances, useful in sun-and-shade areas. May also climb somewhat. Deep green leaves often turn red in winter. Grows about 1 foot (300 mm) tall, sometimes taller; a single plant may spread 4–5 feet (about 1.5 m) wide. Likes rich soil, moderate water. Excellent street-median plant.
Grows Best: Statewide.

Bearberry cotoneaster

Dichondra

Creeping euonymus

Germander (wall germander)

Teucrium chamaedrys 'Prostratum'
Spanish: *Teucrio.*

Teucrium, or germander, is an exotic member of the mint family. In southern and central New Mexico it reaches 6 inches (150 mm) in height, spreading to about 1.5 feet (450 mm) wide. Likes full sun, average soil. Good in small areas or as an accent. Produces reddish flowers. May show cold damage, for which a light pruning will help. Light watering.
Grows Best: Statewide, in small, semi-shaded spaces.

Honeysuckle

Lonicera japonica and varieties
Spanish: *Madreselva.*

A rank-growing, often sweet-smelling, exotic evergreen or semi-evergreen vine or ground cover. Aggressive, fast-spreading, mostly indifferent to soils. Creamy-white flowers produced in spring and summer. Prefers full sun, moderate water. Will cover ground completely in a season or two planted at 3 feet (1 m) o.c. As a ground cover may be 2–3 feet (about 1 m) high. Excellent large-area ground cover, but invasive. Many varieties; Hall's is perhaps the most common. *Lonicera sempervirens,* trumpet honeysuckle, has extraordinary purple-red, bugle-like flowers, small, deep-red fruit, fast growth.
Grows Best: Statewide.

Horizontalis junipers

Juniperus horizontalis and varieties
Spanish: *Enebro.*

Highly useful, hardy, low-growing, exotic ground covers. Generally indifferent to soils, tolerant of dry conditions, and slow-growing, these small junipers rarely exceed a foot (300 mm) or so in height. They can spread a great distance, however, sometimes reaching a diameter of 10 feet (3 m) or more. Colorful. Plant in sun or partial shade. Best varieties for New Mexico include:

Andorra juniper, *Juniperus horizontalis* 'Plumosa.' Rarely exceeds a foot/300 mm in height in New Mexico, spreads to 9–10 feet (about 3 m) in diameter. Very attractive, muted purple color in winter. Moderate rate of growth. Leggy and thin if grown in too much shade. Generally rounded at branch tips. Plant at 3 feet (1 m) o.c.

Bar Harbor juniper, *Juniperus horizontalis* 'Bar Harbor.' May reach 8 inches (200 mm) in height, about 6 feet (2 m) in spread. Attractive bluish color. Moderate to fast growth rate. Unobtrusive; "hugs" contours of a slope in a striking way. May thin with age in New Mexico's high altitude. Plant at 2.5–3 feet (about 1 m) o.c.

Wilton carpet juniper, *Juniperus horizontalis* 'Wiltonii.' An unbelievably low-growing (only about 4 inches/100 mm) ground cover, it can still spread 6 feet (2 m) or more. Beautiful shiny blue color. Good in small (under 100 square feet), sunny open spaces, but don't expect it to grow quickly. Light blue berries add a great deal to the plant's overall appearance.
Grows Best: Statewide.

Germander

Honeysuckle

Wilton carpet juniper

San Jose juniper

Tam juniper

Kinnickinnick

Sabina junipers

Juniperus sabina and varieties
Spanish: *Enebro.*

Excellent, extremely hardy, fast-growing, utilitarian, exotic junipers. A mainstay of New Mexican landscapes for decades, sabina juniper varieties are handsome, ubiquitous shrubs used as mass ground covers, root-cooling elements in tree planters, and unassuming background evergreens in flower settings. Can take virtually any soil. Prefer full or partial sun and moderate watering but can withstand great drought. Long-lived and very widely grown. The most popular varieties are:

Broadmoor juniper, *Juniperus sabina* 'Broadmoor.' Deep green foliage. Usually grows no higher than a foot (300 mm) but spreads to 6 feet (2 m) or more. Good evergreen cover under trees, as it can withstand a great deal of shade. Plant at 3–4 feet (1–1.2 m) o.c.

Buffalo juniper, *Juniperus sabina* 'Buffalo.' Not as widely available as the Broadmoor and tam junipers. Frequently only 8 inches (200 mm) tall, but spreads quickly to 5 feet (1.5 m) or more. Eye-catching, intense green color. Plant at 3–4 feet (about 1 m) o.c.

Tam juniper, *Juniperus sabina* 'Tamariscifolia.' Also called tammy and tamarix juniper. Probably the most widely planted juniper of any kind in New Mexico. Grows up to 2.5 feet (750 mm) tall (sometimes taller) and spreads to 10 feet (3 m) or more. Mounds sharply at center. Extraordinary as ground cover, low hedge, background, or low specimen. Bright green and very fast-growing. Always available. Any soil, but good manuring and light watering dramatically speeds growth. Virtually carefree, as is Broadmoor juniper. Tam juniper composes beautifully with granite boulders and decomposed granite mulch.
Grows Best: Statewide.

San Jose juniper

Juniperus chinensis 'San Jose'
Spanish: *Enebro.*

Very hardy, low-growing (about 2 feet/600 mm or less), drought-tolerant ground cover. One plant can easily spread to 4 feet (1.2 m) or more. Deep green, exotic. Likes full sun and will grow in any soil, but performs best on gravelly slopes with moderate watering and well-manured backfill. Fills in well. Usually slow-growing. Reliable and neat in appearance. Easy to maintain.
Grows Best: Statewide.

Kinnickinnick

Arctostaphylos uva-ursi
Spanish: *Gayuba.*

Also called mountain bearberry and Indian tobacco, this strikingly attractive but modest native ground cover is about 6 inches (150 mm) tall, spreading 2–3 feet (600 mm to 1 m) or more. Needs well-manured garden soil, shade or partial shade, a good deal of water, and time. Good-looking leaves, pink flowers, and richly red berries. A delightful but low-key plant. Grows slowly, loves high country. Good in rock gardens.
Grows Best: High altitudes and partial shade, statewide.

Blue leadwort

Ceratostigma plumbaginoides
Spanish: *Belesa azúl.*

Hardy, sun or shade, exotic ground cover, good under trees and shrubs. A substantial plant, often growing up to a foot (300 mm) tall. Each plant will quickly spread to 3 feet (1 m) or so, so blue leadwort should be set in place at 2–3 feet (about 1 m) o.c. Use blue leadwort to cover small- or medium-sized beds. Good-looking blue or bluish-violet flowers, summer or fall. Moderate water, well-manured soil. Seems to like dry soils. Handsome foliage; looks good in borders.
Grows Best: Throughout New Mexico.

Blue leadwort

Compact nandina

Liriope (lily turf)

Liriope muscari
Spanish: *Liriope.*

Increasingly popular exotic ground cover, growing to about 1 foot (300 mm) tall, spreading wider. Looks like a robust grass. Flowers in late summer, usually in shades of lighter purple or lavender but sometimes white. Grows quickly. Likes half-sun, well-manured soil, moderate watering. Somewhat drought-resistant. Looks good by water. Mow occasionally (set blades high) for better appearance and growth.
Grows Best: Statewide.

Creeping mahonia

Mahonia repens
Spanish: *Acebo falso, algerita.*

This small but very colorful native ground cover prefers rich, somewhat acidic soil, lots of moisture, shade, and high altitude. It grows best in leaf mulch under shrubs and trees. Its natural habitat is in the high spruce, aspen, and fir forests of the state's mountain ranges. Very low; rarely exceeds 6 inches (150 mm) in height, spreading 6 inches to 1 foot (150–300 mm). Produces edible blue berries, usually pubescent. Popular in small, shady garden spaces.
Grows Best: High altitude small spaces, statewide.

Compact nandina

Nandina domestica 'Harbor dwarf'
Spanish: *Bambú celestial.*

Colorful, small (up to 2 feet/600 mm tall, and as wide), slow-growing exotic, often used as an accent ground cover. Compact nandina likes full sun and well-manured soil but will tolerate some shade and drought once established. Moderate water requirements. Round; green in summer, pink-red-scarlet in fall and winter. Plant at 18 inches/450 mm o.c. in small areas for pleasing ground-cover effect.
Grows Best: Southern New Mexico as far north as Albuquerque.

Periwinkle

Vinca major (large-leaf); *Vinca minor* (small-leaf)
Spanish: *Pervencha* or *pervinca.*

Evergreen, exotic vine or ground cover, with violet flowers in summer. Trailing growth habit. Likes well-manured soil and partial shade. Periwinkle is not fond of hot, high-altitude sun. Moderate growth habit. Needs a fair amount of consistent water to flourish. May reach 1 foot (300 mm) in height, but a single plant can grow to a diameter of 4 feet (1.2 m) or more. Low vertical growth as a vine. *Vinca minor* is hardiest.
Grows Best: Statewide, in slightly shaded areas.

Pussytoes ✱ Beautiful in wild.

Antennaria parviflora
Spanish: *Deditos de gato* (colloquial).

Tiny, native ground cover found in mountainous areas of New Mexico. A fine touch in rock gardens or alongside waterfalls. Barely reaches 1–2 inches (about 50 mm) in height. Spreads at a moderate rate. Minute white flowers in spring. Use in semi-shaded areas. Appreciates manured soil, moderate watering. Evergreen, greenish-gray, delicate.
Grows Best: Statewide, in small, somewhat shaded areas.

Rosemary

Rosmarinus officinalis
Spanish: *Romero.*

This exotic, evergreen trailing plant is often placed in raised planters or containers to accentuate its cascading effect. Likes full sun and any soil that drains well. Moderate water. Variety *R. o.* 'Prostratus,' the dwarf rosemary, is best choice for a ground cover. May reach 2 feet (600 mm) in height but can spread to 6 feet (2 m) or more. Pale purple-blue flowers. Variety *R. o.* 'Huntington Blue' is also good and somewhat smaller. Place plants about 2 feet (600 mm) o.c. for complete coverage. Individual rosemary plants are cultivated as herbs. Plant is best used to cover modest-sized areas.
Grows Best: Albuquerque; southern New Mexico.

Liriope (lily turf)

Creeping mahonia

Periwinkle

Rosemary

Pussytoes

Gray santolina (left)

Pachysandra (Japanese spurge)

Green santolina (middle)   Strawberry(below)

Santolina (lavender cotton and green lavender cotton)

Santolina spp.
Spanish: *Abrótano hembra.*

Extremely aromatic, low-growing, evergreen, shrub-like ground covers. Santolinas like full sun, very little watering. Fast, mounded growth; yellow flowers in summer. Any soil. Must be well-mulched, clipped regularly (after flowers are spent), and kept relatively dry to flourish. These two species are exotics, but they look like and mix well with many native species. Not completely cold-hardy north of Albuquerque. *Santolina chamaecyparissus* (gray) grows up to 2 feet (600 mm) tall, equally wide; *Santolina virens* (green) is a few inches shorter. Striking plants; *S. chamaecyparissus* may be pruned as a low, pungent hedge.
Grows Best: Southern New Mexico, as far north as Albuquerque.

Sedum (stonecrop)

Sedum spp.
Spanish: *Fabacrasa.*

Native and exotic species of often tiny (12 inches/300 mm or less), succulent, flowering ground covers. Generally, sedums do best in rock gardens. They like well-drained, moist, sandy soils with full or partial sun and spread at a moderate rate. Use sedums in small areas. The native New Mexican species of stonecrop sedums are rose crown (*Sedum rhodanthum*) and roseroot (*Sedum integrifolium*), both found in stony outcrops along high mountain creeks and ridges. 'Dragonsblood' is a very popular exotic sedum for general garden use.
Grows Best: Statewide.

Sedum

(Japanese) spurge

Pachysandra terminalis
Spanish: *Paquisandra.*

But needs more water & manure

This evergreen exotic displays an unusually strong form in its small, shiny rosettes that spread by means of underground runners. Spurge loves shade and moist, well-manured soil. Provides an excellent and striking ground cover under aspens in northern New Mexico. Reaches a foot (300 mm) or less in height and should be planted at about 1 foot (300 mm) o.c. Grows quickly. Extraordinary structure makes it a good border plant in shady or semi-shady areas. Variegated varieties are also available.
Grows Best: Statewide, in small, shady areas.

Strawberry

Fragaria spp.
Spanish: *Fresa.*

Delicate, low-growing (about 8 inches/200 mm), semi-deciduous, vining ground cover. Native and exotic species are both useful. Native species prefers moist, mulch soil and semi-shade. Most of the cultivated species and varieties like somewhat acidic soil, mulch, and full sun. Quick to spread; will produce a great deal of exceptionally delicious fruit. Water-loving. Plant in a small area; don't expect strawberries to replace a lawn. Strawberries attract snails, slugs, and potato bugs (roly-polies) in profusion. Set out new plants about every three to four years.
Grows Best: Statewide.

GRASSES

GRASSES
TRADITIONAL TURF SPECIES

Bentgrass

Bentgrass

Agrostis spp.
Spanish: *Hierba doblada* (colloquial).

Fussy exotic primarily used for golf greens. Spreads rapidly by runners. Needs much water, well-prepared soil, full sun, and extraordinary care. Generally cut to half an inch (10–20 mm) height, bentgrass has the finest and smoothest of all grass textures. May be used as a lawn grass, but is best restricted to playing greens. Colonial bent, *Agrostis tenuis*, is commonly used in New Mexico. Creeping bent, *Agrostis stolonifera*, is also frequently found both as the species itself and its varieties. Seed or sod.
Grows Best: Statewide, in sunny areas.

Bermuda grass

Cynodon dactylon spp.
Spanish: *Pata de gallo.*

Extremely hardy, extremely aggressive, warm-season turf grass, best cultivated in southern New Mexico but found nearly everywhere. Bermuda spreads from seed or stolons or is planted as sod. Grows quickly to form an impenetrable mat of tough roots and dense blades. An exotic, it is rapidly naturalizing, especially along ditches. Smooth, pleasing appearance with proper fertilization and close (1 inch/25 mm) mowing. Moderate to heavy watering is necessary. Long dormant season; may be overseeded with Manhattan rye for winter color. Invades planters, vegetable gardens, containers, other border areas. Available in a large number of varieties developed for color, lack of allergy-producing pollen, fine leaf blades, and other desirable qualities. Often displaces bluegrass and fescue in old lawns. At its best in heat and growing in well-manured seedbed.

Bermuda is frequently classified as common (coarse) bermuda and African (fine-bladed) bermuda, *Cynodon transvaalensis*, the species most often hybridized.
Grows Best: Southern New Mexico.

Bluegrass

Poa pratensis
Spanish: *Zacate, zacate azul.*

Naturalized, classic cool-season lawn grass. Grown everywhere in North America. Likes full sun, well-manured soil, moderate to heavy watering. Fine-bladed, long-lived. Available in many varieties as seed or sod. Perennial. Often planted in pure stands or mixed with fescues for sports fields. Although it is a tremendous oxygen producer, its appetite for water is likely to confine it largely to field athletics in the near future. Hardy, but does not tolerate drought. Ideal mowing height is 1.5–2 inches (about 50 mm). At its best in spring, fall. Semi-evergreen. Does not flourish in hot deserts. Spreads via underground stems. *Poa annua*, annual bluegrass, is a common, bright green sight in the winter landscapes of New Mexico. Bluegrasses are found throughout the state in highland meadows.
Grows Best: Above 4500 feet (1400 m) statewide.

African bermuda

Bluegrass

Manhattan rye

Fescue

Fescue

Festuca spp.
Spanish: *Cañuela.*

Widely used, cool-season, exotic turfgrass, often mixed with bluegrass in traditional New Mexican lawns. Generally hardy, medium-bladed, and shade-tolerant. Needs consistent watering, well-manured soils to flourish. Grows best in spring, fall. Sometimes available as pure sod; usually planted as seed. Species include:

Red fescue, *Festuca rubra.* Fine-bladed and very commonly mixed with bluegrasses. This grass clumps if not kept short (mowed at about 2 inches/50 mm). Rich, deep green. Red fescue is a good "starter" crop for such slope-holding ground covers as crown vetch because it germinates very quickly. It is later shaded out by the taller permanent ground cover. It can also be used as a winter overseed for bermuda grass in southern New Mexico.

Tall fescue, *Festuca elatior.* Frequently used pasture grass. Makes good hay. Tall fescue comes in many varieties, a number of which are fine-bladed and suitable for lawns. Often mixed with bluegrasses. The old-fashioned "K-31" lawn mixture for New Mexico is tall fescue. Very good on slopes to stop erosion. Typically forms clumps, is medium-bladed and very hardy.

Blue fescue, *Festuca caesia.* An ice-blue, mounding fescue species frequently used as a specialty ground cover. Please see "Grasses: Ornamental species."
Grows Best: Shady and sunny areas, statewide.

Ryegrass (rye)

Lolium spp.
Spanish: *Centeno, grama de centeno.*

Tough, coarse-bladed, exotic, cool-season lawn grass, typically growing in clumps. Often mixed with bluegrass, fescue, or both to form turf. Good erosion control, soil retainer, revegetation plant. Likes full sun, well-manured soil, consistent watering. Like bluegrass and fescue, rye is best mown at 1.5–2 inches (about 50 mm). Not often available as sod, as seed is plentiful, quick to germinate, and cheap. The following types do well in New Mexico:

Common rye, *Lolium multiflorum* and hybrids. Big, coarse, clumping, rough-bladed grass. Frequently used as a winter bermuda overseed in the warm-season grass areas of southern New Mexico.

Perennial rye, *Lolium perenne.* Also a winter overseed grass, perennial rye is generally a fine-textured grass (some varieties, such as 'Manhattan' and 'Pennfine,' are finer than bluegrass) that is so tenacious it quickly supplants bermuda as the principal year-round turf species in many southern New Mexico lawns. Like other ryes, it germinates very fast. Shiny, attractive blades. Long-lived.
Grows Best: Statewide.

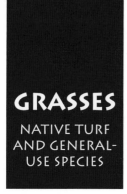

GRASSES
NATIVE TURF AND GENERAL-USE SPECIES

Buffalo grass

Buchlöe dactyloides
Spanish: *Zacate chino.*

Tough, superb, native lawn and pasture grass growing only to 4–5 inches (about 100 mm) tall. Cool, fine-textured, light green or green-blue in color. Makes an excellent turf, especially when planted with blue grama (*Bouteloua gracilis*). Needs full sun, light to moderate watering, and about two full growing seasons to fill in. Grows thicker and faster in manured soil with consistent watering but will also do well with no watering at all.

Buffalo grass is attractive mowed or unmowed. Hardy enough for light play and recreational use. Usually planted from seed, but sod is increasingly available. Like bermuda, sometimes planted from sprigs. Very good choice to replace water-gulping bluegrass in most situations. Cultivated varieties are available.
Grows Best: Statewide.

Galleta

Hilaria jamesii
Spanish: *Galleta.*

Very hardy native, warm-season, sod-forming grass. Common in ranges and along roadsides. Grows up to 2 feet (600 mm) tall, with attractive seed heads. Blue-green color. Roots form an excellent erosion-control mat. May be mowed to form a rough turf grass. Full sun, any soil. Spreads by rhizomes. Found naturally on clay soils as a bunchgrass. Variety *H. j.* 'Viva' is exceptionally drought-resistant.
Grows Best: Statewide, up to 7500 feet/2300 m.

Buffalo grass

Black grama

Bouteloua eriopoda
Spanish: *Navajita negra.*

Tall, native grama, very useful in erosion control and tolerant of long dry spells. Widespread in the Southwest. Grows up to 2 feet (600 mm) and forms an incomplete or light sod. Warm-season grass. Likes full sun, prefers plains or foothills locations. Most soils. Grayish-green in color. Can remain dormant for long periods. Typically reproduces vegetatively by rooting at the nodes of its stems or via stolons. Good choice for revegetation.
Grows Best: Statewide.

Galleta

Blue grama

Mixed blue grama/buffalo grass lawn

Sideoats grama

Blue grama

Bouteloua gracilis
Spanish: *Navajita azul.*
   Very widespread native bunchgrass, often used alone or with buffalo grass to create a good, low-water lawn. Full sun, light watering, and lightly enriched soil will create a good turf within a couple of growing seasons. Good pasture grass—a favorite of New Mexico ranchers. Gray-green color, straw-like when dormant. A warm-season grass. Grows well with no water or care, but will remain bunchy. Tall (up to 1–2 feet/600 mm), extremely tough, and with very handsome seedheads. Several varieties are available; *B. g.* 'Hatchita' is most drought-tolerant.
Grows Best: Statewide.

Sideoats grama

Bouteloua curtipendula
Spanish: *Banderita.*
   Tough, tall, widespread, native grass, very drought-tolerant, usually grown as a bunchgrass. The Spanish name comes from the flag- or pennant-like appearance of the culms or seed stems, which can grow up to about 3 feet (1 m) tall. Sideoats may also spread by rhizomes under favorable conditions. Often found growing alongside blue grama and buffalo grass on the slopes of rocky foothills. Good as a pasture grass or for erosion control. Full sun, any soil. Cultivated varieties adapted to distinct geographic areas are available.
Grows Best: Statewide.

Western wheatgrass (bluestem)

Agropyron smithii
Spanish: *Zacate de llano.*
   This hardy native (up to about 2.5 feet/750 mm tall) is widespread throughout the West. It grows well in full sun in areas with very low annual precipitation. Forms a good sod; spreads quickly via rhizomes. Pale, cool blue when in season (spring, fall); tawny in winter. Excellent choice for erosion control. Likes most soils. Appreciates a little water in deep summer. Available in several cultivated varieties.
   Other wheatgrasses, such as *Agropyron desertorum/Agropyron cristatum* (crested wheatgrass, an exotic), and *Agropyron trichophorum* (pubescent wheatgrass, also an exotic), are also widely available and in use as erosion-control and revegetation species.
Grows Best: Statewide.

Blue grama

Western wheatgrass (Above and right)

GRASSES
ORNAMENTAL SPECIES

Blue fescue

Alkali sacaton

Sporobolus airoides
Spanish: *Zacatón alcalino.*

An extraordinarily beautiful native warm-season bunchgrass common in alkaline soils, especially in central and southern New Mexico. Tough, highly drought-resistant, and sometimes impressively large—up to 2 1/2 feet/750 mm tall and just as wide, with a variety that grows much taller. Has attractive, filigreed seed structures and stems. Blue-green color in summer, tawny yellow in fall and winter. No care needed. Closely related to sand dropseed and other sacaton grasses. Excellent as a cultivated "curiosity" specimen or in masses. The wide sacaton range east of Socorro near Carthage is perhaps the most unusually beautiful grassland in New Mexico.
Grows Best: Statewide, under 6500 feet (2000 m).

Sand dropseed

Sporobolus cryptandrus
Spanish: *Zacatón.*

A very tall (up to 4 feet/1.25 m, but often shorter), somewhat unkempt, sand-loving native grass, often found in natural association with Indian ricegrass, galleta, and the gramas. Tough, hardy, sun-loving, and extremely drought-resistant. Strong ornamental quality. Pale green when growing, and often a light, tawny yellow in the off-season. A strong root system makes sand dropseed a good choice for revegetation and erosion control. Easy to start from seed, sand dropseed is a warm-season bunchgrass.
Grows Best: Sandy or rocky soils, statewide.

Fountain grass

Blue fescue   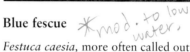 *mod. to low water.*

Festuca caesia, more often called out as *Festuca ovina glauca*
Spanish: *Cañuela azúl.*

Whimsical, mounding, exotic grass, pale blue with ornamental flowers. Blue fescue is used as a ground cover or curiosity plant. Excellent cold-hardiness. Moderate watering needed, but will become highly drought-resistant. Tolerates alkaline soils. Prefers full sun or partial shade. About 1 foot (300 mm) tall and wide. Moderate growth rate.
Grows Best: Statewide.

Fountain grass

Pennisetum spp.
Spanish: *Hierba de fuente* (colloquial).

This graceful exotic, available in a number of species, typically grows from 2–3 feet (about 1 m) tall, spreading to perhaps twice as wide. Fountain grass has attractive, muted green foliage but is valued chiefly for its many bright, feathery plumes, which vary in color from copper (*Pennisetum setaceum*) to silvery-yellow (*Pennisetum alopecuroides*). Likes full sun, well-manured soil, moderate water. Fast-growing. *Pennisetum alopecuroides* is the hardiest general choice for New Mexico landscapes. The foliage of *P. setaceum* also has characteristic rust-colored undertones.
Grows Best: Southern New Mexico, as far north as Albuquerque.

Sand dropseed

Alakali sakaton

River cane

Indian ricegrass

Pampas grass

Pampas grass

Cortaderia selloana
Spanish: *Carrizo de la pampa.*

 Fast-growing, exotic, clump grass used as a border mass or accent specimen. Pampas grass can be either a deciduous or evergreen shrub, depending on its geographic or microclimatic location. Showy, spiky flowers, razor-edged leaves. Pampas makes a very good curiosity species or may be planted in groups as a border, flowering background, or driveway shrub. Up to 6 feet (about 2 m) tall, and as wide. Semi- or fully evergreen in south. Full sun. Very drought-resistant and hardy once established.
Grows Best: Virtually anywhere up to 6500 feet or 2000 m.

Purple threeawn

Indian ricegrass

Oryzopsis hymenoides
Spanish: *Hierba arroz* (colloquial).

 This beautiful bunch grass is perhaps the most ornamental of New Mexico's native grass species. Occurs in deserts, desert uplands, and foothills throughout central and southern New Mexico. Grows up to 1 1/2 feet (450 mm) tall, spreading as wide. Edible seeds or their husks cover the plant from late spring through fall. Excellent as soil stabilizer, accent planting, or in cut floral arrangements. No special soil amendments or water required for good cultivation. Full sun.
Grows Best: In sandy soils, statewide up to 7500 feet/2300 m.

River cane

Arundo donax
Spanish: *Caña.*

 Bamboo-like in appearance, river cane is really a giant grass. This naturalized plant grows along ditch banks in much of southern and central New Mexico, forming an intense screen up to 15 feet (5 m) high. Semi-evergreen, with a showy, tassel-like flower. Sometimes strong-smelling. Spreads by means of an aggressive root system. Grows in any soil. Light to heavy water user. Prefers full sun but will withstand partial shade. Fast-growing.

 As the canes in a stand tend to die back during the cold months, river cane looks best when older canes are cut back to the ground in late winter or early spring.
Grows Best: Statewide up to 6000 feet/1800 m.

Purple threeawn

Aristida longiseta (Aristida purpurea)
Spanish: *Tres aristas.*

 Usually found in sandy or gravelly growing conditions, this extraordinarily beautiful native warm-season grass produces a purplish or reddish effect in massed plantings. Grows about 1 foot/ 300 mm tall in full sun. Bunchgrass. Good for erosion control, revegetation, or curiosity planting in a domestic or residential landscape. Light watering during establishment and thereafter to maintain in prime condition. No particular soil preparation needed. At its peak in late spring.
Grows Best: Statewide.

VINES
DECIDUOUS

ALL PLANTS IN THIS SECTION ARE IDENTIFIED AS NATIVE, EXOTIC, OR NATURALIZED.

Canyon grape

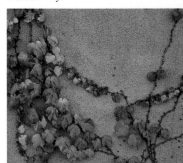

Boston ivy

Boston ivy

Parthenocissus tricuspidata
Spanish: *Hiedra de Boston.*
    An exotic vine, prized for its attractive, often glossy leaves and scarlet fall color. Grows quickly; can spread 10 feet (3 m) or more in a single season. Prefers moderate watering. Often mixed with English ivy for a good effect through all seasons. Closely related to the native Virginia creeper. Likes sun or partial shade, fences, walls with texture. No pests of note.
Grows Best: Statewide.

Canyon grape

Vitis arizonica
Spanish: *Uva.*
    This small, beautiful native prefers springs and watercourses in the Chihuahuan and Sonoran desert reaches of New Mexico. Rich green, glossy leaves, deciduous, and red or orange in the fall. May spread quickly 6–9 feet (about 2–3 m) over rocks, shrubs, trees, or other local support. Likes sun or sun-and-shade. The small grapes are inedible; otherwise, this is a good trellis plant. Likes moderate to heavy water, alkaline soils. Not widely available yet from nurseries.
Grows Best: Statewide.

Carolina jessamine

Gelsimium sempervirens
Spanish: *Jazmín.*
    Exotic, semi-evergreen vine noted for its yellow flowers. Exceptionally striking on wooden fences, trellises, or posts. Likes well-manured soil in sun or partial shade with moderate, consistent water. Hardy once established, average growth. Aromatic. May be used in small areas as ground cover, especially in southern New Mexico.
Grows Best: Southern New Mexico, as far north as Albuquerque.

Clematis

Clematis spp.
Spanish: *Clemátide.*
    Large number of species of hardy, small vines, some exotic, some native. The old adage "feet in the shade, head in the sun" is quite true: for the very best effect, plant clematis on the north side of a short fence or wall in wet, well-manured soil. Grows to about 10 feet (3 m). Cultivated species have rich, bright colors. *Clematis* 'Jackmanii' is a favorite with purple sepals. The wild native *Clematis ligusticifolia* (western virginsbower) is notable for its pale yellow, gossamer, seed-covering threads in late summer, early fall.
Grows Best: Statewide.

Carolina jessamine

Clematis

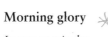

Morning glory

Trumpet vine

Silverlace vine

Morning glory ✳

Ipomoea tricolor
Spanish: *Dondiego* or *dondiego de día.*

   Exotic tropical vine with brilliant blue or blue-violet flowers that open against bright green leaves. Stunning, old-fashioned effect. Morning glory is more properly a tender annual or perennial, growing to 8–10 feet (about 3 m) tall. Tolerates dry soil, blooms all summer and into fall, and loves the sun. Modest watering is helpful. Spread widely by birds.
Grows Best: Statewide, sunny places.

Silverlace vine

Polygonum aubertii
Spanish: *Polígono.*

   A first-rate vine for hiding unsightly fences, utility pole braces, or walls. Exotic. Rampant growth to 25–30 feet (8–9 m). Profuse, tiny white flowers follow thick leaf growth in spring and persist all summer. Thrives in virtually any New Mexican soil. Likes full sun, tolerates drought. Old woody growth may need to be pruned back.
Grows Best: Statewide.

Trumpet vine ✳

Campsis radicans
Spanish: *Jazmín trompeta.*

   Quick-growing exotic with red or reddish-orange, trumpet-like flowers, attractive to hummingbirds. Likes full sun and manured soil. Needs a fence or trellis. Compound leaves, glossy and deep green. Tough, very hardy. Seed cases (canoe-shaped) are also attractive.
Grows Best: Statewide.

Virginia creeper (woodbine) ✳

Parthenocissus quinquefolia
Spanish: *Trepadora virginiana.*

   Fast-spreading naturalized vine with excellent red or red and pink fall color. Closely related to the native Rocky Mountain woodbine, *Parthenocissus inserta,* from which it is virtually indistinguishable. Used as a trellis and fence cover or as a ground cover. Very hardy; indifferent to soils, takes any amount of water. Virginia creeper produces a number of dark purple, grape-like, inedible fruits. Grows readily from seeds, which are spread by birds. Sun or shade. A single plant may spread 40 feet (12 m) or more.
Grows Best: Statewide.

Wisteria ✳ *but mod. water / manure*

Wisteria sinensis
Spanish: *Vistaria.*

   Wisteria is a highly ornamental, fragrant, spring-flowering (lavender or violet) vine. Generally blooms in May. Exotic. Compound, light green leaves are very handsome. Excellent as a trellis or shade-structure plant, but may also be trained as a shrub, small tree, or ground cover. Dependable and hardy. Full sun, well-manured soil, moderate water. Grows rapidly. *Wisteria sinensis* 'Alba' *produces white flowers.*
Grows Best: Statewide.

Virginia creeper

Wisteria

VINES
EVERGREEN

Algerian ivy

Algerian ivy

Hedera canariensis
Spanish: *Hiedra.*

Large-leafed exotic ground cover or vine. One plant covers an impressive territory (200 square feet or more); susceptible to cold. Good plant for texture and intense, shiny green color. Rich soil, moderate water, lots of sun. Robust grower once established. Not for central and northern New Mexico, where varieties of English ivy should be substituted. Fast-growing. *Grows Best:* Extreme southern New Mexico, El Paso.

English ivy ✱ shade

Hedera helix
Spanish: *Hiedra inglesa.*

An unimaginably tenacious, shade-loving ground cover and vine, fast-growing, invasive, tough, and drought-resistant. English ivy will grow but not normally flourish in the sun. Likes rich soil but will adapt to alkaline conditions. Exotic. Water when young. May reach out to 50 feet (15 m) or more. Winter-hardy. Flowers rarely. Good as a fence or wall cover. May become woody with age. Generates large quantities of tiny, intrusive, aerial roots. Excellent winter color. Spectacular in fall mixed with Virginia creeper or Boston ivy. Varieties *H. h.* 'Baltica' and *H. h.* 'Needlepoint,' smaller-leafed and very attractive, are popular.
Grows Best: Statewide.

English ivy

Honeysuckle

Lonicera spp.
Spanish: *Madreselva.*

For a description, please see "Evergreen Ground Covers."

Honeysuckle

FLOWERS
ANNUAL

PLEASE NOTE THAT THE ABBREVIATION "O.C." STANDS FOR "ON CENTER," THE DISTANCE FROM THE MIDDLE OF ONE PLANT TO THE MIDDLE OF THE NEXT. ALL PLANTS IN THIS SECTION ARE IDENTIFIED AS NATIVE, EXOTIC, OR NATURALIZED.

Ageratum

Bedding begonia

Ageratum (floss flower)

Ageratum houstonianum
Spanish: *Agérato.*

Favorite exotic bedding and border annual usually grown for its purple or blue blooms. Usually only 1 foot/300 mm or so in height, perhaps half as wide. Plant in sun or shade and in well-manured soil. Transplants readily. Numerous cultivars also provide white and pink as well as blue or lavender flowers. Attractive foliage. Easy to care for.
Grows Best: Statewide.

Purple aster

Aster bigelovii 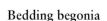 *natural area*
Spanish: *Aster.*

Native, extraordinary, fall-blooming aster, commonly found in sandy or hilly sites throughout the state. Profuse bloomer; flower color runs from lavender to purple to deep red. Grows to about 3 feet (1 m), reseeds easily. May occur as a biennial or an annual, with a semi-woody lower stem. No soil preparation or care are needed. Full sun. Flowers better with some watering. Cheerful, plentiful, and hardy. Usually grown from seed.
Grows Best: Statewide.

Purple aster

Bedding begonia

Begonia spp.
Spanish: *Begonia.*

Hardy exotic annuals grown in shade or partial shade in New Mexico. Leaves are characteristically toothed, glossy, and often deep red in color. Flowers are small and white, pink, or red; they are often produced in profusion from late spring to late fall. Very good in pots. Begonias respond well to rich soil, adequate water. Generally 6 inches (150 mm) or so in height and spread.

Many other groups of begonias are available for garden and landscape use, some of which are rhizomatous or tuberous.
Grows Best: Statewide, in partial shade.

Coleus

Coleus (garden coleus)

Coleus x hybridus
Spanish: *Coleo.*

Colorful, annual herb, grown chiefly for its multi-hued foliage. Exotic. Leaves are usually red and green, with other colors as accents. Coleus grows quickly in near-full sun in moist, well-manured topsoil. May reach 1.5 feet (450 mm) or taller. Small bluish-purple flowers are usually pinched off. Many varieties available, and nearly all may be propagated easily from seed or cuttings.
Grows Best: Statewide.

Cosmos

Cosmos spp. *mod. water.*
Spanish: *Cosmos.*

Tall, widely popular garden annuals, generally pink, white, or deep red and profusely blooming. Daisy family relationship is striking. Exotics from Mexico. May reach 6 feet (2 m) in height. Bloom in summer. Prefer sunny locations, lightly manured soil, and moderate watering. Extraordinarily beautiful against adobe walls. Easy to cultivate, drought-resistant once started. Delicate, lacy, leggy foliage. *Cosmos bipinnatus* is most commonly cultivated and comes in many varieties. *Cosmos sulphureus*, the yellow cosmos, is less common.
Grows Best: Statewide.

Four o'clocks

Four o'clocks

Mirabilis jalapa
Spanish: *Dondiego de noche.*

Four o'clocks are dark pink or light purple in flower. They are profusely blooming exotics from the tropics, very popular as carefree, traditional garden species. Can grow up to 3 feet (1 m) tall, equally wide. Mounding. The foliage has a very pleasing texture. The plant may last through the cold months to bloom again the following year. Likes adequate watering but takes droughts well. Prefers full sun, responds to well-manured soil. Reseeds freely, and the tuberous roots may be dug and stored for planting the following year. Many varieties; also available in yellow, white, red. Flowers resemble small trumpets. *Mirabilis multiflora,* the desert four o'clock, is now easier to find commercially. A very hardy perennial, it typically is covered with reddish-purple blossoms in summer afternoons. Low (up to 2 feet/600 mm) and mounding.
Grows Best: Statewide.

Gaillardia (blanket flower, firewheel)

Gaillardia pulchella
Spanish: *Gaillardia.*

Very colorful and profusely blooming native, up to about 2 feet/600 mm high. Grows quickly from seed or bedding plants, even in dry areas. Red or yellow, or combinations of these. Likes full sun, is not particular about soil. Light or no watering. Unusual natural distribution makes it native to half the United States. Hardy. Wild original specimens, though colorful, are generally half the size of commercial seed gaillardias.
Grows Best: Statewide.

Geranium

Pelargonium hortorum
Spanish: *Geranio.*

Common geranium is extremely popular and showy in windowsills throughout northern New Mexico. Often planted as a bright red summer annual in well-manured soils. Fast-growing, with velvety, somewhat pungent leaves. May reach 3 feet (1 m) in height, and as wide. Grows in partial sun or shade outside; inside, it prefers sunny windows. Medium water. May burn in small, above-ground containers. Widely used in gardens up and down the Rockies from Canada to Mexico.
Grows Best: Statewide.

Impatiens (balsam, dizzy Lizzie)

Impatiens spp.
Spanish: *Balsamina.*

Exotic, shade-loving, long-blooming, multi-colored annuals, fond of rich, moist soil and copious water. Excellent—in fact, unsurpassed —for eastern and northern, shaded or semi-shaded areas. Flowers from late April to late October. May be clipped and grown indoors as a house plant. Grows up to 2 feet (600 mm) tall and as wide. Mounding, with attractive, deep-green foliage. *Impatiens wallerana,* the dizzy Lizzie, is the most popular species, but *Impatiens balsamina* (balsam) and several other species are also common.
Grows Best: Statewide.

Lisianthus (tulip gentian)

Eustoma grandiflorum
Spanish: *Eústoma.*

Actually a Western native, though now bred-up or heavily hybridized, this spectacular biennial grown as an annual produces long, reedy stems topped by bright purple, tulip-like blooms. The flowers may also be pink or white. Very faint, delicate odor. Good cutting flowers, with somewhat succulent, pale green stems and leaves. The purple flower color is actually a rich amethyst. Likes full sun, well-manured soil, adequate water. Cut flowers continually to keep lisianthus blooming all summer.
Grows Best: Statewide.

Gaillardia

Geranium

Impatiens

Cosmos

Lisianthus

Marigold

Pansy

Petunia

Marigold

Tagetes spp.
Spanish: *Maravilla.*

The marigold is a strong-scented, easy-to-grow, very popular exotic ranging in color from deep red to rich yellow. It is usually bright orange. Sprouts readily from seed and frequently reseeds itself. Likes full sun, well-manured soil, and moderate water, but will survive in semi-shade and poor soil. Prefers heat. Most modern marigolds are hybrids of *Tagetes erecta*, the African marigold, and *Tagetes patula*, French marigold.
Grows Best: Statewide.

Pansy

Viola x Wittrockiana
Spanish: *Pensamiento.*

Spectacular, low-growing exotic annual, available in many colors, flourishing in full or partial sun and very hardy. Modern pansies are hybrids derived from *Viola tricolor, Viola altaica,* and other specific lines. The flowers are broad and often multi-colored. Blue, red, yellow, white, orange, purple, and many tones of these are available, and several colors may be present in a single flower. Pansies like moist, well-manured soil and do well in winter beds. May become leggy, so clip off spent flowers. Closely related to violas, violets.
Grows Best: Statewide.

Petunia

Petunia x hybrida
Spanish: *Petunia.*

Colorful, sweet-scented exotic, often planted in large, billowing masses. Pink, purple, white, lavender, and numerous other colors are available. Easy to grow in full sun; likes well-manured, moist soil. Sticky leaves and stems, pale green. May grow up to 1.5 feet (450 mm) tall, about 1 foot (300 mm) wide. Much-hybridized. Good choice for commercial and public landscapes— as well as home gardens—as an accent color planting. Loves heat.
Grows Best: Statewide.

Salvia (sage)

Salvia spp.
Spanish: *Salvia.*

Salvias are striking exotics, members of the mint family. Showy foliage combines with attractive, somewhat delicate, spike-like flowers to make a first-rate garden annual. Grows as tall as 1.5 feet (450 mm), spreads wider. Robust and adaptable; likes heat and half-sun or shade, adequate water. Not fussy about soil. Many species and colors are available. Scarlet sage (*Salvia splendens*) and *Salvia viridis* are popular annuals; red, orange, lavender, and white are common colors. Salvia is also grown as a shrub and an herb.
Grows Best: Statewide.

Salvia

Lobelias and marigolds

Common sunflower

Snapdragon

Antirrhinum majus
Spanish: *Becerra.*

Mediterranean exotic with smoky-hued but bright late-spring and early-summer flowers in red, orange, white, yellow, pink, and related shades. Phenomenal flower-producer. May grow to 3 feet (1 m) tall and as wide. Loves full sun, rich soil, moderate water. Dependable for cut flowers. Use surface irrigation to prevent plant rust from destroying massed beds. Many strains are available as bedding plants. Easy to care for. Snapdragons, petunias, pansies, impatiens, and marigolds are probably the five most widely used and comprehensively satisfying of all exotic annuals present in New Mexico landscapes and gardens.
Grows Best: Statewide.

Common sunflower

Helianthus annuus
Spanish: *Girasol.*

Wonderful but brash and tall native annual. Very colorful, with tasty seeds. (Even the wild sunflower's tiny seeds, when roasted, are delicious.) May reach 12 feet (4 m) in height, spreading to 2–3 feet (about 1 m). Very hardy. Likes sun and prefers occasional water, any soil. Not fussy. Flowers are generally yellow but may also be orange, reddish, or multi-colored. Fast-growing and cheerful. Best in informal situations.

Sunflower likes to colonize disturbed areas and is often found along roadsides. Large, sticky leaves and stalks; agreeable, oily scent.
Grows Best: Anywhere, statewide.

Annual vinca (Madagascar periwinkle)

Catharanthus roseus
Spanish: *Pervencha anual.*

Tropical exotic with glossy leaves and profuse, showy pink or white flowers. Grows to about 2 feet/600 mm tall and about as wide. Likes full sun, well-manured soil, moderate water. Thrives in heat, does not tolerate cold. Remarkably similar to *Vinca major* (periwinkle) but does not spread as a vine or ground cover.
Grows Best: Statewide.

Viola (Johnny jump-ups)

Viola tricolor
Spanish: *Viola.*

Popular, delicately made garden annuals, usually a mixture of purple, white, and yellow. May reach 1 foot (300 mm) in height and spread as wide. Generally likes semi-sun or light shade in New Mexico. Very hardy; will often winter over, as do pansies, and produce cheerful color during the cold months of the year. Johnny jump-ups like moderate water, very well-manured soil. Profusely flowering; flowers often have tiny, discernible "faces." Easy to care for but generally fade in summer heat.
Grows Best: Statewide.

Western wallflower

Erysimum capitatum
Spanish: *Erísimo.*

Handsome, tall annual or biennial with delicate orange and yellow umbelliferous flowers. Grows at both low and high elevations. Native. Takes full or partial sun. Not picky about soil. Moderate water. A native, wallflower can grow to about 2.5 feet (750 mm) tall. Hardy.
Grows Best: Statewide.

Snapdragon

Viola

Western wallflower

Annual vinca

FLOWERS
PERRENIALS

Desert baileya (left)

Carnation

Bear's breech

Desert baileya (desert marigold)

Baileya multiradiata
Spanish: *Baileya.*

Spectacular summer-blooming biennial or annual with yellow flowers and whitish leaves. At its best in early fall. Long-stemmed and showy in dryland plantings. Native; likes full sun and sandy soils but is very tolerant of most planting conditions. Very little care required. Water little to not at all. Looks very good next to adobe structures. Often found with *Dalea* spp., rubber rabbitbrush, saltbush, Indian ricegrass.
Grows Best: Statewide up to 7000 feet/2135 m, sandy areas.

Bear's breech

Acanthus mollis
Spanish: *Acanto.*

Handsome, very unusual, broad-leafed herbaceous plant grown for its enormous flowers and spectacular foliage. Exotic. Sun of any duration wilts it, but it will recover; needs shade, rich soil, adequate water. Not completely cold-hardy but will grow back from roots. The hardiest variety of *Acanthus, A. mollis 'Latifolius,'* is probably the best selection for New Mexico. Grows to 2–3 feet (about 1 m) tall and as wide; flower to 5 feet (1.5 m).
Grows Best: Southern New Mexico, as far north as Albuquerque, in deep shade.

California poppy

Eschscholzia californica
Spanish: *Adormidera* or *amapola california.*

Brilliant naturalized perennial, generally yellow or orange-yellow. Full sun. Very drought-resistant but will respond to water. Lacy, gray-green leaves. Sandy or gravelly soils are best. Blooms throughout the growing season. Typically 6 inches (150 mm) tall. Spreads readily through reseeding. Closely related to the Mexican poppy, *Eschscholzia mexicana,* an equally desirable native.
Grows Best: Statewide.

Carnation

Dianthus caryophyllus et al.
Spanish: *Clavel.*

Cheerful perennial and excellent red, pink, white, or yellow cut flower, often blooming strongly its second season in the ground. Exotic. Sun or partial shade. Likes water, rich soil. Attractive, pale green or green-gray foliage. Wonderful, full scent. May be 1 foot (300 mm) tall and about as wide.
Grows Best: Statewide.

California poppy

Chrysanthemum

Chrysanthemum morifolium
Spanish: *Crisantemo.*
    The color range of chrysanthemums is extraordinary, including yellows, reds, purples, and many shades in between. Exotic. These slow-growing, divisible daisies are noted for providing late-summer and fall color. Mums need good soil, full sun, water, and attention. May reach 1 foot (300 mm) or taller, equally wide.
Grows Best: Statewide.

Columbine

Aquilegia caerulea (blue and white);
Aquilegia chrysantha (light yellow);
Aquilegia formosa (red)
Spanish: *Aguileña* or *pajarilla.*
    These native and exotic perennials have extraordinary trailing blooms that are a colorful combination of sepals and petals. The native species likes dappled sunshine and grows in moist, rich soil pockets in stony canyons. Columbines are large but delicate flowers, sometimes 3 feet (1 m) tall. Excellent accents. Good in small drifts among rocks.
Grows Best: Partial shade, statewide.

Coneflower (Mexican hat)

Ratibida columnifera
Spanish: *Ratíbida.*

natural area

    Beautifully structured native perennial, often growing to 30 inches (750 mm) and found in open grassy deserts as well as pine woods throughout the state. Central flower core is brownish, with appended petals yellow or a rich, rusty red. Striking accent planting. Not particular about soil. Needs very little water. Full sun or partial shade.
Grows Best: Statewide.

Chrysanthemum

Columbine

Daylily (asphodel)

Hemerocallis spp.
Spanish: *Asfódelo.*
    The daylilies, exotic evergreens and deciduous perennials, are frequently grown as ground covers and late-spring/early-summer massed color plants or accents. The commonest old-fashioned species are *Hemerocallis fulva,* or orange daylily, and *Hemerocallis lilioasphodelus,* or lemon daylily. Many hybrids are available. Tall, bold plants (up to 5 feet/1.5 m with *H. fulva*) with attractive, sword-like foliage. Daylily likes manured soil but is not fussy; full sun, moderate water. Plant at 3 feet o.c. for an excellent ground cover.
Grows Best: Statewide.

Coneflower

Daylily

Delphinium

Dusty miller

Delphinium

Delphinium belladonna
Spanish: *Delfínio, espuella de caballero.*

Blue, cockled, exotic perennial with handsome lobed leaves and tall (up to 3 feet/1 m) flower stalks. Likes sun, well-manured soil, and adequate water. Comes in varieties with differing chromatic tones. Late-summer color plant. May be cut back for second bloom. *Delphinium elatum*, a very tall, purple-flowering species, is also common. Several native delphiniums are available from seed.
Grows Best: Statewide.

Fendler's sundrops

Geranium

Blue flax

Dusty miller

Senecio cineraria
Spanish: *Senecio.*

Exotic perennial grown for its dusty gray foliage as well as its button-like, yellow flowers. Up to 1–2 feet (300–600 mm) in height, equally wide. Likes sun, mild watering. Responds to manured soil. Dusty miller is one of the rare species that are useful in night gardens. Extraordinarily beautiful in silver moonlight. Combines well with many native species in the garden.
Grows Best: Statewide, in full sun.

Fendler's sundrops

Calylophus hartwegii fendleri
Spanish: *Gotas del sol* (colloquial).

This perennial may be the most eye-catching roadside flower in New Mexico. A native, it's "drop-dead" beautiful. Likes full sun, stony, sandy, or gravelly soil, some extra water. Grows well in roadside swales. Yellow, reddish-pink (salmon), and white, sometimes all mixed on the same plant. About 1 foot (300 mm) tall, 1.5 feet (450 mm) wide. An evening primrose. Spectacular in the Gila River Valley in late May, early June. Fendler's sundrops are available mostly as seed.
Grows Best: Statewide.

Blue flax

Linum perenne
Spanish: *Lino azúl.*

Delicate perennial with pale blue flowers. Fast-growing; often lasts several seasons in a domestic planting. Likes water but can withstand drought. Native. Grows in poor to moderately improved soils. Easy to cultivate. Best as an accent. Full sun or partial shade.
Grows Best: Anywhere, but prefers full sun.

Geranium (cranesbill)

Geranium richardsonii
Spanish: *Geranio.*

A rather modest but cheerful native flower, white with a purplish cast, occurring on the ponderosa forest floor and higher in New Mexico's mountains. Likes moist, mulched soil, adequate water, partial shade. Up to 1 foot (300 mm) in height. Hardy.
Grows Best: Statewide, shady locations; best at higher elevations.

Hollyhock

Globemallow

Sphaeralcea spp.
Spanish: *Malva*

Tall, striking, native wildflower, frequently found in grassy desert country throughout New Mexico. Orange, red, pink, other colors. Several species. Thin stalks may reach 5 feet (1.5 m) and bloom profusely throughout the summer. Full sun; very drought-tolerant, but blooms better with a bit of water. Creeping variety (*Sphaeralcea grossulariefolia*) makes a good ground cover. Any soil.
Grows Best: Statewide in dry places.

Hollyhock

Alcea rosea
Spanish: *Malva hortense* or *Malva loca.*

Pinkish, white, or red, this tall (up to 9 feet /3 m), traditional exotic is a favorite in old New Mexican gardens. Spectacular against an adobe wall. Sticky stalks and pale green leaves, all rather coarse. Usually reliably hardy and perennial. Fast-growing. Hollyhocks like full sun, well-manured soil, medium watering. Available in numerous colors and cultivars. Often pinkish. Very easy to cultivate. Sometimes naturalizes.
Grows Best: Statewide.

Indian paintbrush

Castilleja integra
Spanish: *Brocha india, castilleja.*

Dusty orange and frequently no more than 6–8 inches tall (about 200 mm) in the wild. Unassuming, very hardy native. Likes sun or part shade. Hard to grow except from seed. It prefers a clump of grass or another herb nearby, as it may take advantage of the second plant's root system to establish itself. Little to no water. No particular soil requirements, but it seems to do best on well-drained sites. A legendary Southwestern flower with many other related *Castilleja* species.
Grows Best: Statewide.

Jimsonweed (datura, sacred datura)

Datura meteloides
Spanish: *Datura.*

An enormous, spectacular, perennial native (up to about 4.5 feet/1.5 m tall, and as wide) growing in hilly or mountainous areas of New Mexico, often on gravelly hillsides. White flowers are very striking and emerge at night. Likes full sun, very modest amounts of water. Tolerates any soil. Broad, coarse, pointed leaves are sometimes evil-smelling, and the entire plant is poisonous. Related to potatoes, tomatoes. Best as an accent next to block or adobe walls, but do not plant near children. Fast-growing.
Grows Best: Statewide.

Globemallow

Jimsonweed

Indian paintbrush

112

Lobelia   *Penstemon*

Maximilian's daisy

Sand penstemon

Lobelia

Lobelia erinus
Spanish: *Lobelia.*

Notable as a good edging and feature annual, this short (about 8 inches/200 mm), splashy exotic flower is easy to cultivate and prolifically colorful. Likes rich soil and medium moisture, as well as half-sun. Violet or bluish-violet selections can be stunning in masses, particularly when placed next to complementary orange-flowering annuals such as marigolds. May also be used in containers.
Grows Best: Statewide.

Maximilian's daisy

Helianthus maximiliani
Spanish: *Margarita de Maximiliano, girasol.*

Naturalized perennial covered with yellow sunflower heads that emerge in late summer and last until frost. May be 7 feet (2 m) tall or taller and as wide. Not particular about soil, likes sun, needs little care and water. Foliage is as interesting as flowers; can serve as temporary screen. Blooms all up and down its stems. Cut old growth to ground in winter.
Grows Best: Statewide.

Paperflower

Psilostrophe tagetina
Spanish: *Psílostrofe.*

Paperflower is a delicately structured, yellow-blossomed native perennial common in sandy foothills and deserts around New Mexico. Needs full sun; likes well-drained, dry soil. Rounded and bushy in form (perhaps 1.5 feet/450 mm high, 3 feet/1 m wide). Summer-blooming, fast-growing. Very similar to groundsel. Good for dry flower arrangements.
Grows Best: Sandy areas, statewide.

Penstemon

Penstemon spp.
Spanish: *Penstemón* (colloquial).

Very showy group of native perennials, available in a wide range of colors, sizes, and plant types. Very hardy. Most penstemons prefer full sun, are not particular about soil, and require light to moderate watering. Many cultivated and wild species and their varieties are available as both plants and seed. The blue-purple flowering *Penstemon strictus* 'Benth' (Rocky Mountain penstemon) is a fine choice for long bloom. Sand penstemon (*Penstemon ambiguus*) is a 2–3 foot (about 1 m) shrub covered with light pink phlox-like flowers in the spring.
Grows Best: Statewide.

Phlox

Phlox paniculata, Phlox subulata
Spanish: *Flox.*

Creeping phlox, *Phlox subulata*, has pink flowers and is a springtime favorite. A tiny exotic plant, it rarely exceeds 4 inches (100 mm) in height but spreads much wider. Garden phlox, *Phlox paniculata*, comes in a multitude of colors and is widely hybridized. It ranges from a few inches to over a foot (300 mm) in height. Phlox needs good soil, lots of sun, and moderate water. Dependable and hardy.
Grows Best: Statewide, except in high mountains.

Paperflower

Red rocket

Primrose

Primrose

Primula spp.
Spanish: *Primavera*.

Large number of exotic perennial favorite garden species, of which perhaps the most common are the polyanthus primroses, *Primula polyantha*, and English primrose, *Primula vulgaris*. Often grows well in shade. Up to 1 foot (300 mm) or so in height. Likes adequate water, well-prepared soil. Many flower colors and good-looking foliage.
Grows Best: Statewide.

Red rocket or scarlet gilia

Ipomopsis aggregata (formerly *Gilia aggregata*)
Spanish: *Gilia*.

Very common native flower in New Mexico's forested mountains. Frequently found in meadows. Brilliant red, well-formed flowers. Likes a bit of moisture and appreciates a manured soil that drains well. Sun or partial shade. May reach 2 feet (600 mm) tall. *Ipomopsis* and *Gilia* are both genera in the phlox family, and there are many related native species. However, red rocket is the most widely available in both plants and as seed.
Grows Best: Statewide.

Shasta daisies

Chrysanthemum maximum
Spanish: *Crisantemo de Shasta, maya de Shasta*.

A white-blooming (with yellow centers), tough perennial used as a "backbone" plant in many seasonal gardens. Exotic; frequently blooms all summer and into early fall. It's a good idea to cut off old flower heads for continuing bloom. Likes sun, well-manured ground, moderate water. Easily started from seed; may grow to 3 feet (1 m) or more in height and width. Many varieties. Makes excellent cut flowers. Divide plants every second year or so.
Grows Best: Statewide.

Spectaclepod

Dithyrea wislizenii
Spanish: *Dithyrea*.

Very handsome, modest, unassuming native perennial with whitish-yellow flowers and curious spectacle-like seed pods. Loves sandy deserts, full sun, no water. Produces flowers all summer. May reach 2 feet (600 mm) but more commonly 1–1.5 feet (300–450 mm) tall. Very pleasant summer accent; use it in small areas. Hardy and easy to grow. Frequently revegetates disturbed slopes.
Grows Best: Statewide, but best in sandy situations.

Spectaclepod

Phlox

Shasta daisies

Violet

Yarrow

Violet

Viola odorata
Spanish: *Violeta, alelí.*

    Exotic and native species, low-growing (up to 6 inches/150 mm), fond of wet, shady spots under trees or shrubs. Heart-shaped leaves and violet, purple, white, or bluish-purple flowers, often very pleasantly scented. Violets like moisture and rich (well-manured) soil. Often found along the banks of small streams in pine or fir forests. The native species include *Viola canadensis* (Canada violet, white bloom), *Viola adunca* (Hook violet, usually blue), and *Viola nephrophylla* (Wanderer violet, violet or purple). Beware of snails in domestic gardens.
Grows Best: Shady areas, statewide.

Yarrow

Achillea spp.
Spanish: *Milhojas* or *milenrama.*

    Native and exotic species, widely adaptable, sun-loving, continuously blooming, very low-care perennials. Yarrows generally divide well and can survive droughts; however, they grow nicely with moderate watering. Common yarrow, *Achillea millefolium*, has yellow flowers and grows to 3 feet (about 1 m); wooly yarrow, *Achillea tomentosa*, is also pale yellow at about 1 foot (300 mm) tall; the native western yarrow, *Achillea lanulosa*, is white-flowered and reaches 2 feet (600 mm) or more in height.
Grows Best: Statewide.

FLOWERS
BULBS

PLEASE NOTE THAT THE ABBREVIATION "O.C." STANDS FOR "ON CENTER," THE DISTANCE FROM THE MIDDLE OF ONE PLANT TO THE MIDDLE OF THE NEXT. ALL PLANTS IN THIS SECTION ARE IDENTIFIED AS NATIVE, EXOTIC, OR NATURALIZED.

Canna

Canna spp.
Spanish: Pico de perico.
　　Huge, exotic, tuberous flowers that bloom profusely in summer. Red, orange, yellow, and related flower colors are the most common. Cannas are grown also for the strong tropical effect of their large leaves. Must have full sun, deeply manured soil, and a great deal of water. Tuberous roots may be dug and stored after blooming to assure next season's quality. Ultimate size may exceed 6 feet (2 m).
Grows Best: Statewide.

Common hyacinth

Hyacinthus orientalis
Spanish: *Jacinto.*
　　Exotic. Excellent choice for cold winter areas of New Mexico and surrounding region. Mid-spring bloomers; may reach 1 foot (300 mm) in height when planted in well-manured soil. Typically bloom in purple, salmon, white, or white shades. Very sweet aroma, lasting one to two weeks. Plant in masses. Water well.
Grows Best: Statewide.

Daffodil

Narcissus spp.
Spanish: *Narciso.*
　　This adaptable and showy exotic spring flower blooms in yellow, white, orange, and mixtures of these and other colors. Flourishes in enriched soils throughout New Mexico year after year. Extremely hardy but needs substantial watering. Does well in full sun. Divide every two to three years. Groups of daffodils with similar characteristics are called "divisions." Daffodils grow up to about 10 inches (250 mm).
　　Many varieties, including an excellent selection of new hybrids, are available. 'King Alfred,' 'Golden Ducat,' 'Cheerfulness' are widely planted, sturdy, and very dependable.
Grows Best: Statewide.

Dutch crocus

Crocus vernus
Spanish: *Azafrán.*
　　This tiny exotic (about 3 inches/75 mm tall) is not a bulb but a corm. Although several other crocus species grow in New Mexico, this one is the most universally planted. Likes rich but well-drained soil, lots of sun, adequate water. Blooms occur in late winter and are generally weaker in successive years. Plants should be divided about every third year. Hardy; responds well to cold winters.
Grows Best: Statewide.

Crocus

Daffodil

Canna

Common hyacinth

Gladiolus

Garden gladiolus

Gladiolus hortulanus
Spanish: *Estoque*; also *gladiolo, gladiola*.

An old-fashioned, exotic corm. Very popular, buoyant, summer-blooming hybrid; tall (up to 6 feet/2 m), with an amazing range of color. Often used as cheery cut flowers or as backdrops for smaller annuals or perennials. Full sun, rich soil, moderate water. Spent corms need to be dug and stored to maintain blooming health.
Grows Best: Statewide.

Grape hyacinth

Grape hyacinth

Muscari armeniacum
Spanish: *Sueldacostilla*.

Tiny, exotic bulb (about 6 inches/150 mm tall) with flower clusters somewhat resembling a bunch of bright blue grapes—hence the name. Delicate appearance; good in sunny or slightly shady spots. Prefers deep, rich soil and moderate watering. Leaves may emerge in late fall; flowers appear as early as January in New Mexico. Cheerful appearance. Other species are equally attractive but much larger.
Grows Best: Statewide.

Ranunculus

Tulip

Iris

Iris spp.
Spanish: *Flor de lis, iris, lirio*.

Native or exotic bulb or rhizome. Long-time garden favorite; richly scented, wide range of color, excellent spring performance. Most (especially bearded varieties) like good soil and adequate water but will also survive drought, neglect, and heavy shade.

Native species (*Iris missouriensis*) grows in beautiful drifts in moist mountains. Very adaptable landscape plant; sometimes used for foliage development as ground cover. Should be divided periodically after bloom for best results.
Grows Best: Statewide.

Ranunculus

Ranunculus asiaticus
Spanish: *Ranúnculo*.

Exotic, spring-blooming flower, usually yellow or red, grown from tuberous roots. Grows up to 18 inches (450 mm) tall, and the broad, multi-petaled flowers may reach 4 inches (about 100 mm) in diameter. The bulb itself has a curious structure, resembling a tiny bird's nest. Ranunculus grows best in New Mexico in very well-manured beds in full sun. Somewhat temperamental, but the strikingly rich, shimmering colors and texture of the double flowers are worth the effort. Water well.
Grows Best: Statewide.

Tulip

Tulipa spp.
Spanish: *Tulipán*.

A solid, dependable, and very popular mid-spring exotic bulb, available in a variety of sizes up to 2.5 feet (750 mm) tall. Tulips like much water, a lot of sun, and manured soil that is porous enough to drain quickly. Respond very notably to sun direction and intensity. Available in a tremendous variety of colors, shapes, and sizes, and easy to grow.

Like daffodils, tulips are arranged for convenience into a number of divisions. Long-stemmed Darwin varieties are quite popular, as are single earlies, parrots, and cottage tulips.
Grows Best: Statewide.

Iris

Section Four

CITIES AND TOWNS

PLANT
RECOMMENDATIONS
AND NOTES

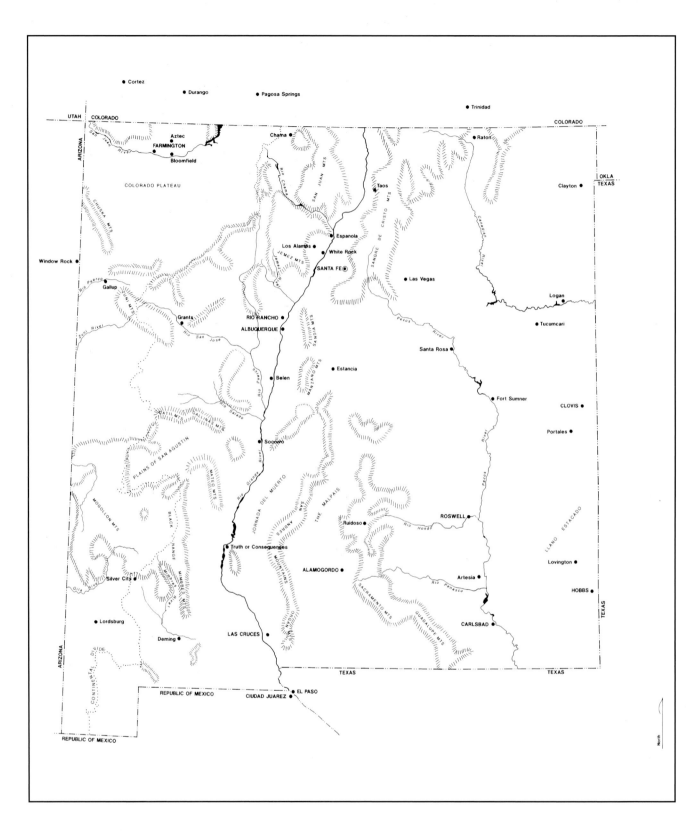

PRINCIPAL CITIES AND TOWNS OF NEW MEXICO AND
SELECTED CITIES IN SURROUNDING STATES

A foothills garden

INTRODUCTORY NOTE

Most cities and towns in New Mexico and neighboring areas of Colorado and Texas were founded and built in the foothills or on the alluvial plains of mountain ranges or along river bottoms. Some settlements were also created near springs or wells on the high plains. Few towns exist in the high mountains. The great geographical diversity of the South-west has led, of course, to planting diversity. Each city or town has its own natural land-scape and individual agricultural patterns. These elements contribute strongly to local domestic landscapes and gardens. Even in the late twentieth century, technology can only carry the garden so far. We must work with the soils, water, slopes, and (as we have recently begun to realize) the native or well-adapted plants that we have at hand. Most if not all of our settlements also have historic man-made landscapes that were planted in local or imported (exotic) species of plants that may well remain very useful to us. These landscapes (plazas, parks, patios, courthouse squares, gardens, and their relatives) have in many cases remained intact and quite beautiful, and they continue to charm us as we near the millennium's end. Santa Fe Plaza, the gardens and terraces of Cimarron's Philmont Scout Ranch, and the wonderful grounds of Fort Bayard near Silver City are only a few examples.

Landscape architects have been busy creating exciting new planting designs for the late twentieth century as well. The number of city, county, state, and national parks (as well as other kinds of public and private landscapes) in New Mexico has easily doubled in the last quarter-century as a result of these efforts. New Mexicans and other Southwesterners of all walks of life now understand that with limited water, unusual young soils, and high altitude, our landscape planning must be better adapted to the region. More New Mexicans than ever are looking for concentrated green space, plants that flourish on minimal moisture, and ease of care in their new landscapes.

Yet it is important to retain local character. The creation of local specialty landscapes that incorporate the concept of the "foothills garden" is becoming more and more popular. As a source of inspiration, New Mexico's typical foothills plant community is essentially a woodland that can easily be replicated in a designed landscape. Typical "foothills garden" New Mexican landscapes now include:

1. Gently rolling hills (berms) or grade changes in some or all parts of the landscape.
2. Local stones or boulders used as character elements or for terracing.
3. Low, rounded evergreen trees (native oak, Mexican elder, juniper, tree-size mountain mahogany, or similar species) that accent the berms.
4. Native or naturalized ornamental grasses used for soil stabilization and as "eye-catchers."
5. Small "dripping spring" water features to attract wildlife and add interest.

6. Native succulents (cacti, sotols, agaves, ocotillos, or yuccas) for color and contrast.
7. Seasonally blooming wildflowers in well-grouped masses.
8. Incidental native or naturalized shade or flowering ornamental trees to provide welcome coolness and relief from glare.
9. Unobtrusive supplemental irrigation.

These features are frequently integrated in the landscape with nearby buffalo or blue grama grass lawns for a very effective, low-care site development.

The ideal foothills garden obviously cannot suit every site and planting situation in New Mexico and surrounding areas. After all, every New Mexican town has its favorite and pre-eminent plants. There are surprising variations in rainfall and elevation around the state and throughout the Southwest. Soils also differ widely. However, most soils are alkaline, and the majority of our popular landscape plant species will benefit from the addition of locally produced aged manure, sawdust, compost, sewage sludge, bark, and sulphur to the soil. (If you use manure, cut it 50/50 with bark or sawdust before adding it to the soil.) Mixing in these soil "amendments" (as the landscape architects call them) in planting areas is also an excellent way to recycle local waste products, although they should not be placed in too great a concentration. Use roughly 3 to 4 inches (100 mm) of soil amendments thoroughly tilled in to a depth of 1 foot (300 mm)

when first preparing a planting area. Be sure to moisten completely. You may also wish to add a pound or two of sulphur to the mixture per 100 square feet. Planting areas containing recycled organic additives and surface mulches hold water better and help to prevent erosion.

Many plant species (such as palms, oleanders, Mexican elders, or ocotillos) that grow well in the southern part of the state do not flourish in the northern part. This problem is not really due to latitude; it is caused by altitude, which along with wind is probably the greatest scourge of new plantings in our area. As you look at a plant species to determine its usefulness in your city, please cross-check it in the New Mexico Plant File for hardiness, tenderness, and other special plant conditions. Remember that your growing season may be too short or your town too high for fast plant growth. Patience in landscaping, as in fishing, often brings good results.

But don't worry too much about these or other incidental plant problems. New Mexican landscapes can be exciting, colorful, and—yes—*unusual* with just a little care and patience. Use your creative instincts wisely with plants and you'll be well rewarded for many years to come.

Hillside stones and cactus

A wild foothills garden

ALAMOGORDO

including La Luz and Tularosa

Alamogordo is a rare "planned community" in New Mexico. It was carefully laid out at the east edge of the Tularosa Basin in 1898 by two brothers, John and Charles Eddy.

The city is in a spectacular setting. From the nearby western foothills of the Sacramento Mountains, the long purple line of the San Andrés Range is visible to the west just beyond the White Sands. The Sacramentos themselves are an imposing mountain mass that defines the eastern boundary of the city.

Alameda Park and Zoo, a linear greensward along the prominent north-south railroad line, and the grounds of the New Mexico School for the Blind, just across U.S. 54 from the park, are among the outstanding public landscapes. Cottonwoods, fruitless mulberries, and Italian cypresses are commonly found around the city and tend to dominate the skyline. Alamogordo enjoys a generally warm climate, mild even in wintertime. California and Mexican fan palms, along with agaves, ocotillos, sotols, Torrey yuccas, oleanders, and birds of paradise are frequently planted desert and subtropical accent species. Soils in Alamogordo actually improve in the hilly eastern residential areas, where there is well-draining alluvium and not as much concentrated gypsum as in the flatter western sections of the city.

Alamogordo lies at a relatively high 4350 feet (1330 m), but its southerly location at the rim of a hot desert basin provides for a long growing season of 209 days. Annual precipitation is between 10 and 11 inches (250–275 mm). Livestock grazing is a major agricultural activity in Otero County. Key crops include fruits and pecans, and there is an emerging pistachio nut industry. All agriculture in the county is heavily irrigated, and nut groves continue to expand into desert areas at the periphery of the Tularosa Basin.

The original Alamogordo landscape was typical of the southern New Mexico foothills: mesquite, creosote, and saltbush were (and continue to be) predominant shrubs, with alkali sacaton, various gramas, Indian ricegrass, and many annual and perennial flowers the typical ground-cover plants. Succulents such as sotols, yuccas, agaves, ocotillos, prickly pear, and claret cup (hedgehog) cactus have always been common in the area. The only native trees of consequence are cottonwoods and desert willows. The high mountains, with their greater rainfall, support vast forests of ponderosa, piñon, and other pines, as well as white fir, aspen, Douglas fir, maples, walnuts, and associated species. The original natural vegetation of the region is still widespread near Alamogordo.

Extraordinary collections of succulents in highly original layouts may be found in several eastern neighborhoods of the city. In the nearby village of La Luz, delightful groves of edible figs, irrigated by a sparkling desert stream, are grown as curiosities and for the shade and delicious fruits that they produce.

Alamogordo street scene

SELECTED BEST PLANTS
FOR ALAMOGORDO

These plant species grow very well in
and around Alamogordo. For the sake of
convenience and quick reference, each plant
is listed as native (N), naturalized (NZ),
or exotic (E). Other plants also will perform
well in landscape and garden situations in the
Alamogordo area. Please see the New Mexico
Plant File for these species.

TREES

A. Deciduous Shade, Street, and Specialty Trees

Ash
    a. Arizona ash—*Fraxinus velutina* (N)
    b. Modesto ash—*Fraxinus velutina* 'Modesto' (Arizona ash variety) (N)
    c. Green ash—*Fraxinus pennsylvanica* and varieties (E)
    d. White ash—*Fraxinus americana* and varieties (E)
Chinaberry—*Melia azedarach* (E)
Cottonwood, Aspen, and Poplar: Trees of the Genus *Populus*
    a. Carolina poplar—*Populus canadensis* (E)
    b. Lanceleaf cottonwood—*Populus acuminata* (N)
    c. Lombardy poplar—*Populus nigra* 'Italica' (E)
    d. Rio Grande cottonwood—*Populus fremontii* 'Wislizeni' (N)
Elm
    a. Siberian elm—*Ulmus pumila* (NZ; best in rural areas)
    b. Chinese elm—*Ulmus parvifolia* (E)
Honey locust—*Gleditsia triacanthos inermis* varieties (E)
Japanese pagoda—*Sophora japonica* (E)
Black locust—*Robinia pseudoacacia* (NZ)
Osage orange—*Maclura pomifera* (E)
Pecan—*Carya illinoiensis* (E)
Pistache—Pistachio
    a. Chinese pistache—*Pistacia chinensis* (E)
    b. Pistachio—*Pistacia vera* (E)
Silk tree—*Albizia jilibrissin* (E)
Sycamore (plane tree)
    a. American sycamore—*Platanus occidentalis* (E)
    b. Arizona sycamore—*Platanus wrightii* (N)
Tree of heaven—*Ailanthus altissima* (NZ, used for shade in very difficult areas)
Walnut
    a. Arizona walnut—*Juglans major* (N)
    b. English (Carpathian) walnut—*Juglans regia* (E)
Willow
    a. Globe Navajo willow—*Salix matsudana* 'Navajo' (E)
    b. Weeping willow—*Salix babylonica* (and other weeping willow species, E)

B. Flowering Ornamental Trees

Flowering crab—*Malus* 'Hopa' et al (E)
Desert willow—*Chilopsis linearis* (N)
Mexican elder—*Sambucus caerulea neomexicana* (N)
Bradford pear—*Pyrus calleryana* (E)
Purpleleaf plum—*Prunus cerasifera* (E)
Salt cedar—*Tamarix chinensis* (NZ)
Smoke tree—*Cotinus coggygria* (E)
Vitex (chaste tree)—*Vitex agnus-castus* (E)

C. Evergreen Trees

Cedar
    a. Atlas cedar—*Cedrus atlantica* (E)
    b. Cedar of Lebanon—*Cedrus libani* (E)
    c. Deodar cedar—*Cedrus deodara* (E)
Cypress
    a. Arizona cypress—*Cupressus arizonica* (N)
    b. Italian cypress—*Cupressus sempervirens* (E)
Juniper
Rocky Mountain juniper—*Juniperus scopulorum* varieties (N)
Magnolia
    a. Southern magnolia—*Magnolia grandiflora* (E)
Palm
    a. California fan palm—*Washingtonia filifera* (E)
    b. Chinese windmill palm—*Trachycarpus fortunei* (E)
    c. Mexican fan palm—*Washingtonia robusta* (E)
    d. Mediterranean fan palm—*Chamaerops humilis* (E)
Pine
    a. Afghan pine—*Pinus eldarica* (E)
    b. Aleppo pine—*Pinus halepensis* (E)
    c. Japanese black pine—*Pinus thunbergiana* (E)
    d. Piñon pine—*Pinus edulis* (N)
Blue spruce—*Picea pungens* (N)
Yucca
    a. Joshua tree—*Yucca brevifolia* (E)
    b. Palm yucca—*Yucca torreyi* (N)
    c. Soaptree yucca—*Yucca elata* (N)

SHRUBS

A. Deciduous

Althea (rose of Sharon)—*Hibiscus syriacus* (E)
Golden bamboo—*Phyllostachys aurea* (E)
Bird of paradise—*Caesalpinia gilliesii* (NZ)
Common butterfly bush—*Buddleia davidii* (E)
Cotoneaster
    a. Rock cotoneaster—*Cotoneaster horizontalis* (E)
    b. Rockspray cotoneaster—*Cotoneaster microphyllus* (E)
Edible fig—*Ficus carica* (E)
Shrub or Tatarian honeysuckle—*Lonicera tatarica* (E)
Flowering jasmine—*Jasminum nudiflorum* (E)
Screwbean mesquite—*Prosopis pubescens* (N)
Pomegranate—*Punica granatum* (E)
Privet—*Ligustrum* spp. (E)
Rose—*Rosa* spp. (E, N)

B. Evergreen

Agave (century plant, mescal)
    a. Century plant—*Agave americana* (N)
    b. Parry agave—*Agave parryi* (N)
    c. Lechugilla—*Agave lechugilla* (N)
Cactus
    a. Claret cup—*Echinocereus triglochidiatus* (N)
    b. Common cholla—*Opuntia imbricata* (N); other cholla species and varieties also grow well
    c. Prickly pear—*Opuntia chlorotica* or *O. engelmannii* (N)
Parney cotoneaster—*Cotoneaster lacteus* (E)
Creosotebush—*Larrea tridentata* (N)
India hawthorn—*Rhaphiolepis indica* (E)
Chinese junipers
    a. Armstrong juniper—*Juniperus chinensis* 'Armstrong' (E)
    b. Pfitzer juniper—*Juniperus chinensis* 'Pfitzerana' (E)
    c. Sea Green juniper—*Juniperus chinensis* 'Sea Green' (E)
Mahonia
    a. Algerita—*Mahonia haematocarpa* (N)
    b. Agritos—*Mahonia trifoliolata* (N)

c. Oregon grape—*Mahonia aquifolium* (E)
Nandina (heavenly bamboo)—*Nandina domestica* (E)
Ocotillo—*Fouquieria splendens* (N)
Oleander—*Nerium oleander* (E)
Photinia
    a. Chinese photinia—*Photinia serrulata* (E)
    b. Fraser's photinia—*Photinia fraseri* (E)
Pittosporum (tobira)—*Pittosporum tobira* (E)
Pyracantha (firethorn)—*Pyracantha* spp. (E)
Fourwing saltbush—*Atriplex canescens* (N)
Sotol—*Dasylirion wheeleri* (N)
Texas ranger—*Leucophyllum frutescens* (E)
Yucca
    a. Softblade yucca—*Yucca recurvifolia* (*Yucca pendula*) (E)
    b. Spanish bayonet—*Yucca baccata* (N)
    c. Coral-flower yucca—*Hesperaloe parviflora* (E)

GROUND COVERS

A. Deciduous

Clover—*Trifolium* spp. (E)
Cranberry cotoneaster—*Cotoneaster apiculatus* (E)
Crown vetch—*Coronilla varia* (E)
Prairie sage—*Artemisia ludoviciana* (N)
Snow-in summer—*Cerastium tomentosum* (E)

B. Evergreen

Dwarf coyotebrush—*Baccharis pilularis* (E)
Dichondra—*Dichondra micrantha* (E)
Germander—*Teucrium chamaedrys* 'Prostratum' (E)
Honeysuckle—*Lonicera japonica* varieties (E)
Sabina junipers
    a. Broadmoor juniper—*Juniperus sabina* 'Broadmoor' (E)
    b. Buffalo juniper—*Juniperus sabina* 'Buffalo' (E)
    c. Tam (tammy) juniper—*Juniperus sabina* 'Tamariscifolia' (E)
Blue leadwort—*Ceratostigma plumbaginoides* (E)
Lilyturf (liriope)—*Liriope spicata* (E)
Rosemary—*Rosmarinus officinalis* (E)
Santolina
    a. Green santolina—*Santolina virens* (E)
    b. Gray santolina—*Santolina chamaecyparissus* (E)
Dragonsblood sedum (stonecrop)—*Sedum* spp. (E)

GRASSES

A. Traditional Turf Species

Common bermuda—*Cynodon dactylon* (E)
Ryegrass—*Lolium* spp. (E)

B. Native Turf And General-Use Species

Buffalo grass—*Buchlöe dactyloides* (N)
Grama (N)
    a. Black grama—*Bouteloua eriopoda*
    b. Blue grama—*Bouteloua gracilis*
    c. Sideoats grama—*Bouteloua curtipendula*

C. Ornamental Species

Alkali sacaton—*Sporobolus airoides* (N)
Sand dropseed—*Sporobolus cryptandrus* (N)
Fountain grass—*Pennisetum* spp. (E)
Pampas grass—*Cortaderia selloana* (E)
Indian ricegrass—*Oryzopsis hymenoides* (N)
River cane—*Arundo donax* (NZ)

VINES

A. Deciduous

Carolina jessamine—*Gelsemium sempervirens* (E)
Morning glory—*Ipomoea tricolor* (E)
Trumpet vine—*Campsis radicans* (E)
Virginia creeper—*Parthenocissus quinquefolia* (NZ)
Wisteria—*Wisteria sinensis* (E)

B. Evergreen

Algerian ivy—*Hedera canariensis* (E)
English ivy—*Hedera helix* (E)
Honeysuckle—*Lonicera* spp. (E)

FLOWERS

A. Annuals

Ageratum—*Ageratum houstonianum* (E)
Purple aster—*Aster bigelovii* (E)
Coleus—*Coleus x hybridus* (E)
Cosmos—*Cosmos* spp. (E)
Four o'clock—*Mirabilis jalapa* (E)
Gaillardia (blanketflower, firewheel)—*Gaillardia pulchella* (N)
Impatiens—*Impatiens wallerana*
Marigold—*Tagetes* spp. (E)
Pansy—*Viola wittrockiana* (E)
Petunia—*Petunia* spp. (E)
Salvia—*Salvia* spp. (E)
Snapdragon—*Antirrhinum majus* (E)
Sunflower—*Helianthus annuus* (N)
Annual vinca (Madagascar periwinkle)—*Catharanthus roseus* (E)

B. Perennials

Desert baileya—*Baileya multiradiata* (N)
Carnation—*Dianthus caryophyllus* (E)
Coneflower—*Ratibida columnifera* (N)
Daylily (asphodel)—*Hemerocallis* spp. (E)
Delphinium—*Delphinium belladonna* (E,N)
Dusty miller—*Senecio cineraria* (E)
Fendler's sundrops—*Calylophus hartwegii fendleri* (N)
Globemallow—*Sphaeralcea incana* (scarlet) (N)
Hollyhock—*Alcea rosea* (NZ)
Indian paintbrush—*Castilleja integra* (N)
Jimsonweed (datura, sacred datura)—*Datura meteloides* (N)
Lobelia—*Lobelia erinus* (E)
Maximilian's daisy—*Helianthus maximiliani* (NZ)
Paperflower—*Psilostrophe tagetina* (N)
Phlox—*Phlox* spp. (E,N)
California poppy—*Eschscholzia californica* (and *E. mexicana*) (N)
Red rocket (scarlet gilia)—*Ipomopsis aggregata* (N)
Shasta daisy—*Chrysanthemum maximum* (E)
Spectaclepod—*Dithyrea wislizenii* (N)

C. Bulbs

Canna—*Canna* spp. (E)
Daffodil—*Narcissus* 'King Alfred' and other varieties (E)
Dutch crocus—*Crocus verus* (E)
Garden gladiolus—*Gladiolus hortulanus* (E)
Iris—*Iris* spp. (E, N)
Ranunculus—*Ranunculus asiaticus* (E)
Tulip—*Tulipa* spp. (E)

A residential garden

ALBUQUERQUE

(settled in 1706), including Rio Rancho, Belen, Placitas, Sandia, Santa Ana, San Felipe, Zia, and Isleta Pueblos, Tomé, Bosque Farms, Algodones, Corrales, Los Lunas, and Bernalillo

Despite its long history, modern Albuquerque is really a boomtown that experienced most of its growth after World War II. There are four natural landscape types in the general metropolitan area:

1. The valley, north and south. This is the old Rio Grande floodplain. Once covered mostly in cottonwoods and willows, it has been cultivated since the thirteenth or fourteenth century, beginning with the Anasazi, in a series of open, irrigated fields. For many centuries, it was roughly half cottonwood forest and half agricultural land.

2. The west mesa. This area includes the sandy western reaches of the city stretching to approximately the top of Nine Mile Hill —the long ridge dividing the Puerco and Rio Grande valleys. Trees here include only scattered singleseed junipers and short runs of desert willows in the dry washes. The west mesa is (or was) actually mostly desert grassland, with Indian ricegrass and sand dropseed predominating. Dalea (indigobush), threadleaf sage, and fourwing saltbush have been the most common shrubs for thousands of years.

3. The east mesa. The area of the city's greatest growth in the last forty years, it is actually a plain covered with shortgrass species such as grama, dropseed, wheatgrass, Indian ricegrass, fluffgrass, and galleta. These survive now only in isolated pockets. Shrubs occurred naturally here mainly in arroyos, where Apache plume and rubber rabbitbrush (chamisa) were abundant. This open plain also supported succulents such as prickly pear and cholla and such flowers as groundsel, globemallow, yellow daisies, desert baileya, purple aster, and paperflower. The only indigenous trees (very occasional) were desert willow and singleseed juniper.

4. The foothills. The lower flanks of the Sandia and Manzano mountains are very stony, with loose, alluvial soil. Such spectacular local species as evergreen oaks, beargrass, algerita, alligator juniper, rubber rabbitbrush, Spanish dagger, and piñon are found here. Near Belen, mesquite even occurs in sparse, low clumps up to the foot of the Manzano Range. Rio Grande and narrowleaf cottonwoods, as well as New Mexico locust and box elder, are found along the ephemeral streams. There is an abundance of native bunchgrasses and both wildflowers and flowering shrubs.

Albuquerque's elevation varies from 4900 feet (1500 m) in the South Valley to over 6000 feet (1830 m) in the Sandia foothills. With an average annual rainfall of only 8 inches (about 200 mm), it is one of the driest places in New Mexico. However, the city is blessed both with the wetter mountains to the east and the Rio Grande—a legendary western river—running through its heart.

Albuquerque is a point of natural intersection for several geographic provinces. The dry, hot Chihuahuan Desert, the southern Rocky Mountains, the Colorado Plateau, and the Great Plains all influence the city's climate and make possible the active cultivation of by far the largest number of ornamental species in the state. It is possible in Albuquerque to grow Chinese windmills, the hardiest of palms, and aspens, the most impressive of Rocky Mountain hardwoods, side by side, though both are at the limits of their range.

Albuquerque has a respectably long growing season of 194 days. Virtually all of its croplands —as well as its domestic, commercial, and public landscapes—are irrigated. The amount of irrigated cropland is falling as the city and its suburbs grow. Livestock, including cattle, pigs, and sheep, are still widely raised in Bernalillo County. The county is second only to Doña Ana County in the number of chickens raised. Substantial quantities of chile, fruit, corn, and alfalfa are also produced in and around Albuquerque.

Bernalillo, southern Sandoval, and (to some extent) Valencia counties have seen a recent dramatic increase in commercial tree, shrub, and bedding plant operations. The growing urban market for ornamental plant specimens from Belen to Santa Fe holds great promise for the expanding production of a large number of species for both the wholesale and retail plant trade.

Shade trees—including ashes, sycamores, honey locusts, golden rain trees, cottonwoods, Russian olives, desert willows, and other species —are widely planted in Albuquerque. Flowering ornamental trees, such as purpleleaf plums, pears, cherries, peaches, apricots, and an infinite variety of crabapples, are found everywhere. Pines—Austrian, Scotch, Italian stone, Afghan, and the native ponderosa, piñon, and limber pines—are used both commercially and residentially, as are cypress, spruce, and cedar. Junipers, cotoneaster, saltbush, rubber rabbitbrush (chamisa), forsythia, snowball viburnum, nandina, photinia, pyracantha, cane and prickly pear cactus, and yucca are commonly used shrubs throughout the city. An enormous selection of annuals, perennials, bulbs, ground covers, and vines are also found in Albuquerque and the towns surrounding it. There is a

general modern tendency toward use of water-saving and attractive native and naturalized species in the landscapes and gardens of the city, and this trend will no doubt continue to gain in popularity in the future.

Exemplary historical landscapes in Albuquerque include Roosevelt Park, a CCC-era creation (1930s); Old Town Plaza, originally laid out in 1706, much revised, and now once again very shady and appealing; the grounds of the old V.A. Hospital; and the central campus of the University of New Mexico, first established in 1889. The brand-new (1992) University Arboretum offers excellent self-guided and accompanied tours of the campus that touch on over 200 native, exotic, and naturalized plant species. Ridgecrest Boulevard in the Southeast Heights offers views of many well-established residential and parkway landscape species. And the recently upgraded grounds of the Rio Grande Zoo are planted in dozens of unusual species of plants that are as well identified and intriguing as the many animal species that are the principal attractions of the place.

SELECTED BEST PLANTS FOR ALBUQUERQUE

These plant species grow very well in and around Albuquerque. For the sake of convenience and quick reference, each plant is listed as native (N), naturalized (NZ), or exotic (E). Other plants also will perform well in landscape and garden situations in the Albuquerque area. Please see the New Mexico Plant File for these species.

TREES

A. Deciduous Shade, Street, and Specialty Trees

Arizona alder—*Alnus oblongifolia* (N)
Ash
    a. Arizona ash—*Fraxinus velutina* (N)
    b. Modesto ash—*Fraxinus velutina* 'Modesto' (Arizona ash variety) (N)
    c. Green ash—*Fraxinus pennsylvanica* and varieties (E)
    d. Raywood ash—*Fraxinus oxycarpa* 'Raywood' (E)
Paper birch—*Betula papyrifera* (E)
Catalpa
    a. Umbrella catalpa—*Catalpa bignonioides* 'Nana' (E)
    b. Western catalpa—*Catalpa speciosa* (E)
Western chokecherry—*Prunus virginiana* (N)
Cottonwood, Aspen, and Poplar: Trees of the Genus *Populus*
    a. Aspen—*Populus tremuloides* (N, select heights locations only)
    b. Bolleana poplar—*Populus alba* 'Pyramidalis' (E)

c. Carolina poplar—*Populus canadensis* (E)
d. Lombardy poplar—*Populus nigra* 'Italica' (E)
e. Plains cottonwood—*Populus sargenti* (N)
f. Rio Grande cottonwood—*Populus fremontii* 'Wislizeni' (N)
g. White (silver) poplar—*Populus alba* (E)
Elm
    a. American elm—*Ulmus americana* (E)
    b. Chinese elm—*Ulmus parvifolia* (E)
Ginkgo (Maidenhair tree)—*Ginkgo biloba* (E)
Hackberry
    a. Common hackberry—*Celtis occidentalis* (E)
    b. Netleaf hackberry—*Celtis reticulata* (N)
Honey locust—*Gleditsia triacanthos inermis* varieties
    a. 'Moraine' (E)
    b. 'Shademaster' (E)
    c. 'Sunburst' (E)
Locust
    a. Black locust—*Robinia pseudoacacia* (NZ)
    b. New Mexico locust—*Robinia neomexicana* (N)
Maple and Box elder
    a. Bigtooth maple—*Acer grandidentatum* (N)
    b. Japanese maple—*Acer palmatum* (E)
    c. Norway maple—*Acer platanoides* (E)
    d. Rocky Mountain maple—*Acer glabrum* (N)
    e. Silver maple—*Acer saccharinum* (E)
    f. Sycamore-leaf maple—*Acer pseudoplatanus* (E)
Mulberry
    a. Fruitless mulberry—*Morus alba* (E)
    b. Weeping mulberry—*Morus alba* 'Pendula' (E)
Oak
    a. Pin oak—*Quercus palustris* (E)
    b. Southern live oak—*Quercus virginiana* (E)
    c. Texas oak—*Quercus texana* (E)
Osage orange—*Maclura pomifera* (NZ)
Pecan—*Carya illinoiensis* (E)
Chinese pistache—*Pistacia chinensis* (E)
Russian olive—*Elaeagnus angustifolia* (NZ)
Sycamore (plane tree)
    a. Arizona sycamore—*Platanus wrightii* (N)
    b. California sycamore—*Platanus racemosa* (E)
    c. London plane tree—*Platanus acerifolia* (E)
    d. Oriental plane tree—*Platanus orientalis* (E)
Walnut
    a. Arizona walnut—*Juglans major* (N)
    b. English (Carpathian) walnut—*Juglans regia* (E)
Willow
    a. Corkscrew willow—*Salix matsudana* 'Tortuosa' (E)
    b. Globe Navajo willow—*Salix matsudana* 'Navajo' (E)
    c. Peachleaf willow—*Salix amygdaloides* (N)
    d. Weeping willow—*Salix babylonica* (and other weeping willow species, E)

B. Flowering Ornamental Trees

Flowering apricot—*Prunus armeniaca* (E)
Flowering cherry—*Prunus serrulata* et al (E)
Flowering crab—*Malus* 'Hopa' et al (E)
Desert willow—*Chilopsis linearis* (N)
Mexican elder—*Sambucus caerulea neomexicana* (N)
Hawthorn—*Crataegus* spp. (E, N)
Flowering peach—*Prunus persica* (E)
Bradford pear—*Pyrus calleryana* (E)
Purpleleaf plum—*Prunus cerasifera* (E)
Eastern redbud—*Cercis canadensis* (E)
Golden rain tree—*Koelreuteria paniculata* (E)
Salt cedar—*Tamarix chinensis* (NZ)
Smoke tree—*Cotinus coggygria* (E)

C. Evergreen Trees

Cedar
    a. Atlas cedar—*Cedrus atlantica* (E)
    b. Deodar cedar—*Cedrus deodara* (E)
Cypress
    a. Arizona cypress—*Cupressus arizonica* (N)
    b. Italian cypress—*Cupressus sempervirens* (E)
Douglas fir—*Pseudotsuga menziesii* (N)
White fir—*Abies concolor* (N, well-drained locations only)
Juniper
    a. Alligator juniper—*Juniperus deppeana* (N)
    b. Chinese juniper—*Juniperus chinensis* varieties (E)
    c. Eastern red cedar—*Juniperus virginiana* varieties (E)
    d. Rocky Mountain juniper—*Juniperus scopulorum* varieties (N)
    e. Singleseed (one-seed) juniper—*Juniperus monosperma* (N)
Leyland false cypress—*Cupressocyparis leylandii* (E)
Magnolia (warm patios only)
    a. Southern magnolia—*Magnolia grandiflora* (E)
    b. Saucer magnolia—*Magnolia soulangiana* (E)
Chinese windmill palm—*Trachycarpus fortunei* (E)
Pine
    a. Afghan pine—*Pinus eldarica* (E)
    b. Austrian pine—*Pinus nigra* (E)
    c. Italian stone pine—*Pinus pinea* (E)
    d. Japanese black pine—*Pinus thunbergiana* (E)
    e. Limber pine—*Pinus flexilis* (N)
    f. Piñon pine—*Pinus edulis* (N)
    g. Ponderosa pine—*Pinus ponderosa* (N)
    h. Scotch pine—*Pinus sylvestris* (E)
Giant redwood (sequoia)—*Sequoiadendron giganteum* (E)
Spruce
    a. Blue spruce—*Picea pungens* (N)
    b. Engelmann spruce—*Picea engelmanni* (N)
Western red cedar—*Thuja plicata* (E)
Yucca
    a. Joshua tree—*Yucca brevifolia* (E)
    b. Palm yucca—*Yucca torreyi* (N)
    c. Soaptree yucca—*Yucca elata* (N)

SHRUBS

A. Deciduous

Glossy abelia—*Abelia grandiflora* (E)
Flowering almond—*Prunus glandulosa* (E)
Althea (Rose of Sharon)—*Hibiscus syriacus* (E)
Apache plume—*Fallugia paradoxa* (N)
Golden bamboo—*Phyllostachys aurea* (NZ)
Bird of paradise—*Caesalpinia gilliesii* (NZ)
Common butterfly bush—*Buddleia davidii* (E)
Shrubby cinquefoil—*Potentilla fruticosa* (N)
Cotoneaster
    a. Cranberry cotoneaster—*Cotoneaster apiculatus* (E)
    b. Rock cotoneaster—*Cotoneaster horizontalis* (E)
    c. Rockspray cotoneaster—*Cotoneaster microphyllus* (E)
Currant and gooseberry—*Ribes* spp. (E)
Red osier dogwood—*Cornus stolonifera* (N)
Edible fig—*Ficus carica* (E)
Forsythia—*Forsythia* spp. (E)
Common lilac—*Syringa vulgaris* (E)
Mountain mahogany—*Cercocarpus montanus* (E)
New Mexico olive—*Forestiera neomexicana* (N)

Cistena plum—*Prunus cistena* (E)
Sand plum—*Prunus americana* (N)
Privet—*Ligustrum* spp. (E)
Flowering quince—*Chaenomeles speciosa* (E)
Raspberry—*Rubus* spp. (E)
Rose—*Rosa* spp. (N, E)
Snakeweed—*Gutierrezia sarothrae* (N)
Snowball—*Viburnum opulus* 'Roseum' (E)
Spirea
    a. Bridal wreath—*Spiraea prunifolia* (E)
    b. Van Houtte—*Spiraea vanhouttei* (E)
    c. Anthony Waterer—*Spiraea bumalda* 'Anthony
       Waterer' (E)
Sumac
    a. Skunkbush—*Rhus trilobata* (N)
    b. Smooth sumac—*Rhus glabra* (N)
    c. Staghorn sumac—*Rhus typhina* (E)
Weigela—*Weigela florida* (E)
Coyote willow—*Salix exigua* (N)
Winterfat—*Ceratoides lanata* (N)

B. Evergreen

Agave (century plant, mescal)
    a. Century plant—*Agave americana* (N)
    b. Parry agave—*Agave parryi* (N)
    c. Lechugilla—*Agave lechugilla* (N)
Aucuba—*Aucuba japonica* (E)
Barberry
    a. Japanese barberry—*Berberis thunbergii* (E)
    b. Three-spine barberry—*Berberis wisleyensis* (E)
    c. Wintergreen barberry—*Berberis julianae* (E)
Beargrass—*Nolina microcarpa* (N)
Cactus
    a. Prickly pear—*Opuntia chlorotica* or *O.
       engelmannii* (N)
    b. Claret cup—*Echinocereus triglochidiatus* (N)
    c. Common cholla—*Opuntia imbricata* (N)
Parney cotoneaster—*Cotoneaster lacteus* (E)
Holly
    a. Burford holly—*Ilex cornuta* 'Burfordii' (E)
    b. Wilson holly—*Ilex altaclarensis* 'Wilsonii' (E)
    c. Yaupon holly—*Ilex vomitoria* (E)
India hawthorn—*Rhaphiolepis indica* (E)
Chinese junipers
    a. Armstrong juniper—*Juniperus chinensis*
       'Armstrong' (E)
    b. Pfitzer juniper—*Juniperus chinensis* 'Pfitzerana' (E)
    c. Sea Green juniper—*Juniperus chinensis* 'Sea
       Green' (E)
Common juniper—*Juniperus communis* (N)
Mormon tea—*Ephedra* spp. (N)
Nandina (heavenly bamboo)—*Nandina domestica* (E)
Ocotillo—*Fouquieria splendens* (N)
Photinia
    a. Chinese photinia—*Photinia serrulata* (E)
    b. Fraser's photinia—*Photinia fraseri* (E)
Mugo pine—*Pinus mugo* (E)
Pyracantha (firethorn)—*Pyracantha* spp. (E)
Rubber rabbitbrush—*Chrysothamnus nauseosus* (N)
Sage
    a. Big sage (sagebrush)—*Artemisia tridentata* (N)
    b. Sand sage—*Artemisia filifolia* (N)
Fourwing saltbush—*Atriplex canescens* (N)
Seepwillow —*Baccharis sarothroides* (N)
Silverberry—*Elaeagnus pungens* (E)
Sotol—*Dasylirion wheeleri* (N)
Alberta spruce—*Picea glauca* 'Conica' (*Picea
    albertiana*) (E)

Yucca
    a. Softblade yucca—*Yucca recurvifolia* (*Yucca
       pendula*) (E)
    b. Spanish bayonet—*Yucca baccata* (N)
    c. Coral-flower yucca—*Hesperaloe parviflora* (E)

GROUND COVERS

A. Deciduous

Spring cinquefoil—*Potentilla tabernaemontani* (E)
Clover—*Trifolium* spp. (NZ, N)
Cranberry cotoneaster—*Cotoneaster apiculatus* (E)
Crown vetch—*Coronilla varia* (E, NZ)
Mint—*Mentha* spp. (E, N, NZ)
Prairie sage—*Artemisia ludoviciana* (N)
Memorial rose (vine)—*Rosa wichuriana* (E)
Snow-in summer—*Cerastium tomentosum* (E)

B. Evergreen

Creeping euonymus—*Euonymus fortunei* (E)
Horizontalis junipers
    a. Bar Harbor juniper—*Juniperus horizontalis* 'Bar
       Harbor' (E)
    b. Wilton carpet juniper—*Juniperus horizontalis*
       'Wiltonii' (E)
Sabina junipers
    a. Broadmoor juniper—*Juniperus sabina* 'Broadmoor'
       (E)
    b. Buffalo juniper—*Juniperus sabina* 'Buffalo' (E)
    c. Tam (tammy) juniper—*Juniperus sabina*
       'Tamariscifolia' (E)
San Jose juniper—*Juniperus chinensis* 'San Jose' (E)
Blue leadwort—*Ceratostigma plumbaginoides* (E)
Lilyturf (liriope)—*Liriope spicata* (E)
Compact nandina—*Nandina domestica* 'Harbor
    dwarf' (E)
Periwinkle—*Vinca major* and *Vinca minor* (E)
Rosemary—*Rosmarinus officinalis* (E)
Sedum (stonecrop)—*Sedum* spp. (E)
Japanese spurge—*Pachysandra terminalis* (E)
Strawberry—*Fragaria* spp. (N,E)

GRASSES

A. Traditional Turf Species

Bluegrass—*Poa pratensis* (E, NZ)
Fescue—*Festuca* spp. (E, N)
Ryegrass—*Lolium* spp. (E)

B. Native Turf And General-Use Species

Buffalo grass—*Buchlöe dactyloides* (N)
Galleta—*Hilaria jamesii* (N)
Grama
    a. Black grama—*Bouteloua eriopoda* (N)
    b. Blue grama—*Bouteloua gracilis* (N)
    c. Sideoats grama—*Bouteloua curtipendula* (N)
Wheatgrass
    a. Western wheatgrass—*Agropyron smithii* (N)
    b. Crested wheatgrass—*Agropyron desertorum*
       (E, NZ)
    c. Pubescent wheatgrass—*Agropyron tricho-
       phorum* (E)

C. Ornamental Species

Alkali sacaton—*Sporobolus airoides* (N)
Sand dropseed—*Sporobolus cryptandrus* (N)
Blue fescue—*Festuca caesia* (E)
Fountain grass—*Pennisetum* spp. (E)
Pampas grass—*Cortaderia selloana* (E)
Indian ricegrass—*Oryzopsis hymenoides* (N)
River cane—*Arundo donax* (NZ)
Purple threeawn—*Aristida longiseta* (N)

VINES

A. Deciduous

Boston ivy—*Parthenocissus tricuspidata* (E)
Canyon grape—*Vitis arizonica* (N)
Carolina jessamine—*Gelsemium sempervirens* (E)
Clematis—*Clematis jackmanni* (E), and others
Morning glory—*Ipomoea tricolor* (E)
Trumpet vine—*Campsis radicans* (E)
Virginia creeper (et al)—*Parthenocissus quinquefolia* (N, E)
Wisteria—*Wisteria sinensis* (E)

B. Evergreen

English ivy—*Hedera helix* (E)
Honeysuckle—*Lonicera* spp. (E)

FLOWERS

A. Annuals

Ageratum—*Ageratum houstonianum* (E)
Purple aster—*Aster bigelovii* (N)
Cosmos—*Cosmos* spp. (E)
Four o'clock—*Mirabilis jalapa* (E, N)
Gaillardia (blanketflower, firewheel)—*Gaillardia pulchella* (N)

Geranium—*Pelargonium hortorum* (N, E)
Pansy—*Viola wittrockiana* (E)
Petunia—*Petunia* spp. (E)
Snapdragon—*Antirrhinum majus* (E)
Sunflower—*Helianthus annuus* (N)
Annual vinca (Madagascar periwinkle)—*Catharanthus roseus* (E)
Viola (Johnny jump-ups)—*Viola* spp. (E)

B. Perennials

Desert baileya—*Baileya multiradiata* (N)
Bear's breech—*Acanthus mollis* (E)
Carnation—*Dianthus caryophyllus* (E)
Chrysanthemum—*Chrysanthemum morifolium* (E)
Colorado columbine—*Aquilegia* spp. (N)
Delphinium—*Delphinium belladonna* (N)
Blue flax—*Linum perenne* (N, E)
Jimsonweed (datura, sacred datura)—*Datura meteloides* (N)
Lobelia—*Lobelia erinus* (E)
Maximilian's daisy—*Helianthus maximiliani* (N)
Penstemon—*Penstemon* spp. (N)
Primrose—*Primula vulgaris* (E)
Red rocket (scarlet gilia)—*Ipomopsis aggregata* (N)
Shasta daisy—*Chrysanthemum maximum* (E)
Spectaclepod—*Dithyrea wislizenii* (N)
Violet—*Viola odorata* (N, E)
Wooly yarrow—*Achillea* spp. (N, E).

C. Bulbs

Canna—*Canna* spp. (E)
Daffodil—*Narcissus* 'King Alfred' (E)
Garden gladiolus—*Gladiolus hortulanus* (E)
Grape hyacinth—*Muscari armeniacum* (E)
Iris—*Iris* spp. (N, E)
Ranunculus—*Ranunculus asiaticus* (E)
Tulip—*Tulipa* spp. (E)

Foothills garden

Small park at residential intersection, Artesia

ARTESIA

(settled in 1903)

There are lots of pecan trees scattered about this quiet town near the Pecos River. Sturdy Siberian elms have also long been a mainstay of shade-tree planting in Artesia.

Rainfall in this area can frequently be considerable by New Mexico standards, at times nearing 18 inches (450 mm) or more a year, although 12–15 inches (about 350 mm) are more common. Artesia lies at 3800 feet (1160 m) of elevation, and the growing season is about 210 days a year.

The high plains end here. Grama, buffalo, and wheatgrass species are common, as are the native mesquite and desert willow, which flourish along the Pecos itself and in the draws leading to the river. Creosote, yuccas, agave, various cacti, and striking specimen plants such as sotols are also common features of the nearby open countryside.

Domestic landscapes in Artesia are commonly planted in pecans, elms, chinaberries, flowering crabs, Torrey yuccas, ashes, Austrian pines, globe willows, and river cane. Popular shrubs include Spanish broom, coral-flower yucca, fourwing saltbush, various junipers, and figs. Bermuda species are often found as lawn grasses. Irrigated farms producing nuts, alfalfa, cotton, barley, chile, and other crops are common near Artesia. The nearby rangeland is also very productively used to raise cattle.

Historic Central Park, with its pleasant green open spaces, and Eagle Draw are among Artesia's favorite outdoor recreation areas.

SELECTED BEST PLANTS FOR ARTESIA

These plant species grow very well in Artesia. For the sake of convenience and quick reference, each plant is listed as native (N), naturalized (NZ), or exotic (E). Other plants also will perform well in landscape and garden situations in and around Artesia. Please see the New Mexico Plant File for these species.

TREES

A. Deciduous Shade, Street, and Specialty Trees

Ash
    a. Modesto ash—*Fraxinus velutina* 'Modesto' (Arizona ash variety) (N)
    b. Green ash—*Fraxinus pennsylvanica* and varieties (E)
Catalpa
    a. Western catalpa—*Catalpa speciosa* (E)
    b. Umbrella catalpa—*Catalpa bignonioides* 'Nana' (E)
Chinaberry—*Melia azedarach* (E)
Cottonwood, Aspen, and Poplar: Trees of the Genus *Populus*
    a. Carolina poplar—*Populus canadensis* (E)
    b. Fremont cottonwood—*Populus fremontii* (N)
    c. Lanceleaf cottonwood—*Populus acuminata* (N)
    d. Lombardy poplar—*Populus nigra* 'Italica' (E)
    e. Rio Grande cottonwood—*Populus fremontii* 'Wislizeni' (N)
    f. Silver (white) poplar—*Populus alba* (NZ)
Elm
    a. American elm—*Ulmus americana* (E)
    b. Siberian elm—*Ulmus pumila* (NZ; best in rural areas)
Honey locust—*Gleditsia triacanthos inermis* varieties (E)
Locust
    a. Black locust—*Robinia pseudoacacia* (NZ)
    b. Hybrid locusts—*Robinia ambigua* varieties (E)
    c. New Mexico locust—*Robinia neomexicana* (N)
Mesquite—*Prosopis glandulosa* (N)
Mulberry
    a. Fruitless mulberry—*Morus alba* (E)
    b. Weeping mulberry—*Morus alba* 'Pendula' (E)
    c. Paper mulberry—*Broussonetia papyrifera* (E)
Oak
    a. Southern live oak—*Quercus virginiana* (E)

b. Texas oak—*Quercus texana* (E)
Pecan—*Carya illinoiensis* (E)
Pistache—Pistachio
    a. Chinese pistache—*Pistacia chinensis* (E)
    b. Pistachio—*Pistacia vera* (E)
Russian olive—*Elaeagnus angustifolia* (NZ)
Silk tree—*Albizia jilibrissin* (E)
Western soapberry—*Sapindus drummondii* (N)
Sycamore
    a. American sycamore—*Platanus occidentalis* (E)
    b. Arizona sycamore—*Platanus wrightii* (N)
Arizona walnut—*Juglans major* (N)
Willow
    a. Globe Navajo willow—*Salix matsudana* '
      Navajo' (E)
    b. Weeping willow—*Salix babylonica* (and other
      weeping willow species, E)

B. Flowering Ornamental Trees

Flowering apricot—*Prunus armeniaca* (E)
Flowering crab—*Malus* 'Hopa' et al (E)
Desert willow—*Chilopsis linearis* (N)
Mexican elder—*Sambucus caerulea neomexicana* (N)
Hawthorn—*Crataegus* spp. (E,N)
Flowering peach—*Prunus persica* (E)
Purpleleaf plum—*Prunus cerasifera* (E)
Eastern redbud—*Cercis canadensis* (E)
Golden rain tree—*Koelreuteria paniculata* (E)
Smoke tree—*Cotinus coggygria* (E)

C. Evergreen Trees

Deodar cedar—*Cedrus deodara* (E)
Cypress
    a. Arizona cypress—*Cupressus arizonica* (N)
    b. Italian cypress—*Cupressus sempervirens* (E)
Juniper
    a. Alligator juniper—*Juniperus deppeana* (N)
    b. Chinese juniper—*Juniperus chinensis* varieties (E)
    c. Eastern red cedar—*Juniperus virginiana*
      varieties (E)
    d. Rocky Mountain juniper—*Juniperus scopulorum*
      varieties (N)
Chinese windmill palm—*Trachycarpus fortunei* (E)
Pine
    a. Afghan pine—*Pinus eldarica* (E)
    b. Austrian pine—*Pinus nigra* (E)
    c. Japanese black pine—*Pinus thunbergiana* (E)
    d. Piñon pine—*Pinus edulis* (N)
Yucca
    a. Joshua tree—*Yucca brevifolia* (E)
    b. Palm yucca—*Yucca torreyi* (N)
    c. Soaptree yucca—*Yucca elata* (N)

SHRUBS

A. Deciduous

Flowering almond—*Prunus glandulosa* (E)
Althea (rose of Sharon)—*Hibiscus syriacus* (E)
Apache plume—*Fallugia paradoxa* (N)
Golden bamboo—*Phyllostachys aurea* (E)
Bird of paradise—*Caesalpinia gilliesii* (NZ)
Spanish broom—*Spartium junceum* (E)
Common butterfly bush—*Buddleia davidii* (E)
Cotoneaster
    a. Cranberry cotoneaster—*Cotoneaster apiculatus* (E)
    b. Rock cotoneaster—*Cotoneaster horizontalis* (E)
    c. Rockspray cotoneaster—*Cotoneaster*
      microphyllus (E)
Crape myrtle—*Lagerstroemia indica* (E)

Winged enonymus—*Euonymus alata* (E)
Cliff fendlerbush—*Fendlera rupicola* (N)
Fernbush—*Chamaebatiaria millefolium* (N)
Edible fig—*Ficus carica* (E)
Forsythia—*Forsythia* spp. (E)
Shrub or tatarian honeysuckle—*Lonicera tatarica* (E)
Flowering jasmine—*Jasminum nudiflorum* (E)
Common lilac—*Syringa vulgaris* (E)
Screwbean mesquite—*Prosopis pubescens* (N)
Mock orange
    a. Sweet mock orange—*Philadelphus coronarius* (E)
    b. Littleleaf mock orange—*Philadelphus*
      microphyllus (N)
New Mexico olive—*Forestiera neomexicana* (N)
Sand plum—*Prunus americana* (N)
Pomegranate—*Punica granatum* (E)
Privet—*Ligustrum* spp. (E)
Raspberry—*Rubus* spp. (N,E)
Rose—*Rosa* spp. (N, E)
Snowball—*Viburnum opulus* 'Roseum' (E)
Spirea
    a. Bridal wreath—*Spiraea prunifolia* (E)
    b. Van Houtte—*Spiraea vanhouttei* (E)
    c. Anthony Waterer—*Spiraea bumalda* 'Anthony
      Waterer' (E)
Sumac
    a. Littleleaf sumac—*Rhus microphylla* (N)
    b. Skunkbush—*Rhus trilobata* (N)
    c. Smooth sumac—*Rhus glabra* (N)
    d. Staghorn sumac—*Rhus typhina* (E)
Weigela—*Weigela florida* (E)
Willow
    a. Coyote willow—*Salix exigua* (N)
    b. Pussywillow—*Salix discolor* (N)
Winterfat—*Ceratoides lanata* (N)

B. Evergreen

Agave (century plant, mescal)
    a. Century plant—*Agave americana* (N)
    b. Parry agave—*Agave parryi* (N)
    c. Lechugilla—*Agave lechugilla* (N)
Japanese barberry—*Berberis thunbergii* (E)
Cactus
    a. Claret cup—*Echinocereus triglochidiatus* (N)
    b. Common cholla—*Opuntia imbricata* (N)
    c. Prickly pear—*Opuntia chlorotica* or *O.*
      engelmannii (N)
Parney cotoneaster—*Cotoneaster lacteus* (E)
Creosotebush—*Larrea tridentata* (N)
India hawthorn—*Rhaphiolepis indica* (E)
Holly
    a. English holly—*Ilex aquifolium* (E)
    b. Yaupon holly—*Ilex vomitoria* (E)
Chinese junipers
    a. Armstrong juniper—*Juniperus chinensis*
      'Armstrong' (E)
    b. Pfitzer juniper—*Juniperus chinensis* 'Pfitzerana' (E)
    c. Sea Green juniper—*Juniperus chinensis* 'Sea
      Green' (E)
Mahonia
    a. Algerita—*Mahonia haematocarpa* (N)
    b. Agritos—*Mahonia trifoliolata* (N)
    c. Oregon grape—*Mahonia aquifolium* (E, NZ)
Nandina (heavenly bamboo)—*Nandina domestica* (E)
Ocotillo—*Fouquieria splendens* (N)
Pyracantha (firethorn)—*Pyracantha* spp. (E)
Fourwing saltbush—*Atriplex canescens* (N)
Texas ranger—*Leucophyllum frutescens* (E)
Yucca
    a. Narrowleaf yucca—*Yucca glauca* (N)
    b. Softblade yucca—*Yucca recurvifolia* (*Yucca*
      pendula) (E)

c. Spanish bayonet—*Yucca baccata* (N)
d. Coral-flower yucca—*Hesperaloe parviflora* (E)

GROUND COVERS

A. Deciduous

Spring cinquefoil—*Potentilla tabernaemontani* (E)
Clover—*Trifolium* spp. (NZ)
Cranberry cotoneaster—*Cotoneaster apiculatus* (E)
Crown vetch—*Coronilla varia* (E, NZ)
Prairie sage—*Artemisia ludoviciana* (N)

B. Evergreen

Ajuga (bugleweed)—*Ajuga reptans* (E)
Creeping euonymus—*Euonymus fortunei* (E)
Germander—*Teucrium chamaedrys* 'Prostratum' (E)
Honeysuckle—*Lonicera japonica* varieties (E)
Horizontalis junipers
   a. Andorra juniper—*Juniperus horizontalis plumosa* (E)
   b. Bar Harbor juniper—*Juniperus horizontalis* 'Bar Harbor' (E)
   c. Wilton carpet juniper—*Juniperus horizontalis* 'Wiltonii' (E)
Sabina junipers
   a. Broadmoor juniper—*Juniperus sabina* 'Broadmoor' (E)
   b. Buffalo juniper—*Juniperus sabina* 'Buffalo' (E)
   c. Tam (tammy) juniper—*Juniperus sabina* 'Tamariscifolia' (E)
San Jose juniper—*Juniperus chinensis* 'San Jose' (E)
Blue leadwort—*Ceratostigma plumbaginoides* (E)
Lilyturf (liriope)—*Liriope spicata* (E)
Rosemary—*Rosmarinus officinalis* (E)
Santolina
   a. Green santolina—*Santolina virens* (E)
   b. Gray santolina—*Santolina chamaecyparissus* (E)
Sedum (stonecrop)—*Sedum* spp. (E,N)
Japanese spurge—*Pachysandra terminalis* (E)

GRASSES

A. Traditional Turf Species

Bermuda
   a. African bermuda—*Cynodon transvaalensis* (E, NZ)
   b. Common bermuda—*Cynodon dactylon* (E)
Ryegrass—*Lolium* spp. (E)

B. Native Turf and General-Use Species

Buffalo grass—*Buchlöe dactyloides* (N)
Grama
   a. Black grama—*Bouteloua eriopoda* (N)
   b. Blue grama—*Bouteloua gracilis* (N)
   c. Sideoats grama—*Bouteloua curtipendula* (N)
Wheatgrass
   a. Western wheatgrass—*Agropyron smithii* (N)
   b. Crested wheatgrass—*Agropyron desertorum* (E, NZ)

C. Ornamental Species

Alkali sacaton—*Sporobolus airoides* (N)
Blue fescue—*Festuca caesia* (E)
Fountain grass—*Pennisetum* spp. (E)
Pampas grass—*Cortaderia selloana* (E)
River cane—*Arundo donax* (NZ)

VINES

A. Deciduous

Canyon grape—*Vitis arizonica* (N)
Carolina jessamine—*Gelsemium sempervirens* (E)
Clematis—*Clematis jackmanni* (E)
Trumpet vine—*Campsis radicans* (E)
Virginia creeper (et al)—*Parthenocissus quinquefolia* (NZ)
Wisteria—*Wisteria sinensis* (E)

B. Evergreen

English ivy—*Hedera helix* (E)
Honeysuckle—*Lonicera* spp. (E)

FLOWERS

A. Annuals

Purple aster—*Aster bigelovii* (N)
Cosmos—*Cosmos* spp. (E)
Four o'clock—*Mirabilis jalapa* (E)
Gaillardia (blanketflower, firewheel)—*Gaillardia pulchella* (N)
Impatiens—*Impatiens wallerana* (E)
Marigold—*Tagetes* spp. (E)
Petunia—*Petunia* spp. (E)
Salvia—*Salvia* spp. (E)
Snapdragon—*Antirrhinum majus* (E)
Sunflower—*Helianthus annuus* (N)
Annual vinca (Madagascar periwinkle)—*Catharanthus roseus* (E)
Wallflower—*Erysimum capitatum* (N)

B. Perennials

Bear's breech—*Acanthus mollis* (E)
Carnation—*Dianthus caryophyllus* (E)
Chrysanthemum—*Chrysanthemum morifolium* (E)
Colorado columbine—*Aquilegia* spp. (N)
Coneflower—*Ratibida columnifera* (N)
Daylily (asphodel)—*Hemerocallis* spp. (E)
Dusty miller—*Senecio cineraria* (E)
Fendler's sundrops—*Calylophus hartwegii fendleri* (N)
Globemallow—*Sphaeralcea incana* (scarlet) (N)
Hollyhock—*Alcea rosea* (NZ)
Indian paintbrush—*Castilleja integra* (N)
Phlox—*Phlox* spp. (E)
California poppy—*Eschscholzia californica* (and *E. mexicana*) (E,N)
Primrose—*Primula vulgaris* (E)
Shasta daisy—*Chrysanthemum maximum* (E)

C. Bulbs

Canna—*Canna* spp. (E)
Daffodil—*Narcissus* 'King Alfred' (E)
Garden gladiolus—*Gladiolus hortulanus* (E)
Iris—*Iris* spp. (E, N)
Ranunculus—*Ranunculus asiaticus* (E)
Tulip—*Tulipa* spp. (E)

Mexican alder in a residential area, Carlsbad

CARLSBAD

(settled about 1888)

The local hot springs reminded early settlers of a famous Central European spa, thus providing Carlsbad with its name. The city has always been identified as well with the nearby Carlsbad Caverns National Park. At 3100 feet (930 m), it is the lowest in elevation of New Mexico's cities.

Carlsbad has unusual flora. The startlingly beautiful Texas madrone grows here, as does the California fan palm, desert ceanothus, yaupon holly, and even an occasional ornamental banana tree. Carlsbad's location on the Pecos River has also led to the creation of a riverside *resaca* (cul-de-sac river "bayou") neighborhood, complete with boat landings and very pleasant residential landscapes. *Resacas* are normally features of such lower Rio Grande Valley cities as Brownsville, Texas. Carlsbad's *resaca* is unique in New Mexico.

Cotton, chile, and pecans are among the principal agricultural crops of the surrounding Eddy County. Cattle are also widely grazed near Carlsbad. A long growing season of 216 days contributes to both agriculture and ornamental horticulture in Carlsbad. Average rainfall is about 12–24 inches (300–600 mm) per year, very good for New Mexico.

Much of the countryside near Carlsbad is desert. Ocotillo, sotol, desert ceanothus, *tornillo* (screwbean) mesquite, creosote, and cactus are frequently found here. Common river basin species include cottonwood, salt cedar, desert willow, shrub willows, and many grass species. To the east, the sandy low plains are frequently

covered in shimmering green shin oak, a ground-cover *Quercus* species that prefers low hillocks. Soils in the area tend to be stony and limey.

In Carlsbad itself, Siberian elm and ailanthus (the tree of heaven) are widely grown as shade trees. Chinaberry, pecan, Afghan pine, pear, ash, soapberry, Aleppo pine, and cottonwood are also popular tree species. Texas ranger, oleander, sotol, various cacti, bird of paradise, and vitex are favorite shrubs.

Riverside Park and Municipal Beach Park, laid out along Lake Carlsbad, are influential historical landscapes. The grounds of the Eddy County Courthouse are among the most impressive and best-maintained courthouse squares in New Mexico. The nearby Living Desert Zoological and Botanical State Park displays substantial collections of native landscape species taken from the surrounding Chihuahuan Desert and the Guadalupe Mountains.

SELECTED BEST PLANTS FOR CARLSBAD

These plant species grow very well in and around Carlsbad. For the sake of convenience and quick reference, each plant is listed as native (N), naturalized (NZ), or exotic (E). Other plants also will perform well in landscape and garden situations in the Carlsbad area. Please see the New Mexico Plant File for these species.

TREES

A. Deciduous Shade, Street, and Specialty Trees

Ash
  a. Arizona ash—*Fraxinus velutina* (N)
  b. Modesto ash—*Fraxinus velutina* 'Modesto' (Arizona ash variety) (N)
Chinaberry—*Melia azedarach* (E)
Cottonwood, Aspen, and Poplar: Trees of the Genus *Populus*
  a. Lanceleaf cottonwood—*Populus acuminata* (N)
  b. Rio Grande cottonwood—*Populus fremontii* 'Wislizeni' (N)
  c. Silver (white) poplar—*Populus alba* (NZ)
Chinese elm—*Ulmus parvifolia* (E)
Honey locust—*Gleditsia triacanthos inermis* varieties (E)
Japanese pagoda—*Sophora japonica* (E)
Littleleaf linden—*Tilia cordata* (E)
Locust
  a. Black locust—*Robinia pseudoacacia* (NZ)
  b. Hybrid locusts—*Robinia ambigua* varieties (E)
Maple and Box elder
  a. Rocky Mountain maple—*Acer glabrum* (N)
  b. Sycamore-leaf maple—*Acer pseudoplatanus* (E)
Mesquite—*Prosopis glandulosa* (N)
Mulberry
  a. Fruitless mulberry—*Morus alba* (E)
  b. Weeping mulberry—*Morus alba* 'Pendula' (E)
Oak
  a. Southern live oak—*Quercus virginiana* (E)
  b. Texas oak—*Quercus texana* (E)
Osage orange—*Maclura pomifera* (E)
Pecan—*Carya illinoiensis* (E)
Silk tree—*Albizia jilibrissin* (E)
Western soapberry—*Sapindus drummondii* (N)
Sycamore (plane tree)
  a. American sycamore—*Platanus occidentalis* (E)
  b. Arizona sycamore—*Platanus wrightii* (N)
Tree of heaven—*Ailanthus altissima* (NZ, used for shade in very difficult areas)
Arizona walnut—*Juglans major* (N)
Willow
  a. Corkscrew willow—*Salix matsudana* 'Tortuosa' (E)
  b. Globe Navajo willow—*Salix matsudana* 'Navajo' (E)
  c. Peachleaf willow—*Salix amygdaloides* (N)
  d. Weeping willow—*Salix babylonica* (and other weeping willow species also, E)

B. Flowering Ornamental Trees

Flowering crab—*Malus* 'Hopa' et al (E)
Desert willow—*Chilopsis linearis* (N)
Mexican elder—*Sambucus caerulea neomexicana* (N)
Flowering peach—*Prunus persica* (E)
Bradford pear—*Pyrus calleryana* (E)
Purpleleaf plum—*Prunus cerasifera* (E)
Eastern redbud—*Cercis canadensis* (E)
Salt cedar—*Tamarix chinensis* (NZ)
Vitex (chaste tree)—*Vitex agnus-castus* (E)

C. Evergreen Trees

Cedar
  a. Atlas cedar—*Cedrus atlantica* (E)
  b. Deodar cedar—*Cedrus deodara* (E)
Cypress
  a. Arizona cypress—*Cupressus arizonica* (N)
  b. Italian cypress—*Cupressus sempervirens* (E)
Juniper
  a. Alligator juniper—*Juniperus deppeana* (N)
  b. Eastern red cedar—*Juniperus virginiana* varieties (E)
  c. Rocky Mountain juniper—*Juniperus scopulorum* varieties (N)
Leyland false cypress—*Cupressocyparis leylandii* (E)
Madrone—*Arbutus texana* (N)
Magnolia
  a. Southern magnolia—*Magnolia grandiflora* (E)
  b. Saucer magnolia—*Magnolia soulangiana* (E)
Palm
  a. California fan palm—*Washingtonia filifera* (E)
  b. Chinese windmill palm—*Trachycarpus fortunei* (E)
  c. Mediterranean fan palm—*Chamaerops humilis* (E)
Pine
  a. Afghan pine—*Pinus eldarica* (E)
  b. Aleppo pine—*Pinus halepensis* (E)
  c. Japanese black pine—*Pinus thunbergiana* (E)
  d. Limber pine—*Pinus flexilis* (N)
  e. Piñon pine—*Pinus edulis* (N)
  f. Ponderosa pine—*Pinus ponderosa* (N)
Blue spruce—*Picea pungens* (E)
Western red cedar—*Thuja plicata* (E)
Yucca
  a. Palm yucca—*Yucca torreyi* (N)
  b. Soaptree yucca—*Yucca elata* (N)

SHRUBS

A. Deciduous

Apache plume—*Fallugia paradoxa* (N)
Bird of paradise—*Caesalpinia gilliesii* (NZ)
Cotoneaster
  a. Cranberry cotoneaster—*Cotoneaster apiculatus* (E)
  b. Rock cotoneaster—*Cotoneaster horizontalis* (E)
  c. Rockspray cotoneaster—*Cotoneaster microphyllus* (E)
Crape myrtle—*Lagerstroemia indica* (E)
Winged enonymus—*Euonymus alata* (E)
Edible fig—*Ficus carica* (E)
Shrub or Tatarian honeysuckle—*Lonicera tatarica* (E)
Flowering jasmine—*Jasminum nudiflorum* (E)
Screwbean mesquite—*Prosopis pubescens* (N)
Mountain mahogany—*Cercocarpus montanus* (N)
New Mexico olive—*Forestiera neomexicana* (N)
Cistena plum—*Prunus cistena* (E)
Privet—*Ligustrum* spp. (E)
Rose—*Rosa* spp. (N, E)
Spirea
  a. Bridal wreath—*Spiraea prunifolia* (E)
  b. Van Houtte—*Spiraea vanhouttei* (E)
  c. Anthony Waterer—*Spiraea bumalda* 'Anthony Waterer' (E)
Sumac
  a. Littleleaf sumac—*Rhus microphylla* (N)
  b. Skunkbush—*Rhus trilobata* (N)
  c. Smooth sumac—*Rhus glabra* (N)
  d. Staghorn sumac—*Rhus typhina* (NZ)

B. Evergreen

Agave (century plant, mescal)
  a. Century plant—*Agave americana* (N)
  b. Parry agave—*Agave parryi* (N)
  c. Lechugilla—*Agave lechugilla* (N)
Wintergreen barberry—*Berberis julianae* (E)
Beargrass—*Nolina microcarpa* (N)
Cactus
  a. Common cholla—*Opuntia imbricata* (N)
  b. Prickly pear—*Opuntia chlorotica* or *O. engelmannii* (N)
Creosotebush—*Larrea tridentata* (N)
Yaupon holly—*Ilex vomitoria* (E)
Chinese junipers
  a. Armstrong juniper—*Juniperus chinensis* 'Armstrong' (E)

b. Pfitzer juniper—*Juniperus chinensis* 'Pfitzerana' (E)

c. Sea Green juniper—*Juniperus chinensis* 'Sea Green' (E)

Nandina (heavenly bamboo)—*Nandina domestica* (E)

Ocotillo—*Fouquieria splendens* (N)

Oleander—*Nerium oleander* (E)

Chinese photinia—*Photinia serrulata* (E)

Pyracantha (firethorn)—*Pyracantha* spp. (E)

Seepwillow -*Baccharis sarothroides* (N)

Silverberry—*Elaeagnus pungens* (E)

Sotol—*Dasylirion wheeleri* (N)

Texas ranger—*Leucophyllum frutescens* (E)

Yucca

a. Narrowleaf yucca—*Yucca glauca* (N)

b. Softblade yucca—*Yucca recurvifolia* (*Yucca pendula*) (E)

c. Spanish bayonet—*Yucca baccata* (N)

d. Coral-flower yucca—*Hesperaloe parviflora* (E)

GROUND COVERS

A. Deciduous

Clover—*Trifolium* spp. (NZ)

Cranberry cotoneaster—*Cotoneaster apiculatus* (E)

Crown vetch—*Coronilla varia* (E)

Prairie sage—*Artemisia ludoviciana* (N)

B. Evergreen

Bearberry cotoneaster—*Cotoneaster dammeri* (E)

Dwarf coyotebrush—*Baccharis pilularis* (E)

Dichondra—*Dichondra micrantha* (E)

Germander—*Teucrium chamaedrys* 'Prostratum' (E)

Honeysuckle—*Lonicera japonica* varieties (E)

Horizontalis junipers

a. Andorra juniper—*Juniperus horizontalis plumosa* (E)

b. Bar Harbor juniper—*Juniperus horizontalis* 'Bar Harbor' (E)

c. Wilton carpet juniper—*Juniperus horizontalis* 'Wiltonii' (E)

Sabina junipers

a. Broadmoor juniper—*Juniperus sabina* 'Broadmoor' (E)

b. Buffalo juniper—*Juniperus sabina* 'Buffalo' (E)

c. Tam (tammy) juniper—*Juniperus sabina* 'Tamariscifolia' (E)

Lilyturf (liriope)—*Liriope spicata* (E)

Compact nandina—*Nandina domestica* 'Harbor dwarf' (E)

Periwinkle—*Vinca major* and *Vinca minor* (E)

Rosemary—*Rosmarinus officinalis* (E)

Santolina

a. Green santolina—*Santolina virens* (E)

b. Gray santolina—*Santolina chamaecyparissus* (E)

GRASSES

A. Traditional Turf Species

Common bermuda—*Cynodon dactylon* (NZ)

Fescue—*Festuca* spp. (E)

Ryegrass—*Lolium* spp. (E)

B. Native Turf And General-Use Species

Buffalo grass—*Buchlöe dactyloides* (N)

Grama

a. Black grama—*Bouteloua eriopoda* (N)

b. Blue grama—*Bouteloua gracilis* (N)

Wheatgrass

a. Western wheatgrass—*Agropyron smithii* (N)

b. Pubescent wheatgrass—*Agropyron trichophorum* (N)

C. Ornamental Species

Alkali sacaton—*Sporobolus airoides* (N)

Blue fescue—*Festuca caesia* (E)

Fountain grass—*Pennisetum* spp. (E)

Pampas grass—*Cortaderia selloana* (E)

Indian ricegrass—*Oryzopsis hymenoides* (N)

River cane—*Arundo donax* (NZ)

Purple threeawn—*Aristida longiseta* (N)

VINES

A. Deciduous

Canyon grape—*Vitis arizonica* (N)

Carolina jessamine—*Gelsemium sempervirens* (E)

Trumpet vine—*Campsis radicans* (E)

Virginia creeper (et al)—*Parthenocissus quinquefolia* (N)

Wisteria—*Wisteria sinensis* (E)

B. Evergreen

Algerian ivy—*Hedera canariensis* (E)

Honeysuckle—*Lonicera* spp. (E)

FLOWERS

A. Annuals

Ageratum—*Ageratum houstonianum* (E)

Purple aster—*Aster bigelovii* (N)

Coleus—*Coleus x hybridus* (E)

Cosmos—*Cosmos* spp. (E)

Gaillardia (blanketflower, firewheel)—*Gaillardia pulchella* (N)

Geranium—*Pelargonium hortorum* (E)

Lisianthus—*Eustoma grandiflorum* (E)

Marigold—*Tagetes* spp. (E)

Sunflower—*Helianthus annuus* (N)

Annual vinca (Madagascar periwinkle)—*Catharanthus roseus* (E)

Viola (Johnny jump-ups)—*Viola* spp. (E)

B. Perennials

Desert baileya—*Baileya multiradiata* (N)

Chrysanthemum—*Chrysanthemum morifolium* (E)

Daylily (asphodel)—*Hemerocallis* spp. (E)

Delphinium—*Delphinium belladonna* (E)

Dusty miller—*Senecio cineraria* (E)

Fendler's sundrops—*Calylophus hartwegii fendleri* (N)

Globemallow—*Sphaeralcea incana* (scarlet) (N)

Indian paintbrush—*Castilleja integra* (N)

Jimsonweed (datura, sacred datura)—*Datura meteloides* (N)

Lobelia—*Lobelia erinus* (E)

Paperflower—*Psilostrophe tagetina* (N)

Phlox—*Phlox* spp.(E)

California poppy—*Eschscholzia californica* (and E. mexicana) (E, N)

Primrose—*Primula vulgaris* (E)

Red rocket (scarlet gilia)—*Ipomopsis aggregata* (N)

Shasta daisy—*Chrysanthemum maximum* (E)

C. Bulbs

Canna—*Canna* spp. (E)

Common hyacinth—*Hyacinthus orientalis* (E)

Daffodil—*Narcissus* 'King Alfred' (E)

Garden gladiolus—*Gladiolus hortulanus* (E)

Iris—*Iris* spp. (E, N)

CHAMA

(settled about 1800), including Dulce and Tierra Amarilla

Chama is an old lumber town just south of the Colorado line. Its high altitude (7830 feet/2400 m) and spectacular setting in the southern San Juan Mountains have also made it popular in the twentieth century as a fishing resort and, recently, as the New Mexico railhead for the Cumbres and Toltec Scenic Railway.

Exotics and colorful local natives combine to make Chama's gardens notably attractive. Sand plums bloom in the spring, followed by lilacs. Daylilies and sweet peas are very popular summer flowers. Ponderosa pine, very frequently accompanied by its natural undergrowth of Gambel oak and currants, is found throughout the town. Narrowleaf cottonwood, red osier dogwood, peachleaf willow, and white fir are frequently found as secondary or specimen plantings. Austrian copper rose, irises, and native yarrow are colorful accents.

The Chama landscape of rolling, grassy parkland spotted with individual or clustered ponderosa pines is the surprisingly pleasant result of years of hard logging. Agriculture in this part of Rio Arriba County is largely centered on stock grazing and the cultivation of fruit trees and alfalfa. Chama receives over 20 inches (500 mm) of rainfall per year; local soils, though clayey, are rich and very supportive of landscape gardening with very little extra irrigation.

The short growing season of only 83 days is comparable to those of the other high-altitude towns of the San Juans in Colorado, which Chama much resembles. In these mountain communities, columbine, beebalm, yellow clover, and lupines are notable for colorfully completing their growing lives in less than three months.

SELECTED BEST PLANTS FOR CHAMA

These plant species grow very well in and around Chama. For the sake of convenience and quick reference, each plant is listed as native (N), naturalized (NZ), or exotic (E). Other plants also will perform well in landscape and garden situations in the Chama area. Please see the New Mexico Plant File for these species.

TREES

A. Deciduous Shade, Street, and Specialty Trees

Cottonwood, Aspen, and Poplar: Trees of the Genus
  Populus
  a. Aspen—*Populus tremuloides* (N)
  b. Carolina poplar—*Populus canadensis* (E)
  c. Lombardy poplar—*Populus nigra* 'Italica' (E)
  d. Narrowleaf cottonwood—*Populus angustifolia* (N)
  f. White (silver) poplar—*Populus alba* (NZ)

High altitude garden with a stone wall, Chama

Siberian elm—*Ulmus pumila* (NZ)
Honey locust—*Gleditsia triacanthos inermis* varieties (E)
Locust
    a. Black locust—*Robinia pseudoacacia* (NZ)
    b. New Mexico locust—*Robinia neomexicana* (N)
Maple and Box elder
    a. Box elder—*Acer negundo* (N)
    b. Rocky Mountain maple—*Acer glabrum* (N)
Gambel oak—*Quercus gambelii* (N)
Russian olive—*Elaeagnus angustifolia* (NZ)

B. Flowering Ornamental Trees

Apple—*Malus sylvestris* varieties (NZ)
Flowering crab—*Malus* 'Hopa' et al (E)
Hawthorn—*Crataegus* spp. (N)
Flowering peach—*Prunus persica* (E)

C. Evergreen Trees

Douglas fir—*Pseudotsuga menziesii* (N)
White fir—*Abies concolor* (N)
Rocky Mountain juniper—*Juniperus scopulorum*
          varieties (N)
Pine
    a. Austrian pine—*Pinus nigra* (E)
    b. Limber pine—*Pinus flexilis* (N)
    c. Ponderosa pine—*Pinus ponderosa* (N)
    d. Scotch pine—*Pinus sylvestris* (E)
Spruce
    a. Blue spruce—*Picea pungens* (N)
    b. Engelmann spruce—*Picea engelmanni* (N)

SHRUBS

A. Deciduous

Shrubby cinquefoil—*Potentilla fruticosa* (N)
Currant and gooseberry—*Ribes* spp. (N)
Red osier dogwood—*Cornus stolonifera* (N)
Common lilac—*Syringa vulgaris* (E)
Mountain mahogany—*Cercocarpus montanus* (N)
Cistena plum—*Prunus cistena* (E)
Sand plum—*Prunus americana* (N)
Rose—*Rosa* spp. (E, N)
Skunkbush—*Rhus trilobata* (N)
Snowball—*Viburnum opulus* 'Roseum' (E)

B. Evergreen

Colorado barberry—*Berberis fendleri* (N)
Common juniper—*Juniperus communis* (N)
Waxleaf privet (ligustrum)—*Ligustrum japonicum* (E)
Big sage (sagebrush)—*Artemisia tridentata* (N)

GROUND COVERS

A. Deciduous

Spring cinquefoil—*Potentilla tabernaemontani* (E)
Clover—*Trifolium* spp. (NZ)
Mint—*Mentha* spp. (E)

B. Evergreen

Bearberry cotoneaster—*Cotoneaster dammeri* (E)
Honeysuckle—*Lonicera japonica* varieties (E)
Sabina junipers
    a. Broadmoor juniper—*Juniperus sabina*
       'Broadmoor' (E)
    b. Buffalo juniper—*Juniperus sabina* 'Buffalo' (E)
    c. Tam (tammy) juniper—*Juniperus sabina*
       'Tamariscifolia' (E)

Kinnickinnick (mountain bearberry)—*Arctostaphylos
    uva-ursi* (N)
Creeping mahonia—*Mahonia repens* (N)
Strawberry—*Fragaria* spp. (N,E)

GRASSES

A. Traditional Turf Species

Bluegrass—*Poa pratensis* (NZ)
Fescue—*Festuca* spp. (E,N)
Ryegrass—*Lolium* spp. (E)

B. Native Turf and General-Use Species

Galleta—*Hilaria jamesii* (N)

C. Ornamental Species

Blue fescue—*Festuca caesia* (E)

VINES

A. Deciduous

Clematis—*Clematis jackmanni* (E)
Morning glory—*Ipomoea tricolor* (E)
Trumpet vine—*Campsis radicans* (E)
Virginia creeper (et al)—*Parthenocissus quinquefolia* (N)

B. Evergreen

English ivy—*Hedera helix* (E)
Honeysuckle—*Lonicera* spp. (E)

FLOWERS

A. Annuals

Four o'clock—*Mirabilis jalapa* (E)
Impatiens—*Impatiens wallerana* (E)
Marigold—*Tagetes* spp. (E)
Pansy—*Viola wittrockiana* (E)
Petunia—*Petunia* spp. (E)
Salvia—*Salvia* spp. (E)
Snapdragon—*Antirrhinum majus* (E)
Sunflower—*Helianthus annuus* (N)
Annual vinca (Madagascar periwinkle)—*Catharanthus
    roseus* (E)

B. Perennials

Colorado columbine—*Aquilegia* spp. (N)
Coneflower—*Ratibida columnifera* (N)
Daylily (asphodel)—*Hemerocallis* spp. (E)
Delphinium—*Delphinium belladonna* (E)
Dusty miller—*Senecio cineraria* (E)
Hollyhock—*Alcea rosea* (N)
Maximilian's daisy—*Helianthus maximiliani* (NZ)
Penstemon—*Penstemon* spp. (N)
Red rocket (scarlet gilia)—*Ipomopsis aggregata* (N)
Shasta daisy—*Chrysanthemum maximum* (E)
Wooly yarrow—*Achillea* spp. (N)

C. Bulbs

Garden gladiolus—*Gladiolus hortulanus* (E)
Common hyacinth—*Hyacinthus orientalis* (E)
Daffodil—*Narcissus* 'King Alfred' (E)
Iris—*Iris* spp. (N, E)

CLAYTON

(founded in 1887)

Court Street, with native grass turf and Siberian elms
Clayton is a statewide leader in the use of native grasses in lawns
(Photo by Elizabeth C. Reardon)

A picturesque plains town beneath Rabbit Ears Mountain, Clayton lies at the edge of the spectacular Kiowa National Grasslands on the Oklahoma and Texas borders. At 4970 feet (1500 m), Clayton can experience great temperature extremes in the winter. Its rainfall averages between 15 and 20 inches (400–500 mm) a year. The growing season is about 164 days.

Buffalo grass, gramas, bromes, and wheatgrasses dominate the nearby grassy range. Sunflowers, yucca, thistles, gumweed, prairie cottonwoods, and singleseed junipers also are commonly found in draws, on hillsides, or in disturbed places. Wheat and hay are widely grown, as are sorghum and corn. Union County leads the state in cattle production, and hogs are also produced in considerable quantity.

In Clayton, a remarkable series of home gardens stretches down Court Street and along Pine Street from Second Street to Clayton High School. These and other private landscapes in town feature black locusts, soapberries, piñons, Rocky Mountain junipers, Austrian pines, walnuts, willows, spruces, and the ubiquitous Siberian elm as key trees. Purpleleaf plum, salt cedar, lilac, pyracantha, cholla, iris, peach, four o'clocks, sand plum, spirea, and Shasta daisies are commonly used for seasonal color.

Historically, the private gardens of Clayton have been influenced by three primary public and private landscapes that exist in a rough "triangle" inside the town. At the north is the heavily shaded campus of the high school and its appealing courtyards, constructed, like the school itself, by an extraordinary, volunteer public effort earlier in this century. To the south is the old Union County Courthouse Square, a historic landscape whose heyday was the 1920s and 1930s. The courthouse itself was built in 1910. At the west end of Clayton stands a substantial private mansion with interesting gardens, probably Union County's best "Country Place" Era (1870– 1930) home grounds.

Many of the town's domestic and commercial landscapes reflect the pervasive influence of these three exemplary open spaces. Clayton is also notable for having the best collection of domestic blue grama–buffalo grass lawns in New Mexico. Nurtured with a little water, recycled local manure, and consistent care, these legendary prairie grasses of the Old West are likely to become the state's most popular turf grasses in the twenty-first century.

SELECTED BEST PLANTS FOR CLAYTON

These plant species grow very well in Clayton. For the sake of convenience and quick reference, each plant is listed as native (N), naturalized (NZ), or exotic (E). Other plants also will perform well in landscape and garden situations in and around Clayton. Please see the New Mexico Plant File for these species.

TREES

A. Deciduous Shade, Street, and Specialty Trees

Green ash—*Fraxinus pennsylvanica* and varieties (E)
Paper birch—*Betula papyrifera* (E)
Western catalpa—*Catalpa speciosa* (E)
Western chokecherry—*Prunus virginiana* (N)
Cottonwood, Aspen, and Poplar: Trees of the Genus *Populus*
    a. Carolina poplar—*Populus canadensis* (E)
    b. Lombardy poplar—*Populus nigra* 'Italica' (E)
    c. Narrowleaf cottonwood—*Populus angustifolia* (N)
    d. Plains cottonwood—*Populus sargenti* (N)
    e. White (silver) poplar—*Populus alba* (NZ)
Siberian elm—*Ulmus pumila* (NZ)
Hackberry

    a. Common hackberry—*Celtis occidentalis* (E)
    b. Netleaf hackberry—*Celtis reticulata* (E, N)
Honey locust—*Gleditsia triacanthos inermis* varieties (E)
Black locust—*Robinia pseudoacacia* (NZ)
Maple and Box elder
    a. Box elder—*Acer negundo* (N)
    b. Norway maple—*Acer platanoides* (E)
    c. Silver maple—*Acer saccharinum* (E)
Russian olive—*Elaeagnus angustifolia* (NZ)
Silk tree—*Albizia jilibrissin* (E)
Tree of heaven—*Ailanthus altissima* (NZ, used for shade in very difficult areas) Willow
    a. Corkscrew willow—*Salix matsudana* 'Tortuosa' (E)
    b. Globe Navajo willow—*Salix matsudana* 'Navajo' (E)
    c. Peachleaf willow—*Salix amygdaloides* (N)
    d. Weeping willow—*Salix babylonica* (and other weeping willow species, E)

B. Flowering Ornamental Trees

Flowering crab—*Malus* 'Hopa' et al (E)
Hawthorn—*Crataegus* spp. (E,N)
Flowering peach—*Prunus persica* (E)
Purpleleaf plum—*Prunus cerasifera* (E)
Eastern redbud—*Cercis canadensis* (E)
Salt cedar—*Tamarix chinensis* (NZ)
Smoke tree—*Cotinus coggygria* (E)

C. Evergreen Trees

Arizona cypress—*Cupressus arizonica* (N)
Douglas fir—*Pseudotsuga menziesii* (N)
White fir—*Abies concolor* (N)
Juniper
    a. Chinese juniper—*Juniperus chinensis* varieties (E)
    b. Eastern red cedar—*Juniperus virginiana* varieties (E)
    c. Rocky Mountain juniper—*Juniperus scopulorum* varieties (N)
    d. Singleseed (one-seed) juniper—*Juniperus monosperma* (N)
Leyland false cypress—*Cupressocyparis leylandii* (E)
Pine
    a. Austrian pine—*Pinus nigra* (E)
    b. Piñon pine—*Pinus edulis* (N)
    c. Ponderosa pine—*Pinus ponderosa* (N)
Blue spruce—*Picea pungens* (N)
Palm yucca—*Yucca torreyi* (N)

SHRUBS

A. Deciduous

Althea (Rose of Sharon)—*Hibiscus syriacus* (E)
Common butterfly bush—*Buddleia davidii* (E)
Shrubby cinquefoil—*Potentilla fruticosa* (N)
Cotoneaster
    a. Cranberry cotoneaster—*Cotoneaster apiculatus* (E)
    b. Rock cotoneaster—*Cotoneaster horizontalis* (E)
    c. Rockspray cotoneaster—*Cotoneaster microphyllus* (E)
Common lilac—*Syringa vulgaris* (E)
Mock orange
    a. Sweet mock orange—*Philadelphus coronarius* (E)
    b. Littleleaf mock orange—*Philadelphus microphyllus* (E)
Mountain mahogany—*Cercocarpus montanus* (N)
New Mexico olive—*Forestiera neomexicana* (N)
Cistena plum—*Prunus cistena* (E)
Sand plum—*Prunus americana* (N)
Rose—*Rosa* spp. (E, N)
Snakeweed—*Gutierrezia sarothrae* (N)
Spirea
    a. Bridal wreath—*Spiraea prunifolia* (E)

b. Anthony Waterer—*Spiraea bumalda* 'Anthony Waterer' (E)
Sumac
    a. Skunkbush—*Rhus trilobata* (N)
    b. Staghorn sumac—*Rhus typhina* (E)
Willow
    a. Coyote willow—*Salix exigua* (N)
    b. Pussywillow—*Salix discolor* (E)
Winterfat—*Ceratoides lanata* (N)

B. Evergreen

Aucuba—*Aucuba japonica* (E)
Barberry
    a. Colorado barberry—*Berberis fendleri* (N)
    b. Japanese barberry—*Berberis thunbergii* (E)
    c. Three-spine barberry—*Berberis wisleyensis* (E)
    d. Wintergreen barberry—*Berberis julianae* (E)
Cactus
    a. Common cholla—*Opuntia imbricata* (N)
    b. Prickly pear—*Opuntia chlorotica* or
      O. engelmannii (N)
Chinese junipers
    a. Armstrong juniper—*Juniperus chinensis*
      'Armstrong' (E)
    b. Pfitzer juniper—*Juniperus chinensis* 'Pfitzerana' (E)
Common juniper—*Juniperus communis* (N)
Mahonia
    a. Algerita—*Mahonia haematocarpa* (N)
    b. Agritos—*Mahonia trifoliolata* (N)
    c. Oregon grape—*Mahonia aquifolium* (E)
Mormon tea—*Ephedra* spp. (N)
Nandina (heavenly bamboo)—*Nandina domestica* (E)
Mugo pine—*Pinus mugo* (E)
Photinia
    a. Chinese photinia—*Photinia serrulata* (E)
    b. Fraser's photinia—*Photinia fraseri* (E)
Pyracantha (firethorn)—*Pyracantha* spp. (E)
Sage
    a. Big sage (sagebrush)—*Artemisia tridentata* (N)
    b. Sand sage—*Artemisia filifolia* (N)
Narrowleaf yucca—*Yucca glauca* (N)

GROUND COVERS

A. Deciduous

Spring cinquefoil—*Potentilla tabernaemontani* (E)
Cranberry cotoneaster—*Cotoneaster apiculatus* (E)
Crown vetch—*Coronilla varia* (E, NZ)
Prairie sage—*Artemisia ludoviciana* (N)
Snow-in summer—*Cerastium tomentosum* (E)

B. Evergreen

Bearberry cotoneaster—*Cotoneaster dammeri* (E)
Creeping euonymus—*Euonymus fortunei* (E)
Honeysuckle—*Lonicera japonica* varieties (E)
Sabina junipers
    a. Broadmoor juniper—*Juniperus sabina* 'Broadmoor'
      (E)
    b. Buffalo juniper—*Juniperus sabina* 'Buffalo' (E)
    c. Tam (tammy) juniper—*Juniperus sabina*
      'Tamariscifolia' (E)
Blue leadwort—*Ceratostigma plumbaginoides* (E)
Creeping mahonia—*Mahonia repens* (N)
Periwinkle—*Vinca major* and *Vinca minor* (E)
Rosemary—*Rosmarinus officinalis* (E)
Santolina
    a. Green santolina—*Santolina virens* (E)
    b. Gray santolina—*Santolina chamaecyparissus* (E)
Sedum (stonecrop)—*Sedum* spp. (N, E)

GRASSES

A. Traditional Turf Species

Common bermuda—*Cynodon dactylon* (NZ)
Bluegrass—*Poa pratensis* (NZ)
Fescue—*Festuca* spp. (E)
Ryegrass—*Lolium* spp. (E)

B. Native Turf And General-Use Species

Buffalo grass—*Buchlöe dactyloides* (N)
Grama
    a. Blue grama—*Bouteloua gracilis* (N)
    b. Sideoats grama—*Bouteloua curtipendula* (N)
Wheatgrass
    a. Western wheatgrass—*Agropyron smithii* (N)
    b. Crested wheatgrass—*Agropyron desertorum* (E)

C. Ornamental Species

Sand dropseed—*Sporobolus cryptandrus* (N)
Blue fescue—*Festuca caesia* (E)
Pampas grass—*Cortaderia selloana* (E)
Indian ricegrass—*Oryzopsis hymenoides* (N)
Purple threeawn—*Aristida longiseta* (N)

VINES

A. Deciduous

Trumpet vine—*Campsis radicans* (E)
Virginia creeper (et al)—*Parthenocissus quinquefolia* (N)

B. Evergreen

English ivy—*Hedera helix* (E)
Honeysuckle—*Lonicera* spp. (E)

FLOWERS

A. Annuals

Purple aster—*Aster bigelovii* (N)
Cosmos—*Cosmos* spp. (E)
Four o'clock—*Mirabilis jalapa* (E, N)
Impatiens—*Impatiens wallerana* (E)
Marigold—*Tagetes* spp. (E)
Sunflower—*Helianthus annuus* (NZ)

B. Perennials

Carnation—*Dianthus caryophyllus* (E)
Chrysanthemum—*Chrysanthemum morifolium* (E)
Colorado columbine—*Aquilegia* spp. (N)
Coneflower—*Ratibida columnifera* (N)
Daylily (asphodel)—*Hemerocallis* spp. (E)
Globemallow—*Sphaeralcea incana* (scarlet) (N)
Hollyhock—*Alcea rosea* (E)
Indian paintbrush—*Castilleja integra* (N)
Maximilian's daisy—*Helianthus maximiliani* (NZ)
Penstemon—*Penstemon* spp. (N)
Phlox—*Phlox* spp. (E)
Shasta daisy—*Chrysanthemum maximum* (E)
Wooly yarrow—*Achillea* spp. (N, E)

C. Bulbs

Common hyacinth—*Hyacinthus orientalis* (E)
Daffodil—*Narcissus* 'King Alfred' (E)
Dutch crocus—*Crocus verus* (E)
Garden gladiolus—*Gladiolus hortulanus* (E)
Iris—*Iris* spp. (E, N)
Tulip—*Tulipa* spp. (E)

Hillcrest Park and golf course

CLOVIS

(founded in 1907), Melrose, and nearby communities

The countryside around Clovis is primarily a well-developed agricultural landscape. Curry County is a leading New Mexico farming area, with production almost evenly split between livestock and crops. Only Union County raises more cattle and calves. Curry is the state's leading wheat, sorghum, barley, and corn producer. Peanuts are also a major crop. Pleasant cultivated fields and pastures cover most of the land in the county. Much of the topography is somewhat flat or gently rolling plains.

The roads into Clovis are lined with aging rows of tough Siberian elms—good as windbreaks and welcome shade producers in the heat of summer. At 4260 feet (1300 m), the city is high and can be cold in the winter. The growing season is long, however (192 days on average), and annual rainfall is from 17 to 27 inches (425–675 mm) per year—quite high for New Mexico. Soils are typically rich and productive.

Globe willows are popular shade trees in Clovis. Texas oak, silver poplar, silver maple, desert willow, several ash species, purpleleaf plum, Austrian pine, Italian cypress, and mag-nolia are common landscape trees. Hawthorn, sotol, black-eyed Susan, Japanese barberry, agave, gladiolus, daylily, and flowering almond are widely planted shrub and accent species. The older high plains landscape of grama, buffalo grass, wheatgrass, yucca, and related species of the same plant association is almost nowhere reflected in the modern, man-made landscape. Undoubtedly the most influential historical landscape in Clovis (in all of eastern New Mexico, for that matter) is Hillcrest Park, an enormous regional public garden that contains a classic prairie park, multiple ballfields, a children's amusement ground, and a golf course. The oldest section of Hillcrest—the CCC/New Deal Frontier Pastoral Park—dates from the 1930s. It features extraordinary stonework, tiers of Siberian elms planted in grids, bluegrass lawns, a fenced sunken garden, and a locomotive. The golf course has attractive water features and very well-maintained tree plantings.

A growing number of new private homes around the city also feature attractive, often large gardens.

SELECTED BEST PLANTS FOR CLOVIS

These plant species grow very well in Clovis. For the sake of convenience and quick reference, each plant is listed as native (N), naturalized (NZ), or exotic (E). Other plants also will perform well in landscape and garden situations in and around Clovis. Please see the New Mexico Plant File for these species.

TREES

A. Deciduous Shade, Street, and Specialty Trees

Ash
  a. Modesto ash—*Fraxinus velutina* 'Modesto' (Arizona ash variety) (N)
  b. Green ash—*Fraxinus pennsylvanica* and varieties (E)
Paper birch—*Betula papyrifera* (E)
Catalpa
  a. Umbrella catalpa—*Catalpa bignonioides* 'Nana' (E)
  b. Western catalpa—*Catalpa speciosa* (E)
Chinaberry—*Melia azedarach* (E)
Cottonwood, Aspen, and Poplar: Trees of the Genus *Populus*
  a. Aspen—*Populus tremuloides* (N)
  b. Carolina poplar—*Populus canadensis* (E)
  c. Fremont cottonwood—*Populus fremontii* (N)
  d. Lanceleaf cottonwood—*Populus acuminata* (N)
  e. Plains cottonwood—*Populus sargenti* (N)
  f. White (silver) poplar—*Populus alba* (NZ)
American elm—*Ulmus americana* (E)
Ginkgo (maidenhair tree)—*Ginkgo biloba* (E)
Hackberry
  a. Common hackberry—*Celtis occidentalis* (E)
  b. Netleaf hackberry -*Celtis reticulata* (N)
Honey locust—*Gleditsia triacanthos inermis* varieties (E)
Locust
  a. Black locust—*Robinia pseudoacacia* (NZ)
  b. Hybrid locusts—*Robinia ambigua* varieties (E)
  c. New Mexico locust—*Robinia neomexicana* (N)
Maple and Box elder
  a. Box elder—*Acer negundo* (N)
  b. Rocky Mountain maple—*Acer glabrum* (N)
  c. Silver maple—*Acer saccharinum* (E)
Mulberry
  a. Fruitless mulberry—*Morus alba* (E)
  b. Weeping mulberry—*Morus alba* 'Pendula' (E)
Oak
  a. Southern live oak—*Quercus virginiana*(E)
  b. Texas oak—*Quercus texana* (E)
Pecan—*Carya illinoiensis* (E)
Russian olive—*Elaeagnus angustifolia* (NZ)
Silk tree—*Albizia jilibrissin* (E)
Western soapberry—*Sapindus drummondii* (N)
Sweet gum—*Liquidambar styraciflua* (E)
Sycamore (plane tree)
  a. American sycamore—*Platanus occidentalis* (E)
  b. London plane tree—*Platanus acerifolia* (E)
  c. Oriental plane tree—*Platanus orientalis* (E)
Willow
  a. Corkscrew willow—*Salix matsudana* 'Tortuosa' (E)
  b. Globe Navajo willow—*Salix matsudana* 'Navajo' (E)
  c. Peachleaf willow—*Salix amygdaloides* (N)
  d. Weeping willow—*Salix babylonica* (and other weeping willow species, E)

B. Flowering Ornamental Trees

Flowering crab—*Malus* 'Hopa' et al (E)
Desert willow—*Chilopsis linearis* (N)
Flowering peach—*Prunus persica* (E)
Bradford pear—*Pyrus calleryana* (E)
Purpleleaf plum—*Prunus cerasifera* (E)
Eastern redbud—*Cercis canadensis* (E)
Golden rain tree—*Koelreuteria paniculata* (E)
Salt cedar—*Tamarix chinensis* (NZ)
Smoke tree—*Cotinus coggygria* (E)

C. Evergreen Trees

Arizona cypress—*Cupressus arizonica* (N)
Douglas fir—*Pseudotsuga menziesii* (N)
Juniper
  a. Alligator juniper—*Juniperus deppeana* (N)
  b. Chinese juniper—*Juniperus chinensis* varieties (E)
  c. Eastern red cedar—*Juniperus virginiana* varieties (E)
  d. Rocky Mountain juniper—*Juniperus scopulorum* varieties (N)
Leyland false cypress—*Cupressocyparis leylandii* (E)
Magnolia
  a. Southern magnolia—*Magnolia grandiflora* (E)
  b. Saucer magnolia—*Magnolia soulangiana* (E)
Chinese windmill palm—*Trachycarpus fortunei* (E)
Pine
  a. Afghan pine—*Pinus eldarica* (E)
  b. Austrian pine—*Pinus nigra* (E)
  c. Japanese black pine—*Pinus thunbergiana* (E)
  d. Piñon pine—*Pinus edulis* (N)
  e. Scotch pine—*Pinus sylvestris* (E)
Spruce
  a. Blue spruce—*Picea pungens* (N)
  b. Engelmann spruce—*Picea engelmanni* (N)
Yucca
  a. Joshua tree—*Yucca brevifolia* (E)
  b. Palm yucca—*Yucca torreyi* (E)

SHRUBS

A. Deciduous

Flowering almond—*Prunus glandulosa* (E)
Althea (rose of Sharon)—*Hibiscus syriacus* (E)
Shrubby cinquefoil—*Potentilla fruticosa* (N)
Cotoneaster
  a. Cranberry cotoneaster—*Cotoneaster apiculatus* (E)
  b. Rock cotoneaster—*Cotoneaster horizontalis* (E)
  c. Rockspray cotoneaster—*Cotoneaster microphyllus* (E)
Currant and gooseberry—*Ribes* spp. (N, E)
Crape myrtle—*Lagerstroemia indica* (E)
Winged enonymus—*Euonymus alata* (E)
Shrub or tatarian honeysuckle—*Lonicera tatarica* (E)
Hop tree—*Ptelea trifoliolata* (N)
Flowering jasmine—*Jasminum nudiflorum* (E)
Common lilac—*Syringa vulgaris* (E)
Mountain mahogany—*Cercocarpus montanus* (N)
New Mexico olive—*Forestiera neomexicana* (N)
Rose—*Rosa* spp. (N, E)
Snowball—*Viburnum opulus* 'Roseum' (E)
Spirea
  a. Bridal wreath—*Spiraea prunifolia* (E)
  b. Van Houtte—*Spiraea vanhouttei* (E)
  c. Anthony Waterer—*Spiraea bumalda* 'Anthony Waterer' (E)
Sumac
  a. Skunkbush—*Rhus trilobata* (N)
  b. Smooth sumac—*Rhus glabra* (N)
  c. Staghorn sumac—*Rhus typhina* (E)
Weigela—*Weigela florida* (E)
Winterfat—*Ceratoides lanata* (N)

B. Evergreen

Aucuba—*Aucuba japonica* (E)

142

Barberry
    a. Colorado barberry—*Berberis fendleri* (N)
    b. Japanese barberry—*Berberis thunbergii* (E)
    c. Three-spine barberry—*Berberis wisleyensis* (E)
    d. Wintergreen barberry—*Berberis julianae* (E)
Beargrass—*Nolina microcarpa* (N)
Century plant—*Agave americana* (N)
Prickly pear—*Opuntia chlorotica* or *O. engelmannii* (N)
Parney cotoneaster—*Cotoneaster lacteus* (E)
Holly
    a. Wilson holly—*Ilex altaclarensis* 'Wilsonii' (E)
    b. Yaupon holly—*Ilex vomitoria* (E)
India hawthorn—*Rhaphiolepis indica* (E)
Chinese junipers
    a. Armstrong juniper—*Juniperus chinensis* 'Armstrong' (E)
    b. Pfitzer juniper—*Juniperus chinensis* 'Pfitzerana' (E)
    c. Sea Green juniper—*Juniperus chinensis* 'Sea Green' (E)
Common juniper—*Juniperus communis* (N)
Mahonia
    a. Algerita—*Mahonia haematocarpa* (N)
    b. Agritos—*Mahonia trifoliolata* (N)
    c. Oregon grape—*Mahonia aquifolium* (E, NZ)
    d. Creeping mahonia—*Mahonia repens* (E)
Nandina (heavenly bamboo)—*Nandina domestica* (E)
Ocotillo—*Fouquieria splendens* (N)
Photinia
    a. Chinese photinia—*Photinia serrulata* (E)
    b. Fraser's photinia—*Photinia fraseri* (E)
Mugo pine—*Pinus mugo* (E)
Waxleaf privet (ligustrum)—*Ligustrum japonicum* (E)
Silverberry—*Elaeagnus pungens* (E)
Sotol—*Dasylirion wheeleri* (N)
Yucca
    a. Spanish bayonet—*Yucca baccata* (N)
    b. Coral-flower yucca—*Hesperaloe parviflora* (E)

GROUND COVERS

A. Deciduous

Spring cinquefoil—*Potentilla tabernaemontani* (E)
Clover—*Trifolium* spp. (NZ, N)
Crown vetch—*Coronilla varia* (E, NZ)
Prairie sage—*Artemisia ludoviciana* (N)
Snow-in summer—*Cerastium tomentosum* (E)

B. Evergreen

Creeping euonymus—*Euonymus fortunei* (E)
Honeysuckle—*Lonicera japonica* varieties (E)
Horizontalis junipers
    a. Bar Harbor juniper—*Juniperus horizontalis* 'Bar Harbor' (E)
    b. Wilton carpet juniper—*Juniperus horizontalis* 'Wiltonii' (E)
Sabina junipers
    a. Broadmoor juniper—*Juniperus sabina* 'Broadmoor' (E)
    b. Tam (tammy) juniper—*Juniperus sabina* 'Tamariscifolia' (E)
Periwinkle—*Vinca major* and *Vinca minor* (E)
Santolina
    a. Green santolina—*Santolina virens* (E)
    b. Gray santolina—*Santolina chamaecyparissus* (E)
Sedum (stonecrop)—*Sedum* spp. (E, N)

GRASSES

A. Traditional Turf Species

Bluegrass—*Poa pratensis* (E, NZ)
Fescue—*Festuca* spp. (E, N)
Ryegrass—*Lolium* spp. (E)

B. Native Turf And General-Use Species

Buffalo grass—*Buchlöe dactyloides* (N)
Grama
    a. Black grama—*Bouteloua eriopoda* (N)
    b. Blue grama—*Bouteloua gracilis* (N)
    c. Sideoats grama—*Bouteloua curtipendula* (N)
Wheatgrass
    a. Western wheatgrass—*Agropyron smithii* (N)
    b. Crested wheatgrass—*Agropyron desertorum* (E, NZ)
    c. Pubescent wheatgrass—*Agropyron trichophorum* (N)

C. Ornamental Species

Sand dropseed—*Sporobolus cryptandrus* (N)
Blue fescue—*Festuca caesia* (E)
Fountain grass—*Pennisetum* spp. (E)
Pampas grass—*Cortaderia selloana* (E)
River cane—*Arundo donax* (NZ)
Purple threeawn—*Aristida longiseta* (N)

VINES

A. Deciduous

Morning glory—*Ipomoea tricolor* (E)
Silver lace vine—*Polygonum aubertii* (E)
Virginia creeper (et al)—*Parthenocissus quinquefolia* (N)
Wisteria—*Wisteria sinensis* (E)

B. Evergreen

English ivy—*Hedera helix* (E)
Honeysuckle—*Lonicera* spp. (E)

FLOWERS

A. Annuals

Purple aster—*Aster bigelovii* (N)
Geranium—*Pelargonium hortorum* (E)
Impatiens—*Impatiens wallerana* (E)
Marigold—*Tagetes* spp. (E)
Pansy—*Viola wittrockiana* (E)
Petunia—*Petunia* spp. (E)
Salvia—*Salvia* spp. (E)
Sunflower—*Helianthus annuus* (N)

B. Perennials

Desert baileya—*Baileya multiradiata* (N)
Carnation—*Dianthus caryophyllus* (E)
Colorado columbine—*Aquilegia* spp. (N)
Coneflower—*Ratibida columnifera* (N)
Daylily (asphodel)—*Hemerocallis* spp. (E)
Delphinium—*Delphinium belladonna* (E, N)
Geranium (cranesbill)—*Geranium* spp. (N)
Hollyhock—*Alcea rosea* (E, NZ)
Indian paintbrush—*Castilleja integra* (N)
Maximilian's daisy—*Helianthus maximiliani* (NZ)
Paperflower—*Psilostrophe tagetina* (N)
Penstemon—*Penstemon* spp. (N)
Phlox—*Phlox* spp. (E)
Primrose—*Primula vulgaris* (E)
Shasta daisy—*Chrysanthemum maximum* (E)

C. Bulbs

Canna—*Canna* spp. (E)
Daffodil—*Narcissus* 'King Alfred' (E)
Garden gladiolus—*Gladiolus hortulanus* (E)
Grape hyacinth—*Muscari armeniacum* (E)
Iris—*Iris* spp. (N, E)
Tulip—*Tulipa* spp. (E)

Colorful salvia, poppies, and green santolina against a backdrop of mugo pines and staghorn sumac in a Cortez courtyard

CORTEZ

(founded in 1886)

Cortez, Colorado, has the classic landscape features of the twentieth-century Rocky Mountain town. Siberian elm and Russian olive, ponderosa pine and globe willow, silver maple and Rocky Mountain juniper are found in private yards and business landscapes throughout the city. Green rabbitbrush, black locust, limber pine, currants, lobelia, columbine, pyracantha, various cotoneasters, and sunflowers are frequently found accents.

Most of Cortez's landscapes are modest home gardens. The city boasts a quite striking streetscape along Montezuma Avenue and a beautiful roadside park at the east end of town along U.S. 160. The wild landscape nearby is hilly or mountainous. Utah juniper, piñon pine, white fir, purshia, Gambel oak, snowberry, currants, New Mexico locust, rabbitbrush, various yuccas, and sand plum are among the most common plant species. The soils in the Montezuma Valley are fertile. This valley and the mesas and canyons near Cortez were the home of the Anasazi, the most sophisticated city-builders of ancient North America, who farmed it extensively to produce corn, beans, and squash. The Anasazi may also have produced crops of amaranth and Indian ricegrass, and they certainly harvested piñon nuts and sand plums. Modern farmers in Montezuma County have made a specialty of intensive pinto bean production.

Cortez sits at an elevation of 6200 feet (about 1900 m). The growing season is approximately 125 days, and average annual rainfall is about 13 inches (325 mm).

SELECTED BEST PLANTS FOR CORTEZ

These plant species grow very well in and around Cortez. For the sake of convenience and quick reference, each plant is listed as native (N), naturalized (NZ), or exotic (E). Other plants also will perform well in landscape and garden situations in the Cortez area. Please see the New Mexico Plant File for these species.

TREES

A. Deciduous Shade, Street, and Specialty Trees

Ash
    a. Green ash—*Fraxinus pennsylvanica* and varieties (E)
    b. White ash—*Fraxinus americana* and varieties (E)
Western catalpa—*Catalpa speciosa* (E)
Western chokecherry—*Prunus virginiana* (N)
Cottonwood, Aspen, and Poplar: Trees of the Genus *Populus*
    a. Aspen—*Populus tremuloides* (N)
    b. Carolina poplar—*Populus canadensis* (E)
    c. Lombardy poplar—*Populus nigra* 'Italica' (E)
    d. Narrowleaf cottonwood—*Populus angustifolia* (N)
Elm
    a. American elm—*Ulmus americana* (E)
    b. Siberian elm—*Ulmus pumila* (NZ, useful in very difficult situations)
Honey locust—*Gleditsia triacanthos inermis* varieties (E)
Locust
    a. Black locust—*Robinia pseudoacacia* (NZ)
    b. New Mexico locust—*Robinia neomexicana* (N)
Maple and Box elder
    a. Box elder—*Acer negundo* (E)
    b. Rocky Mountain maple—*Acer glabrum* (N)
    c. Silver maple—*Acer saccharinum* (E)
Gambel oak—*Quercus gambelii* (N)
Russian olive—*Elaeagnus angustifolia* (NZ)
Tree of heaven—*Ailanthus altissima* (NZ, used for shade in very difficult areas)
Willow
    a. Globe Navajo willow—*Salix matsudana* 'Navajo' (E)
    b. Weeping willow—*Salix babylonica* (and other weeping willow species, E)

B. Flowering Ornamental Trees

Flowering crab—*Malus* 'Hopa' et al (E)
Flowering peach—*Prunus persica* (E)
Purpleleaf plum—*Prunus cerasifera* (E)
Salt cedar—*Tamarix chinensis* (NZ)

C. Evergreen Trees

Douglas fir—*Pseudotsuga menziesii* (N)
Juniper
    a. Eastern red cedar—*Juniperus virginiana* varieties (E)
    b. Rocky Mountain juniper—*Juniperus scopulorum* varieties (N)
    c. Utah juniper—*Juniperus osteosperma* (N)

Pine
    a. Austrian pine—*Pinus nigra* (E)
    b. Bristlecone pine—*Pinus aristata* (N)
    c. Limber pine—*Pinus flexilis* (N)
    d. Piñon pine—*Pinus edulis* (N)
    e. Ponderosa pine—*Pinus ponderosa* (N)
    f. Scotch pine—*Pinus sylvestris* (E)
Spruce
    a. Blue spruce—*Picea pungens* (N)
    b. Engelmann spruce—*Picea engelmanni* (N)

SHRUBS

A. Deciduous

Althea (rose of Sharon)—*Hibiscus syriacus* (E)
Apache plume—*Fallugia paradoxa* (N)
Common butterfly bush—*Buddleia davidii* (E)
Shrubby cinquefoil—*Potentilla fruticosa* (N)
Rock cotoneaster—*Cotoneaster horizontalis* (E)
Currant and gooseberry—*Ribes* spp. (N)
Red osier dogwood—*Cornus stolonifera* (N)
Winged enonymus—*Euonymus alata* (E)
Fernbush—*Chamaebatiaria millefolium* (N)
Common lilac—*Syringa vulgaris* (E)
Mountain mahogany—*Cercocarpus montanus* (N)
New Mexico olive—*Forestiera neomexicana* (N)
Sand plum—*Prunus americana* (N)
Raspberry—*Rubus* spp. (E, N)
Rose—*Rosa* spp. (N, E)
Bridal wreath spirea—*Spiraea prunifolia* (N)
Sumac
    a. Skunkbush—*Rhus trilobata* (N)
    b. Smooth sumac—*Rhus glabra* (N)
    c. Staghorn sumac—*Rhus typhina* (E)

B. Evergreen

Japanese barberry—*Berberis thunbergii* (E)
Beargrass—*Nolina microcarpa* (N)
Chinese junipers
    a. Armstrong juniper—*Juniperus chinensis* 'Armstrong' (E)
    b. Pfitzer juniper—*Juniperus chinensis* 'Pfitzerana' (E)
Common juniper—*Juniperus communis* (N)
Oregon grape—*Mahonia aquifolium* (E)
Pyracantha (firethorn)—*Pyracantha* spp. (E)
Rubber rabbitbrush—*Chrysothamnus nauseosus* (N)
Sage
    a. Big sage (sagebrush)—*Artemisia tridentata* (N)
    b. Sand sage—*Artemisia filifolia* (N)
Fourwing saltbush—*Atriplex canescens* (N)
Yucca
    a. Narrowleaf yucca—*Yucca glauca* (N)
    b. Softblade yucca—*Yucca recurvifolia* (*Yucca pendula*) (N)
    c. Spanish bayonet—*Yucca baccata* (N)
    d. Coral-flower yucca—*Hesperaloe parviflora* (E)

GROUND COVERS

A. Deciduous

Spring cinquefoil—*Potentilla tabernaemontani* (E)
Clover—*Trifolium* spp. (NZ, N)
Cranberry cotoneaster—*Cotoneaster apiculatus* (E)
Mint—*Mentha* spp. (E, N, NZ)
Prairie sage—*Artemisia ludoviciana* (N)

B. Evergreen

Honeysuckle—*Lonicera japonica* varieties (E)
Juniper
Horizontalis junipers
    a. Andorra juniper—*Juniperus horizontalis plumosa* (E)
    b. Bar Harbor juniper—*Juniperus horizontalis* 'Bar Harbor' (E)c. Wilton carpet juniper—*Juniperus horizontalis* 'Wiltonii' (E)
Sabina junipers
    a. Broadmoor juniper—*Juniperus sabina* 'Broadmoor' (E)
    b. Buffalo juniper—*Juniperus sabina* 'Buffalo' (E)
    c. Tam (tammy) juniper—*Juniperus sabina* 'Tamariscifolia' (E)
Kinnickinnick (mountain bearberry)—*Arctostaphylos uva-ursi* (N)
Creeping mahonia—*Mahonia repens* (N)
Strawberry—*Fragaria* spp. (N, E)

GRASSES

A. Traditional Turf Species

Bluegrass—*Poa pratensis* (N)
Fescue—*Festuca* spp. (E)
Ryegrass—*Lolium* spp. (E)

B. Native Turf And General-Use Species

Buffalo grass—*Buchlöe dactyloides* (N)
Galleta—*Hilaria jamesii* (N)
Blue grama—*Bouteloua gracilis* (N)

C. Ornamental Species

Blue fescue—*Festuca caesia* (E)
Purple threeawn—*Aristida longiseta* (N)

VINES

A. Deciduous

Clematis—*Clematis jackmanni* (N, E)
Trumpet vine—*Campsis radicans* (E)
Virginia creeper (et al)—*Parthenocissus quinquefolia* (N, E)
Wisteria—*Wisteria sinensis* (E)

B. Evergreen

English ivy—*Hedera helix* (E, NZ)
Honeysuckle—*Lonicera* spp. (E)

FLOWERS

A. Annuals

Ageratum—*Ageratum houstonianum* (E)
Purple aster—*Aster bigelovii* (N)
Coleus—*Coleus x hybridus* (E)
Four o'clock—*Mirabilis jalapa* (E)
Gaillardia (blanketflower, firewheel)—*Gaillardia pulchella* (E)
Impatiens—*Impatiens wallerana* (E)
Lisianthus—*Eustoma grandiflorum* (E)
Marigold—*Tagetes* spp. (E)
Petunia—*Petunia* spp. (E)
Snapdragon—*Antirrhinum majus* (E)
Sunflower—*Helianthus annuus* (E)
Annual vinca (Madagascar periwinkle)—*Catharanthus roseus* (E)
Viola (Johnny jump-ups)—*Viola* spp. (E)
Wallflower—*Erysimum capitatum* (N)

B. Perennials

Colorado columbine—*Aquilegia* spp(N)
Delphinium—*Delphinium belladonna* (E, N)
Dusty miller—*Senecio cineraria* (E)
Blue flax—*Linum perenne* (N)
Indian paintbrush—*Castilleja integra* (N)
Jimsonweed (datura, sacred datura)—*Datura meteloides* (N)
Lobelia—*Lobelia erinus* (E)
Maximilian's daisy—*Helianthus maximiliani* (NZ)
Penstemon—*Penstemon* spp. (N)
Phlox—*Phlox* spp. (E)
California poppy—*Eschscholzia californica* (and *E. mexicana*) (E)
Shasta daisy—*Chrysanthemum maximum* (E)
Violet—*Viola odorata* (N, E)

C. Bulbs

Common hyacinth—*Hyacinthus orientalis* (E)
Dutch crocus—*Crocus verus* (E)
Daffodil—*Narcissus* 'King Alfred' (E)
Garden gladiolus—*Gladiolus hortulanus* (E)
Grape hyacinth—*Muscari armeniacum* (E)
Iris—*Iris* spp. (N, E)
Tulip—*Tulipa* spp. (E)

Luna County Court-house Square, with its quite large native soapberry trees

DEMING

(founded about 1880), including Columbus, New Mexico, and Palomas, Chihuahua

A great deal of fruit and vegetable farming is carried on around Deming thanks to irrigation, but the town was founded in a natural dry grassland in the northern reaches of the Chihuahuan Desert.

The nearby landscape is quite spectacular. Local mountain ranges hold stands of alligator juniper, Arizona cypress, Arizona alder, netleaf hackberry, Arizona ash, Arizona walnut, ocotillo, and multiple species of oaks. Desert willow, seepwillow, soapberry, very tall soaptree yucca, beargrass, and several species of cacti are found in the desert and its washes. Alkali sacaton, sand dropseed, Indian ricegrass, gramas, and the ubiquitous mesquite and creosote are also common in the countryside near Deming.

Deming has a growing season of 193 days, very few of them cloudy. The city lies at 4305 feet (1300 m). Annual rainfall can fluctuate wildly from as little as 8.5 inches (220 mm) to nearly 17 inches (425 mm). Typical soils are thin and alkaline. Deming is at the edge of a closed basin. The Rio Mimbres, normally dry, flows south past Deming from the Black Range after periods of heavy rain or snow.

Luna County ranks seventh in the state in agricultural production. Farm output is nearly evenly split between livestock and crops. A great deal of cotton is raised in the county, along with much chile, vegetables, and increasing crops of nuts. Cattle and calves are widely grazed.

Pecan, desert willow, mulberries, Italian cypress, Aleppo pine, white poplar, cottonwoods, cedar of Lebanon, deodar cedar, and Afghan pine are popular landscape trees. Agave, barrel, prickly pear, and cholla cactus, various juniper species, saltbush, sotol, ocotillo, Texas ranger, bird of paradise, and pampas grass are widely grown ornamental shrubs. The Arizona sycamore and Arizona cypress are commonly used and well-adapted native trees. California poppies, tulips, cannas, trumpet vines, and California and Chinese windmill palms are frequently used local accent plants.

South Granite Street has a pleasant, well-established residential streetscape, with old street trees in a center median edged by low stone walls. But easily the most impressive historical landscape in Deming is the courthouse square, shaded by the most enormous western soapberry trees in New Mexico. The square is irrigated by an elaborate open sluice and ditch system, now aging rapidly. It is probably the most popular and influential open space in Luna County.

SELECTED BEST PLANTS FOR DEMING

These plant species grow very well in and around Deming. For the sake of convenience and quick reference, each plant is listed as native (N), naturalized (NZ), or exotic (E). Other plants also will perform well in landscape and garden situations in the Deming area. Please see the New Mexico Plant File for these species.

TREES

A. Deciduous Shade, Street, and Specialty Trees

Ash
    a. Arizona ash—*Fraxinus velutina* (N)
    b. Modesto ash—*Fraxinus velutina* 'Modesto' (Arizona ash variety) (N)
    c. White ash—*Fraxinus americana* and varieties (E)
Catalpa
    a. Umbrella catalpa—*Catalpa bignonioides* 'Nana' (E)
    b. Western catalpa—*Catalpa speciosa* (E)
Chinaberry—*Melia azedarach* (E)
Cottonwood, Aspen, and Poplar: Trees of the Genus *Populus*
    a. Carolina poplar—*Populus canadensis* (E)
    b. Fremont cottonwood—*Populus fremontii* (N)
    c. Rio Grande cottonwood—*Populus fremontii* 'Wislizeni' (N)
    d. White (silver) poplar—*Populus alba* (NZ)
Elm
    a. American elm—*Ulmus americana* (E)
    b. Chinese elm—*Ulmus parvifolia* (E)
Honey locust—*Gleditsia triacanthos inermis* varieties (E)
Black locust—*Robinia pseudoacacia* (NZ)
Mesquite—*Prosopis glandulosa* (N)
Mulberry
    a. Fruitless mulberry—*Morus alba* (E)
    b. Weeping mulberry—*Morus alba* 'Pendula' (E)
Osage orange—*Maclura pomifera* (NZ)
Pecan—*Carya illinoiensis* (E)
Pistache—Pistachio
    a. Chinese pistache—*Pistacia chinensis* (E)
    b. Pistachio—*Pistacia vera* (E)
Russian olive—*Elaeagnus angustifolia* (NZ)
Silk tree—*Albizia jilibrissin* (E)
Sycamore (plane tree)
    a. Arizona sycamore—*Platanus wrightii* (N)
    b. London plane tree—*Platanus acerifolia* (E)
Tree of heaven—*Ailanthus altissima* (NZ, used for shade in very difficult locales)
Arizona walnut—*Juglans major* (N)
Willow
    a. Corkscrew willow—*Salix matsudana* 'Tortuosa' (E)
    b. Globe Navajo willow—*Salix matsudana* 'Navajo' (E)
    c. Peachleaf willow—*Salix amygdaloides* (N)
    d. Weeping willow—*Salix babylonica* (and other weeping willow species, E)

B. Flowering Ornamental Trees

Flowering Crab—*Malus* 'Hopa' et al (E)
Mexican elder—*Sambucus caerulea neomexicana* (N)
Flowering peach—*Prunus persica* (E)
Purpleleaf plum—*Prunus cerasifera* (E)
Eastern redbud—*Cercis canadensis* (E)
Salt cedar—*Tamarix chinensis* (NZ)
Smoke tree—*Cotinus coggygria* (E)
Vitex (chaste tree)—*Vitex agnus-castus* (E)

C. Evergreen Trees

Cedar
    a. Atlas cedar—*Cedrus atlantica* (E)
    b. Cedar of Lebanon—*Cedrus libani* (E)
    c. Deodar cedar—*Cedrus deodara* (E)
Cypress
    a. Arizona cypress—*Cupressus arizonica* (N)
    b. Italian cypress—*Cupressus sempervirens* (E)
Eucalyptus (cider gum)—*Eucalyptus gunnii* (E)
Juniper
    a. Alligator juniper—*Juniperus deppeana* (N)
    b. Chinese juniper—*Juniperus chinensis* varieties (E)
    c. Eastern red cedar—*Juniperus virginiana* varieties (E)
    d. Rocky Mountain juniper—*Juniperus scopulorum* varieties (N)
Leyland false cypress—*Cupressocyparis leylandii* (E)
Madrone—*Arbutus texana* (N)
Magnolia
    a. Southern magnolia—*Magnolia grandiflora* (E)
    b. Saucer magnolia—*Magnolia soulangiana* (E)
Palm
    a. California fan palm—*Washingtonia filifera* (E)
    b. Chinese windmill palm—*Trachycarpus fortunei* (E)
    c. Mediterranean fan palm—*Chamaerops humilis* (E)
Pine
    a. Afghan pine—*Pinus eldarica* (E)
    b. Aleppo pine—*Pinus halepensis* (E)
    c. Italian stone pine—*Pinus pinea* (E)
    d. Japanese black pine—*Pinus thunbergiana* (E)
    e. Piñon pine—*Pinus edulis* (N)
Yucca
    a. Palm yucca—*Yucca torreyi* (N)
    b. Soaptree yucca—*Yucca elata* (N)

SHRUBS

A. Deciduous

Althea (Rose of Sharon)—*Hibiscus syriacus* (E)
Bird of paradise—*Caesalpinia gilliesii* (NZ)
Spanish broom—*Spartium junceum* (E)
Cotoneaster
    a. Cranberry cotoneaster—*Cotoneaster apiculatus* (E)
    b. Rock cotoneaster—*Cotoneaster horizontalis* (E)
    c. Rockspray cotoneaster—*Cotoneaster microphyllus* (E)

Crape myrtle—*Lagerstroemia indica* (E)
Winged enonymus—*Euonymus alata* (E)
Cliff fendlerbush—*Fendlera rupicola* (N)
Fernbush—*Chamaebatiaria millefolium* (N)
Edible fig—*Ficus carica* (E)
Forsythia—*Forsythia* spp. (E)
Flowering jasmine—*Jasminum nudiflorum* (E)
Common lilac—*Syringa vulgaris* (E)
Screwbean mesquite—*Prosopis pubescens* (N)
Mountain mahogany—*Cercocarpus montanus* (N)
New Mexico olive—*Forestiera neomexicana* (N)
Pomegranate—*Punica granatum* (E)
Cistena plum—*Prunus cistena* (E)
Pomegranate—*Punica granatum* (E)
Rose—*Rosa* spp. (E, N)
Bridal wreath—*Spiraea prunifolia* (E)
Sumac
    a. Littleleaf sumac—*Rhus microphylla* (N)
    b. Skunkbush—*Rhus trilobata* (N)
    c. Smooth sumac—*Rhus glabra* (N)

B. Evergreen

Agave (century plant, mescal)
    a. Century plant—*Agave americana* (N)
    b. Parry agave—*Agave parryi* (N)
    c. Lechugilla—*Agave lechugilla* (N)
Cactus
    a. Claret cup—*Echinocereus triglochidiatus* (N)
    b. Common cholla—*Opuntia imbricata* (N)
    c. Prickly pear—*Opuntia chlorotica* or *O. engelmannii* (N)
Creosotebush—*Larrea tridentata* (N)
Yaupon holly—*Ilex vomitoria* (E)
India hawthorn—*Rhaphiolepis indica* (E)
Chinese junipers
    a. Armstrong juniper—*Juniperus chinensis* 'Armstrong' (E)
    b. Pfitzer juniper—*Juniperus chinensis* 'Pfitzerana' (E)
    c. Sea Green juniper—*Juniperus chinensis* 'Sea Green' (E)
Mahonia
    a. Algerita—*Mahonia haematocarpa* (N)
    b. Agritos—*Mahonia trifoliolata* (N)
Mormon tea—*Ephedra* spp. (N)
Nandina (heavenly bamboo)—*Nandina domestica* (E)
Ocotillo—*Fouquieria splendens* (N)
Oleander—*Nerium oleander* (E)
Chinese photinia—*Photinia serrulata* (E)
Pittosporum (tobira)—*Pittosporum tobira* (E)
Pyracantha (firethorn)—*Pyracantha* spp. (E)
Rubber rabbitbrush—*Chrysothamnus nauseosus* (N)
Sage
    a. Big sage (sagebrush)—*Artemisia tridentata* (N)
    b. Sand sage—*Artemisia filifolia* (N)
Fourwing saltbush—*Atriplex canescens* (N)
Seepwillow -*Baccharis sarothroides* (N)
Sotol—*Dasylirion wheeleri* (N)
Texas ranger—*Leucophyllum frutescens* (E)
Yucca
    a. Coral-flower yucca—*Hesperaloe parviflora* (E)
    b. Softblade yucca—*Yucca recurvifolia* (*Yucca pendula*) (E)
    c. Spanish bayonet—*Yucca baccata* (N)

GROUND COVERS

A. Deciduous

Clover—*Trifolium* spp. (NZ, N)
Cranberry cotoneaster—*Cotoneaster apiculatus* (E)
Crown vetch—*Coronilla varia* (E, NZ)
Prairie sage—*Artemisia ludoviciana* (N)
Snow-in summer—*Cerastium tomentosum* (E)

B. Evergreen

Bearberry cotoneaster—*Cotoneaster dammeri* (E)
Dwarf coyotebrush—*Baccharis pilularis* (E)
Creeping euonymus—*Euonymus fortunei* (E)
Dichondra—*Dichondra micrantha* (E)
Germander—*Teucrium chamaedrys* 'Prostratum' (E)
Honeysuckle—*Lonicera japonica* varieties (E)
Horizontalis junipers
    a. Andorra juniper—*Juniperus horizontalis plumosa* (E)
    b. Bar Harbor juniper—*Juniperus horizontalis* 'Bar Harbor' (E)
    c. Wilton carpet juniper—*Juniperus horizontalis* 'Wiltonii' (E)
Sabina junipers
    a. Broadmoor juniper—*Juniperus sabina* 'Broadmoor' (E)
    b. Buffalo juniper—*Juniperus sabina* 'Buffalo' (E)
    c. Tam (tammy) juniper—*Juniperus sabina* 'Tamariscifolia' (E)
San Jose juniper—*Juniperus chinensis* 'San Jose' (E)
Lilyturf (liriope)—*Liriope spicata* (E)
Compact nandina—*Nandina domestica* 'Harbor dwarf' (E)
Periwinkle—*Vinca major* and *Vinca minor* (E)
Pussytoes—*Antennaria parviflora* (N)
Rosemary—*Rosmarinus officinalis* (E)
Santolina
    a. Green santolina—*Santolina virens* (E)
    b. Gray santolina—*Santolina chamaecyparissus* (E)
Sedum (stonecrop)—*Sedum* spp. (N, E)
Japanese spurge—*Pachysandra terminalis* (E)

GRASSES

A. Traditional Turf Species

Bermuda
    a. African bermuda—*Cynodon transvaalensis* (E, NZ)
    b. Common bermuda—*Cynodon dactylon* (E, NZ)
Ryegrass—*Lolium* spp. (E)

B. Native Turf And General-Use Species

Galleta—*Hilaria jamesii* (N)
Grama
    a. Black grama—*Bouteloua eriopoda* (N)
    b. Blue grama—*Bouteloua gracilis* (N)
    c. Sideoats grama—*Bouteloua curtipendula* (N)
Wheatgrass
    a. Western wheatgrass—*Agropyron smithii* (N)
    b. Pubescent wheatgrass—*Agropyron trichophorum* (E)

Rio Mimbres near Deming

C. Ornamental Species

Alkali sacaton—*Sporobolus airoides* (N)
Sand dropseed—*Sporobolus cryptandrus* (N)
Pampas grass—*Cortaderia selloana* (E)
River cane—*Arundo donax* (NZ)
Purple threeawn—*Aristida longiseta* (N)

VINES

A. Deciduous

Boston ivy—*Parthenocissus tricuspidata* (E)
Trumpet vine—*Campsis radicans* (E)
Virginia creeper (et al)—*Parthenocissus quinquefolia* (N)

B. Evergreen

Algerian ivy—*Hedera canariensis* (E)
English ivy—*Hedera helix* (E)
Honeysuckle—*Lonicera* spp. (E)

FLOWERS

A. Annuals

Ageratum—*Ageratum houstonianum* (E)
Purple aster—*Aster bigelovii* (N)
Bedding begonia (wax begonia)—*Begonia* spp. (E)
Coleus—*Coleus x hybridus* (E)
Cosmos—*Cosmos* spp. (E)
Four o'clock—*Mirabilis jalapa* (E)
Gaillardia (blanketflower, firewheel)—*Gaillardia pulchella* (N)
Impatiens—*Impatiens wallerana* (E)
Pansy—*Viola wittrockiana* (E)
Petunia—*Petunia* spp. (E)
Snapdragon—*Antirrhinum majus* (E)
Sunflower—*Helianthus annuus* (N)
Annual vinca (Madagascar periwinkle)—*Catharanthus roseus* (E)
Wallflower—*Erysimum capitatum* (N)

B. Perennials

Desert baileya—*Baileya multiradiata* (N)
Chrysanthemum—*Chrysanthemum morifolium* (E)
Colorado columbine—*Aquilegia* spp. (N)
Coneflower—*Ratibida columnifera* (N)
Daylily (asphodel)—*Hemerocallis* spp. (E)
Delphinium—*Delphinium belladonna* (E, N)
Dusty miller—*Senecio cineraria* (E)
Fendler's sundrops—*Calylophus hartwegii fendleri* (N)
Geranium (cranesbill)—*Geranium* spp.(N)
Globemallow—*Sphaeralcea incana* (scarlet) (N)
Hollyhock—*Alcea rosea* (E, NZ)
Indian paintbrush—*Castilleja integra* (N)
Jimsonweed (datura, sacred datura)—*Datura meteloides* (N)
Lobelia—*Lobelia erinus* (E)
Maximilian's daisy—*Helianthus maximiliani* (NZ)
Paperflower—*Psilostrophe tagetina* (N)
Penstemon—*Penstemon* spp. (N)
Phlox—*Phlox* spp. (E)
California poppy—*Eschscholzia californica* (& *E. mexicana*) (E, N)
Primrose—*Primula vulgaris* (E)
Shasta daisy—*Chrysanthemum maximum* (E)
Spectaclepod—*Dithyrea wislizenii* (N)
Wooly yarrow—*Achillea* spp. (N, E).

C. Bulbs

Canna—*Canna* spp. (E)
Daffodil—*Narcissus* 'King Alfred' (E)
Garden gladiolus—*Gladiolus hortulanus* (E)
Iris—*Iris* spp. (E, N)
Tulip—*Tulipa* spp. (E)

Park in Durango

DURANGO
(founded in 1880)

Durango sits in a very appealing location on a clear river at the foot of the La Plata Mountains in southwestern Colorado. The piñon-juniper uplands of northern New Mexico and southern Colorado give way here on three sides to the typical Transition Zone ponderosa pine-Gambel oak forests of the higher mountains.

Livestock grazing and bean and alfalfa farming, as well as some fruit growing, are common agricultural activities in La Plata County. Water in dependable quantity is usually available because of good annual precipitation in the nearby mountains. The growing season is, however, relatively short at a little over 100 days. Soils can be fertile but may be stony, alkaline, or clayey as well. Durango's altitude is quite high at 6500 feet (2000 m).

Silver maple, box elder, Siberian elm, American elm, blue spruce, Engelmann spruce, flowering crab, and narrowleaf cottonwood are very widely planted landscape trees. They are resistant to cold and grow well in Durango's climate. The city is awash in flowers in spring and summer. Wild purple thistles, columbines, lilies, roses, sunflowers, snapdragons, daylilies, spirea, yarrow, shrubby cinquefoil, scarlet bugler, beebalm, and Rocky Mountain penstemons are among the most popular of these. Frequent late-summer showers also benefit serviceberry, currants, scrub oak, mugo pine, skunkbush, snowberry, New Mexico locust, and other shrubs that flourish here. Dusty miller is a consistent garden favorite.

The most influential historic landscapes in Durango are undoubtedly the city's old parks, some dating to the 1920s or earlier, which are often planted in American and other elm species. Fassbinder Park is a good example. Durango's parks are typically small but intensely green, very shady, and informal. Lush streetscapes such as those found along Third Avenue add a great deal to the landscape quality of the city.

Good contemporary landscapes include many small private or commercial gardens, often planted in bright annuals. Foxtail (bristlecone) pine, limber pine, alpine fir, and mountain ash are found as extraordinary accent trees. The campus of Fort Lewis College also contains several appealing and well-maintained open spaces filled with good selections of trees, shrubs, and grasses.

SELECTED BEST PLANTS FOR DURANGO

These plant species grow very well in Durango. For the sake of convenience and quick reference, each plant is listed as native (N), naturalized (NZ), or exotic (E). Other plants also will perform well in landscape and garden situations in and around Durango. Please see the New Mexico Plant File for these species.

TREES

A. Deciduous Shade, Street, and Specialty Trees

Green ash—*Fraxinus pennsylvanica* and varieties (E)
Paper birch—*Betula papyrifera* (E)
Western catalpa—*Catalpa speciosa* (E)
Western chokecherry—*Prunus virginiana* (N)
Cottonwood, Aspen, and Poplar: Trees of the Genus *Populus*
    a. Aspen—*Populus tremuloides* (N)
    b. Narrowleaf cottonwood—*Populus angustifolia* (N)
    c. Rio Grande cottonwood—*Populus fremontii* 'Wislizeni' (N)
    d. White (silver) poplar—*Populus alba* (NZ)
American elm—*Ulmus americana* (E)
Hawthorn—*Crataegus* spp. (E,N)
Honey locust—*Gleditsia triacanthos inermis* varieties (E)
Littleleaf linden—*Tilia cordata* (E)
Locust
    a. Black locust—*Robinia pseudoacacia* (NZ)
    b. New Mexico locust—*Robinia neomexicana* (N)
Maple and Box elder
    a. Box elder—*Acer negundo* (N)
    b. Norway maple—*Acer platanoides* (E)
    c. Silver maple—*Acer saccharinum* (E)
    d. Sycamore-leaf maple—*Acer pseudoplatanus* (E)
European mountain ash—*Sorbus aucuparia* (E)
Gambel oak—*Quercus gambelii* (N)
Russian olive—*Elaeagnus angustifolia* (NZ)
Willow
    a. Corkscrew willow—*Salix matsudana* 'Tortuosa' (E)
    b. Globe Navajo willow—*Salix matsudana* 'Navajo' (E)
    c. Peachleaf willow—*Salix amygdaloides* (N)
    d. Weeping willow—*Salix babylonica* (and other weeping willow species E)

B. Flowering Ornamental Trees

Flowering cherry—*Prunus serrulata* et al (E)
Flowering crab—*Malus* 'Hopa' et al (E)
Hawthorn—*Crataegus* spp. (E,N)
Flowering peach—*Prunus persica* (E)
Bradford pear—*Pyrus calleryana* (E)
Purpleleaf plum—*Prunus cerasifera* (E)
Salt cedar—*Tamarix chinensis* (NZ)
Smoke tree—*Cotinus coggygria* (E)

C. Evergreen Trees

Douglas fir—*Pseudotsuga menziesii* (N)
White fir—*Abies concolor* (N)
Leyland false cypress—*Cupressocyparis leylandii* (E)
Pine
    a. Austrian pine—*Pinus nigra* (E)
    b. Bristlecone pine—*Pinus aristata* (N)
    c. Limber pine—*Pinus flexilis* (N)
    d. Piñon pine—*Pinus edulis* (N)
    e. Ponderosa pine—*Pinus ponderosa* (N)
    f. Scotch pine—*Pinus sylvestris* (E)
Spruce
    a. Blue spruce—*Picea pungens* (N)
    b. Engelmann spruce—*Picea engelmanni* (N)

SHRUBS

A. Deciduous

Althea (Rose of Sharon)—*Hibiscus syriacus* (E)
Apache plume—*Fallugia paradoxa* (N)
Shrubby cinquefoil—*Potentilla fruticosa* (N)
Cotoneaster
    a. Cranberry cotoneaster—*Cotoneaster apiculatus* (E)
    b. Rock cotoneaster—*Cotoneaster horizontalis* (E)
    c. Rockspray cotoneaster—*Cotoneaster microphyllus* (E)
Forsythia—*Forsythia* spp. (E)
Shrub or Tatarian honeysuckle—*Lonicera tatarica* (E)
Flowering jasmine—*Jasminum nudiflorum* (E)
Common lilac—*Syringa vulgaris* (E)
Mountain mahogany—*Cercocarpus montanus* (N)
Cistena plum—*Prunus cistena* (E)
Sand plum—*Prunus americana* (N)
Rose—*Rosa* spp. (N, E)
Spirea
    a. Bridal wreath—*Spiraea prunifolia* (E)
    b. Anthony Waterer—*Spiraea bumalda* 'Anthony Waterer' (E)
Sumac
    a. Skunkbush—*Rhus trilobata* (N)
    b. Smooth sumac—*Rhus glabra* (N)
    c. Staghorn sumac—*Rhus typhina* (E)
Winterfat—*Ceratoides lanata* (N)

B. Evergreen

Barberry
    a. Colorado barberry—*Berberis fendleri* (N)
    b. Japanese barberry—*Berberis thunbergii* (E)
    c. Three-spine barberry—*Berberis wisleyensis* (E)
    d. Wintergreen barberry—*Berberis julianae* (E)
Chinese junipers
    a. Armstrong juniper—*Juniperus chinensis* 'Armstrong' (E)
    b. Pfitzer juniper—*Juniperus chinensis* 'Pfitzerana' (E)
Common juniper—*Juniperus communis* (N)
Oregon grape—*Mahonia aquifolium* (E)
Mugo pine—*Pinus mugo* (E)
Photinia
    a. Chinese photinia—*Photinia serrulata* (E)
    b. Fraser's photinia—*Photinia fraseri* (E)
Pyracantha (firethorn)—*Pyracantha* spp. (E)
Rubber rabbitbrush—*Chrysothamnus nauseosus* (N)
Big sage (sagebrush)—*Artemisia tridentata* (N)
Yucca
    a. Narrowleaf yucca—*Yucca glauca* (N)
    b. Spanish bayonet—*Yucca baccata* (N)

GROUND COVERS

A. Deciduous

Spring cinquefoil—*Potentilla tabernaemontani* (E)
Clover—*Trifolium* spp. (NZ, N)
Cranberry cotoneaster—*Cotoneaster apiculatus* (E)
Mint—*Mentha* spp. (E, N, NZ)
Prairie sage—*Artemisia ludoviciana* (N)

B. Evergreen

Bearberry cotoneaster—*Cotoneaster dammeri* (N)
Horizontalis junipers
    a. Andorra juniper—*Juniperus horizontalis
       plumosa* (E)
    b. Bar Harbor juniper—*Juniperus horizontalis* 'Bar
       Harbor' (E)c. Wilton carpet juniper—*Juniperus
       horizontalis* 'Wiltonii' (E)
Sabina junipers
    a. Broadmoor juniper—*Juniperus sabina*
       'Broadmoor' (E)
    b. Buffalo juniper—*Juniperus sabina* 'Buffalo' (E)
    c. Tam (tammy) juniper—*Juniperus sabina*
       'Tamariscifolia' (E)
San Jose juniper—*Juniperus chinensis* 'San Jose' (E)
Kinnickinnick (mountain bearberry)—*Arctostaphylos
    uva-ursi* (N)
Blue leadwort—*Ceratostigma plumbaginoides* (E)
Creeping mahonia—*Mahonia repens* (N)
Periwinkle—*Vinca major* and *Vinca minor* (E)
Strawberry—*Fragaria* spp. (N)

GRASSES

A. Traditional Turf Species

Bentgrass—*Agrostis* spp. (E)
Bluegrass—*Poa pratensis* (NZ)
Fescue—*Festuca* spp. (E, N)
Ryegrass—*Lolium* spp. (E)

B. Native Turf And General-Use Species

Galleta—*Hilaria jamesii* (N)
Grama
    a. Blue grama—*Bouteloua gracilis* (N)
    b. Sideoats grama—*Bouteloua curtipendula* (N)
Wheatgrass
    a. Western wheatgrass—*Agropyron smithii* (N)
    b. Crested wheatgrass—*Agropyron desertorum*
       (E, NZ)
    c. Pubescent wheatgrass—*Agropyron
       trichophorum* (N)

C. Ornamental Species

Blue fescue—*Festuca caesia* (E)
Indian ricegrass—*Oryzopsis hymenoides* (N)
Purple threeawn—*Aristida longiseta* (N)

VINES

A. Deciduous

Clematis—*Clematis jackmanni* (E)
Morning glory—*Ipomoea tricolor* (E)
Trumpet vine—*Campsis radicans* (E)
Virginia creeper (et al)—*Parthenocissus quinquefolia*
    (N, E)
Wisteria—*Wisteria sinensis* (E)

B. Evergreen

English ivy—*Hedera helix* (E)
Honeysuckle—*Lonicera* spp. (E)

FLOWERS

A. Annuals

Ageratum—*Ageratum houstonianum* (E)
Gaillardia (blanketflower, firewheel)—*Gaillardia
    pulchella* (N)
Geranium—*Pelargonium hortorum* (E)
Impatiens—*Impatiens wallerana* (E)
Lisianthus—*Eustoma grandiflorum* (E)
Marigold—*Tagetes* spp. (E)
Pansy—*Viola wittrockiana* (E)
Petunia—*Petunia* spp. (E)
Snapdragon—*Antirrhinum majus* (E)
Sunflower—*Helianthus annuus* (N)
Annual vinca (Madagascar periwinkle)—*Catharanthus
    roseus* (E)

B. Perennials

Colorado columbine—*Aquilegia* spp. (N)
Blue flax—*Linum perenne* (N)
Geranium (cranesbill)—*Geranium* spp. (N)
Globemallow—*Sphaeralcea incana* (scarlet) (N)
Daylily (asphodel)—*Hemerocallis* spp. (E)
Delphinium—*Delphinium belladonna* (N)
Hollyhock—*Alcea rosea* (E, NZ)
Indian paintbrush—*Castilleja integra* (N)
Lobelia—*Lobelia erinus* (E)
Maximilian's daisy—*Helianthus maximiliani* (NZ)
Penstemon—*Penstemon* spp. (N)
California poppy—*Eschscholzia californica* (and *E.
    mexicana*, E; also
Iceland poppies, *Papaver nudicaule*)
Shasta daisy—*Chrysanthemum maximum* (E)
Wooly yarrow—*Achillea* spp. (N)

C. Bulbs

Common hyacinth—*Hyacinthus orientalis* (E)
Daffodil—*Narcissus* 'King Alfred' (E)
Dutch crocus—*Crocus verus* (E)
Garden gladiolus—*Gladiolus hortulanus* (E)
Iris—*Iris* spp. (N, E)
Ranunculus—*Ranunculus asiaticus* (E)
Tulip—*Tulipa* spp. (E)

*Courtyard garden
with palms as a feature*

EL PASO

including Ciudad Juárez, Chihuahua

El Paso, Texas, is an enormous Southwestern city wrapped around the southern tip of the Franklin Mountains. Although a nearby mission was established in 1682, El Paso proper dates from about 1827. Its climate is dry and sunny. Annual precipitation ranges from about 8 to 14 inches (200 mm to 350 mm). Soils tend to be thin and stony, alkaline, and often clayey. The growing season is around 200 days. The city sits at an altitude of 3762 feet (1150 m), which frequently leads to spells of snow and cold rain in the winter.

Directly across the Rio Grande is Ciudad Juárez, the largest city in the state of Chihuahua and also the largest Mexican city on the U.S. border. Its climate, of course, is the same as El Paso's.

The countryside around El Paso is largely made up of desert and mountains. Sotol, desert willow, several agave species, Torrey yucca, prickly pear, ocotillo, cholla, soaptree yucca, Spanish dagger, and *tornillo* (screwbean mesquite) are common upland plants. Creosote, mesquite, littleleaf sumac, snakeweed, alkali sacaton, various cacti, fourwing saltbush, a number of grama species, buffalo grass, Mormon tea (*cañutillo*), sunflower, vine mesquite, and globemallow are frequently found in the foothills and lowland areas. Along the Rio Grande, which is rigidly channeled here, Rio Grande cottonwood, willows, seepwillow, salt cedar, saltgrass, and fourwing saltbush are the typical vegetation. Dalea species, blackfoot daisy, paperflower, and spectaclepod are common summer accents in the foothills and along the benches above the river.

The lower Mesilla Valley and the general El Paso Valley area are quite fertile. A great deal of dairy farming and cattle and calf production is carried on here. Agricultural crops include cotton, alfalfa, onions, chile, cantaloupes, lettuce, tomatoes, and other truck garden crops. Much poultry is also raised. Virtually all agriculture in El Paso and nearby counties, as well as in the border regions of Chihuahua, is highly dependent on irrigation water from the Rio Grande and wells.

There is a growing nursery industry in the area that produces significant quantities of trees, shrubs, bedding plants, and other landscape specialty species.

The most widely used trees in and around El Paso are probably Italian cypress, with its striking tall and narrow profile, fruitless mulberry, and weeping willow. Globe willow, with its distinctive balloon-like form, and the native Mexican elder provide lime-green accents in early spring. Live oak, a native of the Texas hill country, is also common here, as are California and Mexican fan palms as well as date palms. Oleander, a popular Mediterranean shrub, tends to burn somewhat in cold winters, as do the fan and date palms; however, all these plants generally recover quickly with the arrival of warm weather.

Redbuds provide a great deal of spring color. Desert willow, vitex, various ash species, and Aleppo and Afghan pines are also planted frequently as accent and feature trees. True European olive, *Olea europaea*, is also occasionally used as a curiosity; the Russian olive, *Elaeagnus angustifolia*, much like it in form and color, is more reliable in El Paso's climate.

El Paso has numerous private and public plantings of agave, cactus, sotol, dwarf coyotebush, beargrass, shrub bird of paradise (*Caesalpinia*), and tree mesquite. Cannas, gazanias, California poppies, petunias, desert baileyas, gaillardias, verbenas, and various honeysuckle species are often planted for seasonal color, as are virtually all the spring bulbs. Favorite shrubs include, among others, various juniper species, Texas ranger, saltbush, threadleaf sage, loquat, privet, barberry, Spanish bayonet, pittosporum, and fig.

Some of El Paso's best private landscapes may be found near Memorial Park. Here many home gardens are cultivated to produce an intensely green "oasis" effect. Memorial Park itself is one of the city's finest historical landscapes. Its modern form dates from the great New Deal landscape era of the 1930s. The park features excellent stonework, imaginative terracing, and extraordinarily large specimen mesquite trees. The downtown plaza, the campus of the University of Texas at El Paso, the El Paso Art Museum, and many individual gardens and landscapes in the Sunset Heights Historic District are also noteworthy examples of El Paso's cultural landscape history.

A prime example of streetscape in the city is the graceful Airway Boulevard median and parkway landscape, designed by the distinguished twentieth-century landscape architect, Garrett Eckbo, FASLA, as the main approach to El Paso International Airport.

Most landscapes and gardens in El Paso are planted in very hardy species that can resist a demanding climate and poor soils. Often the background to many of these plantings is a beautiful gray or whitish limestone that is used in walls, terraces, and riprap around the city.

In Ciudad Juárez, the general landscape, through comprising almost identical plants, has a more subtropical character. Palms, mulberries, oleanders, and even bougainvillaea frequently are used with bright flowers in tiled courtyard and patio gardens of great charm and character. The sprawling Chamizal Park near downtown is heavily planted in shady cottonwoods and willows. For much of its intriguing history, the old Cathedral Plaza has usually featured a restrained number of mulberries, chinaberries, or other unassuming foliage trees to shelter its benches and shade its many visitors.

SELECTED BEST PLANTS FOR EL PASO

These plant species grow very well in and around El Paso. For the sake of convenience and quick reference, each plant is listed as native (N), naturalized (NZ), or exotic (E). Other plants also will perform well in landscape and garden situations in the El Paso area. Please see the New Mexico Plant File for these species.

TREES

A. Deciduous Shade, Street, and Specialty Trees

Ash
    a. Arizona ash—*Fraxinus velutina* (N)
    b. Modesto ash—*Fraxinus velutina* 'Modesto' (Arizona ash variety) (N)
    c. Green ash—*Fraxinus pennsylvanica* and varieties (E)
Catalpa
    a. Umbrella catalpa—*Catalpa bignonioides* 'Nana' (E)
    b. Western catalpa—*Catalpa* speciosa (E)
Chinaberry—*Melia azedarach* (E)
Cottonwood, Aspen, and Poplar: Trees of the Genus *Populus*
    a. Carolina poplar—*Populus canadensis* (E)
    b. Lombardy poplar—*Populus nigra* 'Italica' (E)
    c. Rio Grande cottonwood—*Populus fremontii* 'Wislizeni' (N)
    d. White (silver) poplar—*Populus alba* (NZ)
Ginkgo (Maidenhair tree)—*Ginkgo biloba* (E)
Honey locust—*Gleditsia triacanthos inermis* varieties (E)
Japanese pagoda—*Sophora japonica* (E)
Black locust—*Robinia pseudoacacia* (E)
Silver maple—*Acer saccharinum* (E)
Mesquite—*Prosopis glandulosa* (N)
European mountain ash—*Sorbus aucuparia* (E)
Mulberry
    a. Fruitless mulberry—*Morus alba* (E)
    b. Weeping mulberry—*Morus alba* 'Pendula' (E)
    c. Paper mulberry—*Broussonetia papyrifera* (E)
Oak
    a. Cork oak—*Quercus suber* (E)
    b. Southern live oak—*Quercus virginiana* (E)
    c. Texas oak—*Quercus texana* (E)
Pecan—*Carya illinoiensis* (E)
Pistache—Pistachio
    a. Chinese pistache—*Pistacia chinensis* (E)
    b. Pistachio—*Pistacia vera* (E)
Russian olive—*Elaeagnus angustifolia* (NZ)
Silk tree—*Albizia jilibrissin* (E)
Arizona sycamore—*Platanus wrightii* (N)
Arizona walnut—*Juglans major* (N)
Willow
    a. Globe Navajo willow—*Salix matsudana* 'Navajo' (E)
    b. Weeping willow—*Salix babylonica* (and other weeping willow species, E)

B. Flowering Ornamental Trees

Flowering apricot—*Prunus armeniaca* (E)
Flowering cherry—*Prunus serrulata* et al (E)
Flowering crab—*Malus* 'Hopa' et al (E)
Desert willow—*Chilopsis linearis* (N)
Mexican elder—*Sambucus caerulea neomexicana* (N)
Flowering peach—*Prunus persica* (E)
Purpleleaf plum—*Prunus cerasifera* (E)
Eastern redbud—*Cercis canadensis* (E)
Golden rain tree—*Koelreuteria paniculata* (E)
Salt cedar—*Tamarix chinensis* (NZ)
Vitex (chaste tree)—*Vitex agnus-castus* (E)

C. Evergreen Trees

Cedar
    a. Atlas cedar—*Cedrus atlantica* (E)
    b. Cedar of Lebanon—*Cedrus libani* (E)
    c. Deodar cedar—*Cedrus deodara* (E)

Cypress
    a. Arizona cypress—*Cupressus arizonica* (N)
    b. Italian cypress—*Cupressus sempervirens* (E)
Eucalyptus (cider gum)—*Eucalyptus gunnii* (E)
Juniper
    a. Alligator juniper—*Juniperus deppeana* (N)
    b. Eastern red cedar—*Juniperus virginiana*
       varieties (E)
    c. Rocky Mountain juniper—*Juniperus scopulorum*
       varieties (E)
Madrone—*Arbutus texana* (N)
Magnolia
    a. Southern magnolia—*Magnolia grandiflora* (E)
    b. Saucer magnolia—*Magnolia soulangiana* (E)
Palm
    a. California fan palm—*Washingtonia filifera* (E)
    b. Chinese windmill palm—*Trachycarpus fortunei* (E)
    c. Date palm—Phoenix dactylifera (E)
    d. Mexican fan palm—*Washingtonia robusta* (E)
Pine
    a. Afghan pine—*Pinus eldarica* (E)
    b. Aleppo pine—*Pinus halepensis* (E)
    c. Austrian pine—*Pinus nigra* (E)
    d. Italian stone pine—*Pinus pinea* (E)
    e. Japanese black pine—*Pinus thunbergiana* (E)
    f. Piñon pine—*Pinus edulis* (N)
    g. Scotch pine—*Pinus sylvestris* (E)
Blue spruce—*Picea pungens* (E)
Yucca
    a. Joshua tree—*Yucca brevifolia* (E)
    b. Palm yucca—*Yucca torreyi* (N)
    c. Soaptree yucca—*Yucca elata* (N)

SHRUBS

A. Deciduous

Glossy abelia—*Abelia grandiflora* (E)
Althea (Rose of Sharon)—*Hibiscus syriacus* (E)
Golden bamboo—*Phyllostachys aurea* (E)
Bird of paradise—*Caesalpinia gilliesii* (NZ)
Common butterfly bush—*Buddleia davidii* (E)
Cotoneaster
    a. Rock cotoneaster—*Cotoneaster horizontalis* (E)
    b. Rockspray cotoneaster—*Cotoneaster micro-*
       phyllus (E)
Crape myrtle—*Lagerstroemia indica* (E)
Edible fig—*Ficus carica* (E)
Forsythia—*Forsythia* spp.(E)
Shrub or tatarian honeysuckle—*Lonicera tatarica* (E)
Flowering jasmine—*Jasminum nudiflorum* (E)
Screwbean mesquite—*Prosopis pubescens* (N)
Mountain mahogany—*Cercocarpus montanus* (N)
Pomegranate—*Punica granatum* (E)
Rose—*Rosa* spp. (E)
Snakeweed—*Gutierrezia sarothrae* (N)
Snowball—*Viburnum opulus* 'Roseum' (E)
Bridal wreath—*Spiraea prunifolia* (E)
Sumac
    a. Littleleaf sumac—*Rhus microphylla* (N)
    b. Skunkbush—*Rhus trilobata* (N)
    c. Staghorn sumac—*Rhus typhina* (E)

B. Evergreen

Agave (century plant, mescal)
    a. Century plant—*Agave americana* (N)
    b. Parry agave—*Agave parryi* (N)
    c. Lechugilla—*Agave lechugilla* (N)
Barberry
    a. Colorado barberry—*Berberis fendleri* (N)
    b. Japanese barberry—*Berberis thunbergii* (E)

A colorful residential garden

    c. Three-spine barberry—*Berberis wisleyensis* (E)
Beargrass—*Nolina microcarpa* (N)
Cactus
    a. Claret cup—*Echinocereus triglochidiatus* (N)
    b. Common cholla—*Opuntia imbricata* (N)
    c. Prickly pear—*Opuntia chlorotica* or *O.*
       engelmannii (E)
Parney cotoneaster—*Cotoneaster lacteus* (E)
Creosotebush—*Larrea tridentata* (N)
Yaupon holly—*Ilex vomitoria* (E)
India hawthorn—*Rhaphiolepis indica* (E)
Chinese junipers
    a. Pfitzer juniper—*Juniperus chinensis* 'Pfitzerana' (E)
    b. Sea Green juniper—*Juniperus chinensis* 'Sea
       Green' (E)
Mahonia
    a. Algerita—*Mahonia haematocarpa* (N)
    b. Agritos—*Mahonia trifoliolata* (N)
Mormon tea—*Ephedra* spp. (N)
Nandina (heavenly bamboo)—*Nandina domestica* (E)
Ocotillo—*Fouquieria splendens* (N)
Oleander—*Nerium oleander* (E)
Photinia
    a. Chinese photinia—*Photinia serrulata* (E)
    b. Fraser's photinia—*Photinia fraseri* (E)
Mugo pine—*Pinus mugo* (E)
Pittosporum (tobira)—*Pittosporum tobira* (E)
Waxleaf privet (ligustrum)—*Ligustrum japonicum* (E)
Pyracantha (firethorn)—*Pyracantha* spp. (E)
Sage
    a. Big sage (sagebrush)—*Artemisia tridentata* (N)
    b. Sand sage—*Artemisia filifolia* (N)
Fourwing saltbush—*Atriplex canescens* (N)
Seepwillow -*Baccharis sarothroides* (N)
Silverberry—*Elaeagnus pungens* (E)
Sotol—*Dasylirion wheeleri* (N)
Texas ranger—*Leucophyllum frutescens* (N)
Yucca
    a. Narrowleaf yucca—*Yucca glauca* (N)
    b. Softblade yucca—*Yucca recurvifolia* (*Yucca*
      pendula) (E)

c. Spanish bayonet—*Yucca baccata* (N)
d. Coral-flower yucca—*Hesperaloe parviflora* (E)

GROUND COVERS

A. Deciduous

Clover—*Trifolium* spp. (NZ, N)
Cranberry cotoneaster—*Cotoneaster apiculatus* (E)
Crown vetch—*Coronilla varia* (E, NZ)
Prairie sage—*Artemisia ludoviciana* (N)
Snow-in summer—*Cerastium tomentosum* (E)

B. Evergreen

Dwarf coyotebrush—*Baccharis pilularis* (E)
Dichondra—*Dichondra micrantha* (E)
Germander—*Teucrium chamaedrys* 'Prostratum' (E)
Honeysuckle—*Lonicera japonica* varieties (E)
Juniper
Horizontalis junipers
    a. Andorra juniper—*Juniperus horizontalis plumosa* (E)
    b. Bar Harbor juniper—*Juniperus horizontalis* 'Bar Harbor'(E)
    c. Wilton carpet juniper—*Juniperus horizontalis* 'Wiltonii' (E)
Sabina junipers
    a. Broadmoor juniper—*Juniperus sabina* 'Broadmoor' (E)
    b. Buffalo juniper—*Juniperus sabina* 'Buffalo' (E)
    c. Tam (tammy) juniper—*Juniperus sabina* 'Tamariscifolia' (E)
San Jose juniper—*Juniperus chinensis* 'San Jose' (E)
Lilyturf (liriope)—*Liriope spicata* (E)
Rosemary—*Rosmarinus officinalis* (E)
Santolina
    a. Green santolina—*Santolina virens* (E)
    b. Gray santolina—*Santolina chamaecyparissus* (E)
Sedum (stonecrop)—*Sedum* spp. (N, E)
Strawberry—*Fragaria* spp. (N, E)

GRASSES

A. Traditional Turf Species

Bentgrass—*Agrostis* spp. (E)
Bermuda
    a. African bermuda—*Cynodon transvaalensis* (E, NZ)
    b. Common bermuda—*Cynodon dactylon* (E)
Ryegrass—*Lolium* spp. (E)

B. Native Turf And General-Use Species

Grama
    a. Black grama—*Bouteloua eriopoda* (N)
    b. Blue grama—*Bouteloua gracilis* (N)
    c. Sideoats grama—*Bouteloua curtipendula* (N)

C. Ornamental Species

Alkali sacaton—*Sporobolus airoides* (N)
Sand dropseed—*Sporobolus cryptandrus* (N)
Fountain grass—*Pennisetum* spp. (E)
Indian ricegrass—*Oryzopsis hymenoides* (N)
Pampas grass—*Cortaderia selloana* (E)
Purple threeawn—*Aristida longiseta* (N)
River cane—*Arundo donax* (NZ)

VINES

A. Deciduous

Boston ivy—*Parthenocissus tricuspidata* (E)
Morning glory—*Ipomoea tricolor* (E)
Silver lace vine—*Polygonum aubertii* (E)
Trumpet vine—*Campsis radicans* (E)
Virginia creeper (et al)—*Parthenocissus quinquefolia* (E, N)
Wisteria—*Wisteria sinensis* (E)

B. Evergreen

Algerian ivy—*Hedera canariensis* (E)
English ivy—*Hedera helix* (E)
Honeysuckle—*Lonicera* spp. (E)

FLOWERS

A. Annuals

Cosmos—*Cosmos* spp. (E)
Four o'clock—*Mirabilis jalapa* (E)
Gaillardia (blanketflower, firewheel)—*Gaillardia pulchella* (N)
Geranium—*Pelargonium hortorum* (E)
Impatiens—*Impatiens wallerana* (E)
Marigold—*Tagetes* spp. (E)
Pansy—*Viola wittrockiana* (E)
Salvia—*Salvia* spp. (N)
Sunflower—*Helianthus annuus* (N)
Annual vinca (Madagascar periwinkle)—*Catharanthus roseus* (E)
Viola (Johnny jump-ups)—*Viola* spp. (E)
Wallflower—*Erysimum capitatum* (N)

B. Perennials

Desert baileya—*Baileya multiradiata* (N)
Carnation—*Dianthus caryophyllus* (E)
Coneflower—*Ratibida columnifera* (N)
Daylily (asphodel)—*Hemerocallis* spp. (E)
Delphinium—*Delphinium belladonna* (E, N)
Dusty miller—*Senecio cineraria* (E)
Fendler's sundrops—*Calylophus hartwegii fendleri* (N)
Hollyhock—*Alcea rosea* (NZ)
Jimsonweed (datura, sacred datura)—*Datura meteloides* (N)
Lobelia—*Lobelia erinus* (E)
Maximilian's daisy—*Helianthus maximiliani* (NZ)
Paperflower—*Psilostrophe tagetina* (N)
Penstemon—*Penstemon* spp. (N)
Phlox—*Phlox* spp. (E)
California poppy—*Eschscholzia californica* (and *E. mexicana*) (E,N)
Primrose—*Primula vulgaris* (E)
Spectaclepod—*Dithyrea wislizenii* (N)

C. Bulbs

Canna—*Canna* spp. (E)
Common hyacinth—*Hyacinthus orientalis* (E)
Daffodil—*Narcissus* 'King Alfred' (E)
Garden gladiolus—*Gladiolus hortulanus* (E)
Iris—*Iris* spp. (E)
Ranunculus—*Ranunculus asiaticus* (E)
Tulip—*Tulipa* spp. (E)

A post office opened in Estancia in 1903, but there are many stories of settlers using the site as a watering hole and ranch headquarters for perhaps a century or two before the town itself existed. A wonderful spring continues to flow here, and its pond is the landscape focus of the modern community.

Estancia sits at 6100 feet (1860 m) in the middle of a plain—the Estancia Valley—that receives about 11–14 inches (275 mm to 350 mm) or more of annual precipitation. The land is fertile, but the growing season is short (about 131 days). Agricultural production is split almost evenly in Torrance County between crops and cows. A great deal of hay and corn is raised, along with some wheat and vegetables. In the early decades of this century, Torrance County was famous as the pinto bean "capital" of the state. Bean farming has recently undergone a small renaissance in the county. Most crops are intensely irrigated with well water.

The original plains landscape near Estancia included galleta, muhly, buffalo, grama, and other grasses and such native shrubs as winterfat, big sage, and fourwing saltbush. The original trees beside the spring in the middle of town were probably Rio Grande cottonwoods and willows. In the nearby Manzano Range, the classic foothills vegetation is singleseed juniper and piñon pine, with algerita, mountain mahogany, and Gambel and turbinella oak. Common shrubs include coyote willow, currant, Apache plume and woods rose; western virginsbower, Virginia creeper, columbine, Indian paintbrush, and various penstemon

species are frequently found accents. White fir, bigtooth maple, Engelmann spruce, ponderosa and limber pine, Douglas fir, aspen, and narrowleaf cottonwood are typical larger trees of the higher altitudes in the Manzanos. Amazing small forests of tree-size New Mexico locust exist near the crest of the range.

In Estancia itself, the most common street tree is the Siberian elm. The tree of heaven, peachleaf willow, Russian olive, piñon, Scotch pine, globe willow, American sycamore, Rocky Mountain juniper, green ash, American elm, limber pine, and silver poplar also grow well here. Shrubs such as juniper, lilac, red osier dogwood, arborvitae, forsythia, and coral-flower yucca are often planted in private yards. Most local landscapes and gardens are informal and comfortable.

Estancia Park Lake (also known as Mountain View Little Pond and Arthur Park) is the town's most outstanding landscape feature. Its natural spring, pond, and early ranch setting were reconstructed as a classic New Deal landscape by the Civilian Conservation Corps (CCC) in the 1930s. Today, it is a widely recognized historic landscape. Other extremely fine examples of historic cultural landscapes in the county include the plazas, *atrios* (church forecourts), patios, and gardens of the Salinas missions at Abó, Quarai, and Gran Quivira. These are all located in extraordinarily scenic settings. The quiet, remnant apple orchard next to the great spring (Ojo Gigante) in the town of Manzano is a fine example of a small-scale, traditional mountain village landscape (dating

Estancia Park Lake—a historic New Deal landscape from the 1930s

ESTANCIA

including Tijeras, Stanley, Edgewood, Moriarty, Chililí, Tajique, Torreón, Manzano, Mountainair, Willard, Encino, and Vaughn

from the early nineteenth century) that is vanishing all too quickly from modern New Mexico.

SELECTED BEST PLANTS FOR ESTANCIA

These plant species grow very well in Estancia. For the sake of convenience and quick reference, each plant is listed as native (N), naturalized (NZ), or exotic (E). Other plants also will perform well in landscape and garden situations in Estancia and nearby communities. Please see the New Mexico Plant File for these species.

TREES

A. Deciduous Shade, Street, and Specialty Trees

Green ash—*Fraxinus pennsylvanica* and varieties (E)
Western chokecherry—*Prunus virginiana* (N)
Cottonwood, Aspen, and Poplar: Trees of the Genus *Populus*
    a.Lombardy poplar—*Populus nigra* 'Italica' (E)
    b.Rio Grande cottonwood—*Populus fremontii* 'Wislizeni' (N)
    c.White (silver) poplar—*Populus alba* (NZ)
American elm—*Ulmus americana* (E)
Honey locust—*Gleditsia triacanthos inermis* varieties
    a.'Moraine' (E)
    b.'Shademaster' (E)
    c.'Sunburst' (E)
Common horsechestnut—*Aesculus hippocastanum* (E)
Locust
    a.Black locust—*Robinia pseudoacacia* (NZ)
    b.New Mexico locust—*Robinia neomexicana* (N)
Maple and Box elder
    a.Bigtooth maple—*Acer grandidentatum* (N)
    b.Box elder—*Acer negundo* (N)
    c.Rocky Mountain maple—*Acer glabrum* (N)
Gambel oak—*Quercus gambelii* (N)
Russian olive—*Elaeagnus angustifolia* (NZ)
American sycamore—*Platanus occidentalis* (E)
Willow
    a.Globe Navajo willow—*Salix matsudana* 'Navajo' (N)
    b.Peachleaf willow—*Salix amygdaloides* (N)
    c.Weeping willow—*Salix babylonica* (and other weeping willow species, E)

B. Flowering Ornamental Trees

Flowering cherry—*Prunus serrulata* et al (E)
Flowering crab—*Malus* 'Hopa' et al (E)
Hawthorn—*Crataegus* spp. (E, N)
Bradford pear—*Pyrus calleryana* (E)
Golden rain tree—*Koelreuteria paniculata* (E)
Salt cedar—*Tamarix chinensis* (NZ)

C. Evergreen Trees

Arizona cypress—*Cupressus arizonica* (N)
Douglas fir—*Pseudotsuga menziesii* (N)
White fir—*Abies concolor* (E)
Juniper
    a.Alligator juniper—*Juniperus deppeana* (N)
    b.Chinese juniper—*Juniperus chinensis* varieties (E)
    c.Eastern red cedar—*Juniperus virginiana* varieties (E)
    d.Rocky Mountain juniper—*Juniperus scopulorum* varieties (N)
    e.Singleseed (one-seed) juniper—*Juniperus monosperma* (N)
    f.Utah juniper—*Juniperus osteosperma* (N)
Leyland false cypress—*Cupressocyparis leylandii* (E)
Pine
    a.Austrian pine—*Pinus nigra* (E)
    b.Japanese black pine—*Pinus thunbergiana* (E)
    c.Limber pine—*Pinus flexilis* (N)
    d.Piñon pine—*Pinus edulis* (N)
    e.Ponderosa pine—*Pinus ponderosa* (N)
    f.Scotch pine—*Pinus sylvestris* (E)
Spruce
    a.Blue spruce—*Picea pungens* (N)
    b.Engelmann spruce—*Picea engelmanni* (N)
    c.Black Hills spruce—*Picea glauca densata* (E)

SHRUBS

A. Deciduous

Althea (rose of Sharon)—*Hibiscus syriacus* (E)
Apache plume—*Fallugia paradoxa* (N)
Shrubby cinquefoil—*Potentilla fruticosa* (N)
Cotoneaster
    a.Cranberry cotoneaster—*Cotoneaster apiculatus* (E)
    b.Rock cotoneaster—*Cotoneaster horizontalis* (E)
    c.Rockspray cotoneaster—*Cotoneaster microphyllus* (E)
Red osier dogwood—*Cornus stolonifera* (N)
Fernbush—*Chamaebatiaria millefolium* (N)
Forsythia—*Forsythia* spp. (E)
Shrub or Tatarian honeysuckle—*Lonicera tatarica* (E)
Hop tree—*Ptelea trifoliolata* (N)
Flowering jasmine—*Jasminum nudiflorum* (E)
Common lilac—*Syringa vulgaris* (N, E)
Mountain mahogany—*Cercocarpus montanus* (N)
New Mexico olive—*Forestiera neomexicana* (N)
Rose—*Rosa* spp. (E, N)
Sand plum—*Prunus americana* (N)
Spirea
    a.Bridal wreath—*Spiraea prunifolia* (E)
    b.Van Houtte—*Spiraea vanhouttei* (E)
Sumac
    a.Skunkbush—*Rhus trilobata* (N)
    b.Smooth sumac—*Rhus glabra* (N)
    c.Staghorn sumac—*Rhus typhina* (E)
Winterfat—*Ceratoides lanata* (N)

B. Evergreen

Parry agave—*Agave parryi* (N)
Barberry
    a.Colorado barberry—*Berberis fendleri* (N)
    b.Japanese barberry—*Berberis thunbergii* (E)
    c.Three-spine barberry—*Berberis wisleyensis* (E)
    d.Wintergreen barberry—*Berberis julianae* (E)
Beargrass—*Nolina microcarpa* (N)
Cactus
    a.Common cholla—*Opuntia imbricata* (N)
    b.Prickly pear—*Opuntia chlorotica* or *O. engelmannii* (N)
Parney cotoneaster—*Cotoneaster lacteus* (E)
Chinese junipers
    a.Armstrong juniper—*Juniperus chinensis* 'Armstrong' (E)
    b.Pfitzer juniper—*Juniperus chinensis* 'Pfitzerana' (E)
    c.Sea Green juniper—*Juniperus chinensis* 'Sea Green' (E)
Common juniper—*Juniperus communis* (N)

Mahonia
    a.Algerita—*Mahonia haematocarpa* (N)
    b.Agritos—*Mahonia trifoliolata* (N)
    c.Oregon grape—*Mahonia aquifolium* (E, NZ)
Mormon tea—*Ephedra* spp. (N)
Nandina (heavenly bamboo)—*Nandina domestica* (E)
Mugo pine—*Pinus mugo* (E)
Rubber rabbitbrush—*Chrysothamnus nauseosus* (N)
Sage
    a.Big sage (sagebrush)—*Artemisia tridentata* (N)
    b.Sand sage—*Artemisia filifolia* (N)
Fourwing saltbush—*Atriplex canescens* (N)
Yucca
    a.Narrowleaf yucca—*Yucca glauca* (N)
    b.Spanish bayonet—*Yucca baccata* (N)
    c.Coral-flower yucca—*Hesperaloe parviflora* (E)

GROUND COVERS

A. Deciduous

Spring cinquefoil—*Potentilla tabernaemontani* (E)
Clover—*Trifolium* spp. (NZ, N)
Cranberry cotoneaster—*Cotoneaster apiculatus* (E)
Crown vetch—*Coronilla varia* (E, NZ)
Mint—*Mentha* spp. (E, N, NZ)
Prairie sage—*Artemisia ludoviciana* (N)
Memorial rose (vine)—*Rosa wichuriana* (E)

B. Evergreen

Bearberry cotoneaster—*Cotoneaster dammeri* (E)
Creeping euonymus—*Euonymus fortunei* (E)
Honeysuckle—*Lonicera japonica* varieties (E)
Sabina junipers
    a.Broadmoor juniper—*Juniperus sabina*
      'Broadmoor' (E)
    b.Buffalo juniper—*Juniperus sabina* 'Buffalo' (E)
    c.Tam (tammy) juniper—*Juniperus sabina*
      'Tamariscifolia' (E)
Kinnickinnick (mountain bearberry)—*Arctostaphylos
    uva-ursi* (N)
Blue leadwort—*Ceratostigma plumbaginoides* (E)
Creeping mahonia—*Mahonia repens* (N)
Periwinkle—*Vinca major* and *Vinca minor* (E)
Pussytoes—*Antennaria parviflora* (N)
Sedum (stonecrop)—*Sedum* spp. (N, E)
Strawberry—*Fragaria* spp. (N, E)

GRASSES

A. Traditional Turf Species

Bluegrass—*Poa pratensis* (NZ)
Fescue—*Festuca* spp. (E)
Ryegrass—*Lolium* spp. (E)

B. Native Turf And General-Use Species

Buffalo grass—*Buchlöe dactyloides* (N)
Blue grama—*Bouteloua gracilis* (N)
Galleta—*Hilaria jamesii* (N)
Wheatgrass
    a.Western wheatgrass—*Agropyron smithii* (N)
    b.Crested wheatgrass—*Agropyron desertorum* (E,
      NZ)
    c.Pubescent wheatgrass—*Agropyron
      trichophorum* (N)

C. Ornamental Species

Blue fescue—*Festuca caesia* (E)
Indian ricegrass—*Oryzopsis hymenoides* (N)
Purple threeawn—*Aristida longiseta* (N)

VINES

A. Deciduous

Boston ivy—*Parthenocissus tricuspidata* (E)
Canyon grape—*Vitis arizonica* (N)
Clematis—*Clematis jackmanni* (E)
Morning glory—*Ipomoea tricolor* (E)
Trumpet vine—*Campsis radicans* (E)
Virginia creeper (et al)—*Parthenocissus quinque-
    folia* (N, E)
Wisteria—*Wisteria sinensis* (E)

B. Evergreen

English ivy—*Hedera helix* (E)
Honeysuckle—*Lonicera* spp. (E)

FLOWERS

A. Annuals

Purple aster—*Aster bigelovii* (N)
Bedding begonia—*Begonia* spp. (E)
Cosmos—*Cosmos* spp. (E)
Four o'clock—*Mirabilis jalapa* (E)
Gaillardia (blanketflower, firewheel)—*Gaillardia
    pulchella* (N)
Geranium—*Pelargonium hortorum* (E)
Impatiens—*Impatiens wallerana* (E)
Marigold—*Tagetes* spp. (E)
Pansy—*Viola wittrockiana* (E)
Petunia—*Petunia* spp. (E)
Salvia—*Salvia* spp. (E)
Snapdragon—*Antirrhinum majus* (E)
Sunflower—*Helianthus annuus* (N)
Viola (Johnny jump-ups)—*Viola* spp. (E)
Wallflower—*Erysimum capitatum* (N)

B. Perennials

Bear's breech—*Acanthus mollis* (E)
Carnation—*Dianthus caryophyllus* (E)
Chrysanthemum—*Chrysanthemum morifolium* (E)
Colorado columbine—*Aquilegia* spp. (N)
Coneflower—*Ratibida columnifera* (N)
Daylily (asphodel)—*Hemerocallis* spp. (E)
Delphinium—*Delphinium belladonna* (E, N)
Fendler's sundrops—*Calylophus hartwegii fendleri* (N)
Blue flax—*Linum perenne* (N)
Globemallow—*Sphaeralcea incana* (scarlet) (N)
Hollyhock—*Alcea rosea* (E, NZ)
Indian paintbrush—*Castilleja integra* (N)
Lobelia—*Lobelia erinus* (E)
Maximilian's daisy—*Helianthus maximiliani* (NZ)
Penstemon—*Penstemon* spp. (N)
Phlox—*Phlox* spp. (E)
Red rocket (scarlet gilia)—*Ipomopsis aggregata* (N)
Shasta daisy—*Chrysanthemum maximum* (E)
Violet—*Viola odorata* (N, E)
Wooly yarrow—*Achillea* spp. (N, E).

C. Bulbs

Canna—*Canna* spp. (E)
Common hyacinth—*Hyacinthus orientalis* (E)
Daffodil—*Narcissus* 'King Alfred' (E)
Garden gladiolus—*Gladiolus hortulanus* (E)
Iris—*Iris* spp. (N, E)
Tulip—*Tulipa* spp. (E)

*Riverside Park
(a "spring" park)
in Farmington*

FARMINGTON, BLOOMFIELD, AND AZTEC

including Shiprock, Kirtland, and Fruitland

Farmington was founded in 1879 as a "farming town" near the confluence of the San Juan, Animas, and La Plata rivers. Bloomfield was settled the year before as a cattle-raising center. Aztec, also dating from 1879, was named for a spectacular Chaco Anasazi ruin (mistakenly thought to have been constructed by the legendary Aztecs of central Mexico) located just across the Animas River from the townsite.

All three settlements actually lie in the far southern foothills of Colorado's San Juan Mountains. They are high, at about 5300 to 5700 feet (roughly 1700 m), but dry: the typical rainfall is between 9 and 10 inches (250 mm). The growing season is relatively short at 139 days. Soils tend to be sandy or clayey, alkaline, and thin.

The landscape near Farmington begins to change from the sage-covered uplands of the Colorado Plateau to the outskirts of the Rockies and then the mountains proper. South of Farmington and Bloomfield, singleseed and Utah juniper, piñon, Gambel oak, and mountain mahogany are found in pockets along draws and hillsides. Greasewood is common. An occasional grove of relict ponderosa pine hangs on in the upper reaches of many dry washes. North of Farmington and Aztec the

land gets wetter and higher, and streams with narrowleaf cottonwood, alder, willow, oak, and thickets of occasional New Mexico locust become more common. Ponderosa pine, piñon, singleseed and/or Utah juniper, oak, and purshia (antelope bitterbrush) grow on the ridges and hillsides. Naturalized stands of Russian olive and salt cedar can be found in both the northern uplands and on the Colorado Plateau.

San Juan County is heavily farmed and very productive. Both sheep and cattle are widely grazed. Alfalfa, corn, barley, vegetables, landscape trees, and other crops are produced in great quantity by irrigation. San Juan is also one of the leading wheat-producing counties of New Mexico. The Navajo Irrigation Project has brought vast amounts of fertile desert land into production in recent years.

Despite certain differences in growing seasons (Albuquerque's is longer) and latitude (Farmington is more northerly), Farmington and its companion cities of Aztec and Bloomfield enjoy much the same plant "palette" as Albuquerque. In Farmington and Bloomfield, enormous globe Navajo willows are perhaps the most striking "skyline" trees. Rio Grande (valley) cottonwood, flowering crabapple, western catalpa, corkscrew willow, aspen, honey locust, Russian olive, white fir, Engelmann spruce, western red cedar, Douglas fir, various ash species, and black locust are popular shade, flowering ornamental, and evergreen trees. Big sage, fourwing saltbush, barberry, various juniper species, spirea, forsythia, softblade yucca, and Spanish bayonet are frequently selected shrubs. Most of these plants are found in private gardens as well as in commercial and public landscapes. Winged enonymus is a particularly striking accent shrub in the fall gardens of Farmington.

Aztec seems to have a distinctively strong garden history. Historic streetside canals supply the enormous street trees (cottonwoods, silver maples) of this appealing town with water. Small residential gardens are often laid out below street level, and these are traditionally planted in many colorful types of flowers. Shasta daisies, marigolds, desert baileya, honeysuckle, roses, irises, cannas, trumpet vine, sweet peas, daylilies, hollyhocks, alyssum, and asters are typical favorites.

Aztec's jewel-like private gardens and the splendid Brookside Park in Farmington are among the finest landscapes to be found in northwestern New Mexico.

SELECTED BEST PLANTS FOR FARMINGTON

These plant species grow very well in Farmington. For the sake of convenience and quick reference, each plant is listed as native (N), naturalized (NZ), or exotic (E). Other plants also will perform well in landscape and garden situations in the Farmington area. Please see the New Mexico Plant File for these species.

TREES

A. Deciduous Shade, Street, and Specialty Trees

Ash
    a.Arizona ash—*Fraxinus velutina* (N)
    b.Modesto ash—*Fraxinus velutina* 'Modesto' (Arizona ash variety) (N)
    c.Green ash—*Fraxinus pennsylvanica* and varieties (E)
Paper birch—*Betula papyrifera* (E)
Catalpa
    a.Umbrella catalpa—*Catalpa bignonioides* 'Nana' (E)
    b.Western catalpa—*Catalpa speciosa* (E)
Cottonwood, Aspen, and Poplar: Trees of the Genus *Populus*
    a.Aspen—*Populus tremuloides* (N)
    b.Carolina poplar—*Populus canadensis* (E)
    c.Lanceleaf cottonwood—*Populus acuminata* (N)
    d.Lombardy poplar—*Populus nigra* 'Italica' (E)
    e.Narrowleaf cottonwood—*Populus angustifolia* (N)
    f.Rio Grande cottonwood—*Populus fremontii* 'Wislizeni' (N)
    g.White (silver) poplar—*Populus alba* (NZ)
Elm
    a.American elm—*Ulmus americana* (E)
    b.Chinese elm—*Ulmus parvifolia* (E)
Honey locust—*Gleditsia triacanthos inermis* varieties
    a.'Moraine' (E)
    b.'Shademaster' (E)
    c.'Sunburst' (E)
Horsechestnut
    a.Common horsechestnut—*Aesculus hippocastanum* (E)
    b.California buckeye—*Aesculus californica* (E)
Littleleaf linden—*Tilia cordata* (E)
Locust
    a.Black locust—*Robinia pseudoacacia* (NZ)
    b.Hybrid locusts—*Robinia ambigua* varieties (E)
    c.New Mexico locust—*Robinia neomexicana* (N)
Maple and Box elder
    a.Box elder—*Acer negundo* (N)
    b.Japanese maple—*Acer palmatum* (E)
    c.Norway maple—*Acer platanoides* (E)
    d.Rocky Mountain maple—*Acer glabrum* (N)
    e.Silver maple—*Acer saccharinum* (E)
    f.Sycamore-leaf maple—*Acer pseudoplatanus* (E)
Mulberry
    a.Fruitless mulberry—*Morus alba* (E)
    b.Weeping mulberry—*Morus alba* 'Pendula' (E)
Oak
    a.Gambel oak—*Quercus gambelii* (N)
    b.Texas oak—*Quercus texana* (E)
Pecan—*Carya illinoiensis* (E)
Russian olive—*Elaeagnus angustifolia* (NZ)
Silk tree—*Albizia jilibrissin* (E)
Sycamore (plane tree)
    a.American sycamore—*Platanus occidentalis* (E)
    b.London plane tree—*Platanus acerifolia* (E)
Willow
    a.Corkscrew willow—*Salix matsudana* 'Tortuosa' (E)
    b.Globe Navajo willow—*Salix matsudana* 'Navajo' (E)
    c.Peachleaf willow—*Salix amygdaloides* (N)
    d.Weeping willow—*Salix babylonica* (and other weeping willow species, E)

B. Flowering Ornamental Trees

Flowering apricot—*Prunus armeniaca* (E)
Flowering cherry—*Prunus serrulata* et al (E)
Flowering crab—*Malus* 'Hopa' et al (E)
Bradford pear—*Pyrus calleryana* (E)
Purpleleaf plum—*Prunus cerasifera* (E)
Eastern redbud—*Cercis canadensis* (E)
Golden rain tree—*Koelreuteria paniculata* (E)
Salt cedar—*Tamarix chinensis* (NZ)
Smoke tree—*Cotinus coggygria* (E)

C. Evergreen Trees

Arizona cypress—*Cupressus arizonica* (N)
Douglas fir—*Pseudotsuga menziesii* (N)
White fir—*Abies concolor* (N)
Juniper
    a.Eastern red cedar—*Juniperus virginiana* varieties (E)
    b.Rocky Mountain juniper—*Juniperus scopulorum* varieties (N)
    c.Singleseed (one-seed) juniper—*Juniperus monosperma* (N)
    d.Utah juniper—*Juniperus osteosperma* (N)

Leyland false cypress—*Cupressocyparis leylandii* (E)
Pine
    a. Austrian pine—*Pinus nigra* (E)
    b. Bristlecone pine—*Pinus aristata* (N)
    c. Japanese black pine—*Pinus thunbergiana* (E)
    d. Limber pine—*Pinus flexilis* (N)
    e. Piñon pine—*Pinus edulis* (N)
    f. Ponderosa pine—*Pinus ponderosa* (N)
    g. Scotch pine—*Pinus sylvestris* (E)
Spruce
    a. Blue spruce—*Picea pungens* (N)
    b. Engelmann spruce—*Picea engelmanni* (N)
Western red cedar—*Thuja plicata* (E)

SHRUBS

A. Deciduous

Althea (rose of Sharon)—*Hibiscus syriacus* (E)
Common butterfly bush—*Buddleia davidii* (E)
Shrubby cinquefoil—*Potentilla fruticosa* (N)
Cotoneaster
    a. Rock cotoneaster—*Cotoneaster horizontalis* (E)
    b. Rockspray cotoneaster—*Cotoneaster microphyllus* (E)
Currant and gooseberry—*Ribes* spp. (N, E)
Red osier dogwood—*Cornus stolonifera* (N)
Winged enonymus—*Euonymus alata* (E)
Forsythia—*Forsythia* spp. (E)
Shrub or Tatarian honeysuckle—*Lonicera tatarica* (E)
Hop tree—*Ptelea trifoliolata* (N)
Common lilac—*Syringa vulgaris* (E)
New Mexico olive—*Forestiera neomexicana* (N)
Cistena plum—*Prunus cistena* (E)
Sand plum—*Prunus americana* (N)
Rose—*Rosa* spp. (N, E)
Snakeweed—*Gutierrezia sarothrae* (N)
Snowball—*Viburnum opulus* 'Roseum' (E)
Spirea
    a. Bridal wreath—*Spiraea prunifolia* (E)
    b. Anthony Waterer—*Spiraea bumalda* 'Anthony Waterer' (E)
Sumac
    a. Skunkbush—*Rhus trilobata* (N)
    b. Smooth sumac—*Rhus glabra* (N)
    c. Staghorn sumac—*Rhus typhina* (E)
Willow
    a. Coyote willow—*Salix exigua* (N)
    b. Pussywillow—*Salix discolor* (N, E)
Winterfat—*Ceratoides lanata* (N)

B. Evergreen

Barberry
    a. Colorado barberry—*Berberis fendleri* (N)
    b. Japanese barberry—*Berberis thunbergii* (E)
    c. Three-spine barberry—*Berberis wisleyensis* (E)
    d. Wintergreen barberry—*Berberis julianae* (E)
Cactus
    a. Common cholla—*Opuntia imbricata* (N)
    b. Prickly pear—*Opuntia chlorotica* or *O. engelmannii* (N)
Parney cotoneaster—*Cotoneaster lacteus* (E)
Chinese junipers
    a. Armstrong juniper—*Juniperus chinensis* 'Armstrong' (E)
    b. Pfitzer juniper—*Juniperus chinensis* 'Pfitzerana' (E)
    c. Sea Green juniper—*Juniperus chinensis* 'Sea Green' (E)

Common juniper—*Juniperus communis* (N)
Mahonia
    a. Algerita—*Mahonia haematocarpa* (N)
    b. Agritos—*Mahonia trifoliolata* (N)
    c. Oregon grape—*Mahonia aquifolium* (E, NZ)
    d. Creeping mahonia—*Mahonia repens* (N)
Mormon tea—*Ephedra* spp. (N)
Nandina (heavenly bamboo)—*Nandina domestica* (E)
Photinia
    a. Chinese photinia—*Photinia serrulata* (E)
    b. Fraser's photinia—*Photinia fraseri* (E)
Mugo pine—*Pinus mugo* (E)
Waxleaf privet (ligustrum)—*Ligustrum japonicum* (E)
Pyracantha (firethorn)—*Pyracantha* spp. (E)
Rubber rabbitbrush—*Chrysothamnus nauseosus* (N)
Sage
    a. Big sage (sagebrush)—*Artemisia tridentata* (N)
    b. Sand sage—*Artemisia filifolia* (N)
Fourwing saltbush—*Atriplex canescens* (N)
Seepwillow -*Baccharis sarothroides* (N)
Silverberry—*Elaeagnus pungens* (E)
Alberta spruce—*Picea glauca* 'Conica' (*Picea albertiana*) (E)
Yucca
    a. Narrowleaf yucca—*Yucca glauca* (N)
    b. Softblade yucca—*Yucca recurvifolia* (*Yucca pendula*) (E)
    c. Spanish bayonet—*Yucca baccata* (N)
    d. Coral-flower yucca—*Hesperaloe parviflora* (E)

GROUND COVERS

A. Deciduous

Spring cinquefoil—*Potentilla tabernaemontani* (E)
Clover—*Trifolium* spp. (NZ, N)
Cranberry cotoneaster—*Cotoneaster apiculatus* (E)
Crown vetch—*Coronilla varia* (E, NZ)
Prairie sage—*Artemisia ludoviciana* (N)
Snow-in summer—*Cerastium tomentosum* (E)

B. Evergreen

Bearberry cotoneaster—*Cotoneaster dammeri* (E)
Creeping euonymus—*Euonymus fortunei* (E)
Honeysuckle—*Lonicera japonica* varieties (E)
Junipers
Horizontalis junipers
    a. Andorra juniper—*Juniperus horizontalis plumosa* (E)
    b. Bar Harbor juniper—*Juniperus horizontalis* 'Bar Harbor' (E)
    c. Wilton carpet juniper—*Juniperus horizontalis* 'Wiltonii' (E)
Sabina junipers
    a. Broadmoor juniper—*Juniperus sabina* 'Broadmoor' (E)
    b. Buffalo juniper—*Juniperus sabina* 'Buffalo' (E)
    c. Tam (tammy) juniper—*Juniperus sabina* 'Tamariscifolia' (E)
San Jose juniper—*Juniperus chinensis* 'San Jose' (E)
Kinnickinnick (mountain bearberry)—*Arctostaphylos uva-ursi* (N)
Periwinkle—*Vinca major* and *Vinca minor* (E)
Rosemary—*Rosmarinus officinalis* (E)
Santolina
    a. Green santolina—*Santolina virens* (E)
    b. Gray santolina—*Santolina chamaecyparissus* (E)
Sedum (stonecrop)—*Sedum* spp. (E)
Japanese spurge—*Pachysandra terminalis* (E)
Strawberry—*Fragaria* spp. (N, E)

GRASSES

A. Traditional Turf Species

Bentgrass—*Agrostis* spp. (E)
Bluegrass—*Poa pratensis* (NZ)
Fescue—*Festuca* spp. (E)
Ryegrass—*Lolium* spp. (E)

B. Native Turf And General-Use Species

Buffalo grass—*Buchlöe dactyloides* (N)
Galleta—*Hilaria jamesii* (N)
Grama
    a.Black grama—*Bouteloua eriopoda* (N)
    b.Blue grama—*Bouteloua gracilis* (N)
    c.Sideoats grama—*Bouteloua curtipendula* (N)
Wheatgrass
    a.Western wheatgrass—*Agropyron smithii* (N)
    b.Crested wheatgrass—*Agropyron desertorum*
      (E, NZ)
    c.Pubescent wheatgrass—*Agropyron*
      trichophorum (N)

C. Ornamental Species

Sand dropseed—*Sporobolus cryptandrus* (N)
Blue fescue—*Festuca caesia* (E)
Fountain grass—*Pennisetum* spp. (E)
Pampas grass—*Cortaderia selloana* (E)
Indian ricegrass—*Oryzopsis hymenoides* (N)
River cane—*Arundo donax* (NZ)
Purple threeawn—*Aristida longiseta* (N)

VINES

A. Deciduous

Boston ivy—*Parthenocissus tricuspidata* (E)
Silver lace vine—*Polygonum aubertii* (E)
Trumpet vine—*Campsis radicans* (E)
Virginia creeper (et al)—*Parthenocissus quinquefolia*
    (E, N)
Wisteria—*Wisteria sinensis* (E)

B. Evergreen

English ivy—*Hedera helix* (E)
Honeysuckle—*Lonicera* spp. (E)

FLOWERS

A. Annuals

Purple aster—*Aster bigelovii* (N, E)
Coleus—*Coleus x hybridus* (E)
Cosmos—*Cosmos* spp. (E)
Four o'clock—*Mirabilis jalapa* (E)
Gaillardia (blanketflower, firewheel)—*Gaillardia*
    pulchella (N)
Geranium—*Pelargonium hortorum* (E)
Marigold—*Tagetes* spp. (E)
Petunia—*Petunia* spp. (E)
Snapdragon—*Antirrhinum majus* (E)
Sunflower—*Helianthus annuus* (N)
Annual vinca (Madagascar periwinkle)—*Catharanthus*
    roseus (E)

B. Perennials

Desert baileya—*Baileya multiradiata* (N)
Carnation—*Dianthus caryophyllus* (E)
Chrysanthemum—*Chrysanthemum morifolium* (E)
Colorado columbine—*Aquilegia* spp. (N)
Coneflower—*Ratibida columnifera* (N)
Daylily (asphodel)—*Hemerocallis* spp. (E)
Delphinium—*Delphinium belladonna* (E, N)
Globemallow—*Sphaeralcea incana* (scarlet) (N)
Hollyhock—*Alcea rosea* (E)
Indian paintbrush—*Castilleja integra* (N)
Jimsonweed (datura, sacred datura)—*Datura*
    meteloides (N)
Lobelia—*Lobelia erinus* (E)
Maximilian's daisy—*Helianthus maximiliani* (NZ)
Penstemon—*Penstemon* spp. (N)
Phlox—*Phlox* spp. (E)
California poppy—*Eschscholzia californica* (and *E.*
    mexicana) (N)
Shasta daisy—*Chrysanthemum maximum* (E)
Wooly yarrow—*Achillea* spp. (N, E)

C. Bulbs

Canna—*Canna* spp. (E)
Daffodil—*Narcissus* 'King Alfred' (E)
Dutch crocus—*Crocus verus* (E)
Garden gladiolus—*Gladiolus hortulanus* (E)
Iris—*Iris* spp. (E, N)
Tulip—*Tulipa* spp. (E)

De Baca County Courthouse Square

FORT SUMNER
(founded in 1862)

At an elevation of about 4025 feet (1250 m), Fort Sumner lies beside the Pecos River near the western edge of the Great Plains. The town has a growing season of about 185 days and annual rainfall of 13.5–15 inches (about 360 mm).

Soils in and around Fort Sumner can be quite fertile. Cattle, calves, and some sheep are widely grazed in de Baca County. Hay is commonly grown, along with wheat, fruit, nuts, and other crops. Much of the county's prime cropland lies along the Pecos and is irrigated. Many ornamental tree and shrub species are also grown near Fort Sumner for the landscape trade.

The plains near Fort Sumner are often rolling, hilly, and broken by dry watercourses leading to the Pecos River. Mesquite, prickly pear and cholla cactus, Russian olive, salt cedar, cottonwood, and singleseed juniper are common here. Wheatgrass, various grama species, muhly, and buffalo grass, frequently broken by clusters of snakeweed and narrow-leaf yucca, are also typical native species.

In Fort Sumner itself, there is a surprisingly extensive collection of both native and exotic plants. Siberian elm—a plains favorite since the 1930s—is frequently planted, as are apple trees, fruitless mulberries, western catalpas, Arizona cypress, honey locusts, flowering crabs, pecans, green and Modesto ashes, silver poplars, Scotch pines, genuine Chinese (evergreen) elms (*Ulmus parvifolia*), soapberries, and lindens. Grapes, Boston ivy, cosmos, salvia, figs, softblade yucca, winterfat, white yarrows, big sage, marigolds, currants, butterfly bushes,

and zinnias are planted for color and texture. Bermuda is a very popular and virtually care-free lawn grass.

Arborvitae is a unique local favorite. An unusual but effective use of this sometimes pedestrian evergreen can be seen at the de Baca County Courthouse Square, certainly Fort Sumner's most influential modern public landscape.

SELECTED BEST PLANTS FOR FORT SUMNER

These plant species grow very well in and around Fort Sumner. For the sake of convenience and quick reference, each plant is listed as native (N), naturalized (NZ), or exotic (E). Other plants also will perform well in landscape and garden situations in the Fort Sumner area. Please see the New Mexico Plant File for these species.

TREES

A. Deciduous Shade, Street, and Specialty Trees

Ash
  a. Modesto ash—*Fraxinus velutina* 'Modesto' (Arizona ash variety) (N)
  b. Green ash—*Fraxinus pennsylvanica* and varieties (E)
Paper birch—*Betula papyrifera*
Catalpa
  a. Umbrella catalpa—*Catalpa bignonioides* 'Nana' (E)
  b. Western catalpa—*Catalpa speciosa* (E)
Cottonwood, Aspen, and Poplar: Trees of the Genus *Populus*
  a. Carolina poplar—*Populus canadensis* (E)
  b. Lombardy poplar—*Populus nigra* 'Italica' (E)

c. Rio Grande cottonwood—*Populus fremontii* 'Wislizeni' (N)

d. White (silver) poplar—*Populus alba* (NZ)

Elm

    a. American elm—*Ulmus americana* (E)

    b. Chinese elm—*Ulmus parvifolia* (E)

Honey locust—*Gleditsia triacanthos inermis* varieties (E)

Japanese pagoda—*Sophora japonica* (E)

Jujube—*Zizyphus jujuba* (E)

Littleleaf linden—*Tilia cordata* (E)

Locust

    a. Black locust—*Robinia pseudoacacia* (NZ)

    b. Hybrid locusts—*Robinia ambigua* varieties (E)

    c. New Mexico locust—*Robinia neomexicana* (N)

Maple and Box elder

    a. Bigtooth maple—*Acer grandidentatum* (N)

    b. Box elder—*Acer negundo* (N)

    c. Japanese maple—*Acer palmatum* (E)

    d. Silver maple—*Acer saccharinum* (E)

    e. Sycamore-leaf maple—*Acer pseudoplatanus* (E)

Mesquite—*Prosopis glandulosa* (N)

Fruitless mulberry—*Morus alba* (E)

Texas oak—*Quercus texana* (E)

Pecan—*Carya illinoiensis* (E)

Russian olive—*Elaeagnus angustifolia* (NZ)

Silk tree—*Albizia jilibrissin* (E)

Western soapberry—*Sapindus drummondii* (N)

Sycamore (plane tree)

    a. American sycamore—*Platanus occidentalis* (E)

    b. Arizona sycamore—*Platanus wrightii* (N)

    c. London plane tree—*Platanus acerifolia* (E)

    d. Oriental plane tree—*Platanus orientalis* (E)

Arizona walnut—*Juglans major* (N)

Willow

    a. *Globe Navajo willow*—*Salix matsudana* 'Navajo' (E)

    b. Weeping willow—*Salix babylonica* (and other weeping willow species, E)

B. Flowering Ornamental Trees

Flowering crab—*Malus* 'Hopa' et al (E)

Desert willow—*Chilopsis linearis* (N)

Flowering peach—*Prunus persica* (E)

Bradford pear—*Pyrus calleryana* (E)

Purpleleaf plum—*Prunus cerasifera* (E)

Salt cedar—*Tamarix chinensis* (NZ)

Smoke tree—*Cotinus coggygria* (E)

Vitex (chaste tree)—*Vitex agnus-castus* (E)

C. Evergreen Trees

Cedar

    a. Atlas cedar—*Cedrus atlantica* (E)

    b. Cedar of Lebanon—*Cedrus libani* (E)

Arizona cypress—*Cupressus arizonica* (N)

Douglas fir—*Pseudotsuga menziesii* (N)

Juniper

    a. Alligator juniper—*Juniperus deppeana* (N)

    b. Chinese juniper—*Juniperus chinensis* varieties (E)

    c. Eastern red cedar—*Juniperus virginiana* varieties (E)

    d. Rocky Mountain juniper—*Juniperus scopulorum* varieties (N)

    e. Singleseed (one-seed) juniper—*Juniperus monosperma* (N)

Leyland false cypress—*Cupressocyparis leylandii* (E)

Pine

    a. Afghan pine—*Pinus eldarica* (E)

    b. Japanese black pine—*Pinus thunbergiana* (E)

    c. Piñon pine—*Pinus edulis* (N)

    d. Ponderosa pine—*Pinus ponderosa* (N)

    e. Scotch pine—*Pinus sylvestris* (E)

Dawn redwood—*Metasequoia glyptostroboides* (E)

Blue spruce—*Picea pungens* (N)

Yucca

    a. Joshua tree—*Yucca brevifolia* (E)

    b. Palm yucca—*Yucca torreyi* (N)

    c. Soaptree yucca—*Yucca elata* (N)

SHRUBS

A. Deciduous

Althea (rose of Sharon)—*Hibiscus syriacus* (N)

Apache plume—*Fallugia paradoxa* (N)

Golden bamboo—*Phyllostachys aurea* (E, NZ)

Bird of paradise—*Caesalpinia gilliesii* (NZ)

Common butterfly bush—*Buddleia davidii* (E)

Cotoneaster

    a. Cranberry cotoneaster—*Cotoneaster apiculatus* (E)

    b. Rock cotoneaster—*Cotoneaster horizontalis* (E)

    c. Rockspray cotoneaster—*Cotoneaster microphyllus* (E)

Crape myrtle—*Lagerstroemia indica* (E)

Currant and gooseberry—*Ribes* spp. (E)

Shrub or tatarian honeysuckle—*Lonicera tatarica* (E)

Hop tree—*Ptelea trifoliolata* (E)

Flowering jasmine—*Jasminum nudiflorum* (E)

Common lilac—*Syringa vulgaris* (E)

Privet—*Ligustrum* spp. (E)

Rose—*Rosa* spp. (N, E)

Spirea

    a. Bridal wreath—*Spiraea prunifolia* (E)

    b. Van Houtte—*Spiraea vanhouttei* (E)

    c. Anthony Waterer—*Spiraea bumalda* 'Anthony Waterer' (E)

Sumac

    a. Littleleaf sumac—*Rhus microphylla* (N)

    b. Skunkbush—*Rhus trilobata* (N)

    c. Smooth sumac—*Rhus glabra* (N)

    d. Staghorn sumac—*Rhus typhina* (E)

Weigela—*Weigela florida* (E)

Willow

    a. Coyote willow—*Salix exigua* (N)

    b. Pussywillow—*Salix discolor* (N, E)

Winterfat—*Ceratoides lanata* (N)

B. Evergreen

Agave (century plant, mescal)

    a. Century plant—*Agave americana* (N)

    b. Parry agave—*Agave parryi* (N)

Arborvitae—*Thuja* spp., *Platycladus* spp. (E)

Barberry

    a. Colorado barberry—*Berberis fendleri* (N)

    b. Japanese barberry—*Berberis thunbergii* (E)

    c. Three-spine barberry—*Berberis wisleyensis* (E)

    d. Wintergreen barberry—*Berberis julianae* (E)

Beargrass—*Nolina microcarpa* (N)

Parney cotoneaster—*Cotoneaster lacteus* (E)

Yaupon holly—*Ilex vomitoria* (E)

India hawthorn—*Rhaphiolepis indica* (E)

Chinese junipers

    a. Armstrong juniper—*Juniperus chinensis* 'Armstrong' (E)

    b. Pfitzer juniper—*Juniperus chinensis* 'Pfitzerana' (E)

    c. Sea Green juniper—*Juniperus chinensis* 'Sea Green' (E)

Common juniper—*Juniperus communis* (N)

Mahonia

    a. Algerita—*Mahonia haematocarpa* (N)

    b. Agritos—*Mahonia trifoliolata* (N)

    c. Oregon grape—*Mahonia aquifolium* (E, NZ)

Mormon tea—*Ephedra* spp. (N)

Nandina (heavenly bamboo)—*Nandina domestica* (E)
Mugo pine—*Pinus mugo* (E)
Pyracantha (firethorn)—*Pyracantha* spp. (E)
Sage
    a.Big sage (sagebrush)—*Artemisia tridentata* (N)
    b.Sand sage—*Artemisia filifolia* (N)
Fourwing saltbush—*Atriplex canescens* (N)
Seepwillow -*Baccharis sarothroides* (N)
Yucca
    a.Narrowleaf yucca—*Yucca glauca* (N)
    b.Softblade yucca—*Yucca recurvifolia* (*Yucca pendula*) (E)

GROUND COVERS

A. Deciduous

Spring cinquefoil—*Potentilla tabernaemontani* (E)
Clover—*Trifolium* spp. (NZ, N)
Crown vetch—*Coronilla varia* (E, NZ)
Prairie sage—*Artemisia ludoviciana* (N)
Memorial rose (vine)—*Rosa wichuriana* (E)

B. Evergreen

Bearberry cotoneaster—*Cotoneaster dammeri* (E)
Creeping euonymus—*Euonymus fortunei* (E)
Honeysuckle—*Lonicera japonica* varieties (E)
Horizontalis junipers
    a.Andorra juniper—*Juniperus horizontalis plumosa* (E)
    b.Bar Harbor juniper—*Juniperus horizontalis* 'Bar Harbor' (E)
    c.Wilton carpet juniper—*Juniperus horizontalis* 'Wiltonii' (E)
Sabina junipers
    a.Broadmoor juniper—*Juniperus sabina* 'Broadmoor' (E)
    b.Buffalo juniper—*Juniperus sabina* 'Buffalo' (E)
    c.Tam (tammy) juniper—*Juniperus sabina* 'Tamariscifolia' (E)
Blue leadwort—*Ceratostigma plumbaginoides* (E)
Compact nandina—*Nandina domestica* 'Harbor dwarf' (E)
Periwinkle—*Vinca major* and *Vinca minor* (E)
Pussytoes—*Antennaria parviflora* (N)
Santolina
    a.Green santolina—*Santolina virens* (E)
    b.Gray santolina—*Santolina chamaecyparissus* (E)
Sedum (stonecrop)—*Sedum* spp. (N, E)

GRASSES

A. Traditional Turf Species

Bermuda
    a.African bermuda—*Cynodon transvaalensis* (E, NZ)
    b.Common bermuda—*Cynodon dactylon* (NZ)
Fescue—*Festuca* spp. (E)
Ryegrass—*Lolium* spp. (E)

B. Native Turf And General-Use Species

Buffalo grass—*Buchlöe dactyloides* (N)
Blue grama—*Bouteloua gracilis* (N)
Galleta—*Hilaria jamesii* (N)
Wheatgrass
    a.Western wheatgrass—*Agropyron smithii* (N)
    b.Crested wheatgrass—*Agropyron desertorum* (E, NZ)
    c.Pubescent wheatgrass—*Agropyron trichophorum* (N)

C. Ornamental Species

Alkali sacaton—*Sporobolus airoides* (N)
Fountain grass—*Pennisetum* spp. (E)
Pampas grass—*Cortaderia selloana* (E)
River cane—*Arundo donax* (NZ)

VINES

A. Deciduous

Boston ivy—*Parthenocissus tricuspidata* (E)
Canyon grape—*Vitis arizonica* (N)
Carolina jessamine—*Gelsemium sempervirens* (E)
Clematis—*Clematis jackmanni* (E)
Morning glory—*Ipomoea tricolor* (E)
Trumpet vine—*Campsis radicans* (E)
Virginia creeper (et al)—*Parthenocissus quinquefolia* (N, E)

B. Evergreen

English ivy—*Hedera helix* (E)
Honeysuckle—*Lonicera* spp. (E)

FLOWERS

A. Annuals

Purple aster—*Aster bigelovii* (N)
Cosmos—*Cosmos* spp. (E)
Four o'clock—*Mirabilis jalapa* (E)
Gaillardia (blanketflower, firewheel)—*Gaillardia pulchella* (N)
Geranium—*Pelargonium hortorum* (E)
Impatiens—*Impatiens wallerana* (E)
Marigold—*Tagetes* spp. (E)
Petunia—*Petunia* spp. (E)
Salvia—*Salvia* spp. (E)
Snapdragon—*Antirrhinum majus* (E)
Sunflower—*Helianthus annuus* (N)
Annual vinca (Madagascar periwinkle)—*Catharanthus roseus* (E)

B. Perennials

Desert baileya—*Baileya multiradiata* (N)
Chrysanthemum—*Chrysanthemum morifolium* (E)
Colorado columbine—*Aquilegia* spp. (N)
Coneflower—*Ratibida columnifera* (N)
Daylily (asphodel)—*Hemerocallis* spp. (E)
Fendler's sundrops—*Calylophus hartwegii fendleri* (N)
Hollyhock—*Alcea rosea* (E, NZ)
Indian paintbrush—*Castilleja integra* (N)
Jimsonweed (datura, sacred datura)—*Datura meteloides* (N)
Lobelia—*Lobelia erinus* (E)
Maximilian's daisy—*Helianthus maximiliani* (NZ)
Penstemon—*Penstemon* spp. (N)
Phlox—*Phlox* spp. (E)
California poppy—*Eschscholzia californica* (and *E. mexicana*) (E,N)
Shasta daisy—*Chrysanthemum maximum* (E)
Violet—*Viola odorata* (N, E)
Wooly yarrow—*Achillea* spp. (N, E)

C. Bulbs

Canna—*Canna* spp. (E)
Common hyacinth—*Hyacinthus orientalis* (E)
Daffodil—*Narcissus* 'King Alfred' (E)
Dutch crocus—*Crocus verus* (E)
Garden gladiolus—*Gladiolus hortulanus* (E)
Iris—*Iris* spp. (N, E)
Tulip—*Tulipa* spp. (E)

City Hall, Grants

Gallup and Grants both have short growing seasons of about 120–126 days and an annual rainfall between 9 and 12 inches (225–300 mm) per year. Soils in the two cities can be challenging to gardeners—they are often thin, stony, very high in clay content, and alkaline. Some soils in Grants are also saline. Bedrock frequently lies just below the surface.

The virtually identical high altitude of these cities (6514 feet in Gallup, 6520 feet in Grants—about 2000 m) and their location on the Colorado Plateau often can lead to cold winters. Gallup lies in an exposed location and may experience more temperature extremes than Grants. Most plant species that thrive in Gallup and Grants are hardy and adaptable.

The native landscape near both cities comprises piñon- and juniper-covered foothills. Little pockets of Gambel oak, fourwing saltbush, New Mexico olive, and cottonwoods subsist in small valleys and along arroyos, and small, exotic groves of silver poplar, salt cedar, Russian olive, and Siberian elm are scattered in arroyos and swales. Grama species, buffalo grass, sand dropseed, Indian ricegrass, snakeweed, greasewood, big sage, and yuccas are also commonly found. Ponderosa pine, narrowleaf cottonwood, Douglas fir, coyote willow, white fir, limber pine, and aspen are typical trees in the higher elevations.

Cattle and sheep raising is by far the most important agricultural activity in McKinley and Cibola counties. Limited amounts of alfalfa, corn, vegetables, and other crops are grown through irrigation.

Although the environment surrounding these western New Mexico cities is both colorful and spectacular, landscapes and gardens in Gallup and Grants tend to be small-scale and modest. Favorite trees in both cities include Rio Grande cottonwood, black locust, New Mexico locust, Rocky Mountain juniper, weeping and globe willows, flowering crab, blue spruce, Douglas fir, and the ubiquitous and tough-as-nails Siberian elm. Russian olives are often cultivated very successfully as hedges. White poplars and 'Sunburst' honey locusts are very appealing accent trees. Gladiolas, mums, Shasta daisies, black-eyed Susans, sunflowers, asters, marigolds, gaillardias, lilacs, globemallows, hollyhocks, and snapdragons provide excellent spring and summer color.

In Grants, the native New Mexico olive is particularly attractive in "pocket" landscapes set against the deep black local basalt. Fourwing saltbush is also highly useful in many situations here. *Rosa rugosa* is the most popular flowering shrub in the city in the warm summer months.

Among Gallup's finest modern landscapes are the grounds of Roosevelt Elementary School. In Grants, the new San José River Park near the Municipal Government Complex uses water and an imaginatively refurbished neighborhood setting to create an attractive public open space.

GALLUP AND GRANTS

(both founded in 1882), including Zuni, Laguna, and Acoma pueblos, Milan, and Window Rock, Arizona

SELECTED BEST PLANTS FOR GRANTS AND GALLUP

These plant species grow very well in and around Grants and Gallup. For the sake of convenience and quick reference, each plant is listed as native (N), naturalized (NZ), or exotic (E). Other plants also will perform well in landscape and garden situations in the Grants and Gallup area. Please see the New Mexico Plant File for these species.

TREES

A. Deciduous Shade, Street, and Specialty Trees

Ash
    a.White ash—*Fraxinus americana* and varieties (E)
    b.Green ash—*Fraxinus pennsylvanica* and
       varieties (E)
Paper birch—*Betula papyrifera* (E)
Catalpa
    a.Umbrella catalpa—*Catalpa bignonioides*
       'Nana' (E)
    b.Western catalpa—*Catalpa speciosa* (E)
Cottonwood, Aspen, and Poplar: Trees of the Genus
    Populus
    a.Aspen—*Populus tremuloides* (N)
    b.Carolina poplar—*Populus canadensis* (E)
    c.Fremont cottonwood—*Populus fremontii* (N)
    d.Lombardy poplar—*Populus nigra* 'Italica' (E)
    e.Narrowleaf cottonwood—*Populus*
       angustifolia (N)
    f.Rio Grande cottonwood—*Populus fremontii*
       'Wislizeni' (N)
    g.White (silver) poplar—*Populus alba* (NZ)
American elm—*Ulmus americana* (E)
Honey locust—*Gleditsia triacanthos inermis*
    varieties (E)
Locust
    a.Black locust—*Robinia pseudoacacia* (NZ)
    b.New Mexico locust—*Robinia neomexicana* (N)
Maple and Box elder
    a.Box elder—*Acer negundo* (N)
    b.Rocky Mountain maple—*Acer glabrum* (N)
    c.Silver maple—*Acer saccharinum* (E)
European mountain ash—*Sorbus aucuparia* (E)
Fruitless mulberry—*Morus alba* (E)
Gambel oak—*Quercus gambelii* (N)
Russian olive—*Elaeagnus angustifolia* (NZ)
Willow
    a.Globe Navajo willow—*Salix matsudana*
       'Navajo' (E)
    b.Peachleaf willow—*Salix amygdaloides* (N)
    c.Weeping willow—*Salix babylonica* (and other
       weeping willow species) (E)

B. Flowering Ornamental Trees

Flowering cherry—*Prunus serrulata* et al (E)
Flowering crab—*Malus* 'Hopa' et al (E)
Desert willow—*Chilopsis linearis* (N)
Flowering peach—*Prunus persica* (E)
Purpleleaf plum—*Prunus cerasifera* (E)
Eastern redbud—*Cercis canadensis* (E)
Salt cedar—*Tamarix chinensis* (NZ)
Smoke tree—*Cotinus coggygria* (E)

C. Evergreen Trees

Arizona cypress—*Cupressus arizonica* (N)
Douglas fir—*Pseudotsuga menziesii* (N)
Juniper
    a.Eastern red cedar—*Juniperus virginiana*
       varieties (E)
    b.Rocky Mountain juniper—*Juniperus scopulorum*
       varieties (N)
    c.Singleseed (one-seed) juniper—*Juniperus*
       monosperma (N)
Pine
    a.Austrian pine—*Pinus nigra* (E)
    b.Japanese black pine—*Pinus thunbergiana* (E)
    c.Limber pine—*Pinus flexilis* (N)
    d.Piñon pine—*Pinus edulis* (N)
    e.Ponderosa pine—*Pinus ponderosa* (N)
    f.Scotch pine—*Pinus sylvestris* (E)
Spruce
    a.Blue spruce—*Picea pungens* (N)
    b.Engelmann spruce—*Picea engelmanni* (N)
Soaptree yucca—*Yucca elata* (N)

SHRUBS

A. Deciduous

Althea (rose of Sharon)—*Hibiscus syriacus* (E)
Apache plume—*Fallugia paradoxa* (N)
Shrubby cinquefoil—*Potentilla fruticosa* (N)
Cotoneaster
    a.Cranberry cotoneaster—*Cotoneaster*
       apiculatus (E)
    b.Rock cotoneaster—*Cotoneaster horizontalis* (E)
    c.Rockspray cotoneaster—*Cotoneaster*
       microphyllus (E)
Currant and gooseberry—*Ribes* spp. (N)
Red osier dogwood—*Cornus stolonifera* (N)
Shrub or Tatarian honeysuckle—*Lonicera tatarica* (E)
Common lilac—*Syringa vulgaris* (E)
Mountain mahogany—*Cercocarpus montanus* (N)
New Mexico olive—*Forestiera neomexicana* (N)
Cistena plum—*Prunus cistena* (E)
Sand plum—*Prunus americana* (N)
Privet—*Ligustrum* spp. (E)
Rose—*Rosa* spp. (N, E)
Snakeweed—*Gutierrezia sarothrae* (N)
Snowball—*Viburnum opulus* 'Roseum' (E)
Spirea
    a.Bridal wreath—*Spiraea prunifolia* (E)
    b.Anthony Waterer—*Spiraea bumalda* 'Anthony
       Waterer' (E)
Sumac
    a.Skunkbush—*Rhus trilobata* (N)
    b.Smooth sumac—*Rhus glabra* (N)
    c.Staghorn sumac—*Rhus typhina* (E)
Willow
    a.Coyote willow—*Salix exigua* (N)
    b.Pussywillow—*Salix discolor* (N, E)
Winterfat—*Ceratoides lanata* (N)

B. Evergreen

Agave (century plant)—*Agave americana* (N)
Barberry
    a.Colorado barberry—*Berberis fendleri* (N)
    b.Japanese barberry—*Berberis thunbergii* (E)
    c.Three-spine barberry—*Berberis wisleyensis* (E)
    d.Wintergreen barberry—*Berberis julianae* (E)
Beargrass—*Nolina microcarpa* (N)

Grove of flowering crabs

Cactus
- a. Common cholla—*Opuntia imbricata* (N)
- b. Prickly pear—*Opuntia chlorotica* or *O. engelmannii* (N)

Parney cotoneaster—*Cotoneaster lacteus* (E)

Chinese junipers
- a. Armstrong juniper—*Juniperus chinensis* 'Armstrong' (E)
- b. Pfitzer juniper—*Juniperus chinensis* 'Pfitzerana' (E)
- c. Sea Green juniper—*Juniperus chinensis* 'Sea Green' (E)

Common juniper—*Juniperus communis* (N)

Mahonia
- a. Algerita—*Mahonia haematocarpa* (N)
- b. Agritos—*Mahonia trifoliolata* (N)
- c. Oregon grape—*Mahonia aquifolium* (E, NZ)

Mormon tea—*Ephedra* spp. (N)

Nandina (heavenly bamboo)—*Nandina domestica* (E)

Photinia
- a. Chinese photinia—*Photinia serrulata* (E)
- b. Fraser's photinia—*Photinia fraseri* (E)

Mugo pine—*Pinus mugo* (E)

Pyracantha (firethorn)—*Pyracantha* spp. (E)

Rubber rabbitbrush—*Chrysothamnus nauseosus* (N)

Big sage (sagebrush)—*Artemisia tridentata* (N)

Fourwing saltbush—*Atriplex canescens* (N)

Seepwillow -*Baccharis sarothroides* (N)

Yucca
- a. Narrowleaf yucca—*Yucca glauca* (N)
- b. Softblade yucca—*Yucca recurvifolia* (*Yucca pendula*) (N)
- c. Spanish bayonet—*Yucca baccata* (N)

GROUND COVERS

A. Deciduous

Spring cinquefoil—*Potentilla tabernaemontani* (E)
Clover—*Trifolium* spp. (NZ, N)
Crown vetch—*Coronilla varia* (E, NZ)
Prairie sage—*Artemisia ludoviciana* (N)

B. Evergreen

Creeping euonymus—*Euonymus fortunei* (E)
Honeysuckle—*Lonicera japonica* varieties (E)
Horizontalis junipers
    a.Bar Harbor juniper—*Juniperus horizontalis* 'Bar Harbor' (E)
    b.Wilton carpet juniper—*Juniperus horizontalis* 'Wiltonii' (E)
Sabina junipers
    a.Broadmoor juniper—*Juniperus sabina* 'Broadmoor' (E)
    b.Buffalo juniper—*Juniperus sabina* 'Buffalo' (E)
    c.Tam (tammy) juniper—*Juniperus sabina* 'Tamariscifolia' (E)
Kinnickinnick (mountain bearberry)—*Arctostaphylos uva-ursi* (N)
Blue leadwort—*Ceratostigma plumbaginoides* (E)
Periwinkle—*Vinca major* and *Vinca minor* (E)
Gray santolina—*Santolina chamaecyparissus* (E)

GRASSES

A. Traditional Turf Species

Bluegrass—*Poa pratensis* (NZ)
Fescue—*Festuca* spp. (E)
Ryegrass—*Lolium* spp. (E)

B. Native Turf And General-Use Species

Buffalo grass—*Buchlöe dactyloides* (N)
Galleta—*Hilaria jamesii* (N)
Grama
    a.Blue grama—*Bouteloua gracilis* (N)
    b.Sideoats grama—*Bouteloua curtipendula* (N)
Wheatgrass
    a.Western wheatgrass—*Agropyron smithii* (N)
    b.Pubescent wheatgrass—*Agropyron trichophorum* (N)

C. Ornamental Species

Alkali sacaton—*Sporobolus airoides* (N)
Sand dropseed—*Sporobolus cryptandrus* (N)
Indian ricegrass—*Oryzopsis hymenoides* (N)
Purple threeawn—*Aristida longiseta* (N)

VINES

A. Deciduous

Canyon grape—*Vitis arizonica* (N)
Silver lace vine—*Polygonum aubertii* (E)
Trumpet vine—*Campsis radicans* (E)
Virginia creeper (et al)—*Parthenocissus quinquefolia* (N, E)

B. Evergreen

Honeysuckle—*Lonicera* spp. (E)
English ivy—*Hedera helix* (E)

FLOWERS

A. Annuals

Purple aster—*Aster bigelovii* (N)
Cosmos—*Cosmos* spp. (E)
Four o'clock—*Mirabilis jalapa* (N, E)
Geranium—*Pelargonium hortorum* (E)
Marigold—*Tagetes* spp. (E)
Pansy—*Viola wittrockiana* (E)
Petunia—*Petunia* spp. (E)
Snapdragon—*Antirrhinum majus* (E)
Sunflower—*Helianthus annuus* (N)

B. Perennials

Daylily (asphodel)—*Hemerocallis* spp. (E)
Chrysanthemum—*Chrysanthemum morifolium* (E)
Blue flax—*Linum perenne* (N)
Dusty miller—*Senecio cineraria* (E)
Globemallow—*Sphaeralcea incana* (scarlet) (N)
Hollyhock—*Alcea rosea* (E, NZ)
Lobelia—*Lobelia erinus* (E)
Maximilian's daisy—*Helianthus maximiliani* (N)
Paperflower—*Psilostrophe tagetina* (N)
Shasta daisy—*Chrysanthemum maximum* (E)

C. Bulbs

Canna—*Canna* spp. (E)
Dutch crocus—*Crocus verus* (E)
Daffodil—*Narcissus* 'King Alfred' (E)
Garden gladiolus—*Gladiolus hortulanus* (E)
Iris—*Iris* spp. (N, E)

The campus of New Mexico Junior College in Hobbs

Hobbs (altitude 3625 feet/1100 m), located on the *Llano Estacado* (Staked Plains) in the southeastern corner of New Mexico, is best known as an oil center. Yet Lea County is a highly productive agricultural area as well. The county's growing season is long at 217 days, and rainfall ranges from 15 to 27 inches (375 mm to 675 mm) per year, quite substantial for New Mexico. Most livestock raising is centered on cattle and calves. Wheat and hay are grown, as well as corn, sorghum, cotton, and modest quantities of other crops. Many crops are irrigated. The plains soils are often only a few feet thick and lie above a limestone stratum ("caprock"); though generally productive, they tend to be alkaline.

The general topography is flat or slightly rolling. Native plants include buffalo, wheat-grass, grama, and other prairie grass species, but these have generally been disturbed or modified by exotic introductions. Cholla and prickly pear cactus and narrowleaf yucca are common on the range, as is the very curious shin oak (*Quercus havardii*), a ground-cover oak growing across vast expanses of fields and hillocks throughout Lea County. Mesquite also occurs frequently in low clumps. In general, the countryside is agricultural or outright industrial: pump jacks are everywhere to be seen north and south of Hobbs.

Southern live oak and Texas oak are popular favorites in Hobbs landscapes. Atlas cedar, deodar cedar, and cedar of Lebanon grow extremely well and are outstanding "skyline" trees. *Magnolia grandiflora* grows and flowers better in Hobbs than anywhere else in New

HOBBS

(founded in 1910), including Lovington, Tatum, Jal, and Eunice

Mexico. Many private gardens display redbud, Italian cypress, Arizona cypress, various ash species, lilac, daffodil, althea, fig, windflowers, trumpet vine, yaupon holly, fountain grass, and flowering peach to good advantage. Hobbseans frequently use English ivy, periwinkle, honeysuckle, ajuga, and cotoneasters as ground covers. Popular shade and street trees include honey locust, silver maple, Russian olive, globe willow, catalpa, Bradford pear, and American and Siberian elm. Various nandina varieties may be the city's most popular shrub.

A whimsical pompom juniper "forest" has been for some years a remarkable landscape feature at the Lea County Good Samaritan Center. In Lovington, the Lea County Courthouse Square is an outstanding and influential historic landscape. The campus of New Mexico Junior College, just north of Hobbs, has attractive and well-maintained tree groves, seating areas, and accent plantings.

SELECTED BEST PLANTS FOR HOBBS

These plant species grow very well in and around Hobbs. For the sake of convenience and quick reference, each plant is listed as native (N), naturalized (NZ), or exotic (E). Other plants also will perform well in landscape and garden situations in the Hobbs area. Please see the New Mexico Plant File for these species.

TREES

A. Deciduous Shade, Street, and Specialty Trees

Ash
    a.Green ash—*Fraxinus pennsylvanica* and
       varieties (E)
    b.White ash—*Fraxinus americana* and varieties (E)
Paper birch—*Betula papyrifera* (E)
Catalpa
    a.Umbrella catalpa—*Catalpa bignonioides*
      'Nana' (E)
    b.Western catalpa—*Catalpa speciosa* (E)
Chinaberry—*Melia azedarach* (E)
Cottonwood, Aspen, and Poplar: Trees of the Genus *Populus*
    a.Bolleana poplar—*Populus alba* 'Pyramidalis' (E)
    b.Lombardy poplar—*Populus nigra* 'Italica' (E)
    c.Plains cottonwood—*Populus sargenti* (N)
    d.Rio Grande cottonwood—*Populus fremontii*
      'Wislizeni' (N)
    e.White (silver) poplar—*Populus alba* (E)
American elm—*Ulmus americana* (E)
Locust
    a.Black locust—*Robinia pseudoacacia* (NZ)
    b.Hybrid locusts—*Robinia ambigua* varieties (E)
    c.New Mexico locust—*Robinia neomexicana* (N)
Honey locust—*Gleditsia triacanthos inermis*
    varieties (E)
Silver maple—*Acer saccharinum* (E)
Mesquite—*Prosopis glandulosa* (N)

Mulberry
    a.Fruitless mulberry—*Morus alba* (E)
    b.Weeping mulberry—*Morus alba* 'Pendula' (E)
Oak
    a.Texas oak—*Quercus texana* (E)
    b.Southern live oak—*Quercus virginiana* (E)
Pecan—*Carya illinoiensis* (E)
Russian olive—*Elaeagnus angustifolia* (NZ)
Silk tree—*Albizia jilibrissin* (E)
Western soapberry—*Sapindus drummondii* (N)
Sycamore (plane tree)
    a.American sycamore—*Platanus occidentalis* (E)
    b.London plane tree—*Platanus acerifolia* (E)
Willow
    a.Corkscrew willow—*Salix matsudana*
      'Tortuosa' (E)
    b.Globe Navajo willow—*Salix matsudana*
      'Navajo' (E)
    c.Weeping willow—*Salix babylonica* (and other
      weeping willow species) (E)

B. Flowering Ornamental Trees

Flowering apricot—*Prunus armeniaca* (E)
Flowering crab—*Malus* 'Hopa' et al (E)
Desert willow—*Chilopsis linearis* (N)
Hawthorn—*Crataegus* spp. (E)
Flowering peach—*Prunus persica* (E)
Bradford pear—*Pyrus calleryana* (E)
Purpleleaf plum—*Prunus cerasifera* (E)
Eastern redbud—*Cercis canadensis* (E)
Smoke tree—*Cotinus coggygria* (E)
Vitex (chaste tree)—*Vitex agnus-castus* (E)

C. Evergreen Trees

Cedar
    a.Atlas cedar—*Cedrus atlantica* (E)
    b.Cedar of Lebanon—*Cedrus libani* (E)
    c.Deodar cedar—*Cedrus deodara* (E)
Cypress
    a.Arizona cypress—*Cupressus arizonica* (N)
    b.Italian cypress—*Cupressus sempervirens* (E)
Douglas fir—*Pseudotsuga menziesii* (N)
Juniper
    a.Alligator juniper—*Juniperus deppeana* (N)
    b.Chinese juniper—*Juniperus chinensis* varieties (E)
    c.Eastern red cedar—*Juniperus virginiana*
      varieties (E)
Magnolia
    a.Southern magnolia—*Magnolia grandiflora* (E)
    b.Saucer magnolia—*Magnolia soulangiana* (E)
Chinese windmill palm—*Trachycarpus fortunei* (E)
Pine
    a.Afghan pine—*Pinus eldarica* (E)
    b.Aleppo pine—*Pinus halepensis* (E)
    c.Austrian pine—*Pinus nigra* (E)
    d.Japanese black pine—*Pinus thunbergiana* (E)
    e.Limber pine—*Pinus flexilis* (N)
    f.Pinon pine—*Pinus edulis* (N)
    g.Ponderosa pine—*Pinus ponderosa* (N)
    h.Scotch pine—*Pinus sylvestris* (E)
Dawn redwood—*Metasequoia glyptostroboides* (E)
Spruce
    a.Blue spruce—*Picea pungens* (N)
    b.Engelmann spruce—*Picea engelmanni* (N)
Yucca
    a.Palm yucca—*Yucca torreyi* (N)
    b.Soaptree yucca—*Yucca elata* (N)

SHRUBS

A. Deciduous

Althea (rose of Sharon)—*Hibiscus syriacus* (E)
Golden bamboo—*Phyllostachys aurea* (E)
Spanish broom—*Spartium junceum* (E)
Cotoneaster
    a.Cranberry cotoneaster—*Cotoneaster apiculatus* (E)
    b.Rock cotoneaster—*Cotoneaster horizontalis* (E)
    c.Rockspray cotoneaster—*Cotoneaster microphyllus* (E)
Crape myrtle—*Lagerstroemia indica* (E)
Currant and gooseberry—*Ribes* spp. (N, E)
Edible fig—*Ficus carica* (E)
Forsythia—*Forsythia* spp. (E)
Shrub or Tatarian honeysuckle—*Lonicera tatarica* (E)
Flowering jasmine—*Jasminum nudiflorum* (E)
Common lilac—*Syringa vulgaris* (E)
New Mexico olive—*Forestiera neomexicana* (N)
Cistena plum—*Prunus cistena* (E)
Privet—*Ligustrum* spp. (E)
Flowering quince—*Chaenomeles speciosa* (E)
Rose—*Rosa* spp. (E, N)
Snowball—*Viburnum opulus* 'Roseum' (E)
Spirea
    a.Bridal wreath—*Spiraea prunifolia* (E)
    b.Van Houtte—*Spiraea vanhouttei* (E)
    c.Anthony Waterer—*Spiraea bumalda* 'Anthony Waterer' (E)
Sumac
    a.Skunkbush—*Rhus trilobata* (N)
    b.Staghorn sumac—*Rhus typhina* (E)
Weigela—*Weigela florida* (E)
Willow
    a.Coyote willow—*Salix exigua* (N)
    b.Pussywillow—*Salix discolor* (N, E)
Winterfat—*Ceratoides lanata* (N)

B. Evergreen

Agave (century plant, mescal)
    a.Century plant—*Agave americana* (N)
    b.Parry agave—*Agave parryi* (N)
Aucuba—*Aucuba japonica* (E)
Barberry
    a.Japanese barberry—*Berberis thunbergii* (E)
    b.Three-spine barberry—*Berberis wisleyensis* (E)
Beargrass—*Nolina microcarpa* (N)
Cactus
    a.Common cholla—*Opuntia imbricata* (N)
    b.Prickly pear—*Opuntia chlorotica* or *O. engelmannii* (N)
Parney cotoneaster—*Cotoneaster lacteus* (E)
Holly
    a.Burford holly—*Ilex cornuta* 'Burfordii' (E)
    b.English holly—*Ilex aquifolium* (E)
    c.Wilson holly—*Ilex altaclarensis* 'Wilsonii' (E)
    d.Yaupon holly—*Ilex vomitoria* (E)
India hawthorn—*Rhaphiolepis indica* (E)
Chinese junipers
    a.Armstrong juniper—*Juniperus chinensis* 'Armstrong' (E)
    b.Pfitzer juniper—*Juniperus chinensis* 'Pfitzerana' (E)
Mahonia
    a.Algerita—*Mahonia haematocarpa* (N)
    b.Oregon grape—*Mahonia aquifolium* (E)
Nandina (heavenly bamboo)—*Nandina domestica* (E)
Ocotillo—*Fouquieria splendens* (N)
Photinia
    a.Chinese photinia—*Photinia serrulata* (E)
    b.Fraser's photinia—*Photinia fraseri* (E)
Mugo pine—*Pinus mugo* (E)
Pittosporum (tobira)—*Pittosporum tobira* (E)
Pyracantha (firethorn)—*Pyracantha* spp. (E)
Fourwing saltbush—*Atriplex canescens* (N)
Seepwillow—*Baccharis sarothroides* (N)
Silverberry—*Elaeagnus pungens* (E)
Sotol—*Dasylirion wheeleri* (N)
Alberta spruce—*Picea glauca* 'Conica' (*Picea albertiana*) (E)
Texas ranger—*Leucophyllum frutescens* (N)
Yucca
    a.Softblade yucca—*Yucca recurvifolia* (*Yucca pendula*) (E)
    b.Spanish bayonet—*Yucca baccata* (N)
    c.Coral-flower yucca—*Hesperaloe parviflora* (E)

GROUND COVERS

A. Deciduous

Clover—*Trifolium* spp. (NZ)
Cranberry cotoneaster—*Cotoneaster apiculatus* (E)
Crown vetch—*Coronilla varia* (E, NZ)
Mint—*Mentha* spp. (E, N, NZ)
Prairie sage—*Artemisia ludoviciana* (N)

B. Evergreen

Dichondra—*Dichondra micrantha* (E)
Horizontalis junipers
    a.Andorra juniper—*Juniperus horizontalis plumosa* (E)
    b.Bar Harbor juniper -*Juniperus horizontalis* 'Bar Harbor' (E)
    c.Wilton carpet juniper—*Juniperus horizontalis* 'Wiltonii' (E)
Sabina junipers
    a.Broadmoor juniper—*Juniperus sabina* 'Broadmoor' (E)
    b.Tam (tammy) juniper—*Juniperus sabina* 'Tamariscifolia' (E)
Lilyturf (liriope)—*Liriope spicata* (E)
Compact nandina—*Nandina domestica* 'Harbor dwarf' (E)
Periwinkle—*Vinca major* and *Vinca minor* (E)
Rosemary—*Rosmarinus officinalis* (E)
Santolina
    a.Green santolina—*Santolina virens* (E)
    b.Gray santolina—*Santolina chamaecyparissus* (E)
Sedum (stonecrop)—*Sedum* spp. (N, E)
Japanese spurge—*Pachysandra terminalis* (E)

GRASSES

A. Traditional Turf Species

Bermuda
    a.African bermuda—*Cynodon transvaalensis* (E, NZ)
    b.Common bermuda—*Cynodon dactylon* (NZ)
Fescue—*Festuca* spp. (E)
Ryegrass—*Lolium* spp. (E)

B. Native Turf And General Use Species

Buffalo grass—*Buchlöe dactyloides* (N)
Grama
    a.Black grama—*Bouteloua eriopoda* (N)
    b.Blue grama—*Bouteloua gracilis* (N)
    c.Sideoats grama—*Bouteloua curtipendula* (N)
Wheatgrass
    a.Western wheatgrass—*Agropyron smithii* (N)
    b.Crested wheatgrass—*Agropyron desertorum*
    (E, NZ)

C. Ornamental Species

Alkali sacaton—*Sporobolus airoides* (N)
Blue fescue—*Festuca caesia* (E)
Pampas grass—*Cortaderia selloana* (E)
River cane—*Arundo donax* (NZ)
Purple threeawn—*Aristida longiseta* (N)

VINES

A. Deciduous

Boston ivy—*Parthenocissus tricuspidata* (E)
Clematis—*Clematis jackmanni* (E)
Morning glory—*Ipomoea tricolor* (E)
Trumpet vine—*Campsis radicans* (E)
Virginia creeper (et al)—*Parthenocissus quinque-folia* (N, E)
Wisteria—*Wisteria sinensis* (E)

B. Evergreen

English ivy—*Hedera helix* (E)
Honeysuckle—*Lonicera* spp. (E)

FLOWERS

A. Annuals

Ageratum—*Ageratum houstonianum* (E)
Purple aster—*Aster bigelovii* (N)
Cosmos—*Cosmos* spp. (E)
Four o'clock—*Mirabilis jalapa* (E)
Gaillardia (blanketflower, firewheel)—*Gaillardia pulchella* (N)
Pansy—*Viola wittrockiana* (E)
Salvia—*Salvia* spp. (E)
Snapdragon—*Antirrhinum majus* (E)
Sunflower—*Helianthus annuus* (N)
Annual vinca (Madagascar periwinkle)—*Catharanthus roseus* (E)

B. Perennials

Desert baileya—*Baileya multiradiata* (N)
Bear's breech—*Acanthus mollis* (E)
Carnation—*Dianthus caryophyllus* (E)
Chrysanthemum—*Chrysanthemum morifolium* (E)
Dusty miller—*Senecio cineraria* (E)
Fendler's sundrops—*Calylophus hartwegii fendlerii* (N)
Geranium (cranesbill)—*Geranium* spp. (E)
Lobelia—*Lobelia erinus* (E)
Maximilian's daisy—*Helianthus maximiliani* (NZ)
Paperflower—*Psilostrophe tagetina* (N)
Phlox—*Phlox* spp. (N)
California poppy—*Eschscholzia californica* (and *E. mexicana*) (E,N)
Violet—*Viola odorata* (N, E)

C. Bulbs

Canna—*Canna* spp. (E)
Daffodil—*Narcissus* 'King Alfred' (E)
Dutch crocus—*Crocus verus* (E)
Garden gladiolus—*Gladiolus hortulanus* (E)
Iris—*Iris* spp. (N, E)
Tulip—*Tulipa* spp. (E)

Las Cruces is the center of the greatest agricultural county (Doña Ana) in New Mexico. At 3881 feet (1175 m), the city has a wonderful climate and a long growing season of 198 days. Rainfall varies from about 8 to 14 inches (200–350 mm) annually. Early settlement may have occurred during Spanish colonial times (1540–1821), but the modern city dates from about 1854. Soils in Las Cruces and throughout the Mesilla Valley are frequently deep and highly productive. Chile, pecan, alfalfa, and cotton farming are extremely important in Doña Ana County, which produces large quantities of market vegetables such as onions and lettuce as well.

In years past, the Rio Grande cottonwood was undoubtedly Las Cruces's most popular and widely planted tree. Now that position has been assumed by the pecan, grown primarily for its nuts but also for shade. It is a first-rate, long-lived, excellent choice for landscape situations. Chinaberry, willows, fruitless mulberry, sycamore, ashes of many species, pistache, Russian olive, salt cedar, desert willow, mesquite, hackberry, soapberry, honey locust, and Arizona walnut are also widely planted shade trees.

Las Cruces has a greater variety of evergreen tree species than any city in the state, and many of these are spectacular. Afghan pine, Aleppo pine, piñon, Japanese black pine, magnolia, many species of cedar, Arizona and Italian cypress, bald cypress, alligator juniper, Rocky Mountain juniper, and western red cedar all flourish here. California fan, Mexican fan, Mediterranean fan, date, Chinese windmill, and Mexican blue palms grow well here, as does sabal palmetto, though they may burn somewhat in winter. They generally flourish with very well-manured backfill and deep periodic irrigation.

Native succulents are no less striking. Torrey and soaptree yuccas and Joshua trees like the climate. Giant agave, lechugilla, sotol, ocotillo, Indian fig prickly pear, cholla, barrel cactus, and even (amazingly) saguaro are especially well adapted to the gravelly and sandy uplands of the city. Other natives and naturalized species often found in Las Cruces gardens are creosote, screwbean mesquite (tornillo), dalea, fourwing saltbush, fernbush, Apache plume, sand penstemon, seepwillow, Texas ranger, New Mexico olive (forestiera), Mexican poppy, paperflower, desert baileya, and littleleaf sumac.

Private Las Cruces gardens are often appealing combinations of desert-inspired, shrub-and-tree-based "Southwestern" areas (usually front and side yards) and intensely

New library at New Mexico State University, Dean Krueger Architects. Morrow and Co., Landscape Architects

green, private "oases" (back yards). Mexican elders are used as quick-growing accent trees, as are golden rain trees, birds of paradise, and vitexes. Oleander, coral-flower yucca, wisteria, Spanish broom, Mormon tea, a number of sage species, India hawthorn, junipers, and several cotoneasters are also widely planted as accent shrubs. Clover, honeysuckle, dichondra, crown vetch, rosemary, teucrium, and dwarf coyotebush are popular ground covers.

The lower Hatch and Mesilla valleys are hot in summer, with distinct riverine vegetation. Rio Grande cottonwoods, several willow species, mesquite, *tornillo,* littleleaf sumac, saltgrass, desert willow, netleaf hackberry, and the highly invasive salt cedar are common plants. In the nearby arroyos and foothills, many of these same species plus Arizona grape, Mexican elder, Arizona ash, catclaw acacia, beargrass, algerita, creosote, fourwing saltbush, Arizona walnut, seepwillow, ocotillo, several cactus species, and numerous desert grasses can be found. In such remarkably picturesque local mountain ranges as the Organs, San Andrés, Robledos, and Uvas, there are oaks, soapberries, pines, and alligator junipers as well. The sandy desert plains west of Las Cruces are typically covered in mesquite, alkali sacaton, Indian ricegrass, several grama

LAS CRUCES

including Hatch, Arrey, Garfield, Doña Ana, Radium Springs, Organ, La Mesilla, Mesilla Park, Chamberino, Mesquite, Rodey, and Anthony

species, soaptree yucca, littleleaf sumac, cacti, creosote, snakeweed, and numerous annual and perennial flowers and forbs.

The campus of New Mexico State University has a large number of ornamental landscape plantings in good condition. The grounds of the new library, with its specimen oak, palm, and Arizona sycamore groves, are particularly appealing. Young, Valley View, Four Hills, San José, Apodaca, and Northridge parks all have well-maintained grounds with many good specimen plantings. The Holiday Inn de Las Cruces has an interesting series of palm, willow, oleander, and other accent plantings. Pioneer Park in Las Cruces and the old plaza at La Mesilla are Doña Ana County's most important historic landscapes.

SELECTED BEST PLANTS FOR LAS CRUCES

These plant species grow very well in and around Las Cruces. For the sake of convenience and quick reference, each plant is listed as native (N), naturalized (NZ), or exotic (E). Other plants also will perform well in landscape and garden situations in the Las Cruces area. Please see the New Mexico Plant File for these species.

TREES

A. Deciduous Shade, Street, and Specialty Trees

Ash
    a.Arizona ash—*Fraxinus velutina* (N)
    b.Modesto ash—*Fraxinus velutina* 'Modesto' (Arizona ash variety) (N)
    c.Green ash—*Fraxinus pennsylvanica* and varieties (E)
    d.Raywood ash—*Fraxinus oxycarpa* 'Raywood' (E)
    e.White ash—*Fraxinus americana* and varieties (E)
Catalpa
    a.Umbrella catalpa—*Catalpa bignonioides* 'Nana' (E)
    b.Western catalpa—*Catalpa speciosa* (E)
Chinaberry—*Melia azedarach* (E)
Cottonwood, Aspen, and Poplar: Trees of the Genus *Populus*
    a.Bolleana poplar—*Populus alba* 'Pyramidalis' (E)
    b.Carolina poplar—*Populus canadensis* (E)
    c.Fremont cottonwood—*Populus fremontii* (N)
    d.Lanceleaf cottonwood—*Populus acuminata* (N)
    e.Lombardy poplar—*Populus nigra* 'Italica' (E)
    f.Narrowleaf cottonwood—*Populus angustifolia* (N)
    g.Rio Grande cottonwood—*Populus fremontii* 'Wislizeni' (N)
American elm—*Ulmus americana* (E)
Hackberry
    a.Common hackberry—*Celtis occidentalis* (E)
    b.Netleaf hackberry—*Celtis reticulata* (N)
Honey locust—*Gleditsia triacanthos inermis* varieties (E)

Jujube—*Zizyphus jujuba* (E)
Locust
    a.Black locust—*Robinia pseudoacacia* (E)
    b.Hybrid locusts—*Robinia ambigua* varieties (E)
Mesquite—*Prosopis glandulosa* (N)
Fruitless mulberry—*Morus alba* (E)
Oak
    a.Cork oak—*Quercus suber* (E)
    b.Southern live oak—*Quercus virginiana* (E)
    c.Texas oak—*Quercus texana* (E)
Osage orange—*Maclura pomifera* (E)
Pecan—*Carya illinoiensis* (E)
Pistache—Pistachio
    a.Chinese pistache—*Pistacia chinensis* (E)
    b.Pistachio—*Pistacia vera* (E)
Russian olive—*Elaeagnus angustifolia* (NZ)
Silk tree—*Albizia jilibrissin* (E)
Sycamore (plane tree)
    a.American sycamore—*Platanus occidentalis* (E)
    b.Arizona sycamore—*Platanus wrightii* (N)
    c.California sycamore—*Platanus racemosa* (E)
    d.London plane tree—*Platanus acerifolia* (E)
Arizona walnut—*Juglans major* (N)
Willow
    a.Corkscrew willow—*Salix matsudana* 'Tortuosa' (E)
    b.Globe Navajo willow—*Salix matsudana* 'Navajo' (E)
    c.Peachleaf willow—*Salix amygdaloides* (N)
    d.Weeping willow—*Salix babylonica* (and other weeping willow species, E)

B. Flowering Ornamental Trees

Desert willow—*Chilopsis linearis* (N)
Mexican elder—*Sambucus caerulea neomexicana* (N)
Flowering peach—*Prunus persica* (E)
Bradford pear—*Pyrus calleryana* (E)
Purpleleaf plum—*Prunus cerasifera* (E)
Golden rain tree—*Koelreuteria paniculata* (E)
Salt cedar—*Tamarix chinensis* (NZ)
Smoke tree—*Cotinus coggygria* (E)
Vitex (chaste tree)—*Vitex agnus-castus* (E)

C. Evergreen Trees

Cedar
    a.Atlas cedar—*Cedrus atlantica* (E)
    b.Cedar of Lebanon—*Cedrus libani* (E)
    c.Deodar cedar—*Cedrus deodara* (E)
Cypress
    a.Arizona cypress—*Cupressus arizonica* (N)
    b.Italian cypress—*Cupressus sempervirens* (E)
Eucalyptus (cider gum)—*Eucalyptus gunnii* (E)
Juniper
    a.Alligator juniper—*Juniperus deppeana* (N)
    b.Eastern red cedar—*Juniperus virginiana* varieties (E)
    c.Rocky Mountain juniper -*Juniperus scopulorum* varieties (N)
Leyland false cypress—*Cupressocyparis leylandii* (E)
Madrone—*Arbutus texana* (N)
Southern magnolia—*Magnolia grandiflora* (E)
Palm
    a.California fan palm—*Washingtonia filifera* (E)
    b.Chinese windmill palm—*Trachycarpus fortunei* (E)
    c.Mexican fan palm—*Washingtonia robusta* (E)
    d.Mediterranean fan palm—*Chamaerops humilis* (E)

Pine
- a. Afghan pine—*Pinus eldarica* (E)
- b. Aleppo pine—*Pinus halepensis* (E)
- c. Italian stone pine—*Pinus pinea* (E)
- d. Japanese black pine—*Pinus thunbergiana* (E)
- e. Piñon pine—*Pinus edulis* (N)
- f. Scotch pine—*Pinus sylvestris* (E)

Yucca
- a. Joshua tree—*Yucca brevifolia* (E)
- b. Palm yucca—*Yucca torreyi* (N)
- c. Soaptree yucca—*Yucca elata* (N)

SHRUBS

A. Deciduous

Glossy abelia—*Abelia grandiflora* (E)
Flowering almond—*Prunus glandulosa* (E)
Althea (rose of Sharon)—*Hibiscus syriacus* (E)
Apache plume—*Fallugia paradoxa* (N)
Golden bamboo—*Phyllostachys aurea* (E, NZ)
Bird of paradise—*Caesalpinia gilliesii* (NZ)
Spanish broom—*Spartium junceum* (E)
Common butterfly bush—*Buddleia davidii* (E)
Cotoneaster
- a. Cranberry cotoneaster—*Cotoneaster apiculatus* (E)
- b. Rock cotoneaster—*Cotoneaster horizontalis* (E)
- c. Rockspray cotoneaster—*Cotoneaster microphyllus* (E)

Crape myrtle—*Lagerstroemia indica* (E)
Cliff fendlerbush—*Fendlera rupicola* (N)
Fernbush—*Chamaebatiaria millefolium* (N)
Edible fig—*Ficus carica* (E)
Screwbean mesquite—*Prosopis pubescens* (N)
New Mexico olive—*Forestiera neomexicana* (N)
Pomegranate—*Punica granatum* (E)
Rose—*Rosa* spp. (E, N)
Sumac
- a. Littleleaf sumac—*Rhus microphylla* (N)
- b. Skunkbush—*Rhus trilobata* (N)

Coyote willow—*Salix exigua* (E)

B. Evergreen

Agave (century plant, mescal)
- a. Century plant—*Agave americana* (N)
- b. Parry agave—*Agave parryi* (N)
- c. Lechugilla—*Agave lechugilla* (N)

Aucuba—*Aucuba japonica* (E)
Barberry
- a. Japanese barberry—*Berberis thunbergii* (E)
- b. Three-spine barberry—*Berberis wisleyensis* (E)

Beargrass—*Nolina microcarpa* (N)
Cactus
- a. Claret cup—*Echinocereus triglochidiatus* (N)
- b. Common cholla—*Opuntia imbricata* (N)
- c. Prickly pear—*Opuntia chlorotica* or *O. engelmannii* (N)

Parney cotoneaster—*Cotoneaster lacteus* (E)
Creosotebush—*Larrea tridentata* (N)
Yaupon holly—*Ilex vomitoria* (E)
India hawthorn—*Rhaphiolepis indica* (E)
Chinese junipers
- a. Armstrong juniper—*Juniperus chinensis* 'Armstrong' (E)
- b. Pfitzer juniper—*Juniperus chinensis* 'Pfitzerana' (E)
- c. Sea Green juniper—*Juniperus chinensis* 'Sea Green' (E)

Mahonia
- a. Algerita—*Mahonia haematocarpa* (N)
- b. Agritos—*Mahonia trifoliolata* (N)
- c. Oregon grape—*Mahonia aquifolium* (E, NZ)

Mormon tea—*Ephedra* spp. (N)
Nandina (heavenly bamboo)—*Nandina domestica* (E)
Ocotillo—*Fouquieria splendens* (N)
Oleander—*Nerium oleander* (E)
Photinia
- a. Chinese photinia—*Photinia serrulata* (E)
- b. Fraser's photinia—*Photinia fraseri* (E)

Pittosporum (tobira)—*Pittosporum tobira* (E)
Pyracantha (firethorn)—*Pyracantha* spp. (E)
Sand sage—*Artemisia filifolia* (N)
Fourwing saltbush—*Atriplex canescens* (N)
Seepwillow—*Baccharis sarothroides* (N)
Silverberry—*Elaeagnus pungens* (E)
Sotol—*Dasylirion wheeleri* (N)
Texas ranger—*Leucophyllum frutescens* (E)
Yucca
- a. Softblade yucca—*Yucca recurvifolia* (*Yucca pendula*) (E)
- b. Spanish bayonet—*Yucca baccata* (N)
- c. Coral-flower yucca—*Hesperaloe parviflora* (E)

GROUND COVERS

A. Deciduous

Clover—*Trifolium* spp. (NZ)
Cranberry cotoneaster—*Cotoneaster apiculatus* (E)
Crown vetch—*Coronilla varia* (E, NZ)
Mint—*Mentha* spp. (E, N, NZ)
Prairie sage—*Artemisia ludoviciana* (N)
Snow-in summer—*Cerastium tomentosum* (E)

B. Evergreen

Dwarf coyotebrush—*Baccharis pilularis* (E)
Creeping euonymus—*Euonymus fortunei* (E)
Dichondra—*Dichondra micrantha* (E)
Germander—*Teucrium chamaedrys* 'Prostratum' (E)
Honeysuckle—*Lonicera japonica* varieties (E)
Horizontalis junipers
- a. Andorra juniper—*Juniperus horizontalis plumosa* (E)
- b. Bar Harbor juniper—*Juniperus horizontalis* 'Bar Harbor' (E)
- c. Wilton carpet juniper—*Juniperus horizontalis* 'Wiltonii' (E)

Sabina junipers
- a. Broadmoor juniper—*Juniperus sabina* 'Broadmoor' (E)
- b. Buffalo juniper—*Juniperus sabina* 'Buffalo' (E)
- c. Tam (tammy) juniper—*Juniperus sabina* 'Tamariscifolia' (E)

Blue leadwort—*Ceratostigma plumbaginoides* (E)
Lilyturf (liriope)—*Liriope spicata* (E)
Periwinkle—*Vinca major* and *Vinca minor* (E)
Rosemary—*Rosmarinus officinalis* (E)
Santolina
- a. Green santolina—*Santolina virens* (E)
- b. Gray santolina—*Santolina chamaecyparissus* (E)

Sedum (stonecrop)—*Sedum* spp. (N, E)
Japanese spurge—*Pachysandra terminalis* (E)

*Hotel and drainage
channel landscape,
Las Cruces*

GRASSES

A. Traditional Turf Species

Bermuda
    a.African bermuda—*Cynodon transvaalensis*
      (E, NZ)
    b.Common bermuda—*Cynodon dactylon* (E, NZ)
Fescue—*Festuca* spp. (E, N)
Ryegrass—*Lolium* spp. (E)

B. Native Turf And General-Use Species

Grama
    a.Black grama—*Bouteloua eriopoda* (N)
    b.Blue grama—*Bouteloua gracilis* (N)
    c.Sideoats grama—*Bouteloua curtipendula* (N)
Wheatgrass
    a.Western wheatgrass—*Agropyron smithii* (N)
    b.Crested wheatgrass—*Agropyron desertorum*
      (E, NZ)
    c.Pubescent wheatgrass—*Agropyron tricho-
phorum* (N)

C. Ornamental Species

Alkali sacaton—*Sporobolus airoides* (N)
Sand dropseed—*Sporobolus cryptandrus* (N)
Blue fescue—*Festuca caesia* (E)
Fountain grass—*Pennisetum* spp. (E)
Pampas grass—*Cortaderia selloana* (E)
Indian ricegrass—*Oryzopsis hymenoides* (N)
River cane—*Arundo donax* (NZ)

VINES

A. Deciduous

Canyon grape—*Vitis arizonica* (N)
Carolina jessamine—*Gelsemium sempervirens* (E)
Silver lace vine—*Polygonum aubertii* (E)
Trumpet vine—*Campsis radicans* (E)
Virginia creeper (et al)—*Parthenocissus quinque-
folia* (N, E)
Wisteria—*Wisteria sinensis* (E)

B. Evergreen

Algerian ivy—*Hedera canariensis* (E)
English ivy—*Hedera helix* (E)
Honeysuckle—*Lonicera* spp. (E)

FLOWERS

A. Annuals

Purple aster—*Aster bigelovii* (N)
Coleus—*Coleus x hybridus* (E)
Cosmos—*Cosmos* spp. (E)
Four o'clock—*Mirabilis jalapa* (E)
Gaillardia (blanketflower, firewheel)—*Gaillardia
pulchella* (N)
Impatiens—*Impatiens wallerana* (E)
Lisianthus—*Eustoma grandiflorum* (E)
Marigold—*Tagetes* spp. (E)
Petunia—*Petunia* spp. (E)
Salvia—*Salvia* spp. (E)
Sunflower—*Helianthus annuus* (N)
Annual vinca (Madagascar periwinkle)—*Catharanthus
roseus* (E)

B. Perennials

Desert baileya—*Baileya multiradiata* (N)
Carnation—*Dianthus caryophyllus* (E)
Coneflower—*Ratibida columnifera* (N)
Daylily (asphodel)—*Hemerocallis* spp. (E)
Dusty miller—*Senecio cineraria* (E)
Fendler's sundrops—*Calylophus hartwegii fendleri* (N)
Geranium (cranesbill)—*Geranium* spp. (E)
Hollyhock—*Alcea rosea* (E, NZ)
Indian paintbrush—*Castilleja integra* (N)
Jimsonweed (datura, sacred datura)—*Datura
meteloides* (N)
Lobelia—*Lobelia erinus* (E)
Maximilian's daisy—*Helianthus maximiliani* (NZ)
Phlox—*Phlox* spp. (E)
California poppy—*Eschscholzia californica* (and *E.
mexicana*) (E, N)
Shasta daisy—*Chrysanthemum maximum* (E)
Violet—*Viola odorata* (N, E)

C. Bulbs

Canna—*Canna* spp. (E)
Daffodil—*Narcissus* 'King Alfred' (E)
Dutch crocus—*Crocus verus* (E)
Garden gladiolus—*Gladiolus hortulanus* (E)
Iris—*Iris* spp. (N, E)
Ranunculus—*Ranunculus asiaticus* (E)

Old Las Vegas Plaza

It would be hard to imagine a more pleasant setting than the rolling green meadows of the Gallinas River on the east side of the Sangre de Cristo Range. Las Vegas is high (6470 feet/1990 m) and often cold in the winter, but it is moist (15–22 inches/375–550 mm of annual rainfall), and its soils, though sometimes stony, are fertile. The growing season is a brief 139 days.

For a city of modest size, it has an inordinate number of great historic landscapes. The first of these, of course, is the plaza, dating from about 1833 and strongly developed after the coming of the railroad in the 1870s. Library Park and Lincoln Park are also important open spaces in the history of the city. Both the plaza and the two territorial parks have kept their Victorian-Edwardian integrity throughout the twentieth century.

Trees and shrubs grow well without much additional irrigation in Las Vegas because of the near-ample natural moisture and relatively good soils in and around the city. Livestock raising—particularly of cattle and calves— far outweighs crop production in terms of its importance to the economy of San Miguel County. Alfalfa, fruits, chile, and vegetables are the most important crops. Chickens and some sheep and hogs are also kept. Virtually all crops are irrigated.

Wheatgrasses, gramas, buffalo grass, and other native grass species grow very well on the rolling plains near Las Vegas. Ponderosa, limber, and piñon pine, Gambel oak, white fir, narrowleaf cottonwood, aspen, alder, Douglas fir, Engelmann spruce, chokecherry, sand plum, currant, and Rocky Mountain and singleseed juniper are common trees in the foothills and mountains around Las Vegas. So is the beautiful peachleaf willow. Red osier dogwood, snowberry, mountain mahogany, common juniper, rubber rabbitbrush (chamisa), woods rose, and big sage are common wild shrubs.

Within the city, Siberian elms, several ash species, white firs, and flowering crabs are found everywhere in public and private landscapes. As in Santa Fe and Taos, lilacs and hollyhocks are popular blooming plants. Common landscape annuals and perennials also include Shasta daisies, rudbeckias, cosmos, iris, violets, marigolds, petunias, geraniums, and the spectacular Maximilian's daisies. Most visitors also remark on the landscape color provided by yarrow, four o'clocks, and the many varieties of shrubby cinquefoil found in Las Vegas gardens.

LAS VEGAS
(founded in 1833) including Springer and Mora

SELECTED BEST PLANTS FOR LAS VEGAS

These plant species grow very well in Las Vegas. For the sake of convenience and quick reference, each plant is listed as native (N), naturalized (NZ), or exotic (E). Other plants also will perform well in landscape and garden situations in and around Las Vegas. Please see the New Mexico Plant File for these species.

TREES

A. Deciduous Shade, Street, and Specialty Trees

Arizona alder—*Alnus oblongifolia* (N)
Green ash—*Fraxinus pennsylvanica* and varieties (E)
Catalpa
    a.Umbrella catalpa—*Catalpa bignonioides* 'Nana' (E)
    b.Western catalpa—*Catalpa speciosa* (E)
Western chokecherry—*Prunus virginiana* (N)
Cottonwood, Aspen, and Poplar: Trees of the Genus *Populus*
    a.Aspen—*Populus tremuloides* (N)
    b.Bolleana poplar—*Populus alba* 'Pyramidalis' (E)
    c.Carolina poplar—*Populus canadensis* (NZ)
    d.Lanceleaf cottonwood—*Populus acuminata* (N)
    e.Lombardy poplar—*Populus nigra* 'Italica' (E)
    f.Narrowleaf cottonwood—*Populus angustifolia* (N)
    g.Rio Grande cottonwood—*Populus fremontii* 'Wislizeni' (N)
    h.White (silver) poplar—*Populus alba* (NZ)
American elm—*Ulmus americana* (E)
Honey locust—*Gleditsia triacanthos inermis* varieties (E)
Locust
    a.Black locust—*Robinia pseudoacacia* (NZ)
    b.Hybrid locusts—*Robinia ambigua* varieties (E)
    c.New Mexico locust—*Robinia neomexicana* (N)
Maple and Box elder
    a.Box elder—*Acer negundo* (N)
    b.Silver maple—*Acer saccharinum* (E)
    c.Sycamore-leaf maple—*Acer pseudoplatanus* (E)
Weeping mulberry—*Morus alba* 'Pendula' (E)
Gambel oak—*Quercus gambelii* (N)
Russian olive—*Elaeagnus angustifolia* (NZ)
Sycamore (plane tree)
    a.American sycamore—*Platanus occidentalis* (E)
    b.London plane tree—*Platanus acerifolia* (E)
English (Carpathian) walnut—*Juglans regia* (E)
Willow
    a.Corkscrew willow—*Salix matsudana* 'Tortuosa' (E)
    b.Globe Navajo willow—*Salix matsudana* 'Navajo' (E)
    c.Peachleaf willow—*Salix amygdaloides* (N)
    d.Weeping willow—*Salix babylonica* (and other weeping willow species (E)

B. Flowering Ornamental Trees

Flowering crab—*Malus* 'Hopa' et al (E)
Flowering peach—*Prunus persica* (E)
Purpleleaf plum—*Prunus cerasifera* (E)
Eastern redbud—*Cercis canadensis* (E)
Golden rain tree—*Koelreuteria paniculata* (E)
Salt cedar—*Tamarix chinensis* (NZ)

C. Evergreen Trees

Douglas fir—*Pseudotsuga menziesii* (N)
White fir—*Abies concolor* (N)
Juniper
    a.Rocky Mountain juniper—*Juniperus scopulorum* varieties (N)
    b.Singleseed (one-seed) juniper—*Juniperus monosperma* (N)
Pine
    a.Austrian pine—*Pinus nigra* (E)
    b.Bristlecone pine—*Pinus aristata* (N)
    c.Limber pine—*Pinus flexilis* (N)
    d.Piñon pine—*Pinus edulis* (N)
    e.Ponderosa pine—*Pinus ponderosa* (N)
    f.Scotch pine—*Pinus sylvestris* (E)
Spruce
    a.Blue spruce—*Picea pungens* (N)
    b.Engelmann spruce—*Picea engelmanni* (N)
    c.Black Hills spruce—*Picea glauca densata* (E)
Western red cedar—*Thuja plicata* (E)

SHRUBS

A. Deciduous

Althea (rose of Sharon)—*Hibiscus syriacus* (E)
Apache plume—*Fallugia paradoxa* (N)
Common butterfly bush—*Buddleia davidii* (E)
Shrubby cinquefoil—*Potentilla fruticosa* (N)
Cotoneaster
    a.Cranberry cotoneaster—*Cotoneaster apiculatus* (E)
    b.Rock cotoneaster—*Cotoneaster horizontalis* (E)
    c.Rockspray cotoneaster—*Cotoneaster microphyllus* (E)
Currant and gooseberry—*Ribes* spp. (N)
Red osier dogwood—*Cornus stolonifera* (N)
Fernbush—*Chamaebatiaria millefolium* (N)
Flowering jasmine—*Jasminum nudiflorum* (E)
Forsythia—*Forsythia* spp. (E)
Common lilac—*Syringa vulgaris* (E)
Mountain mahogany—*Cercocarpus montanus* (N)
New Mexico olive—*Forestiera neomexicana* (N)
Sand plum—*Prunus americana* (N)
Rose—*Rosa* spp. (E, N)
Snowball—*Viburnum opulus* 'Roseum' (E)
Spirea
    a.Bridal wreath—*Spiraea prunifolia* (E)
    b.Van Houtte—*Spiraea vanhouttei* (E)
    c.Anthony Waterer—*Spiraea bumalda* 'Anthony Waterer' (E)
Sumac
    a.Skunkbush—*Rhus trilobata* (N)
    b.Staghorn sumac—*Rhus typhina* (E)
Coyote willow—*Salix exigua* (N)
Winterfat—*Ceratoides lanata* (N)

B. Evergreen

Barberry
    a.Japanese barberry—*Berberis thunbergii* (E)
    b.Wintergreen barberry—*Berberis julianae* (E)
Common cholla—*Opuntia imbricata* (N)
Parney cotoneaster—*Cotoneaster lacteus* (E)
Holly
    a.Burford holly—*Ilex cornuta* 'Burfordii' (E)
    b.English holly—*Ilex aquifolium* (E)
Chinese junipers
    a.Armstrong juniper—*Juniperus chinensis* 'Armstrong' (E)
    b.Pfitzer juniper—*Juniperus chinensis* 'Pfitzerana' (E)
Common juniper—*Juniperus communis* (N)
Oregon grape—*Mahonia aquifolium* (E, NZ)
Photinia
    a.Chinese photinia—*Photinia serrulata* (E)
    b.Fraser's photinia—*Photinia fraseri* (E)
Mugo pine—*Pinus mugo* (E)
Rubber rabbitbrush—*Chrysothamnus nauseosus* (N)

Big sage (sagebrush)—*Artemisia tridentata* (N)
Yucca
    a.Narrowleaf yucca—*Yucca glauca* (N)
    b.Spanish bayonet—*Yucca baccata* (N)

GROUND COVERS

A. Deciduous

Spring cinquefoil—*Potentilla tabernaemontani* (E)
Clover—*Trifolium* spp. (NZ, N)
Cranberry cotoneaster—*Cotoneaster apiculatus* (E)
Crown vetch—*Coronilla varia* (E, NZ)
Prairie sage—*Artemisia ludoviciana* (N)
Snow-in summer—*Cerastium tomentosum* (E)

B. Evergreen

Bearberry cotoneaster—*Cotoneaster dammeri* (E)
Creeping euonymus—*Euonymus fortunei* (E)
Honeysuckle—*Lonicera japonica* varieties (E)
Horizontalis junipers
    a.Bar Harbor juniper—*Juniperus horizontalis* 'Bar Harbor' (E)
    b.Wilton carpet juniper—*Juniperus horizontalis* 'Wiltonii' (E)
Sabina junipers
    a.Broadmoor juniper—*Juniperus sabina* 'Broadmoor' (E)
    b.Buffalo juniper—*Juniperus sabina* 'Buffalo' (E)
    c.Tam (tammy) juniper—*Juniperus sabina* 'Tamariscifolia' (E)
Kinnickinnick (mountain bearberry)—*Arctostaphylos uva-ursi* (N)
Creeping mahonia—*Mahonia repens* (N)
Compact nandina—*Nandina domestica* 'Harbor dwarf' (E)
Periwinkle—*Vinca major* and *Vinca minor* (E)
Pussytoes—*Antennaria parviflora* (N)
Sedum (stonecrop)—*Sedum* spp. (N, E)
Strawberry—*Fragaria* spp. (N, E)

GRASSES

A. Traditional Turf Species

Bentgrass—*Agrostis* spp. (E)
Bluegrass—*Poa pratensis* (NZ)
Fescue—*Festuca* spp. (E)
Ryegrass—*Lolium* spp. (E)

B. Native Turf And General-Use Species

Galleta—*Hilaria jamesii* (N)
Buffalo grass—*Buchlöe dactyloides* (N)
Grama
    a.Blue grama—*Bouteloua gracilis* (N)
    b.Sideoats grama—*Bouteloua curtipendula* (N)
Wheatgrass
    a.Western wheatgrass—*Agropyron smithii* (N)
    b.Crested wheatgrass—*Agropyron desertorum* (E, NZ)
    c.Pubescent wheatgrass—*Agropyron trichophorum* (N)

C. Ornamental Species

Blue fescue—*Festuca caesia* (E)
Fountain grass—*Pennisetum* spp. (E)
Purple threeawn—*Aristida longiseta* (N)

VINES

A. Deciduous

Boston ivy—*Parthenocissus tricuspidata* (E)
Clematis—*Clematis jackmanni* (E)
Morning glory—*Ipomoea tricolor* (E)
Silver lace vine—*Polygonum aubertii* (E)
Trumpet vine—*Campsis radicans* (E)
Virginia creeper (et al)—*Parthenocissus quinquefolia* (N, E)

Wall with perennials near Mora (Photo by Elizabeth C. Reardon)

B. Evergreen

English ivy—*Hedera helix* (E)
Honeysuckle—*Lonicera* spp. (E)

FLOWERS

A. Annuals

Ageratum—*Ageratum houstonianum* (E)
Purple aster—*Aster bigelovii* (N)
Cosmos—*Cosmos* spp. (E)
Four o'clock—*Mirabilis jalapa* (E)
Gaillardia (blanketflower, firewheel)—*Gaillardia pulchella* (N)
Geranium—*Pelargonium hortorum* (E)
Impatiens—*Impatiens wallerana* (E)
Lisianthus—*Eustoma grandiflorum* (E)
Marigold—*Tagetes* spp. (E)
Pansy—*Viola wittrockiana* (E)
Petunia—*Petunia* spp. (E)
Salvia—*Salvia* spp. (E)
Sunflower—*Helianthus annuus* (N)
Wallflower—*Erysimum capitatum* (N)

B. Perennials

Carnation—*Dianthus caryophyllus* (E)
Chrysanthemum—*Chrysanthemum morifolium* (E)
Colorado columbine—*Aquilegia* spp. (N)
Coneflower—*Ratibida columnifera* (N)
Daylily (asphodel)—*Hemerocallis* spp. (E)
Delphinium—*Delphinium belladonna* (E, N)
Blue flax—*Linum perenne* (N)
Globemallow—*Sphaeralcea incana* (scarlet) (N)
Hollyhock—*Alcea rosea* (E)
Indian paintbrush—*Castilleja integra* (N)
Lobelia—*Lobelia erinus* (E)
Maximilian's daisy—*Helianthus maximiliani* (NZ)
Penstemon—*Penstemon* spp. (N)
Phlox—*Phlox* spp. (E)
Red rocket (scarlet gilia)—*Ipomopsis aggregata* (N)
Shasta daisy—*Chrysanthemum maximum* (E)
Spectaclepod—*Dithyrea wislizenii* (N)
Violet—*Viola odorata* (N, E)
Wooly yarrow—*Achillea* spp. (N, E)

C. Bulbs

Canna—*Canna* spp. (E)
Daffodil—*Narcissus* 'King Alfred' (E)
Garden gladiolus—*Gladiolus hortulanus* (E)
Iris—*Iris* spp. (N, E)
Tulip—*Tulipa* spp. (E)

LORDSBURG
(founded in 1880)

A grove of Emory oak near Lordsburg

At an elevation of 4250 feet (1300 m), Lordsburg has a growing season of 195 days, about the same as Roswell, Las Cruces, Clovis, and Albuquerque. The town expects approximately 10.5 inches (270 mm) of rainfall a year. The soils, though generally alkaline and shallow, can be fertile.

Agriculture in Hidalgo County is heavily dependent on cattle and calves. The county is second in the state in the production of hogs. Crops include alfalfa, cotton, sorghum, wheat, and increasing quantities of chile, vegetables, and nuts (pecans). Virtually all production of crops and livestock is dependent on irrigation from wells.

Within Hidalgo County, the Pyramid, Burro, and Animas mountains are notable extensions of the Mexican Sierra Madres. Beargrass, many species of oaks, numerous interesting cacti, ocotillo, alligator juniper, several pine species, Arizona alder, sotol, mesquite, and netleaf hackberry are common in and near these ranges. Seepwillow, alkali sacaton, desert willow, creosote, ricegrass,

mesquite, and such spectacular flowers as desert baileya and Mexican or California poppy are found in the open desert. Great stands of *Yucca elata*—the soaptree yucca—exist between Deming and Lordsburg. These are probably the finest of their kind in the state.

The native Arizona ash is Lordsburg's most popular street and shade tree. Arizona cypress, silk tree, ocotillo, chinaberry, Mexican elder, Fremont cottonwood, California poppy, forsythia, Spanish dagger, Japanese black pine, peach, plum, and the very beautiful Arizona madrone are popular ornamentals. Oleanders grow well here, as do California fan palms, Afghan pines, hollyhocks, ice plant, Chinese windmill palm, Texas ranger, and Mexican fan palms. River cane, photinia, and yaupon holly are useful hedge and screen plants.

The city's gardens, though generally modest, contain some excellent specimen plants. The grounds of new roadside inns and the impressive stretch of new street trees along the railroad tracks near downtown are among the most attractive of Lordsburg's modern landscapes.

SELECTED BEST PLANTS FOR LORDSBURG

These plant species grow very well in and around Lordsburg. For the sake of convenience and quick reference, each plant is listed as native (N), naturalized (NZ), or exotic (E). Other plants also will perform well in landscape and garden situations in the Lordsburg area. Please see the New Mexico Plant File for these species.

TREES

A. Deciduous Shade, Street, and Specialty Trees

Ash
  a. Arizona ash—*Fraxinus velutina* (N)
  b. Green ash—*Fraxinus pennsylvanica* and varieties (E)
Western catalpa—*Catalpa speciosa* (E)
Chinaberry—*Melia azedarach* (E)
Cottonwood, Aspen, and Poplar: Trees of the Genus *Populus*
  a. Fremont cottonwood—*Populus fremontii* (E)
  b. Lanceleaf cottonwood—*Populus acuminata* (N)
  c. Lombardy poplar—*Populus nigra* 'Italica' (E)
Elm
  a. American elm—*Ulmus americana* (E)
  b. Chinese elm—*Ulmus parvifolia* (E)
Netleaf hackberry—*Celtis reticulata* (N)
Honey locust—*Gleditsia triacanthos inermis* varieties
  a. 'Moraine' (E)
  b. 'Shademaster' (E)
  c. 'Sunburst' (E)
Horsechestnut (E)
California buckeye—*Aesculus californica* (E)
Jujube—*Zizyphus jujuba* (E)
Mesquite—*Prosopis glandulosa* (N)
Mulberry
  a. Fruitless mulberry—*Morus alba* (E)
  b. Weeping mulberry—*Morus alba* 'Pendula' (E)
  c. Paper mulberry—*Broussonetia papyrifera* (E)
Oak
  a. Cork oak—*Quercus suber* (E)
  b. Southern live oak—*Quercus virginiana* (E)
  c. Texas oak—*Quercus texana* (E) (Note: Local oak species such as Emory oak, *Quercus emoryii*, when available, will also thrive here.)
Osage orange—*Maclura pomifera* (E)
Pecan—*Carya illinoiensis* (E)
Pistache—Pistachio
  a. Chinese pistache—*Pistacia chinensis* (E)
  b. Pistachio—*Pistacia vera* (E)
Russian olive—*Elaeagnus angustifolia* (NZ)
Silk tree—*Albizia jilibrissin* (E)
Western soapberry—*Sapindus drummondii* (N)
Sycamore (plane tree)
  a. American sycamore—*Platanus occidentalis* (E)
  b. Arizona sycamore—*Platanus wrightii* (N)
  c. London plane tree—*Platanus acerifolia* (E)
  d. Oriental plane tree—*Platanus orientalis* (E)
Arizona walnut—*Juglans major* (N)
Willow
  a. Corkscrew willow—*Salix matsudana* 'Tortuosa' (E)
  b. Globe Navajo willow—*Salix matsudana* 'Navajo' (E)
  c. Peachleaf willow—*Salix amygdaloides* (N)
  d. Weeping willow—*Salix babylonica* (and other weeping willow species) (E)

B. Flowering Ornamental Trees

Flowering crab—*Malus* 'Hopa' et al (E)
Desert willow—*Chilopsis linearis* (N)
Mexican elder—*Sambucus caerulea neomexicana* (N)
Flowering peach—*Prunus persica* (E)
Bradford pear—*Pyrus calleryana* (E)
Purpleleaf plum—*Prunus cerasifera* (E)
Salt cedar—*Tamarix chinensis* (NZ)
Smoke tree—*Cotinus coggygria* (E)
Vitex (chaste tree)—*Vitex agnus-castus* (E)

C. Evergreen Trees

Cedar
  a. Atlas cedar—*Cedrus atlantica* (E)
  b. Cedar of Lebanon—*Cedrus libani* (E)
  c. Deodar cedar—*Cedrus deodara* (E)
Cypress
  a. Arizona cypress—*Cupressus arizonica* (N)
  b. Italian cypress—*Cupressus sempervirens* (E)
Eucalyptus (cider gum)—*Eucalyptus gunnii* (E)
Juniper
  a. Alligator juniper—*Juniperus deppeana* (N)
  b. Chinese juniper—*Juniperus chinensis* varieties (E)
  c. Eastern red cedar—*Juniperus virginiana* varieties (E)
Leyland false cypress—*Cupressocyparis leylandii* (E)
Madrone—*Arbutus texana* (N) (also Arizona madrone, *Arbutus arizonica*)
Palm
  a. California fan palm—*Washingtonia filifera* (E)
  b. Chinese windmill palm—*Trachycarpus fortunei* (E)
  c. Mexican fan palm—*Washingtonia robusta* (E)
Pine
  a. Afghan pine—*Pinus eldarica* (E)
  b. Aleppo pine—*Pinus halepensis* (E)
  c. Japanese black pine—*Pinus thunbergiana* (E)
  d. Piñon pine—*Pinus edulis* (N)
Yucca
  a. Joshua tree—*Yucca brevifolia* (E)
  b. Palm yucca—*Yucca torreyi* (N)
  c. Soaptree yucca—*Yucca elata* (N)

SHRUBS

A. Deciduous

Flowering almond—*Prunus glandulosa* (E)
Althea (rose of Sharon)—*Hibiscus syriacus* (E)
Apache plume—*Fallugia paradoxa* (N)
Bird of paradise—*Caesalpinia gilliesii* (NZ)
Common butterfly bush—*Buddleia davidii* (E)
Cotoneaster
  a. Cranberry cotoneaster—*Cotoneaster apiculatus* (E)
  b. Rock cotoneaster—*Cotoneaster horizontalis* (E)
  c. Rockspray cotoneaster—*Cotoneaster microphyllus* (E)
Crape myrtle—*Lagerstroemia indica* (E)
Edible fig—*Ficus carica* (E)
Forsythia—*Forsythia* spp. (E)
Shrub or Tatarian honeysuckle—*Lonicera tatarica* (E)
Common lilac—*Syringa vulgaris* (E)
Screwbean mesquite—*Prosopis pubescens* (N)
Mountain mahogany—*Cercocarpus montanus* (N)
New Mexico olive—*Forestiera neomexicana* (N)

Cistena plum—*Prunus cistena* (E)
Pomegranate—*Punica granatum* (E)
Rose—*Rosa* spp. (E, N)
Snakeweed—*Gutierrezia sarothrae* (N)
Sumac
    a.Littleleaf sumac—*Rhus microphylla* (N)
    b.Skunkbush—*Rhus trilobata* (N)

B. Evergreen

Agave (century plant, mescal)
    a.Century plant—*Agave americana* (N)
    b.Parry agave—*Agave parryi* (N)
    c.Lechugilla—*Agave lechugilla* (N)
Beargrass—*Nolina microcarpa* (N)
Cactus
    a.Claret cup—*Echinocereus triglochidiatus* (N)
    b.Common cholla—*Opuntia imbricata* (N)
    c.Prickly pear—*Opuntia chlorotica* or *O. engelmannii* (N)
Parney cotoneaster—*Cotoneaster lacteus* (E)
Creosotebush—*Larrea tridentata* (N)
Yaupon holly—*Ilex vomitoria* (E)
India hawthorn—*Rhaphiolepis indica* (E)
Chinese junipers
    a.Armstrong juniper—*Juniperus chinensis* 'Armstrong' (E)
    b.Pfitzer juniper—*Juniperus chinensis* 'Pfitzerana' (E)
    c.Sea Green juniper—*Juniperus chinensis* 'Sea Green' (E)
Common juniper—*Juniperus communis* (N)
Mahonia
    a.Algerita—*Mahonia haematocarpa* (N)
    b.Agritos—*Mahonia trifoliolata* (N)
Mormon tea—*Ephedra* spp. (N)
Nandina (heavenly bamboo)—*Nandina domestica* (E)
Ocotillo—*Fouquieria splendens* (N)
Oleander—*Nerium oleander* (E)
Chinese photinia—*Photinia serrulata* (E)
Pittosporum (tobira)—*Pittosporum tobira* (E)
Pyracantha (firethorn)—*Pyracantha* spp. (E)
Sand sage—*Artemisia filifolia* (N)
Fourwing saltbush—*Atriplex canescens* (N)
Seepwillow -*Baccharis sarothroides* (N)
Sotol—*Dasylirion wheeleri* (N)
Texas ranger—*Leucophyllum frutescens* (E)
Yucca
    a.Softblade yucca—*Yucca recurvifolia* (*Yucca pendula*) (E)
    b.Spanish bayonet—*Yucca baccata* (N)
    c.Coral-flower yucca—*Hesperaloe parviflora* (E)

GROUND COVERS

A. Deciduous

Clover—*Trifolium* spp. (NZ, N)
Crown vetch—*Coronilla varia* (E, NZ)
Mint—*Mentha* spp. (E, N, NZ)
Prairie sage—*Artemisia ludoviciana* (N)
Memorial rose (vine)—*Rosa wichuriana* (E)

B. Evergreen

Ajuga (bugleweed)—*Ajuga reptans* (E)
Dwarf coyotebrush—*Baccharis pilularis* (E)
Dichondra—*Dichondra micrantha* (E)
Germander—*Teucrium chamaedrys* 'Prostratum' (E)
Honeysuckle—*Lonicera japonica* varieties (E)
Horizontalis junipers
    a.Andorra juniper—*Juniperus horizontalis plumosa* (E)

    b.Bar Harbor juniper—*Juniperus horizontalis* 'Bar Harbor'(E)
    c.Wilton carpet juniper—*Juniperus horizontalis* 'Wiltonii' (E)
Sabina junipers
    a.Broadmoor juniper—*Juniperus sabina* 'Broadmoor' (E)
    b.Buffalo juniper—*Juniperus sabina* 'Buffalo' (E)
    c.Tam (tammy) juniper—*Juniperus sabina* 'Tamariscifolia' (E)
San Jose juniper—*Juniperus chinensis* 'San Jose' (E)
Lilyturf (liriope)—*Liriope spicata* (E)
Periwinkle—*Vinca major* and *Vinca minor* (E)
Pussytoes—*Antennaria parviflora* (N)
Rosemary—*Rosmarinus officinalis* (E)
Santolina
    a.Green santolina—*Santolina virens* (E)
    b.Gray santolina—*Santolina chamaecyparissus* (E)

GRASSES

A. Traditional Turf Species

Bermuda
    a.African bermuda—*Cynodon transvaalensis* (E, NZ)
    b.Common bermuda—*Cynodon dactylon* (NZ)
Ryegrass—*Lolium* spp. (E)

B. Native Turf And General-Use Species

Grama
    a.Black grama—*Bouteloua eriopoda* (N)
    b.Blue grama—*Bouteloua gracilis* (N)
    c.Sideoats grama—*Bouteloua curtipendula* (N)
Wheatgrass
    a.Western wheatgrass—*Agropyron smithii* (N)
    b.Crested wheatgrass—*Agropyron desertorum* (E, NZ)
    c.Pubescent wheatgrass—*Agropyron trichophorum* (N)

C. Ornamental Species

Alkali sacaton—*Sporobolus airoides* (N)
Sand dropseed—*Sporobolus cryptandrus* (N)
Blue fescue—*Festuca caesia* (E)
Fountain grass—*Pennisetum* spp. (E)
Pampas grass—*Cortaderia selloana* (E)
Indian ricegrass—*Oryzopsis hymenoides* (N)
River cane—*Arundo donax* (NZ)
Purple threeawn—*Aristida longiseta* (N)

VINES

A. Deciduous

Canyon grape—*Vitis arizonica* (N)
Carolina jessamine—*Gelsemium sempervirens* (E)
Clematis—*Clematis jackmanni* (E)
Trumpet vine—*Campsis radicans* (E)
Virginia creeper (et al)—*Parthenocissus quinquefolia* (N, E)
Wisteria—*Wisteria sinensis* (E)

B. Evergreen

Algerian ivy—*Hedera canariensis* (E)
English ivy—*Hedera helix* (E)
Honeysuckle—*Lonicera* spp. (E)

FLOWERS

A. Annuals

Purple aster—*Aster bigelovii* (N)
Cosmos—*Cosmos* spp. (E)
Gaillardia (blanketflower, firewheel)—*Gaillardia pulchella* (N)
Lisianthus—*Eustoma grandiflorum* (E)
Marigold—*Tagetes* spp. (E)
Pansy—*Viola wittrockiana* (E)
Petunia—*Petunia* spp. (E)
Salvia—*Salvia* spp. (E)
Sunflower—*Helianthus annuus* (N)
Annual vinca (Madagascar periwinkle)—*Catharanthus roseus* (E)
Wallflower—*Erysimum capitatum* (N)

B. Perennials

Desert baileya—*Baileya multiradiata* (N)
Chrysanthemum—*Chrysanthemum morifolium* (E)
Colorado columbine—*Aquilegia* spp. (N)
Coneflower—*Ratibida columnifera* (N)
Daylily (asphodel)—*Hemerocallis* spp. (E)
Delphinium—*Delphinium belladonna* (E, N)
Dusty miller—*Senecio cineraria* (E)

Fendler's sundrops—*Calylophus hartwegii fendleri* (N)
Blue flax—*Linum perenne* (N)
Geranium (cranesbill)—*Geranium* spp. (N)
Globemallow—*Sphaeralcea incana* (scarlet) (N)
Hollyhock—*Alcea rosea* (E, NZ)
Jimsonweed (datura, sacred datura)—*Datura meteloides* (N)
Lobelia—*Lobelia erinus* (E)
Maximilian's daisy—*Helianthus maximiliani* (NZ)
Paperflower—*Psilostrophe tagetina* (N)
Penstemon—*Penstemon* spp. (N)
Phlox—*Phlox* spp. (E)
California poppy—*Eschscholzia californica* (and *E. mexicana*) (E,N)
Shasta daisy—*Chrysanthemum maximum* (E)
Spectaclepod—*Dithyrea wislizenii* (N)
Wooly yarrow—*Achillea* spp. (N, E)

C. Bulbs

Canna—*Canna* spp. (E)
Daffodil—*Narcissus* 'King Alfred' (E)
Garden gladiolus—*Gladiolus hortulanus* (E)
Iris—*Iris* spp. (N, E)
Ranunculus—*Ranunculus asiaticus* (E)
Tulip—*Tulipa* spp. (E)

Garden scene in Los Alamos

LOS ALAMOS

(founded in 1917 as Los Alamos Ranch School), including White Rock

Los Alamos is both a city and a county at quite high altitude. The city is at 7400 feet (2260 m); its slightly lower suburb of White Rock is at 6300 feet (1920 m). Los Alamos lies in the classic Transition Zone ponderosa pine–Gambel oak forest of the Southwest. The climate and setting are very reminiscent of Ruidoso, Pagosa Springs, and Flagstaff. White Rock lies in the piñon-juniper (Upper Sonoran) zone. The average growing season here is about 115 days. Annual rainfall may total 18 inches (450 mm) or more.

Soils in Los Alamos are typical of the Jemez Mountains as a whole. They can be fertile, but there is great variation in depth, they are often stony, and clay is an abundant component. Many soils are thin and immediately underlain with rock.

In addition to ponderosa pine and Gambel oak, an exceptional abundance of handsome native plants thrive on the Jemez Mountains and Pajarito Plateau. White fir, Douglas fir, Engelmann spruce, New Mexico locust, aspen, narrowleaf cottonwood, snowberry, purshia, mountain mahogany, Arizona alder, western virginsbower, columbine, penstemon, gilia, thistle, wild rose, and currant are among these. The native Rocky Mountain iris is exceptionally beautiful in and around Los Alamos. The mountains also contain extraordinary volcanic rock formations that add color and unusual texture to the local landscape setting.

Los Alamos is unique among New Mexican counties in that it has virtually no agricultural production. No salable crops are grown, although some livestock grazing occurs in the national forest within the county.

Like Aztec, Tucumcari, and several other New Mexican cities, the city of Los Alamos has a garden tradition that is strong and distinct. Residents tend to cultivate both exotics and native plants in abundance on relatively small plots of ground. Lilac, forsythia, snowball viburnum, many rose varieties (including spectacular Austrian coppers and *R. rugosa* spp.), and spirea are spring favorites. These shrubs are often underplanted with peonies, iris, periwinkle, mountain bearberry, common juniper, and small expanses of bluegrass. Ponderosa pine is very common, of course; white fir, another favorite, typically displays a delightful light green or pale blue color. Poppies, Apache plume, serviceberry, New Mexico olive, aspen, and Lombardy poplar are also frequently cultivated. Limber, bristlecone, Austrian, and piñon pines are found as evergreen accents.

White Rock's altitude, its origin (it was carved out of a piñon-juniper forest, whereas Los Alamos proper is set in a ponderosa pine–Gambel oak forest), and its orientation (it faces south-southeast, while Los Alamos lies on the east-facing flank of the Jemez Mountains) give it a slightly different landscape character. Its site is hilly and entirely suburban in character. Aspen, piñon, Austrian pine, green ash, and—surprisingly—the European exotic mountain ash are White Rock's favorite trees. Rose, lilac, and bridalwreath spirea are widely planted shrubs. The native Apache plume, shrubby cinquefoil, rubber rabbitbrush (chamisa), mountain mahogany, Spanish dagger, big sage, cholla, and skunkbush are popular in gardens. Fruit trees and the gracefully beautiful reticulated silver maple are also found here. Shasta daisies, pinks and carnations, gaillardia, red hot poker, columbine, daylily, marigold, and lupine are everywhere under trees and next to shrubs. Most gardens, though casual, are well planned and well cared for.

Los Alamos County's most important historic landscapes are probably the grounds of Fuller Lodge and the serene old orchard and irrigation channels at the headquarters of Bandelier National Monument. Many new projects on the grounds of the Los Alamos National Laboratory have greatly expanded the scope of exemplary public landscapes in the city.

SELECTED BEST PLANTS FOR LOS ALAMOS AND WHITE ROCK

These plant species grow very well in Los Alamos and White Rock. For the sake of convenience and quick reference, each plant is listed as native (N), naturalized (NZ), or exotic (E). Other plants also will perform well in landscape and garden situations in and around Los Alamos and White Rock. Please see the New Mexico Plant File for these species.

TREES

A. Deciduous Shade, Street, and Specialty Trees

Arizona alder—*Alnus oblongifolia* (N)
Green ash—*Fraxinus pennsylvanica* and varieties (E)
Paper birch—*Betula papyrifera* (E)
Western catalpa—*Catalpa speciosa* (E)
Cottonwood, Aspen, and Poplar: Trees of the Genus *Populus*
  a. Aspen—*Populus tremuloides* (N)
  b. Bolleana poplar—*Populus alba* 'Pyramidalis' (E)
  c. Carolina poplar—*Populus canadensis* (E)
  d. Lanceleaf cottonwood—*Populus acuminata* (N)
  e. Lombardy poplar—*Populus nigra* 'Italica' (E)
  f. Narrowleaf cottonwood—*Populus angustifolia* (N)
  g. White (silver) poplar—*Populus alba* (NZ)
Common hackberry—*Celtis occidentalis* (E)
Honey locust—*Gleditsia triacanthos inermis* varieties
  a. 'Moraine' (E)
  b. 'Sunburst' (E)

Common horsechestnut—*Aesculus hippocastanum* (E)
Littleleaf linden—*Tilia cordata* (E)
Maple and Box elder
  a. Bigtooth maple—*Acer grandidentatum* (N)
  b. Box elder—*Acer negundo* (N)
  c. Japanese maple—*Acer palmatum* (E)
  d. Norway maple—*Acer platanoides* (E)
  e. Rocky Mountain maple—*Acer glabrum* (N)
  f. Silver maple—*Acer saccharinum* (E)
  g. Sycamore-leaf maple—*Acer pseudoplatanus* (E)
European mountain ash—*Sorbus aucuparia* (E)
Gambel oak—*Quercus gambelii* (N)
Russian olive—*Elaeagnus angustifolia* (NZ)
London plane tree—*Platanus acerifolia* (E)
English (Carpathian) walnut—*Juglans regia* (E)
Willow
  a. Globe Navajo willow—*Salix matsudana* 'Navajo' (E)
  b. Weeping willow—*Salix babylonica* (oth. spp. also) (E)

B. Flowering Ornamental Trees

Flowering cherry—*Prunus serrulata* et al (E)
Flowering crab—*Malus* 'Hopa' et al (E)
Hawthorn—*Crataegus* spp. (E,N)
Flowering peach—*Prunus persica* (E)
Bradford pear—*Pyrus calleryana* (E)
Purpleleaf plum—*Prunus cerasifera* (E)
Eastern redbud—*Cercis canadensis* (E)
Golden rain tree—*Koelreuteria paniculata* (E)

C. Evergreen Trees

Douglas fir—*Pseudotsuga menziesii* (N)
White fir—*Abies concolor* (N)
Juniper
  a. Rocky Mountain juniper -*Juniperus scopulorum* varieties (N)
  b. Singleseed (one-seed) juniper—*Juniperus monosperma* (N)
Leyland false cypress—*Cupressocyparis leylandii* (E)
Pine
  a. Austrian pine—*Pinus nigra* (E)
  b. Bristlecone pine—*Pinus aristata* (N)
  c. Japanese black pine—*Pinus thunbergiana* (E)
  d. Limber pine—*Pinus flexilis* (N)
  e. Piñon pine—*Pinus edulis* (N)
  f. Ponderosa pine—*Pinus ponderosa* (N)
  g. Scotch pine—*Pinus sylvestris* (E)
Spruce
  a. Blue spruce—*Picea pungens* (N)
  b. Engelmann spruce—*Picea engelmanni* (N)

SHRUBS

A. Deciduous

Althea (rose of Sharon)—*Hibiscus syriacus* (E)
Apache plume—*Fallugia paradoxa* (N)
Common butterfly bush—*Buddleia davidii* (E)
Shrubby cinquefoil—*Potentilla fruticosa* (N)
Cotoneaster
  a. Rock cotoneaster—*Cotoneaster horizontalis* (E)
  b. Rockspray cotoneaster—*Cotoneaster microphyllus* (E)
Currant and gooseberry—*Ribes* spp.(N)
Red osier dogwood—*Cornus stolonifera* (E)
Fernbush—*Chamaebatiaria millefolium* (N)
Forsythia—*Forsythia* spp. (E)
Shrub or Tatarian honeysuckle—*Lonicera tatarica* (E)
Flowering jasmine—*Jasminum nudiflorum* (E)

Common lilac—*Syringa vulgaris* (E)
Mountain mahogany—*Cercocarpus montanus* (N)
New Mexico olive—*Forestiera neomexicana* (N)
Sand plum—*Prunus americana* (N)
Privet—*Ligustrum* spp. (E)
Rose—*Rosa* spp. (N, E)
Snakeweed—*Gutierrezia sarothrae* (N)
Snowball—*Viburnum opulus* 'Roseum' (E)
Spirea
    a.Bridal wreath—*Spiraea prunifolia* (E)
    b.Van Houtte—*Spiraea vanhouttei* (E)
Sumac
    a.Skunkbush—*Rhus trilobata* (N)
    b.Smooth sumac—*Rhus glabra* (N)
    c.Staghorn sumac—*Rhus typhina* (E)
Weigela—*Weigela florida* (E)
Willow
    a.Coyote willow—*Salix exigua* (N)
    b.Pussywillow—*Salix discolor* (N, E)

B. Evergreen

Barberry
    a.Colorado barberry—*Berberis fendleri* (N)
    b.Japanese barberry—*Berberis thunbergii* (E)
    c.Three-spine barberry—*Berberis wisleyensis* (E)
    d.Wintergreen barberry—*Berberis julianae* (E)
Common cholla—*Opuntia imbricata* (N)
Holly
    a.Burford holly—*Ilex cornuta* 'Burfordii' (E)
    b.English holly—*Ilex aquifolium* (E)
    c.Wilson holly—*Ilex altaclarensis* 'Wilsonii' (E)
Chinese junipers
    a.Armstrong juniper—*Juniperus chinensis*
      'Armstrong' (E)
    b.Pfitzer juniper—*Juniperus chinensis* 'Pfitzerana'
      (E)
Common juniper—*Juniperus communis* (N)
Oregon grape—*Mahonia aquifolium* (E)
Chinese photinia—*Photinia serrulata* (E)
Mugo pine—*Pinus mugo* (E)
Pyracantha (firethorn)—*Pyracantha* spp. (E)
Rubber rabbitbrush—*Chrysothamnus nauseosus* (N)
Big sage (sagebrush)—*Artemisia tridentata* (N)
Fourwing saltbush—*Atriplex canescens* (N)
Yucca
    a.Narrowleaf yucca—*Yucca glauca* (N)
    b.Softblade yucca—*Yucca recurvifolia* (*Yucca*
      pendula) (N)
    c.Spanish bayonet—*Yucca baccata* (N)

GROUND COVERS

A. Deciduous

Spring cinquefoil—*Potentilla tabernaemontani* (E)
Clover—*Trifolium* spp. (NZ, N)
Cranberry cotoneaster—*Cotoneaster apiculatus* (E)
Crown vetch—*Coronilla varia* (E, NZ)
Snow-in summer—*Cerastium tomentosum* (E)

B. Evergreen

Ajuga (bugleweed)—*Ajuga reptans* (E)
Creeping euonymus—*Euonymus fortunei* (E)
Germander—*Teucrium chamaedrys* 'Prostratum' (E)
Honeysuckle—*Lonicera japonica* varieties (E)

Horizontalis junipers
    a.Bar Harbor juniper -*Juniperus horizontalis* 'Bar
      Harbor' (E)
    b.Wilton carpet juniper—*Juniperus horizontalis*
      'Wiltonii' (E)
Sabina junipers
    a.Broadmoor juniper—*Juniperus sabina*
      'Broadmoor' (E)
    b.Tam (tammy) juniper—*Juniperus sabina*
      'Tamariscifolia' (E)
Common juniper—*Juniperus communis* (N)
Kinnickinnick (mountain bearberry)—*Arctostaphylos
uva-ursi* (N)
Blue leadwort—*Ceratostigma plumbaginoides* (E)
Creeping mahonia—*Mahonia repens* (N)
Periwinkle—*Vinca major* and *Vinca minor* (E)
Gray santolina—*Santolina chamaecyparissus* (E)
Sedum (stonecrop)—*Sedum* spp. (N, E)

GRASSES

A. Traditional Turf Species

Bluegrass—*Poa pratensis* (E, NZ)
Fescue—*Festuca* spp. (E, N)
Ryegrass—*Lolium* spp. (E)

B. Native Turf And General-Use Species

Buffalo grass—*Buchlöe dactyloides* (N)
Blue grama—*Bouteloua gracilis* (N)
Wheatgrass
    a.Western wheatgrass—*Agropyron smithii* (N)
    b.Crested wheatgrass—*Agropyron desertorum* (N)

C. Ornamental Species

Blue fescue—*Festuca caesia* (E)
Indian ricegrass—*Oryzopsis hymenoides* (N)
Purple threeawn—*Aristida longiseta* (N)

VINES

A. Deciduous

Boston ivy—*Parthenocissus tricuspidata* (E)
Canyon grape—*Vitis arizonica* (N)
Clematis—*Clematis jackmanni* (E)
Morning glory—*Ipomoea tricolor* (E)
Silver lace vine—*Polygonum aubertii* (E)
Trumpet vine—*Campsis radicans* (E)
Virginia creeper (et al)—*Parthenocissus quinque-
folia* (N, E)

B. Evergreen

English ivy—*Hedera helix* (E)
Honeysuckle—*Lonicera* spp. (E)

FLOWERS

A. Annuals

Purple aster—*Aster bigelovii* (N)
Cosmos—*Cosmos* spp. (E)
Four o'clock—*Mirabilis jalapa* (E)
Gaillardia (blanketflower, firewheel)—*Gaillardia pulchella* (N)
Geranium—*Pelargonium hortorum* (E)
Impatiens—*Impatiens wallerana* (E)
Marigold—*Tagetes* spp. (E)
Pansy—*Viola wittrockiana* (E)
Petunia—*Petunia* spp. (E)
Snapdragon—*Antirrhinum majus* (E)
Sunflower—*Helianthus annuus* (N)
Wallflower—*Erysimum capitatum* (N)

B. Perennials

Desert baileya—*Baileya multiradiata* (N)
Carnation—*Dianthus caryophyllus* (E)
Chrysanthemum—*Chrysanthemum morifolium* (E)
Colorado columbine—*Aquilegia* spp. (N)
Coneflower—*Ratibida columnifera* (N)

Daylily (asphodel)—*Hemerocallis* spp. (E)
Delphinium—*Delphinium belladonna* (N)
Dusty miller—*Senecio cineraria* (E)
Blue flax—*Linum perenne* (N)
Hollyhock—*Alcea rosea* (E)
Indian paintbrush—*Castilleja integra* (N)
Jimsonweed (datura, sacred datura)—*Datura meteloides* (N)
Lobelia—*Lobelia erinus* (E)
Penstemon—*Penstemon* spp. (N)
Phlox—*Phlox* spp. (E)
California poppy—*Eschscholzia californica* (and *E. mexicana*) (E)
Shasta daisy—*Chrysanthemum maximum* (E)
Wooly yarrow—*Achillea* spp. (N, E)

C. Bulbs

Common hyacinth—*Hyacinthus orientalis* (E)
Daffodil—*Narcissus* 'King Alfred' (E)
Dutch crocus—*Crocus verus* (E)
Garden gladiolus—*Gladiolus hortulanus* (E)
Iris—*Iris* spp. (N, E)
Ranunculus—*Ranunculus asiaticus* (E)
Tulip—*Tulipa* spp. (E)

Old irrigated orchard at Bandalier National Monument

*Aspen and meadow landscape
near Pagosa Springs*

PAGOSA SPRINGS
(founded in 1891)

At an altitude of almost 7100 feet (2165 m), Pagosa Springs is very high and relatively moist. Rainfall is about 18 inches (440 mm) per year. The growing season is quite short at 60 to 90 days.

In and around Pagosa Springs, the views are often spectacular. The town is situated in a ponderosa pine forest, but many other hardy Rocky Mountain species are cultivated as domestic plants. Gambel oak flourishes here. Peachleaf willow, bristlecone pine, creeping mahonia, narrowleaf cottonwood, aspen, thimbleberry (the local raspberry), skunkbush, currants, shrubby cinquefoil, chokecherry, blue spruce, and several sedges are popular garden species. Sego lily, holly-

hock, New Mexico locust, marigold, lupine, woods rose, and smooth sumac are cultivated for seasonal color. Wheatgrass, bluegrass, and gramas are frequently planted to prevent erosion or for turf.

Most of these species flourish in the forest and woodland soils common in the area. Some alfalfa and small quantities of other crops are grown in Archuleta County, but livestock grazing remains a primary agricultural activity.

Several small, attractive gardens can be found in and around Pagosa Springs. Some very attractive new landscapes, including golf courses, have been built in the resort complexes west of town.

SELECTED BEST PLANTS FOR PAGOSA SPRINGS

These plant species grow very well in Pagosa Springs. For the sake of convenience and quick reference, each plant is listed as native (N), naturalized (NZ), or exotic (E). Other plants also will perform well in landscape and garden situations in and around Pagosa Springs. Please see the New Mexico Plant File for these species.

TREES

A. Deciduous Shade, Street, and Specialty Trees

Paper birch—*Betula papyrifera* (E)
Western chokecherry—*Prunus virginiana* (N)
Cottonwood, Aspen, and Poplar: Trees of the Genus *Populus*
    a. Aspen—*Populus tremuloides* (N)
    b. Narrowleaf cottonwood—*Populus angustifolia* (N)
Locust
    a. Black locust—*Robinia pseudoacacia* (NZ)
    b. Hybrid locusts—*Robinia ambigua* varieties (E)
    c. New Mexico locust—*Robinia neomexicana* (N)
Maple and Box elder
    a. Bigtooth maple—*Acer grandidentatum* (N)
    b. Box elder—*Acer negundo* (N)
    c. Rocky Mountain maple—*Acer glabrum* (N)
Gambel oak—*Quercus gambelii* (N)
Russian olive—*Elaeagnus angustifolia* (NZ)
Willow
    a. Peachleaf willow—*Salix amygdaloides* (N)
    b. Weeping willow—*Salix babylonica* (and other weeping willow species) (E)

B. Flowering Ornamental Trees

Flowering crab—*Malus* 'Hopa' et al (E)
Hawthorn—*Crataegus* spp. (E, N)
Purpleleaf plum—*Prunus cerasifera* (E)

C. Evergreen Trees

Douglas fir—*Pseudotsuga menziesii* (N)
White fir—*Abies concolor* (N)
Rocky Mountain juniper—*Juniperus scopulorum* varieties (N)
Pine
    a. Bristlecone pine—*Pinus aristata* (N)
    b. Limber pine—*Pinus flexilis* (N)
    c. Piñon pine—*Pinus edulis* (N)
    d. Ponderosa pine—*Pinus ponderosa* (N)
Spruce
    a. Engelmann spruce—*Picea engelmanni* (N)
    b. Blue spruce—*Picea pungens* (N)

SHRUBS

A. Deciduous

Common butterfly bush—*Buddleia davidii* (E)
Shrubby cinquefoil—*Potentilla fruticosa* (N)
Cotoneaster
    a. Cranberry cotoneaster—*Cotoneaster apiculatus* (E)
    b. Rock cotoneaster—*Cotoneaster horizontalis* (E)
    c. Rockspray cotoneaster—*Cotoneaster microphyllus* (E)
Currant and gooseberry—*Ribes* spp. (N)
Red osier dogwood—*Cornus stolonifera* (N)
Cliff fendlerbush—*Fendlera rupicola* (N)
Fernbush—*Chamaebatiaria millefolium* (N)
Common lilac—*Syringa vulgaris* (E)
Raspberry—*Rubus* spp. (E, N)
Snowball—*Viburnum opulus* 'Roseum' (E)
Sumac
    a. Skunkbush—*Rhus trilobata* (N)
    b. Smooth sumac—*Rhus glabra* (N)

B. Evergreen

Barberry
    a. Colorado barberry—*Berberis fendleri* (N)
    b. Japanese barberry—*Berberis thunbergii* (E)
Chinese junipers
    a. Armstrong juniper—*Juniperus chinensis* 'Armstrong' (E)
    b. Sea Green juniper—*Juniperus chinensis* 'Sea Green' (E)
Common juniper—*Juniperus communis* (N)
Mahonia
    a. Oregon grape—*Mahonia aquifolium* (E, NZ)
    b. Creeping mahonia—*Mahonia repens* (N)
Chinese photinia—*Photinia serrulata* (E)
Mugo pine—*Pinus mugo* (E)
Rubber rabbitbrush—*Chrysothamnus nauseosus* (N)
Big sage (sagebrush)—*Artemisia tridentata* (N)

GROUND COVERS

A. Deciduous

Spring cinquefoil—*Potentilla tabernaemontani* (E)
Clover—*Trifolium* spp. (NZ, N)
Cranberry cotoneaster—*Cotoneaster apiculatus* (E)
Mint—*Mentha* spp. (E, N, NZ)
Snow-in summer—*Cerastium tomentosum* (E)

B. Evergreen

Bearberry cotoneaster—*Cotoneaster dammeri* (E)
Creeping euonymus—*Euonymus fortunei* (E)
Honeysuckle—*Lonicera japonica* varieties (E)
Horizontalis junipers
Wilton carpet juniper—*Juniperus horizontalis* 'Wiltonii' (E)
Sabina junipers
    a. Buffalo juniper—*Juniperus sabina* 'Buffalo' (E)
    b. Tam (tammy) juniper—*Juniperus sabina* Tamariscifolia' (E)
Kinnickinnick (mountain bearberry)—*Arctostaphylos uva-ursi* (N)
Blue leadwort—*Ceratostigma plumbaginoides* (E)
Creeping mahonia—*Mahonia repens* (N)
Sedum (stonecrop)—*Sedum* spp. (N, E)
Strawberry—*Fragaria* spp. (N, E)

GRASSES

A. Traditional Turf Species

Bentgrass—*Agrostis* spp. (E)
Bluegrass—*Poa pratensis* (NZ)
Fescue—*Festuca* spp. (E, N)
Ryegrass—*Lolium* spp. (E)

B. Native Turf And General-Use Species

Galleta—*Hilaria jamesii* (N)
Crested wheatgrass—*Agropyron desertorum* (N)

C. Ornamental Species

Blue fescue—*Festuca caesia* (E)
Purple threeawn—*Aristida longiseta* (N)

VINES

A. Deciduous

Boston ivy—*Parthenocissus tricuspidata* (E)
Clematis—*Clematis jackmanni* (E)
Morning glory—*Ipomoea tricolor* (E)
Trumpet vine—*Campsis radicans* (E)
Virginia creeper (et al)—*Parthenocissus quinque-folia* (N, E)

B. Evergreen

English ivy—*Hedera helix* (E)
Honeysuckle—*Lonicera* spp. (E)

FLOWERS

A. Annuals

Ageratum—*Ageratum houstonianum* (E)
Purple aster—*Aster bigelovii* (N)
Coleus—*Coleus x hybridus* (E)
Gaillardia (blanketflower, firewheel)—*Gaillardia pulchella* (N)

Geranium—*Pelargonium hortorum* (E)
Marigold—*Tagetes* spp. (E)
Pansy—*Viola wittrockiana* (E)
Petunia—*Petunia* spp. (E)
Salvia—*Salvia* spp. (E)
Snapdragon—*Antirrhinum majus* (E)
Sunflower—*Helianthus annuus* (N)
Wallflower—*Erysimum capitatum* (N)

B. Perennials

Chrysanthemum—*Chrysanthemum morifolium* (E)
Colorado columbine—*Aquilegia* spp. (N)
Coneflower—*Ratibida columnifera* (N)
Daylily (asphodel)—*Hemerocallis* spp. (E)
Delphinium—*Delphinium belladonna* (E, N)
Blue flax—*Linum perenne* (N)
Geranium (cranesbill)—*Geranium* spp. (N)
Globemallow—*Sphaeralcea incana* (scarlet) (N)
Hollyhock—*Alcea rosea* (E, NZ)
Indian paintbrush—*Castilleja integra* (N)
Maximilian's daisy—*Helianthus maximiliani* (NZ)
Penstemon—*Penstemon* spp. (N)
Phlox—*Phlox* spp. (E)
Primrose—*Primula vulgaris* (E)
Red rocket (scarlet gilia)—*Ipomopsis aggregata* (N)
Shasta daisy—*Chrysanthemum maximum* (E)
Wooly yarrow—*Achillea* spp. (N, E)

C. Bulbs

Daffodil—*Narcissus* 'King Alfred' (E)
Dutch crocus—*Crocus verus* (E)
Iris—*Iris* spp. (N, E)

PORTALES

(founded in 1898)

Deposits of wind-blown loess lie all around Portales. This primeval soil material has stabilized into sandy, rolling, reddish hills very characteristic of Roosevelt County. The sandy loam soil is extremely fertile, and Roosevelt is one of New Mexico's principal agricultural counties. At 4070 feet (1240 m), Portales is only slightly lower than next-door Clovis in Curry County, but it has a shorter growing season (178 days). Rainfall ranges from about 16 inches (400 mm) to over 25 inches (625 mm).

The city itself is named after the intriguing Portales Springs, which flow out of caves a few miles south of the townsite. Much of the nearby countryside has been developed since the turn of the century through irrigation into a distinct agricultural landscape. Peanuts are a very important and unique crop, as are sorghum, wheat, corn, onions, and cotton. Cattle and calves are widely raised, but milk cows are essential to the county's economy. Hogs and chickens are also produced.

Cottonwoods in draws were generally the only native trees in the high plains Portales landscape before the development of the great agricultural tracts of Roosevelt County. Narrowleaf yucca, snakeweed, and cholla appear where there have been heavy grazing or other great disturbances. So does the remarkable shin oak (*Quercus havardii*), a distinctive, shrubby, ground-cover plant.

Wheatgrass, grama, buffalo, and other grass species are widespread and provide excellent soil protection. Black locusts have naturalized themselves in small groves in and around Portales. Honey locust, globe willow, eastern red cedar, ashes, Arizona cypress, linden, Russian olive, catalpa, Afghan pine, various poplar species, redbud, and elms are widely used as street, shade, and accent trees in Portales. Pecans grow well here; as in much of New Mexico, these are tremendously under-utilized as shade trees. Popular shrubs and ground covers include junipers, yuccas, santolina, honeysuckle, althea, pampas grass, yaupon holly, roses, lilac, big sage, shrubby cinquefoil, cotoneasters, and butterfly bush. Sunflowers, daylilies, marigolds, lupines, four o'clocks, lobelia, ageratum, and yarrows are favorite local annuals and perennials.

Portales has a large number of well-tended home gardens. Among the city's public gardens, City Park and Rotary Park are shady and very reminiscent of the "Prairie Park" style of the 1930s. The campus quad at Eastern New

Silk tree in a colorful planter on the campus of Eastern New Mexico University, Portales

Mexico University is easily the most ambitious and unique public landscape in Roosevelt County. Its graceful lines of honey locusts, generous open lawns, cool blue central fountains, and bright annual flower accents give it the quality of a refined oasis in the midst of the high plains.

SELECTED BEST PLANTS FOR PORTALES

These plant species grow very well in Portales. For the sake of convenience and quick reference, each plant is listed as native (N), naturalized (NZ), or exotic (E). Other plants also will perform well in landscape and garden situations in and around Portales. Please see the New Mexico Plant File for these species.

TREES

A. Deciduous Shade, Street, and Specialty Trees

Ash
    a. Green ash—*Fraxinus pennsylvanica* and varieties (E)
    b. Raywood ash—*Fraxinus oxycarpa* 'Raywood' (E)
    c. White ash—*Fraxinus americana* and varieties (E)
Catalpa
    a. Umbrella catalpa—*Catalpa bignonioides* 'Nana' (E)
    b. Western catalpa—*Catalpa speciosa* (E)
Cottonwood, Aspen, and Poplar: Trees of the Genus *Populus*

a.Bolleana poplar—*Populus alba* 'Pyramidalis'(E)
b.Carolina poplar—*Populus canadensis* (E)
c.Lanceleaf cottonwood—*Populus acuminata* (N)
d.Lombardy poplar—*Populus nigra* 'Italica' (E)
e.White (silver) poplar—*Populus alba* (NZ)
American elm—*Ulmus americana* (E)
Ginkgo (maidenhair tree)—*Ginkgo biloba* (E)
Common hackberry—*Celtis occidentalis* (E)
Littleleaf linden—*Tilia cordata* (E)
Honey locust—*Gleditsia triacanthos inermis*
          varieties (E)
Locust
a.Black locust—*Robinia pseudoacacia* (E, NZ)
b.Hybrid locusts—*Robinia ambigua* varieties (E)
c.New Mexico locust—*Robinia neomexicana* (N)
Maple and Box elder
a.Box elder—*Acer negundo* (N)
b.Japanese maple—*Acer palmatum* (E)
c.Norway maple—*Acer platanoides* (E)
d.Silver maple—*Acer saccharinum* (E)
e.Sycamore-leaf maple—*Acer pseudoplatanus* (E)
Fruitless mulberry—*Morus alba* (E)
Oak
a.Southern live oak—*Quercus virginiana* (E)
b.Texas oak—*Quercus texana* (E)
Osage orange—*Maclura pomifera* (E)
Pecan—*Carya illinoiensis* (E)
Russian olive—*Elaeagnus angustifolia* (NZ)
Sweet gum—*Liquidambar styraciflua* (E)
Willow
a.Corkscrew willow—*Salix matsudana*
          'Tortuosa' (E)
b.Globe Navajo willow—*Salix matsudana*
          'Navajo' (E)
c.Peachleaf willow—*Salix amygdaloides* (N)
d.Weeping willow—*Salix babylonica* (and other
          weeping willow species) (E)

B. Flowering Ornamental Trees

Flowering apricot—*Prunus armeniaca* (E)
Flowering cherry—*Prunus serrulata* et al (E)
Flowering crab—*Malus* 'Hopa' et al (E)
Desert willow—*Chilopsis linearis* (N)
Hawthorn—*Crataegus* spp. (E, N)
Flowering peach—*Prunus persica* (E)
Bradford pear—*Pyrus calleryana* (E)
Purpleleaf plum—*Prunus cerasifera* (E)
Eastern redbud—*Cercis canadensis* (E)
Golden rain tree—*Koelreuteria paniculata* (E)
Vitex (chaste tree)—*Vitex agnus-castus* (E)

C. Evergreen Trees

Atlas cedar—*Cedrus atlantica* (E)
Arizona cypress—*Cupressus arizonica* (E)
Juniper
a.Eastern red cedar—*Juniperus virginiana*
          varieties (E)
b.Rocky Mountain juniper—*Juniperus scopulorum*
          varieties (N)
Leyland false cypress—*Cupressocyparis leylandii* (E)
Magnolia
a.Southern magnolia—*Magnolia grandiflora* (E)
b.Saucer magnolia—*Magnolia soulangiana* (E)
Pine
a.Afghan pine—*Pinus eldarica* (E)
b.Austrian pine—*Pinus nigra* (E)
c.Piñon pine—*Pinus edulis* (N)
d.Ponderosa pine—*Pinus ponderosa* (N)
e.Scotch pine—*Pinus sylvestris* (E)
Dawn redwood—*Metasequoia glyptostroboides* (E)
Blue spruce—*Picea pungens* (N)

Yucca
a.Palm yucca—*Yucca torreyi* (N)
b.Soaptree yucca—*Yucca elata* (N)

SHRUBS

A. Deciduous

Glossy abelia—*Abelia grandiflora* (E)
Flowering almond—*Prunus glandulosa* (E)
Althea (rose of Sharon)—*Hibiscus syriacus* (E)
Common butterfly bush—*Buddleia davidii* (E)
Shrubby cinquefoil—*Potentilla fruticosa* (N)
Cotoneaster
a.Cranberry cotoneaster—*Cotoneaster
          apiculatus* (E)
b.Rock cotoneaster—*Cotoneaster horizontalis* (E)
c.Rockspray cotoneaster—*Cotoneaster
          microphyllus* (E)
Crape myrtle—*Lagerstroemia indica* (E)
Shrub or Tatarian honeysuckle—*Lonicera tatarica* (E)
Flowering jasmine—*Jasminum nudiflorum* (E)
Common lilac—*Syringa vulgaris* (E)
Mock orange
a.Sweet mock orange—*Philadelphus coronarius* (E)
b.Littleleaf mock orange—*Philadelphus
          microphyllus* (E, N)
Mountain mahogany—*Cercocarpus montanus* (N)
New Mexico olive—*Forestiera neomexicana* (N)
Raspberry—*Rubus* spp. (E, N)
Rose—*Rosa* spp. (N, E)
Snakeweed—*Gutierrezia sarothrae* (N)
Snowball—*Viburnum opulus* 'Roseum' (E)
Spirea
a.Bridal wreath—*Spiraea prunifolia* (E)
b.Anthony Waterer—*Spiraea bumalda* 'Anthony
          Waterer' (E)
Sumac
a.Littleleaf sumac—*Rhus microphylla* (N)
b.Skunkbush—*Rhus trilobata* (N)
c.Smooth sumac—*Rhus glabra* (N)
d.Staghorn sumac—*Rhus typhina* (E)
Pussywillow—*Salix discolor* (N, E)
Winterfat—*Ceratoides lanata* (N)

B. Evergreen

Aucuba—*Aucuba japonica* (E)
Barberry
a.Colorado barberry—*Berberis fendleri* (N)
b.Japanese barberry—*Berberis thunbergii* (E), in-
          cluding redleaf Japanese barberry, *B. japon.*
          'Atropurpurea'
c.Three-spine barberry—*Berberis wisleyensis* (E)
Beargrass—*Nolina microcarpa* (N)
Common cholla—*Opuntia imbricata* (N)
Yaupon holly—*Ilex vomitoria* (E)
Chinese junipers
a.Armstrong juniper—*Juniperus chinensis*
          'Armstrong' (E)
b.Pfitzer juniper—*Juniperus chinensis*
          'Pfitzerana' (E)
Mahonia
a.Algerita—*Mahonia haematocarpa* (N)
b.Oregon grape—*Mahonia aquifolium* (E, NZ)
Mormon tea—*Ephedra* spp. (N)
Nandina (heavenly bamboo)—*Nandina domestica* (E)
Chinese photinia—*Photinia serrulata* (E)
Mugo pine—*Pinus mugo* (E)
Pyracantha (firethorn)—*Pyracantha* spp. (E)
Big sage (sagebrush)—*Artemisia tridentata* (N)

Fourwing saltbush—*Atriplex canescens* (N)
Yucca
    a.Softblade yucca—*Yucca recurvifolia* (*Yucca pendula*) (E)
    b.Coral-flower yucca—*Hesperaloe parviflora* (E)

GROUND COVERS

A. Deciduous

Spring cinquefoil—*Potentilla tabernaemontani* (E)
Clover—*Trifolium* spp. (NZ, N)
Cranberry cotoneaster—*Cotoneaster apiculatus* (E)
Mint—*Mentha* spp. (E, N, NZ)
Prairie sage—*Artemisia ludoviciana* (N)
Snow-in summer—*Cerastium tomentosum* (E)

B. Evergreen

Bearberry cotoneaster—*Cotoneaster dammeri* (E)
Creeping euonymus—*Euonymus fortunei* (E)
Germander—*Teucrium chamaedrys* 'Prostratum' (E)
Honeysuckle—*Lonicera japonica* varieties (E)
Horizontalis junipers
    a.Bar Harbor juniper—*Juniperus horizontalis* 'Bar Harbor'(E)
    b.Wilton carpet juniper—*Juniperus horizontalis* 'Wiltonii' (E)
Sabina junipers
    a.Broadmoor juniper—*Juniperus sabina* 'Broadmoor' (E)
    b.Tam (tammy) juniper -*Juniperus sabina* 'Tamariscifolia' (E)
Blue leadwort—*Ceratostigma plumbaginoides* (E)
Compact nandina—*Nandina domestica* 'Harbor dwarf' (E)
Santolina
    a.Green santolina—*Santolina virens* (E)
    b.Gray santolina—*Santolina chamaecyparissus* (E)
Sedum (stonecrop)—*Sedum* spp. (N, E)
Japanese spurge—*Pachysandra terminalis* (E)
Strawberry—*Fragaria* spp. (N, E)

GRASSES

A. Traditional Turf Species

Bentgrass—*Agrostis* spp. (E)
Bermuda
    a.African bermuda—*Cynodon transvaalensis* (E, NZ)
    b.Common bermuda—*Cynodon dactylon* (NZ)
Bluegrass—*Poa pratensis* (NZ)
Fescue—*Festuca* spp. (NZ)
Ryegrass—*Lolium* spp. (E)

B. Native Turf And General-Use Species

Buffalo grass—*Buchlöe dactyloides* (N)
Grama
    a.Black grama—*Bouteloua eriopoda* (N)
    b.Blue grama—*Bouteloua gracilis* (N)
    c.Sideoats grama—*Bouteloua curtipendula* (N)
Wheatgrass
    a.Western wheatgrass—*Agropyron smithii* (N)
    b.Crested wheatgrass—*Agropyron desertorum* (E, NZ)

C. Ornamental Species

Blue fescue—*Festuca caesia* (E)
Fountain grass—*Pennisetum* spp. (E)
Pampas grass—*Cortaderia selloana* (E)
River cane—*Arundo donax* (NZ)
Purple threeawn—*Aristida longiseta* (N)

VINES

A. Deciduous

Boston ivy—*Parthenocissus tricuspidata* (E)
Canyon grape—*Vitis arizonica* (N)
Carolina jessamine—*Gelsemium sempervirens* (E)
Clematis—*Clematis jackmanni* (E)
Trumpet vine—*Campsis radicans* (E)
Virginia creeper (et al)—*Parthenocissus quinquefolia* (N, E)
Wisteria—*Wisteria sinensis* (E)

B. Evergreen

English ivy—*Hedera helix* (E)
Honeysuckle—*Lonicera* spp. (E)

FLOWERS

A. Annuals

Ageratum—*Ageratum houstonianum* (E)
Coleus—*Coleus x hybridus* (E)
Cosmos—*Cosmos* spp. (E)
Four o'clock—*Mirabilis jalapa* (E)
Gaillardia (blanketflower, firewheel)—*Gaillardia pulchella* (N)
Marigold—*Tagetes* spp. (E)
Petunia—*Petunia* spp. (E)
Snapdragon—*Antirrhinum majus* (E)
Sunflower—*Helianthus annuus* (N)
Annual vinca (Madagascar periwinkle)—*Catharanthus roseus* (E)

B. Perennials

Desert baileya—*Baileya multiradiata* (N)
Chrysanthemum—*Chrysanthemum morifolium* (E)
Colorado columbine—*Aquilegia* spp. (N)
Coneflower—*Ratibida columnifera* (N)
Daylily (asphodel)—*Hemerocallis* spp. (E)
Delphinium—*Delphinium belladonna* (E, N)
Dusty miller—*Senecio cineraria* (E)
Blue flax—*Linum perenne* (N)
Hollyhock—*Alcea rosea* (E, NZ)
Jimsonweed (datura, sacred datura)—*Datura meteloides* (N)
Lobelia—*Lobelia erinus* (E)
Maximilian's daisy—*Helianthus maximiliani* (NZ)
Penstemon—*Penstemon* spp. (N)
Phlox—*Phlox* spp. (E)
Shasta daisy—*Chrysanthemum maximum* (E)
Violet—*Viola odorata* (N, E)

C. Bulbs

Canna—*Canna* spp. (E)
Dutch crocus—*Crocus verus* (E)
Garden gladiolus—*Gladiolus hortulanus* (E)
Iris—*Iris* spp. (N, E)
Ranunculus—*Ranunculus asiaticus* (E)
Tulip—*Tulipa* spp. (E)

Perennial garden at the museum in Folsom

RATON

including also Springer, Wagon Mound, Capulin, Folsom, Des Moines, and Cimarron

In Raton, there is no question that you are in the Rockies. Rocky Mountain juniper, white fir, Gambel oak, ponderosa pine, piñon, spruce, and rubber rabbitbrush are everywhere to be seen. But the plains brush up against Raton's distinctive foothills landscape, too: winterfat, various gramas, buffalo grass, wheatgrass, singleseed juniper, and choke-cherry dot the hill and mesa country to the east and south of town.

Raton is high at 6700 feet (2060 m), and winters can be cold. The growing season is about 148 days. Rainfall is generous by New Mexico standards at 16–23 inches (400–575 mm). Soils are generally fertile but may also be stony and clayey. Relatively deep soil is found in pockets. Most of Colfax County's agricultural production is concentrated in the raising of cattle and calves. Hay is widely grown, along with a modest amount of other crops.

Settled in 1879, Raton lies astride the old Santa Fe Trail at the south end of Raton Pass. The native peachleaf willow is found in many of the town's home landscapes, as are sand plum, althea, snowball viburnum, aspen, narrowleaf cottonwood, forsythia, limber and bristlecone pines, spirea, red osier dogwood, box elder, and Russian olive. Attractive accents include birch, mugo pine, sedums, roses,

currants, Oregon grape, bearberry, and cheerful hollyhocks, columbines, and sunflowers.

Raton has many attractive small gardens. The Colfax County Courthouse grounds feature beautifully maintained white firs and other evergreens. Blue and Engelmann spruces, along with Siberian elms, are perhaps the most common streetside trees. Flowering crabapples are popular. The grounds of the Miners' Hospital continue to be, along with the courthouse square, the most important public landscape in Raton. However, the stately landscape of the Mount Calvary Catholic Cemetery, with its quiet, dignified beauty, perhaps best reflects both the spirit of the Rockies and that of the pioneer miners and railroad workers who built Raton after the turn of the century.

(Please see Trinidad, at the other end of Raton Pass, under its own listing.)

SELECTED BEST PLANTS FOR RATON

These plant species grow very well in Raton. For the sake of convenience and quick reference, each plant is listed as native (N), naturalized (NZ), or exotic (E). Other plants also will perform well in landscape and garden situations in and around Raton. Please see the New Mexico Plant File for these species.

TREES

A. Deciduous Shade, Street, and Specialty Trees

Green ash—*Fraxinus pennsylvanica* and varieties (E)
Paper birch—*Betula papyrifera* (E)
Western chokecherry—*Prunus virginiana* (N)
Cottonwood, Aspen, and Poplar: Trees of the Genus *Populus*
    a.Aspen—*Populus tremuloides* (N)
    b.Bolleana poplar—*Populus alba* 'Pyramidalis' (E)
    c.Carolina poplar—*Populus canadensis* (E)
    d.Lanceleaf cottonwood—*Populus acuminata* (N)
    e.Lombardy poplar—*Populus nigra* 'Italica' (E)
    f.Narrowleaf cottonwood—*Populus angustifolia* (N)
    g.Plains cottonwood—*Populus sargenti* (N)
    h.Rio Grande cottonwood -*Populus fremontii* 'Wislizeni' (N)
    i.White (silver) poplar—*Populus alba* (E)
American elm—*Ulmus americana* (NZ)
Honey locust—*Gleditsia triacanthos inermis* varieties (E)
Common horsechestnut—*Aesculus hippocastanum* (E)
Locust
    a.Black locust—*Robinia pseudoacacia* (NZ)
    b.Hybrid locusts—*Robinia ambigua* varieties (E)
    c.New Mexico locust—*Robinia neomexicana* (N)
Maple and Box elder
    a.Box elder—*Acer negundo* (N)
    b.Rocky Mountain maple—*Acer glabrum* (N)
    c.Silver maple—*Acer saccharinum* (E)
European mountain ash—*Sorbus aucuparia* (E)
Fruitless mulberry—*Morus alba* (E) (and fruiting mulberry, same sp.)
Gambel oak—*Quercus gambelii* (N)
Russian olive—*Elaeagnus angustifolia* (NZ)
Willow
    a.Globe Navajo willow—*Salix matsudana* 'Navajo' (E)
    b.Peachleaf willow—*Salix amygdaloides* (N)

B. Flowering Ornamental Trees

Flowering apricot—*Prunus armeniaca* (E)
Flowering crab—*Malus* 'Hopa' et al (E)
Hawthorn—*Crataegus* spp. (E, N)
Flowering peach—*Prunus persica* (E)
Bradford pear—*Pyrus calleryana* (E)
Purpleleaf plum—*Prunus cerasifera* (E)
Eastern redbud—*Cercis canadensis* (E)
Golden rain tree—*Koelreuteria paniculata* (E)

C. Evergreen Trees

Douglas fir—*Pseudotsuga menziesii* (N)
White fir—*Abies concolor* (N)
Juniper
    a.Eastern red cedar—*Juniperus virginiana* varieties (E)
    b.Rocky Mountain juniper—*Juniperus scopulorum* varieties (N)
    c.Singleseed (one-seed) juniper—*Juniperus monosperma* (N)
Pine
    a.Austrian pine—*Pinus nigra* (E)
    b.Japanese black pine—*Pinus thunbergiana* (E)
    c.Bristlecone pine—*Pinus aristata* (N)
    d.Limber pine—*Pinus flexilis* (N)
    e.Piñon pine—*Pinus edulis* (N)
    f.Ponderosa pine—*Pinus ponderosa* (N)
Spruce
    a.Blue spruce—*Picea pungens* (N)
    b.Engelmann spruce—*Picea engelmanni* (N)
    c.Black Hills spruce—*Picea glauca densata* (E)
Western red cedar—*Thuja plicata* (E)
Soaptree yucca—*Yucca elata* (N)

SHRUBS

A. Deciduous

Althea (rose of Sharon)—*Hibiscus syriacus* (E)
Apache plume—*Fallugia paradoxa* (N)
Common butterfly bush—*Buddleia davidii* (E)
Shrubby cinquefoil—*Potentilla fruticosa* (N)
Cotoneaster
    a.Cranberry cotoneaster—*Cotoneaster apiculatus* (E)
    b.Rock cotoneaster—*Cotoneaster horizontalis* (E)
    c.Rockspray cotoneaster—*Cotoneaster microphyllus* (E)
Currant and gooseberry—*Ribes* spp. (N)
Red osier dogwood—*Cornus stolonifera* (N)
Fernbush—*Chamaebatiaria millefolium* (N)
Forsythia—*Forsythia* spp. (E)
Hop tree—*Ptelea trifoliolata* (N)
Flowering jasmine—*Jasminum nudiflorum* (E)
Common lilac—*Syringa vulgaris* (E)
Mountain mahogany—*Cercocarpus montanus* (N)
New Mexico olive—*Forestiera neomexicana* (N)
Sand plum—*Prunus americana* (N)
Privet—*Ligustrum* spp. (E)
Raspberry—*Rubus* spp. (E, N)
Rose—*Rosa* spp. (N, E)
Snakeweed—*Gutierrezia sarothrae* (N)
Snowball—*Viburnum opulus* 'Roseum' (E)
Spirea
    a.Bridal wreath—*Spiraea prunifolia* (E)
    b.Van Houtte—*Spiraea vanhouttei* (E)
    c.Anthony Waterer—*Spiraea bumalda* 'Anthony Waterer' (E)
Sumac
    a.Skunkbush—*Rhus trilobata* (N)
    b.Smooth sumac—*Rhus glabra* (N)
    c.Staghorn sumac—*Rhus typhina* (E)
Pussywillow—*Salix discolor* (N)
Winterfat—*Ceratoides lanata* (N)

B. Evergreen

Aucuba—*Aucuba japonica* (E)
Barberry
    a.Colorado barberry—*Berberis fendleri* (N)
    b.Japanese barberry—*Berberis thunbergii* (E)
    c.Three-spine barberry—*Berberis wisleyensis* (E)
    d.Wintergreen barberry—*Berberis julianae* (E)
Beargrass—*Nolina microcarpa* (N)
Common cholla—*Opuntia imbricata* (N)
Parney cotoneaster—*Cotoneaster lacteus* (E)
Holly
    a.Burford holly—*Ilex cornuta* 'Burfordii' (E)
    b.English holly—*Ilex aquifolium* (E)
Chinese junipers
    a.Armstrong juniper—*Juniperus chinensis* 'Armstrong' (E)
    b.Pfitzer juniper—*Juniperus chinensis* 'Pfitzerana' (E)
    c.Sea Green juniper—*Juniperus chinensis* 'Sea Green' (E)
Common juniper—*Juniperus communis* (N)
Oregon grape—*Mahonia aquifolium* (E)
Nandina (heavenly bamboo)—*Nandina domestica* (E)
Mugo pine—*Pinus mugo* (E)

Pyracantha (firethorn)—*Pyracantha* spp. (E)
Rubber rabbitbrush—*Chrysothamnus nauseosus* (N)
Big sage (sagebrush)—*Artemisia tridentata* (N)
Fourwing saltbush—*Atriplex canescens* (N)
Alberta spruce—*Picea glauca* 'Conica'
 (*Picea albertiana*) (E)
Yucca
 a.Narrowleaf yucca—*Yucca glauca* (N)
 b.Spanish bayonet—*Yucca baccata* (N)

GROUND COVERS

A. Deciduous

Spring cinquefoil—*Potentilla tabernaemontani* (E)
Clover—*Trifolium* spp. (NZ, N)
Cranberry cotoneaster—*Cotoneaster apiculatus* (E)
Prairie sage—*Artemisia ludoviciana* (N)
Memorial rose (vine)—*Rosa wichuriana* (E)

B. Evergreen

Ajuga (bugleweed)—*Ajuga reptans* (E)
Bearberry cotoneaster—*Cotoneaster dammeri* (E)
Creeping euonymus—*Euonymus fortunei* (E)
Honeysuckle—*Lonicera japonica* varieties (E)
Horizontalis junipers
 a.Wilton carpet juniper—*Juniperus horizontalis*
 'Wiltonii' (E)
Sabina junipers
 a.Broadmoor juniper—*Juniperus sabina*
 'Broadmoor' (E)
 b.Buffalo juniper—*Juniperus sabina* 'Buffalo' (E)
 c.Tam (tammy) juniper—*Juniperus sabina*
 'Tamariscifolia' (E)
Kinnickinnick (mountain bearberry)—*Arctostaphylos*
 uva-ursi (N)
Creeping mahonia—*Mahonia repens* (N)
Periwinkle—*Vinca major* and *Vinca minor* (E)
Pussytoes—*Antennaria parviflora* (N)
Sedum (stonecrop)—*Sedum* spp. (N, E)
Strawberry—*Fragaria* spp. (N, E)

GRASSES

A. Traditional Turf Species

Bluegrass—*Poa pratensis* (NZ)
Fescue—*Festuca* spp. (E)
Ryegrass—*Lolium* spp. (E)

B. Native Turf And General-Use Species

Buffalo grass—*Buchlöe dactyloides* (N)
Galleta—*Hilaria jamesii* (N)
Grama
 a.Black grama—*Bouteloua eriopoda* (N)
 b.Blue grama—*Bouteloua gracilis* (N)
 c.Sideoats grama—*Bouteloua curtipendula* (N)
Wheatgrass
 a.Western wheatgrass—*Agropyron smithii* (N)
 b.Crested wheatgrass—*Agropyron desertorum*
 (E, NZ)
 c.Pubescent wheatgrass—*Agropyron trichophorum* (N)

C. Ornamental Species

Blue fescue—*Festuca caesia* (E)
Fountain grass—*Pennisetum* spp. (E)
Purple threeawn—*Aristida longiseta* (N)

VINES

A. Deciduous

Boston ivy—*Parthenocissus tricuspidata* (E)
Canyon grape—*Vitis arizonica* (N)
Clematis—*Clematis jackmanni* (E)
Morning glory—*Ipomoea tricolor* (E)
Silver lace vine—*Polygonum aubertii* (E)
Trumpet vine—*Campsis radicans* (E)
Virginia creeper (et al)—*Parthenocissus quinquefolia*
 (N, E)
Wisteria—*Wisteria sinensis* (E)

B. Evergreen

English ivy—*Hedera helix* (E)
Honeysuckle—*Lonicera* spp. (E)

FLOWERS

A. Annuals

Purple aster—*Aster bigelovii* (N)
Cosmos—*Cosmos* spp. (E)
Four o'clock—*Mirabilis jalapa* (E)
Gaillardia (blanketflower, firewheel)—*Gaillardia*
 pulchella (N)
Geranium—*Pelargonium hortorum* (E)
Impatiens—*Impatiens wallerana* (E)
Lisianthus—*Eustoma grandiflorum* (E)
Marigold—*Tagetes* spp. (E)
Petunia—*Petunia* spp. (E)
Salvia—*Salvia* spp. (E)
Snapdragon—*Antirrhinum majus* (E)
Sunflower—*Helianthus annuus* (N)
Annual vinca (Madagascar periwinkle)—*Catharanthus*
 roseus (E)
Viola (Johnny jump-ups)—*Viola* spp. (E)
Wallflower—*Erysimum capitatum* (N)

B. Perennials

Carnation—*Dianthus caryophyllus* (E)
Chrysanthemum—*Chrysanthemum morifolium* (E)
Colorado columbine—*Aquilegia* spp. (N)
Coneflower—*Ratibida columnifera* (N)
Daylily (asphodel)—*Hemerocallis* spp. (E)
Delphinium—*Delphinium belladonna* (E, N)
Dusty miller—*Senecio cineraria* (E)
Blue flax—*Linum perenne* (N)
Geranium (cranesbill)—*Geranium* spp. (N)
Globemallow—*Sphaeralcea incana* (scarlet) (N)
Hollyhock—*Alcea rosea* (E, NZ)
Indian paintbrush—*Castilleja integra* (N)
Lobelia—*Lobelia erinus* (E)
Maximilian's daisy—*Helianthus maximiliani* (NZ)
Penstemon—*Penstemon* spp. (N)
Phlox—*Phlox* spp. (E)
Primrose—*Primula vulgaris* (E)
Red rocket (scarlet gilia)—*Ipomopsis aggregata* (N)
Shasta daisy—*Chrysanthemum maximum* (E)
Violet—*Viola odorata* (N, E)
Wooly yarrow—*Achillea* spp. (N, E)

C. Bulbs

Canna—*Canna* spp. (E)
Daffodil—*Narcissus* 'King Alfred' (E)
Dutch crocus—*Crocus verus* (E)
Garden gladiolus—*Gladiolus hortulanus* (E)
Iris—*Iris* spp. (N, E)
Tulip—*Tulipa* spp. (E)

Fulton Water Gardens, Cahoon Park

Roswell is the largest of New Mexico's Pecos River cities. At 3600 feet (1100 m), it has a considerable growing season of 198 days. Rainfall varies from about 12 to 19 inches (300–475 mm) per year. Although much of Roswell lies on thin, limey soils, rich pockets of fertile ground can be found in and around the city. The lowlands near the Pecos itself are intensively farmed.

Chaves County is second only to Doña Ana in terms of the importance of its agriculture to New Mexico's economy. Barley, cotton, hay, alfalfa, pecans, wheat, sorghum, and corn are widely planted. Beef cattle and calves, milk cows, poultry, hogs, and other livestock are raised throughout the county. Chile, vegetables, and fruit are also important agricultural products. Chaves County is the number one sheep producer in New Mexico.

The Chihuahuan Desert extends north into the area around Roswell from West Texas and Chihuahua. Its classic shrub-tree is the mesquite, and this grows in clumpy abundance around the city. So do the desert willows, saltbush, snakeweed, yucca, ocotillo, cactus, alkali sacaton, screwbean, and soapberry trees that also mark this desert. Along the river itself are willows, salt cedar, cottonwood, saltgrass, seepwillow, and netleaf hackberry. The Great Plains touch Roswell from the east, and here shin oak, several grama species, wheatgrass, winterfat, and other low plants are common.

Large groves of pecan trees are found in many of the agricultural areas around Roswell. The traditional streetside trees of twentieth-century Roswell are Siberian elms, ashes, and often silver poplars—all tough and tolerant of shallow, alkaline soils. Cottonwoods, other poplar species, and sycamores are grown for large-scale shade within the city. Bradford pear, Rocky Mountain juniper, Mexican elder, stone fruits, soapberry, honey and black locusts, western red cedar, willows, ponderosa pine, southern live oak, Texas oak, Austrian pine, and Russian olive are favorite cultivated local trees. Redbuds are brilliant here and commonly grown for their spring color. Fig, Spanish dagger, bird of paradise, softblade yucca, golden rain tree, yaupon holly, photinia, saltbush, various junipers, and pyracantha are popular accents.

The Chaves County Courthouse Square and the grounds of the CCC-era Cahoon Park are the city's most influential historic landscapes. Cahoon's sunken Fulton Water Gardens have recently been refurbished and are quite unique in New Mexico. The more formal grounds of the New Mexico Military Institute and miscellaneous parks along the lower Spring River are also important public landscapes.

SELECTED BEST PLANTS FOR ROSWELL

These plant species grow very well in Roswell. For the sake of convenience and quick reference, each plant is listed as native (N), naturalized (NZ), or exotic (E). Other plants also will perform well in landscape and garden situations in and around Roswell. Please see the New Mexico Plant File for these species.

TREES

A. Deciduous Shade, Street, and Specialty Trees

Arizona alder—*Alnus oblongifolia* (N)
Ash
  a.Modesto ash—*Fraxinus velutina* 'Modesto' (Arizona ash variety) (N)
  b.Green ash—*Fraxinus pennsylvanica* and varieties (E)
  c.Raywood ash—*Fraxinus oxycarpa* 'Raywood' (E)
  d.White ash—*Fraxinus americana* and varieties (E)
Catalpa
  a.Umbrella catalpa—*Catalpa bignonioides* 'Nana' (E)
  b.Western catalpa—*Catalpa speciosa* (E)
Chinaberry—*Melia azedarach* (E)
Cottonwood, Aspen, and Poplar: Trees of the Genus *Populus*
  a.Bolleana poplar—*Populus alba* 'Pyramidalis' (E)
  b.Carolina poplar—*Populus canadensis* (NZ)
  c.Lanceleaf cottonwood—*Populus acuminata* (N)
  d.Lombardy poplar—*Populus nigra* 'Italica' (E)
  e.Rio Grande cottonwood—*Populus fremontii* 'Wislizeni' (N)
Elm
  a.American elm—*Ulmus americana* (E)
  b.Chinese elm—*Ulmus parvifolia* (E)
Hackberry
  a.Common hackberry—*Celtis occidentalis* (E)
  b.Netleaf hackberry—*Celtis reticulata* (N)
Honey locust—*Gleditsia triacanthos inermis* varieties (NZ)
Locust
  a.Black locust—*Robinia pseudoacacia* (NZ)
  b.New Mexico locust—*Robinia neomexicana* (N)
Maple and Box elder
  a.Norway maple—*Acer platanoides* (E)
  b.Sycamore-leaf maple—*Acer pseudoplatanus* (E)
Mesquite—*Prosopis glandulosa* (N)
Mulberry
  a.Fruitless mulberry—*Morus alba* (E)
  b.Weeping mulberry—*Morus alba* 'Pendula' (E)
Oak
  a.Pin oak—*Quercus palustris* (E)
  b.Southern live oak—*Quercus virginiana* (E)
  c.Texas oak—*Quercus texana* (E)
Japanese pagoda—*Sophora japonica* (E)
Pecan—*Carya illinoiensis* (E)
Russian olive—*Elaeagnus angustifolia* (NZ)
Silk tree—*Albizia jilibrissin* (E)
Western soapberry—*Sapindus drummondii* (N)
Sycamore (plane tree)
  a.American sycamore—*Platanus occidentalis* (E)
  b.Arizona sycamore—*Platanus wrightii* (N)
  c.London plane tree—*Platanus acerifolia* (E)
  d.Oriental plane tree—*Platanus orientalis* (E)

Walnut
  a.Arizona walnut—*Juglans major* (N)
  b.English (Carpathian) walnut—*Juglans regia* (E)
Willow
  a.Globe Navajo willow—*Salix matsudana* 'Navajo' (E)
  b.Weeping willow—*Salix babylonica* (and other weeping willow species) (E)

B. Flowering Ornamental Trees

Flowering apricot—*Prunus armeniaca* (E)
Flowering cherry—*Prunus serrulata* et al (E)
Flowering crab—*Malus* 'Hopa' et al (E)
Desert willow—*Chilopsis linearis* (N)
Mexican elder—*Sambucus caerulea neomexicana* (N)
Flowering peach—*Prunus persica* (E)
Bradford pear—*Pyrus calleryana* (E)
Purpleleaf plum—*Prunus cerasifera* (E)
Eastern redbud—*Cercis canadensis* (E)
Golden rain tree—*Koelreuteria paniculata* (E)
Salt cedar—*Tamarix chinensis* (NZ)
Vitex (chaste tree)—*Vitex agnus-castus* (E)

C. Evergreen Trees

Cedar
  a.Atlas cedar—*Cedrus atlantica* (E)
  b.Cedar of Lebanon—*Cedrus libani* (E)
Arizona cypress—*Cupressus arizonica* (E)
Juniper
  a.Alligator juniper—*Juniperus deppeana* (E)
  b.Eastern red cedar—*Juniperus virginiana* varieties (E)
  c.Rocky Mountain juniper -*Juniperus scopulorum* varieties (N)
Madrone—*Arbutus texana* (N)
Magnolia
  a.Southern magnolia—*Magnolia grandiflora* (E)
  b.Saucer magnolia—*Magnolia soulangiana* (E)
Chinese windmill palm—*Trachycarpus fortunei* (E)
Pine
  a.Afghan pine—*Pinus eldarica* (E)
  b.Austrian pine—*Pinus nigra* (E)
  c.Bristlecone pine—*Pinus aristata* (N)
  d.Japanese black pine—*Pinus thunbergiana* (E)
  e.Piñon pine—*Pinus edulis* (N)
  f.Ponderosa pine—*Pinus ponderosa* (N)
  g.Scotch pine—*Pinus sylvestris* (E)
Blue spruce—*Picea pungens* (N)
Western red cedar—*Thuja plicata* (E)
Yucca
  a.Joshua tree—*Yucca brevifolia* (E)
  b.Palm yucca—*Yucca torreyi* (N)
  c.Soaptree yucca—*Yucca elata* (N)

SHRUBS

A. Deciduous

Glossy abelia—*Abelia grandiflora* (E)
Apache plume—*Fallugia paradoxa* (N)
Bird of paradise—*Caesalpinia gilliesii* (NZ)
Spanish broom—*Spartium junceum* (E)
Common butterfly bush—*Buddleia davidii* (E)
Cotoneaster
  a.Cranberry cotoneaster—*Cotoneaster apiculatus* (E)
  b.Rock cotoneaster—*Cotoneaster horizontalis* (E)
  c.Rockspray cotoneaster—*Cotoneaster microphyllus* (E)
Crape myrtle—*Lagerstroemia indica* (E)
Currant and gooseberry—*Ribes* spp. (N, E)

Red osier dogwood—*Cornus stolonifera* (N)
Edible fig—*Ficus carica* (E)
Shrub or Tatarian honeysuckle—*Lonicera tatarica* (E)
Common lilac—*Syringa vulgaris* (E)
Screwbean mesquite—*Prosopis pubescens* (N)
New Mexico olive—*Forestiera neomexicana* (N)
Rose—*Rosa* spp. (E, N)
Snakeweed—*Gutierrezia sarothrae* (N)
Spirea
    a.Bridal wreath—*Spiraea prunifolia* (E)
    b.Van Houtte—*Spiraea vanhouttei* (E)
    c.Anthony Waterer—*Spiraea bumalda* 'Anthony
      Waterer' (E)
Sumac
    a.Littleleaf sumac—*Rhus microphylla* (N)
    b.Skunkbush—*Rhus trilobata* (N)
    c.Smooth sumac—*Rhus glabra* (N)
    d.Staghorn sumac—*Rhus typhina* (E)
Weigela—*Weigela florida* (E)
Willow
    a.Coyote willow—*Salix exigua* (N)
    b.Pussywillow—*Salix discolor* (N, E)

B. Evergreen

Agave (century plant, mescal)
    a.Century plant—*Agave americana* (N)
    b.Parry agave—*Agave parryi* (N)
    c.Lechugilla—*Agave lechugilla* (N)
Barberry
    a.Colorado barberry—*Berberis fendleri* (N)
    b.Japanese barberry—*Berberis thunbergii* (E), in-
      cluding redleaf barberry, *B. Japonica*
      'Atropurpurea'
    c.Three-spine barberry—*Berberis wisleyensis* (E)
    d.Wintergreen barberry—*Berberis julianae* (E)
Beargrass—*Nolina microcarpa* (N)
Cactus
    a.Claret cup—*Echinocereus triglochidiatus* (N)
    b.Common cholla—*Opuntia imbricata* (N)
    c.Prickly pear—*Opuntia chlorotica* or *O.
      engelmannii* (N)
Holly
    a.English holly—*Ilex aquifolium* (E)
    b.Yaupon holly—*Ilex vomitoria* (E)
India hawthorn—*Rhaphiolepis indica* (E, N)
Chinese junipers
    a.Armstrong juniper—*Juniperus chinensis*
      'Armstrong' (E)
    b.Pfitzer juniper—*Juniperus chinensis*
      'Pfitzerana' (E)
    c.Sea Green juniper—*Juniperus chinensis* 'Sea
      Green' (E)
Common juniper—*Juniperus communis* (N)
Mahonia
    a.Algerita—*Mahonia haematocarpa* (N)
    b.Agritos—*Mahonia trifoliolata* (N)
    c.Oregon grape—*Mahonia aquifolium* (E, NZ)
Mormon tea—*Ephedra* spp. (N)
Nandina (heavenly bamboo)—*Nandina domestica* (E)
Ocotillo—*Fouquieria splendens* (N)
Photinia
    a.Chinese photinia—*Photinia serrulata* (E)
    b.Fraser's photinia—*Photinia fraseri* (E)
Pyracantha (firethorn)—*Pyracantha* spp. (E)
Sage
    a.Big sage (sagebrush)—*Artemisia tridentata* (N)
    b.Sand sage—*Artemisia filifolia* (N)
Fourwing saltbush—*Atriplex canescens* (N)
Seepwillow -*Baccharis sarothroides* (N)
Silverberry—*Elaeagnus pungens* (E)
Sotol—*Dasylirion wheeleri* (N)
Texas ranger—*Leucophyllum frutescens* (N)

Yucca
    a.Softblade yucca—*Yucca recurvifolia* (*Yucca
      pendula*) (E)
    b.Spanish bayonet—*Yucca baccata* (N)
    c.Coral-flower yucca—*Hesperaloe parviflora* (N)

GROUND COVERS

A. Deciduous

Clover—*Trifolium* spp. (NZ, N)
Cranberry cotoneaster—*Cotoneaster apiculatus* (E)
Crown vetch—*Coronilla varia* (E, NZ)
Prairie sage—*Artemisia ludoviciana* (N)
Memorial rose (vine)—*Rosa wichuriana* (E)

B. Evergreen

Ajuga (bugleweed)—*Ajuga reptans* (E)
Bearberry cotoneaster—*Cotoneaster dammeri* (E)
Creeping euonymus—*Euonymus fortunei* (E)
Honeysuckle—*Lonicera japonica* varieties (E)
Horizontalis junipers
    a.Bar Harbor juniper—*Juniperus horizontalis* 'Bar
      Harbor' (E)b.Wilton carpet juniper—*Juniperus
      horizontalis* 'Wiltonii' (E)
Sabina junipers
    a.Broadmoor juniper—*Juniperus sabina*
      'Broadmoor' (E)
    b.Buffalo juniper—*Juniperus sabina* 'Buffalo' (E)
    c.Tam (tammy) juniper—*Juniperus sabina*
      'Tamariscifolia' (E)
San Jose juniper—*Juniperus chinensis* 'San Jose' (E)
Kinnickinnick (mountain bearberry)—*Arctostaphylos
    uva-ursi* (N)
Blue leadwort—*Ceratostigma plumbaginoides* (E)
Lilyturf (liriope)—*Liriope spicata* (E)
Compact nandina—*Nandina domestica* 'Harbor
    dwarf' (E)
Periwinkle—*Vinca major* and *Vinca minor* (E)
Santolina
    a.Green santolina—*Santolina virens* (E)
    b.Gray santolina—*Santolina chamaecyparissus* (E)

GRASSES

A. Traditional Turf Species

Bentgrass—*Agrostis* spp. (E)
Bermuda
    a.African bermuda—*Cynodon transvaalensis*
      (E, NZ)
    b.Common bermuda—*Cynodon dactylon* (E, NZ)
Bluegrass—*Poa pratensis* (E, NZ)
Fescue—*Festuca* spp. (E, N)
Ryegrass—*Lolium* spp. (E)

B. Native Turf And General-Use Species

Buffalo grass—*Buchlöe dactyloides* (N)
Grama
    a.Black grama—*Bouteloua eriopoda* (N)
    b.Blue grama—*Bouteloua gracilis* (N)
Wheatgrass
    a.Western wheatgrass—*Agropyron smithii* (N)
    b.Crested wheatgrass—*Agropyron desertorum* (E,
      NZ)
    c.Pubescent wheatgrass—*Agropyron tricho-
      phorum* (N)

C. Ornamental Species

Alkali sacaton—*Sporobolus airoides* (N)
Sand dropseed—*Sporobolus cryptandrus* (N)
Blue fescue—*Festuca caesia* (E)
Fountain grass—*Pennisetum* spp. (E)
Pampas grass—*Cortaderia selloana* (E)
River cane—*Arundo donax* (NZ)

VINES

A. Deciduous

Boston ivy—*Parthenocissus tricuspidata* (E)
Canyon grape—*Vitis arizonica* (N)
Clematis—*Clematis jackmanni* (E)
Carolina jessamine—*Gelsemium sempervirens* (E)
Virginia creeper (et al)—*Parthenocissus quinque-folia* (N, E)
Wisteria—*Wisteria sinensis* (E)

B. Evergreen

English ivy—*Hedera helix* (E)
Honeysuckle—*Lonicera* spp. (E)

FLOWERS

A. Annuals

Ageratum—*Ageratum houstonianum* (E)
Purple aster—*Aster bigelovii* (N)
Cosmos—*Cosmos* spp. (E)
Gaillardia (blanketflower, firewheel)—*Gaillardia pulchella* (N)
Impatiens—*Impatiens wallerana* (E)
Lisianthus—*Eustoma grandiflorum* (E)
Marigold—*Tagetes* spp. (E)
Salvia—*Salvia* spp. (E)
Snapdragon—*Antirrhinum majus* (E)
Sunflower—*Helianthus annuus* (N)
Viola (Johnny jump-ups)—*Viola* spp. (E)
Wallflower—*Erysimum capitatum* (N)

B. Perennials

Desert baileya—*Baileya multiradiata* (N)
Chrysanthemum—*Chrysanthemum morifolium* (E)
Colorado columbine—*Aquilegia* spp. (N)
Coneflower—*Ratibida columnifera* (N)
Daylily (asphodel)—*Hemerocallis* spp. (E)
Delphinium—*Delphinium belladonna* (E, N)
Dusty miller—*Senecio cineraria* (E)
Fendler's sundrops—*Calylophus hartwegii fendleri* (N)
Blue flax—*Linum perenne* (N)
Globemallow—*Sphaeralcea incana* (scarlet) (N)
Hollyhock—*Alcea rosea* (E, NZ)
Indian paintbrush—*Castilleja integra* (N)
Jimsonweed (datura, sacred datura)—*Datura meteloides* (N)Maximilian's daisy—*Helianthus maximiliani* (NZ)
Paperflower—*Psilostrophe tagetina* (N)
Phlox—*Phlox* spp. (E)
California poppy—*Eschscholzia californica* (and E. mexicana) (E, N)
Shasta daisy—*Chrysanthemum maximum* (E)
Violet—*Viola odorata* (N, E)
Wooly yarrow—*Achillea* spp. (N, E)

C. Bulbs

Canna—*Canna* spp. (E)
Common hyacinth—*Hyacinthus orientalis* (E)
Daffodil—*Narcissus* 'King Alfred' (E)
Dutch crocus—*Crocus verus* (E)
Garden gladiolus—*Gladiolus hortulanus* (E)
Iris—*Iris* spp. (N, E)

RUIDOSO

(founded in 1882), including Alto, Capitan, Mescalero, San Patricio, Lincoln, and Cloudcroft

Stream pond with cattails and ponderosa pines, Ruidoso

Ruidoso resembles Los Alamos in its high-mountain, ponderosa pine–forest setting. The town lies at the edge of Otero and Lincoln counties at an altitude of about 7000 feet (2135 m).

Ruidoso's canyon locale can be quite spectacular. Gambel oak, limber and piñon pine, Rocky Mountain juniper, currant, skunk-bush, snowberry, bigtooth maple, ptelea (hop tree), white fir, Engelmann spruce, and other classic Western alpine species grow in the town or nearby. Rainfall can reach 23 inches (575 mm) annually, and the growing season is very short at about 90 days. Soils can be deep, moist, and fertile, and most have a relatively low pH. Nearby areas produce a great deal of fruit, alfalfa, hay, and other crops. Horse, cattle, and sheep raising are common.

Ruidoso itself has numerous pleasant single family–home and condominium landscapes or gardens. In many of these, a good attempt has been made to integrate man-made features with the local wild landscape. Ponderosa pine groves, for instance, may be frequently underplanted with bluegrass lawns, holly-hocks, common juniper, snowberry, daylilies, redleaf barberries, forsythia, or shrubby

cinquefoil. Aspen, white fir, Engelmann spruce, New Mexico locust, and currant often appear as accents. The spectacular native alligator juniper is quite commonly found as a well-developed specimen. Daffodil, narcissus, crocus, hyacinth, sunflower, santolina, petunia, penstemon, columbine, and delicate straw-berry are favorite flowers.

The typically small gardens and landscapes of Ruidoso are much different from those of Ruidoso Downs, which is lower, drier, sunnier, and more open. The Upper Canyon has many delightful small-scale gardens. One of the finest small-scale landscapes in the Ruidoso area is the grounds of the old Pippin's Ranch House, Store, and Orchard at Ruidoso Downs. Pfitzer junipers, spruces, lawns, and an apple orchard set off this exceptional domestic landscape.

Farther down the Hondo Valley, the agri-cultural landscape becomes one of the most scenic in New Mexico. Alfalfa fields, extensive plantings of a large number of poplar and cottonwood species, and well-tended fruit orchards characterize this extraordinary corner of Lincoln County. The town of Lincoln has an impressive number of historic landscapes, including some of the best-preserved and most extensive of the American Territorial Period (1848–1912) in New Mexico.

Just outside Ruidoso, the Inn of the Mountain Gods has developed an exceptional hotel landscape that makes very good use of the native ponderosa and white fir forest. Its views of Sierra Blanca are unsurpassed.

SELECTED BEST PLANTS FOR RUIDOSO

These plant species grow very well in Ruidoso. For the sake of convenience and quick reference, each plant is listed as native (N), naturalized (NZ), or exotic (E). Other plants also will perform well in landscape and garden situations in the Ruidoso area. Please see the New Mexico Plant File for these species.

TREES

A. Deciduous Shade, Street, and Specialty Trees

Arizona alder—*Alnus oblongifolia* (N)
Paper birch—*Betula papyrifera* (E)
Cottonwood, Aspen, and Poplar: Trees of the Genus *Populus*
  a.Aspen—*Populus tremuloides* (N)
  b.Carolina poplar—*Populus canadensis* (E)
  c.Fremont cottonwood—*Populus fremontii* (N)
  d.Lanceleaf cottonwood—*Populus acuminata* (N)
  e.Lombardy poplar—*Populus nigra* 'Italica' (E)
  f.Narrowleaf cottonwood—*Populus angustifolia* (N)
  g.Rio Grande cottonwood—*Populus fremontii* 'Wislizeni' (N)
  h.White (silver) poplar—*Populus alba* (E, NZ)
Honey locust—*Gleditsia triacanthos inermis* varieties (E)
Locust
  a.Black locust—*Robinia pseudoacacia* (NZ)
  b.Hybrid locusts—*Robinia ambigua* varieties (E)
  c.New Mexico locust—*Robinia neomexicana* (N)
Maple and Box elder
  a.Bigtooth maple—*Acer grandidentatum* (N)
  b.Box elder—*Acer negundo* (N)
  c.Rocky Mountain maple—*Acer glabrum* (N)
  d.Silver maple—*Acer saccharinum* (E)
European mountain ash—*Sorbus aucuparia* (E)
Gambel oak—*Quercus gambelii* (N)
Russian olive—*Elaeagnus angustifolia* (NZ)
Arizona walnut—*Juglans major* (N)
Willow
  a.Globe Navajo willow—*Salix matsudana* 'Navajo' (E)
  b.Peachleaf willow—*Salix amygdaloides* (N)
  c.Weeping willow—*Salix babylonica* (and other weeping willow species) (E)

B. Flowering Ornamental Trees

Flowering cherry—*Prunus serrulata* et al (E)
Flowering crab—*Malus* 'Hopa' et al (E) (also bearing apple, *Malus sylvatica* varieties)
Hawthorn—*Crataegus* spp. (E, N)
Flowering peach—*Prunus persica* (E)
Bradford pear—*Pyrus calleryana* (E)

Eastern redbud—*Cercis canadensis* (E)
Golden rain tree—*Koelreuteria paniculata* (E)
Salt cedar—*Tamarix chinensis* (NZ)

C. Evergreen Trees

Douglas fir—*Pseudotsuga menziesii* (N)
White fir—*Abies concolor* (N)
Juniper
  a.Alligator juniper—*Juniperus deppeana* (N)
  b.Rocky Mountain juniper—*Juniperus scopulorum* varieties (N)
  c.Singleseed (one-seed) juniper—*Juniperus monosperma* (N)
Pine
  a.Bristlecone pine—*Pinus aristata* (N)
  b.Limber pine—*Pinus flexilis* (N)
  c.Piñon pine—*Pinus edulis* (N)
  d.Ponderosa pine—*Pinus ponderosa* (N)
Dawn redwood—*Metasequoia glyptostroboides* (E)
Spruce
  a.Blue spruce—*Picea pungens* (N)
  b.Engelmann spruce—*Picea engelmanni* (N)

SHRUBS

A. Deciduous

Althea (rose of Sharon)—*Hibiscus syriacus* (E)
Common butterfly bush—*Buddleia davidii* (E)
Shrubby cinquefoil—*Potentilla fruticosa* (N)
Cotoneaster
  a.Rock cotoneaster—*Cotoneaster horizontalis* (E)
  b.Rockspray cotoneaster—*Cotoneaster microphyllus* (E)
Currant and gooseberry—*Ribes* spp. (N)
Red osier dogwood—*Cornus stolonifera* (E)
Fernbush—*Chamaebatiaria millefolium* (N)
Forsythia—*Forsythia* spp. (E)
Hop tree—*Ptelea trifoliolata* (N)
Flowering jasmine—*Jasminum nudiflorum* (E)
Common lilac—*Syringa vulgaris* (E)
Mountain mahogany—*Cercocarpus montanus* (N)
New Mexico olive—*Forestiera neomexicana* (N)
Sand plum—*Prunus americana* (N)
Rose—*Rosa* spp. (N, E)
Snowball—*Viburnum opulus* 'Roseum' (E)
Bridal wreath spirea—*Spiraea prunifolia* (E)
Sumac
  a.Skunkbush—*Rhus trilobata* (N)
  b.Smooth sumac—*Rhus glabra* (N)
  c.Staghorn sumac—*Rhus typhina* (E)
Willow
  a.Coyote willow—*Salix exigua* (N)
  b.Pussywillow—*Salix discolor* (N, E)

B. Evergreen

Barberry
  a.Colorado barberry—*Berberis fendleri* (N)
  b.Japanese barberry—*Berberis thunbergii* (E) (including redleaf Japanese barberry, *B. thunbergii*. 'Atropurpurea'
  c.Wintergreen barberry—*Berberis julianae* (E)
Chinese junipers
  a.Armstrong juniper—*Juniperus chinensis* 'Armstrong' (E)
  b.Pfitzer juniper—*Juniperus chinensis* 'Pfitzerana' (E)
Common juniper—*Juniperus communis* (N)
Mahonia
  a.Algerita—*Mahonia haematocarpa* (N)
  b.Agritos—*Mahonia trifoliolata* (N)
  c.Oregon grape—*Mahonia aquifolium* (E, NZ)

Nandina (heavenly bamboo)—*Nandina domestica* (E)
Mugo pine—*Pinus mugo* (E)
Pyracantha (firethorn)—*Pyracantha* spp. (E)
Rubber rabbitbrush—*Chrysothamnus nauseosus* (E)
Big sage (sagebrush)—*Artemisia tridentata* (N)
Alberta spruce—*Picea glauca* 'Conica' (*Picea albertiana*) (E)
Yucca
    a.Spanish bayonet—*Yucca baccata* (N)
    b.Coral-flower yucca—*Hesperaloe parviflora* (E)

GROUND COVERS

A. Deciduous

Spring cinquefoil—*Potentilla tabernaemontani* (E)
Clover—*Trifolium* spp. (NZ, N)
Cranberry cotoneaster—*Cotoneaster apiculatus* (E)
Mint—*Mentha* spp. (E, N, NZ)
Prairie sage—*Artemisia ludoviciana* (N)
Snow-in summer—*Cerastium tomentosum* (E)

B. Evergreen

Ajuga (bugleweed)—*Ajuga reptans* (E)
Creeping euonymus—*Euonymus fortunei* (E)
Germander—*Teucrium chamaedrys* 'Prostratum' (E)
Honeysuckle—*Lonicera japonica* varieties (E)
Horizontalis junipers
    a.Andorra juniper—*Juniperus horizontalis plumosa* (E)
    b.Bar Harbor juniper -*Juniperus horizontalis* 'Bar Harbor' (E)
    c.Wilton carpet juniper—*Juniperus horizontalis* 'Wiltonii' (E)
Sabina junipers
    a.Broadmoor juniper—*Juniperus sabina* 'Broadmoor' (E)
    b.Buffalo juniper—*Juniperus sabina* 'Buffalo' (E)
    c.Tam (tammy) juniper—Juniperus sabina 'Tamariscifolia' (E)
San Jose juniper—*Juniperus chinensis* 'San Jose' (E)
Kinnikinnick (mountain bearberry)—*Arctostaphylos uva-ursi* (N)
Blue leadwort—*Ceratostigma plumbaginoides* (E)
Lilyturf (liriope)—*Liriope spicata* (E)
Creeping mahonia—*Mahonia repens* (N)
Periwinkle—*Vinca major* and *Vinca minor* (E)
Gray santolina—*Santolina chamaecyparissus* (E)
Sedum (stonecrop)—*Sedum* spp. (N, E)
Strawberry—*Fragaria* spp. (N, E)

GRASSES

A. Traditional Turf Species

Bentgrass—*Agrostis* spp. (E)
Bluegrass—*Poa pratensis* (E, NZ)
Fescue—*Festuca* spp. (E, N)
Ryegrass—*Lolium* spp. (E)

B. Native Turf and General-Use Species

Buffalo grass—*Buchloe dactyloides* (N)
Galleta—*Hilaria jamesii* (N)
Grama
    a.Blue grama—*Bouteloua gracilis* (N)
    b.Sideoats grama—*Bouteloua curtipendula* (N)
Wheatgrass
    a.Western wheatgrass—*Agropyron smithii* (N)
    b.Crested wheatgrass—*Agropyron desertorum* (E, NZ)

C. Ornamental Species

Blue fescue—*Festuca caesia* (E)
Fountain grass—*Pennisetum* spp. (E)
Pampas grass—*Cortaderia selloana* (E)
Indian ricegrass—*Oryzopsis hymenoides* (N)
Purple threeawn—*Aristida longiseta* (N)

VINES

A. Deciduous

Canyon grape—*Vitis arizonica* (N)
Clematis—*Clematis jackmanni* (E)
Morning glory—*Ipomoea tricolor* (E)
Trumpet vine—*Campsis radicans* (E)
Virginia creeper (et al)—*Parthenocissus quinquefolia* (N, E)
Wisteria—*Wisteria sinensis* (E)

B. Evergreen

English ivy—*Hedera helix* (E)
Honeysuckle—*Lonicera* spp. (E)

FLOWERS

A. Annuals

Ageratum—*Ageratum houstonianum* (E)
Purple aster—*Aster bigelovii* (N)
Coleus—*Coleus x hybridus* (E)
Gaillardia (blanketflower, firewheel)—*Gaillardia pulchella* (N)
Geranium—*Pelargonium hortorum* (E)
Impatiens—*Impatiens wallerana* (E)
Lisianthus—*Eustoma grandiflorum* (E)
Marigold—*Tagetes* spp. (E)
Petunia—*Petunia* spp. (E)
Salvia—*Salvia* spp. (E)
Sunflower—*Helianthus annuus* (N)
Viola (Johnny jump-ups)—*Viola* spp. (E)
Wallflower—*Erysimum capitatum* (N)

B. Perennials

Carnation—*Dianthus caryophyllus* (E)
Chrysanthemum—*Chrysanthemum morifolium* (E)
Colorado columbine—*Aquilegia* spp. (N)
Coneflower—*Ratibida columnifera* (N)
Daylily (asphodel)—*Hemerocallis* spp. (E)
Delphinium—*Delphinium belladonna* (E, N)
Fendler's sundrops—*Calylophus hartwegii fendleri* (N)
Blue flax—*Linum perenne* (N)
Geranium (cranesbill)—*Geranium* spp. (N)
Globemallow—*Sphaeralcea incana* (scarlet) (N)
Hollyhock—*Alcea rosea* (E, NZ)
Indian paintbrush—*Castilleja integra* (N)
Lobelia—*Lobelia erinus* (E)
Maximilian's daisy—*Helianthus maximiliani* (NZ)
Penstemon—*Penstemon* spp. (N)
Phlox—*Phlox* spp. (E)
California poppy—*Eschscholzia californica* (and *E. mexicana*) (E, N)
Red rocket (scarlet gilia)—*Ipomopsis aggregata* (N)
Shasta daisy—*Chrysanthemum maximum* (E)
Violet—*Viola odorata* (N, E)
Wooly yarrow—*Achillea* spp. (N, E)

C. Bulbs

Common hyacinth—*Hyacinthus orientalis* (E)
Daffodil—*Narcissus* 'King Alfred' (E)
Dutch crocus—*Crocus verus* (E)
Garden gladiolus—*Gladiolus hortulanus* (E)
Iris—*Iris* spp. (N, E)
Tulip—*Tulipa* spp. (E)

Canyon Road
garden, Santa Fe

SANTA FE

(founded in 1610),
including Española,
Santa Cruz,
Chimayó, and
Pecos

Santa Fe is about as old as an American town can be. It has the greatest concentration of historically important landscapes and gardens in New Mexico. Many of these are still quite stunning and well kept, and they are planted in species that have proven to be hardy and long-lived in this highest (7000 feet/2135 m) of American state capitals.

The soil here is often stony and full of clay, but farming and gardening persistence over the centuries has improved general planting conditions. Fruit and vegetable gardens as well as small farms often produce surprisingly good crops, and ornamentals grow well here. Annual rainfall ranges from almost 14 inches (350 mm) to almost 18 inches (450 mm). The growing season is 158 days.

The city is set, of course, in a piñon-juniper forest that expanding suburbs steadily nibble. The hilly terrain also supports box elders, narrowleaf cottonwoods, willows, and many other species in ravines and gullies. Rubber rabbitbrush (chamisa), fourwing saltbush, Apache plume, snakeweed, and narrowleaf yucca are common shrubs. Buffalo grass, blue grama, wheatgrass, sideoats grama, galleta, and many other native grass species grow in or near the city. White and Douglas fir, aspen, ponderosa and limber pine, Engelmann spruce, elderberry, maples, and Gambel oak are widely distributed in the higher elevations of the Rockies just outside Santa Fe. Red osier dogwood, chokecherry, sand plum, and mountain alder grow along high country streams.

Santa Fe County is noted for its apples. Cattle and calves are widely kept, as well as some milk cows, and sheep and poultry are commonly raised. The county produces a good quantity of hay and some wheat, corn, barley, chile, and vegetables. Much agricultural land in the county is irrigated. Arable soils throughout Santa Fe County vary greatly in quality and availability.

Santa Fe has an excellent concentration of "vignette" or small courtyard landscapes. Many of these are located within a half-mile or so of the Plaza. Terrace gardens are also popular in the city, and these attractive landscape features are often laid out with excellent views of distant mountain ranges or nearby winding streets and their houses. Traditionally, small *acequias,* or communal ditches, have been used to irrigate the Santa Fe landscape. Modest amounts of water in trickling brooks or tiny pools are frequently found in Santa Fe gardens. This custom was started by Bishop Jean Lamy, who built an elaborate water garden at his house near St. Francis Cathedral in early American Territorial days.

Santa Fe fairly explodes with lilacs in spring. Their color and scent often peak just after a cool April shower. Currants, crabtrees, daffodils and other bulbs, forsythia, spirea, and sand plum often bloom at nearly the same time. Apples, peaches, and pears add to the bright garden scene.

Ponderosa, limber, Austrian, Scotch, and even foxtail or bristlecone pines are popular in city landscapes. But white fir and Douglas fir reach truly impressive proportions in Santa Fe —sometimes 60 feet (18 m) or taller. Redwoods grow well in Santa Fe. There are striking specimens in Cornell Park, on the grounds of the state capitol, and at many private residences. Russian olive, honey locust, horse-chestnut, several ash species, aspen, black locust, and the ever-present Siberian elm are common in the city. An exemplary planting of American elms graces the perimeter of the Federal Oval (the U.S. Courthouse Square), one of the finest landscapes of the late Territorial period.

Santa Fe is the center of a native landscape plants industry that continues to grow in popularity and usefulness. Blue grama and buffalo grass are widely planted for low-water lawns; these grasses have a strikingly beautiful, hazy blue-green texture and may be left unmown for long periods. Fernbush, rubber rabbitbrush, beargrass, Apache plume, serviceberry, indigobush, prairie sage, skunkbush, winterfat, cliff fendlerbush, and Mormon tea are among the local shrub species that recently have become quite popular. Such formerly hard-to-find Southwestern trees as New Mexico olive, New Mexico locust, ptelea (hop tree), alligator juniper, singleseed juniper, bigtooth maple, aspen, Gambel oak, and peachleaf willow have begun to appear in commercial landscapes as well as home gardens. Many species of local wildflowers have come into favor as landscape ornamentals; these include, among others, western virginsbower (a strongly vining clematis), Woods rose, Rocky Mountain penstemon, sand penstemon, gilia, columbine, butterflyweed, beebalm, desert baileya, sego lily, coreopsis, coneflowers, gaillardia, delphinium, many sunflower species, lupine, evening primroses, and verbenas. The extraordinary sacred datura (more an event than a flower) and the amazing *Calylophus* (Fendler's sundrops) recently have become widely available.

As is true elsewhere in New Mexico, natives are inconsistent in their availability and quality in Santa Fe. However, their increasing popularity and general ease of care, as well as the dedication of nursery growers in Santa Fe and elsewhere in New Mexico, have finally made it possible to use these wonderful plants in general landscaping with confidence and ease.

Many home landscapes along East Palace Avenue and Canyon Road are exceptionally beautiful in the spring and can be glimpsed from the street while strolling. Sena Plaza and Cathedral Park are good examples of Mexican and U.S. Territorial period landscapes, respectively. The Alameda or River Park and the grounds of the Supreme Court Building are

at their peak in late spring. And the plaza itself, with its eclectic complement of aging cottonwoods, firs, honey locusts, and other trees, still functions as the great central landscape space—the *spirit*, if you will—of New Mexico.

SELECTED BEST PLANTS FOR SANTA FE

These plant species grow very well in Santa Fe. For the sake of convenience and quick reference, each plant is listed as native (N), naturalized (NZ), or exotic (E). Other plants also will perform well in landscape and garden situations in and around Santa Fe. Please see the New Mexico Plant File for these species.

TREES

A. Deciduous Shade, Street, and Specialty Trees

Ash
    a. Green ash—*Fraxinus pennsylvanica* and
        varieties (E)
    b. White ash—*Fraxinus americana* and varieties (E)
Paper birch—*Betula papyrifera* (E)
Western catalpa—*Catalpa speciosa* (E)
Western chokecherry—*Prunus virginiana* (N)
Cottonwood, Aspen, and Poplar: Trees of the Genus
    Populus
    a. Aspen—*Populus tremuloides* (N)
    b. Bolleana poplar—*Populus alba* 'Pyramidalis' (E)
    c. Carolina poplar—*Populus canadensis* (E)
    d. Fremont cottonwood—*Populus fremontii* (N)
    e. Lanceleaf cottonwood—*Populus acuminata* (N)
    f. Lombardy poplar—*Populus nigra* 'Italica (E)
    g. Narrowleaf cottonwood—*Populus angusti-*
        folia (N)
    h. Rio Grande cottonwood—*Populus fremontii*
        'Wislizeni' (N)
    i. White (silver) poplar—*Populus alba* (NZ)
American elm—*Ulmus americana* (E)
Honey locust—*Gleditsia triacanthos inermis* varieties
    a. 'Moraine' (E)
    b. 'Shademaster' (E)
    c. 'Sunburst' (E)
Common horsechestnut—*Aesculus hippocastanum* (E)
Littleleaf linden—*Tilia cordata* (E)
Locust
    a. Black locust—*Robinia pseudoacacia* (NZ)
    b. Hybrid locusts—*Robinia ambigua* varieties (E)
    c. New Mexico locust—*Robinia neomexicana* (N)
Maple and Box elder
    a. Bigtooth maple—*Acer grandidentatum* (N)
    b. Box elder—*Acer negundo* (N)
    c. Japanese maple—*Acer palmatum* (E)
    d. Rocky Mountain maple—*Acer glabrum* (E)
European mountain ash—*Sorbus aucuparia* (E)
Gambel oak—*Quercus gambelii* (N)
Russian olive—*Elaeagnus angustifolia* (NZ)
Sycamore (plane tree)
    a. American sycamore—*Platanus occidentalis* (E)
    b. London plane tree—*Platanus acerifolia* (E)
English (Carpathian) walnut—*Juglans regia* (E)

Willow
- a. Corkscrew willow—*Salix matsudana* 'Tortuosa' (E)
- b. Globe Navajo willow—*Salix matsudana* 'Navajo' (E)
- c. Peachleaf willow—*Salix amygdaloides* (N)
- d. Weeping willow—*Salix babylonica* (and other weeping willow species) (E)

B. Flowering Ornamental Trees

Flowering apricot—*Prunus armeniaca* (E)
Flowering crab—*Malus* 'Hopa' et al (E)
Hawthorn—*Crataegus* spp. (E, N)
Flowering peach—*Prunus persica* (E)
Bradford pear—*Pyrus calleryana* (E)
Eastern redbud—*Cercis canadensis* (E)
Salt cedar—*Tamarix chinensis* (NZ)

C. Evergreen Trees

Arizona cypress—*Cupressus arizonica* (N)
Douglas fir—*Pseudotsuga menziesii* (N)
White fir—*Abies concolor* (N)
Juniper
- a. Eastern red cedar—*Juniperus virginiana* varieties (E)
- b. Rocky Mountain juniper—*Juniperus scopulorum* varieties (N)
- c. Singleseed (one-seed) juniper—*Juniperus monosperma* (N)

Pine
- a. Austrian pine—*Pinus nigra* (E)
- b. Bristlecone pine—*Pinus aristata* (N)
- c. Japanese black pine—*Pinus thunbergiana* (E)
- d. Limber pine—*Pinus flexilis* (N)
- e. Pinon pine—*Pinus edulis* (N)
- f. Ponderosa pine—*Pinus ponderosa* (N)
- g. Scotch pine—*Pinus sylvestris* (E)

Giant redwood (sequoia)—*Sequoiadendron giganteum* (E)
Palm yucca—*Yucca torreyi* (N)

SHRUBS

A. Deciduous

Flowering almond—*Prunus glandulosa* (E)
Apache plume—*Fallugia paradoxa* (N)
Common butterfly bush—*Buddleia davidii* (E)
Shrubby cinquefoil—*Potentilla fruticosa* (N)
Cotoneaster
- a. Cranberry cotoneaster—*Cotoneaster apiculatus* E)
- b. Rock cotoneaster—*Cotoneaster horizontalis* (E)

Currant and gooseberry—*Ribes* spp. (E)
Red osier dogwood—*Cornus stolonifera* (N)
Fernbush—*Chamaebatiaria millefolium* (N)
Forsythia—*Forsythia* spp. (E)
Shrub or tatarian honeysuckle—*Lonicera tatarica* (E)
Hop tree—*Ptelea trifoliolata* (N)
Common lilac—*Syringa vulgaris* (E)
Mountain mahogany—*Cercocarpus montanus* (N)
New Mexico olive—*Forestiera neomexicana* (N)
Sand plum—*Prunus americana* (N)
Raspberry—*Rubus* spp. (E, N)
Rose—*Rosa* spp. (E)
Snowball—*Viburnum opulus* 'Roseum' (E)
Spirea
- a. Bridal wreath—*Spiraea prunifolia* (E)
- b. Anthony Waterer—*Spiraea bumalda* 'Anthony Waterer' (E)

Sumac
- a. Skunkbush—*Rhus trilobata* (N)
- b. Smooth sumac—*Rhus glabra* (N)

Willow
- a. Coyote willow—*Salix exigua* (N)
- b. Pussywillow—*Salix discolor* (N, E)

Winterfat—*Ceratoides lanata* (N)

B. Evergreen

Parry agave—*Agave parryi* (N)
Barberry
- a. Colorado barberry—*Berberis fendleri* (N)
- b. Japanese barberry—*Berberis thunbergii* (E), including redleaf Japanese barberry, *B. japon.* 'Atropurpurea'
- c. Three-spine barberry—*Berberis wisleyensis* (E)

Beargrass—*Nolina microcarpa* (N)
Parney cotoneaster—*Cotoneaster lacteus* (E)
Cactus
- a. Common cholla—*Opuntia imbricata* (N)
- b. Prickly pear—*Opuntia chlorotica* or *O. engelmannii* (N)

Holly
- a. Burford holly—*Ilex cornuta* 'Burfordii' (E)
- b. English holly—*Ilex aquifolium* (E)

Chinese junipers
- a. Armstrong juniper—*Juniperus chinensis* 'Armstrong' (E)
- b. Pfitzer juniper—*Juniperus chinensis* 'Pfitzerana' (E)
- c. Sea Green juniper—*Juniperus chinensis* 'Sea Green' (E)

Common juniper—*Juniperus communis* (N)
Mahonia
- a. Algerita—*Mahonia haematocarpa* (N)
- b. Agritos—*Mahonia trifoliolata* (N)
- c. Oregon grape—*Mahonia aquifolium* (E)

Mormon tea—*Ephedra* spp. (N)
Nandina (heavenly bamboo)—*Nandina domestica* (E)
Photinia
- a. Chinese photinia—*Photinia serrulata* (E)
- b. Fraser's photinia—*Photinia fraseri* (E)

Mugo pine—*Pinus mugo* (E)
Rubber rabbitbrush—*Chrysothamnus nauseosus* (N)
Big sage (sagebrush)—*Artemisia tridentata* (N)
Fourwing saltbush—*Atriplex canescens* (N)
Alberta spruce—*Picea glauca* 'Conica' (*Picea albertiana*) (E)
Yucca
- a. Narrowleaf yucca—*Yucca glauca* (N)
- b. Softblade yucca—*Yucca recurvifolia* (*Yucca pendula*) (E)
- c. Spanish bayonet—*Yucca baccata* (N)
- d. Coral-flower yucca—*Hesperaloe parviflora* (E)

GROUND COVERS

A. Deciduous

Spring cinquefoil—*Potentilla tabernaemontani* (E)
Clover—*Trifolium* spp. (NZ, N)
Cranberry cotoneaster—*Cotoneaster apiculatus* (E)
Mint—*Mentha* spp. (E, N, NZ)
Prairie sage—*Artemisia ludoviciana* (N)
Snow-in summer—*Cerastium tomentosum* (E)

B. Evergreen

Bearberry cotoneaster—*Cotoneaster dammeri* (E)
Creeping euonymus—*Euonymus fortunei* (E)
Honeysuckle—*Lonicera japonica* varieties (E)

Horizontalis junipers
  a. Andorra juniper—*Juniperus horizontalis plumosa* (E)
  b. Bar Harbor juniper—*Juniperus horizontalis* 'Bar Harbor (E)
  c. Wilton carpet juniper—*Juniperus horizontalis* 'Wiltonii' (E)
Sabina junipers
  a. Broadmoor juniper—*Juniperus sabina* 'Broadmoor' (E)
  b. Buffalo juniper—*Juniperus sabina* 'Buffalo' (E)
  c. Tam (tammy) juniper—Juniperus sabina 'Tamariscifolia' (E)
Kinnickinnick (mountain bearberry)—*Arctostaphylos uva-ursi* (N)
Creeping mahonia—*Mahonia repens* (N)
Compact nandina—*Nandina domestica* 'Harbor dwarf' (E)
Periwinkle—*Vinca major* and *Vinca minor* (E)
Pussytoes—*Antennaria parviflora* (N)
Gray santolina—*Santolina chamaecyparissus* (E)
Sedum (stonecrop)—*Sedum* spp. (N, E)
Strawberry—*Fragaria* spp. (N, E)

GRASSES

A. Traditional Turf Species

Bentgrass—*Agrostis* spp. (E)
Bluegrass—*Poa pratensis* (E, NZ)
Fescue—*Festuca* spp. (E, N)
Ryegrass—*Lolium* spp. (E)

B. Native Turf and General-Use Species

Buffalo grass—*Buchloe dactyloides* (N)
Galleta—*Hilaria jamesii* (N)
Grama
  a. Black grama—*Bouteloua eriopoda* (N)
  b. Blue grama—*Bouteloua gracilis* (N)
  c. Sideoats grama—*Bouteloua curtipendula* (N)
Wheatgrass
  a. Western wheatgrass—*Agropyron smithii* (N)
  b. Crested wheatgrass—*Agropyron desertorum* (E, NZ)
  c. Pubescent wheatgrass—*Agropyron trichophorum* (N)

C. Ornamental Species

Sand dropseed—*Sporobolus cryptandrus* (N)
Blue fescue—*Festuca caesia* (E)
Fountain grass—*Pennisetum* spp. (E)
Indian ricegrass—*Oryzopsis hymenoides* (N)
Purple threeawn—*Aristida longiseta* (N)

VINES

A. Deciduous

Boston ivy—*Parthenocissus tricuspidata* (E)
Canyon grape—*Vitis arizonica* (N)
Clematis—*Clematis jackmanni* (E)
Morning glory—*Ipomoea tricolor* (E)
Silver lace vine—*Polygonum aubertii* (E)
Trumpet vine—*Campsis radicans* (E)
Virginia creeper (et al)—*Parthenocissus quinquefolia* (N, E)
Wisteria—*Wisteria sinensis* (E)

B. Evergreen

English ivy—*Hedera helix* (E)
Honeysuckle—*Lonicera* spp. (E)

FLOWERS

A. Annuals

Ageratum—*Ageratum houstonianum* (E)
Purple aster—*Aster bigelovii* (N)
Cosmos—*Cosmos* spp. (E)
Four o'clock—*Mirabilis jalapa* (E)
Gaillardia (blanketflower, firewheel)—*Gaillardia pulchella* (N)
Geranium—*Pelargonium hortorum* (E)
Impatiens—*Impatiens wallerana* (E)
Lisianthus—*Eustoma grandiflorum* (E)
Marigold—*Tagetes* spp. (E)
Petunia—*Petunia* spp. (E)
Salvia—*Salvia* spp. (E)
Snapdragon—*Antirrhinum majus* (E)
Sunflower—*Helianthus annuus* (N)
Annual vinca (Madagascar periwinkle)—*Catharanthus roseus* (E)
Viola (Johnny jump-ups)—*Viola* spp. (E)
Wallflower—*Erysimum capitatum* (N)

B. Perennials

Desert baileya—*Baileya multiradiata* (N)
Chrysanthemum—*Chrysanthemum morifolium* (E)
Colorado columbine—*Aquilegia* spp. (N)
Coneflower—*Ratibida columnifera* (N)
Daylily (asphodel)—*Hemerocallis* spp. (E)
Delphinium—*Delphinium belladonna* (E, N)
Dusty miller—*Senecio cineraria* (E)
Fendler's sundrops—*Calylophus hartwegii fendleri* (N)
Blue flax—*Linum perenne* (N, E)
Geranium (cranesbill)—*Geranium* spp. (E)
Hollyhock—*Alcea rosea* (E, NZ)
Indian paintbrush—*Castilleja integra* (N)
Jimsonweed (datura, sacred datura)—*Datura meteloides* (N)
Lobelia—*Lobelia erinus* (E)
Maximilian's daisy—*Helianthus maximiliani* (NZ)
Paperflower—*Psilostrophe tagetina* (N)
Penstemon—*Penstemon* spp. (N)
Phlox—*Phlox* spp. (E)
Red rocket (scarlet gilia)—*Ipomopsis aggregata* (N)
Shasta daisy—*Chrysanthemum maximum* (E)
Violet—*Viola odorata* (E, N)
Wooly yarrow—*Achillea* spp. (N, E)

C. Bulbs

Common hyacinth—*Hyacinthus orientalis* (E)
Daffodil—*Narcissus* 'King Alfred' (E)
Dutch crocus—*Crocus verus* (E)
Garden gladiolus—*Gladiolus hortulanus* (E)
Iris—*Iris* spp. (N, E)
Tulip—*Tulipa* spp. (E)

Park Lake (above)
Blue Hole (right)

SANTA ROSA

(settled about 1865), including Puerto de Luna

Santa Rosa is very much an oasis in a warm, low pocket on the plains of eastern New Mexico. Its abundance of water from different sources (springs, creeks, the Pecos River) has given it an unusually rich landscape history. Within the city limits, Park Lake and Blue Hole are historic landscapes largely created by the Federal Works Projects Administration as part of the New Deal parks and recreation construction of the 1930s.

At an altitude of roughly 4600 feet (1400 m), Santa Rosa features such "warm zone" native plants as mesquites and desert willows because of its locale on the Pecos River. Its growing season averages approximately 183 days, and Santa Rosa receives between 13 and 18.5 inches (about 325–470 mm) of moisture annually. Soils are generally alkaline. The surrounding plains are often broken by low hills, mesas, and small ravines. The typical wild hillside landscape near the town is piñon-juniper in sparse woodlands, with grasslands stretching across the nearby plains. In the Pecos and its tributary valleys, cottonwoods, soapberries, willows, Russian olives, and salt cedars are abundant. The ubiquitous Siberian elm also is found frequently in both wild and domestic landscapes.

Guadalupe County raises some wheat, hay, and chile, but the main agricultural product is livestock, including cattle, sheep, and poultry. Although the county is quite sparsely populated, the effects of droughts and intense, long-term grazing are sometimes noticeable on ranges that are now overgrown with snakeweed, yucca, and various cactus species.

Santa Rosa has many good examples of ailanthus (the tree of heaven) used well as a street tree. Siberian elm is also used for this purpose, as are several other popular hardwoods, such as ashes, crabs, and honey locusts. The town has a surprising number of small, well-kept gardens. The recently completed landscape at Santa Rosa Mid-School is a successful combination of select pavements and very attractive basic plantings.

The incandescent turquoise pool at Blue Hole, which sits below a limestone ridge still covered in native trees and shrubs, is probably Santa Rosa's most unforgettable landscape feature.

SELECTED BEST PLANTS FOR SANTA ROSA

These plant species grow very well in Santa Rosa. For the sake of convenience and quick reference, each plant is listed as native (N), naturalized (NZ), or exotic (E). Other plants also will perform well in landscape and garden situations in and around Santa Rosa. Please see the New Mexico Plant File for these species.

TREES

A. Deciduous Shade, Street, and Specialty Trees

Ash
  a. Modesto ash—*Fraxinus velutina* 'Modesto' (Arizona ash variety) (N)
  b. Green ash—*Fraxinus pennsylvanica* and varieties (E)
  c. Raywood ash—*Fraxinus oxycarpa* 'Raywood' (E)
Catalpa
  a. Umbrella catalpa—*Catalpa bignonioides* 'Nana' (E)
  b. Western catalpa—*Catalpa speciosa* (E)
Chinaberry—*Melia azedarach* (E)
Western chokecherry—*Prunus virginiana* (N)
Cottonwood, Aspen, and Poplar: Trees of the Genus *Populus*
  a. Carolina poplar—*Populus canadensis* (E)
  b. Fremont cottonwood—*Populus fremontii* (N)
  c. Lanceleaf cottonwood—*Populus acuminata* (N)
  d. Lombardy poplar—*Populus nigra* 'Italica' (E)
  e. Plains cottonwood—*Populus sargenti* (N)
  f. Rio Grande cottonwood—*Populus fremontii* 'Wislizeni' (N)
  g. White (silver) poplar—*Populus alba* (E, NZ)
Elm
  a. American elm—*Ulmus americana* (E)
  b. Chinese elm—*Ulmus parvifolia* (E)
Hackberry
  a. Common hackberry—*Celtis occidentalis* (E)
  b. Netleaf hackberry—*Celtis reticulata* (N)
Honey locust—*Gleditsia triacanthos inermis* varieties
  a. 'Moraine' (E)
  b. 'Shademaster' (E)
  c. 'Sunburst' (E)
Locust
  a. Black locust—*Robinia pseudoacacia* (E)
  b. New Mexico locust—*Robinia neomexicana* (N)
Maple and Box elder
  a. Box elder—*Acer negundo* (N)
  b. Sycamore-leaf maple—*Acer pseudoplatanus* (E)
Mesquite—*Prosopis glandulosa* (N)
Mulberry
  a. Fruitless mulberry—*Morus alba* (E)
  b. Weeping mulberry—*Morus alba* 'Pendula' (E)
  c. Paper mulberry—*Broussonetia papyrifera* (E)
Oak
  a. Gambel oak—*Quercus gambelii* (N)
  b. Southern live oak—*Quercus virginiana* (E)
  c. Texas oak—*Quercus texana* (E)
Osage orange—*Maclura pomifera* (E)
Pecan—*Carya illinoiensis* (E)
Pistache–Pistachio
  a. Chinese pistache—*Pistacia chinensis* (E)
  b. Pistachio—*Pistacia vera* (E)

Russian olive—*Elaeagnus angustifolia* (NZ)
Silk tree—*Albizia jilibrissin* (E)
Western soapberry—*Sapindus drummondii* (N)
Sycamore (plane tree)
  a. Arizona sycamore—*Platanus wrightii* (N)
  b. London plane tree—*Platanus acerifolia* (E)
  c. Oriental plane tree—*Platanus orientalis* (E)
Tree of heaven—*Ailanthus altissima* (NZ, useful under extremely harsh planting conditions)
Arizona walnut—*Juglans major* (N)
Willow
  a. Globe Navajo willow—*Salix matsudana* 'Navajo' (E)
  b. Peachleaf willow—*Salix amygdaloides* (N)
  c. Weeping willow—*Salix babylonica* (other spp. also, E)

B. Flowering Ornamental Trees

Flowering apricot—*Prunus armeniaca* (E)
Flowering crab—*Malus* 'Hopa' et al (E)
Mexican elder—*Sambucus caerulea neomexicana* (N)
Desert willow—*Chilopsis linearis* (N)
Hawthorn—*Crataegus* spp. (E, N)
Flowering peach—*Prunus persica* (E)
Bradford pear—*Pyrus calleryana* (E)
Purpleleaf plum—*Prunus cerasifera* (E)
Golden rain tree—*Koelreuteria paniculata* (E)
Salt cedar—*Tamarix chinensis* (NZ)
Smoke tree—*Cotinus coggygria* (E)
Vitex (chaste tree)—*Vitex agnus-castus* (E)

C. Evergreen Trees

Arizona cypress—*Cupressus arizonica* (N)
Juniper
  a. Alligator juniper—*Juniperus deppeana* (N)
  b. Chinese juniper—*Juniperus chinensis* varieties (E)
  c. Eastern red cedar—*Juniperus virginiana* varieties (E)
  d. Rocky Mountain juniper—*Juniperus scopulorum* varieties (N)
  e. Singleseed (one-seed) juniper—*Juniperus monosperma* (N)
Leyland false cypress—*Cupressocyparis leylandii* (E)
Pine
  a. Afghan pine—*Pinus eldarica* (E)
  b. Austrian pine—*Pinus nigra* (E)
  c. Japanese black pine—*Pinus thunbergiana* (E)
  d. Piñon pine—*Pinus edulis* (N)
  e. Ponderosa pine—*Pinus ponderosa* (N)
Dawn redwood—*Metasequoia glyptostroboides* (E)
Spruce
  a. Blue spruce—*Picea pungens* (N)
  b. Engelmann spruce—*Picea engelmanni* (N)
  c. Black Hills spruce—*Picea glauca densata* (E)
Western red cedar—*Thuja plicata* (E)
Yucca
  a. Joshua tree—*Yucca brevifolia* (E)
  b. Palm yucca—*Yucca torreyi* (N)
  c. Soaptree yucca—*Yucca elata* (N)

SHRUBS

A. Deciduous

Althea (rose of Sharon)—*Hibiscus syriacus* (E)
Apache plume—*Fallugia paradoxa* (N)
Bird of paradise—*Caesalpinia gilliesii* (NZ)
Spanish broom—*Spartium junceum* (E)
Common butterfly bush—*Buddleia davidii* (E)
Shrubby cinquefoil—*Potentilla fruticosa* (N)

Cotoneaster
    a.Cranberry cotoneaster—*Cotoneaster apiculatus* (E)
    b.Rock cotoneaster—*Cotoneaster horizontalis* (E)
Crape myrtle—*Lagerstroemia indica* (E)
Currant and gooseberry—*Ribes* spp. (N, E)
Red osier dogwood—*Cornus stolonifera* (N)
Edible fig—*Ficus carica* (E)
Forsythia—*Forsythia* spp. (E)
Common lilac—*Syringa vulgaris* (E)
Mountain mahogany—*Cercocarpus montanus* (N)
New Mexico olive—*Forestiera neomexicana* (N)
Sand plum—*Prunus americana* (N)
Pomegranate—*Punica granatum* (E)
Raspberry—*Rubus* spp. (E, N)
Rose—*Rosa* spp. (N, E)
Bridal wreath—*Spiraea prunifolia* (E)
Sumac
    a.Skunkbush—*Rhus trilobata* (N)
    b.Staghorn sumac—*Rhus typhina* (E)
Coyote willow—*Salix exigua* (N)
Winterfat—*Ceratoides lanata* (N)

B. Evergreen

Agave (century plant, mescal)
    a.Century plant—*Agave americana* (N)
    b.Parry agave—*Agave parryi* (N)
    c.Lechugilla—*Agave lechugilla* (N)
Barberry
    a.Colorado barberry—*Berberis fendleri* (N)
    b.Japanese barberry—*Berberis thunbergii* (E)
Beargrass—*Nolina microcarpa* (N)
Cactus
    a.Claret cup—*Echinocereus triglochidiatus* (N)
    b.Common cholla—*Opuntia imbricata* (N)
    c.Prickly pear—*Opuntia chlorotica* or *O. engelmannii* (N)
Yaupon holly—*Ilex vomitoria* (E)
Chinese junipers
    a.Pfitzer juniper—*Juniperus chinensis* 'Pfitzerana' (E)
    b.Sea Green juniper—*Juniperus chinensis* 'Sea Green' (E)
Common juniper—*Juniperus communis* (N)
Mahonia
    a.Algerita—*Mahonia haematocarpa* (N)
    b.Agritos—*Mahonia trifoliolata* (N)
Mormon tea—*Ephedra* spp. (N)
Nandina (heavenly bamboo)—*Nandina domestica* (E)
Photinia
    a.Chinese photinia—*Photinia serrulata* (E)
    b.Fraser's photinia—*Photinia fraseri* (E)
Mugo pine—*Pinus mugo* (E)
Pyracantha (firethorn)—*Pyracantha* spp. (E)
Rubber rabbitbrush—*Chrysothamnus nauseosus* (N)
Sage
    a.Big sage (sagebrush)—*Artemisia tridentata* (N)
    b.Sand sage—*Artemisia filifolia* (N)
Fourwing saltbush—*Atriplex canescens* (N)
Seepwillow -*Baccharis sarothroides* (N)
Sotol—*Dasylirion wheeleri* (N)
Texas ranger—*Leucophyllum frutescens* (N)
Yucca
    a.Narrowleaf yucca—*Yucca glauca* (N)
    b.Softblade yucca—*Yucca recurvifolia* (*Yucca pendula*) (E)
    c.Spanish bayonet—*Yucca baccata* (N)

GROUND COVERS

A. Deciduous

Spring cinquefoil—*Potentilla tabernaemontani* (E)
Clover—*Trifolium* spp. (NZ, N)
Cranberry cotoneaster—*Cotoneaster apiculatus* (E)
Crown vetch—*Coronilla varia* (E, NZ)
Prairie sage—*Artemisia ludoviciana* (N)
Memorial rose (vine)—*Rosa wichuriana* (E)

B. Evergreen

Ajuga (bugleweed)—*Ajuga reptans* (E)
Bearberry cotoneaster—*Cotoneaster dammeri* (E)
Dwarf coyotebrush—*Baccharis pilularis* (E)
Creeping euonymus—*Euonymus fortunei* (E)
Honeysuckle—*Lonicera japonica* varieties (E)
Horizontalis junipers
    a.Bar Harbor juniper—*Juniperus horizontalis* 'Bar Harbor' (E)
    b.Wilton carpet juniper—*Juniperus horizontalis* 'Wiltonii' (E)
Sabina junipers
    a.Broadmoor juniper—*Juniperus sabina* 'Broadmoor' (E)
    b.Buffalo juniper—*Juniperus sabina* 'Buffalo' (E)
    c.Tam (tammy) juniper—*Juniperus sabina* 'Tamariscifolia' (E)
Kinnickinnick (mountain bearberry)—*Arctostaphylos uva-ursi* (N)
Periwinkle—*Vinca major* and *Vinca minor* (E)
Pussytoes—*Antennaria parviflora* (N)
Santolina
    a.Green santolina—*Santolina virens* (E)
    b.Gray santolina—*Santolina chamaecyparissus* (E)
Sedum (stonecrop)—*Sedum* spp. (N, E)
Strawberry—*Fragaria* spp. (N, E)

GRASSES

A. Traditional Turf Species

Bermuda
    a.African bermuda—*Cynodon transvaalensis* (E, NZ)
    b.Common bermuda—*Cynodon dactylon* (E)
Bluegrass—*Poa pratensis* (N)
Fescue—*Festuca* spp. (E)
Ryegrass—*Lolium* spp. (E)

B. Native Turf and General-Use Species

Buffalo grass—*Buchlöe dactyloides* (N)
Galleta—*Hilaria jamesii* (N)
Grama
    a.Blue grama—*Bouteloua gracilis* (N)
    b.Sideoats grama—*Bouteloua curtipendula* (N)
Western wheatgrass—*Agropyron smithii* (N)

C. Ornamental Species

Alkali sacaton—*Sporobolus airoides* (N)
Sand dropseed—*Sporobolus cryptandrus* (N)
Blue fescue—*Festuca caesia* (E)
Fountain grass—*Pennisetum* spp. (E)
Pampas grass—*Cortaderia selloana* (E)
Indian ricegrass—*Oryzopsis hymenoides* (N)
Purple threeawn—*Aristida longiseta* (N)

VINES

A. Deciduous

Canyon grape—*Vitis arizonica* (N)
Carolina jessamine—*Gelsemium sempervirens* (E)
Clematis—*Clematis jackmanni* (E)
Morning glory—*Ipomoea tricolor* (E)
Trumpet vine—*Campsis radicans* (E)
Virginia creeper (et al)—*Parthenocissus
     quinquefolia* (N)
Wisteria—*Wisteria sinensis* (E)

B. Evergreen

English ivy—*Hedera helix* (E)
Honeysuckle—*Lonicera* spp. (E)

FLOWERS

A. Annuals

Purple aster—*Aster bigelovii* (N)
Bedding begonia—*Begonia* spp. (E)
Cosmos—*Cosmos* spp. (E)
Four o'clock—*Mirabilis jalapa* (E)
Gaillardia (blanketflower, firewheel)—*Gaillardia
     pulchella* (N)
Geranium—*Pelargonium hortorum* (E)
Marigold—*Tagetes* spp. (E)
Pansy—*Viola wittrockiana* (E)
Petunia—*Petunia* spp. (E)
Salvia—*Salvia* spp. (E)
Snapdragon—*Antirrhinum majus* (E)
Sunflower—*Helianthus annuus* (N)

B. Perennials

Desert baileya—*Baileya multiradiata* (N)
Chrysanthemum—*Chrysanthemum morifolium* (E)
Colorado columbine—*Aquilegia* spp. (N)
Coneflower—*Ratibida columnifera* (N)
Daylily (asphodel)—*Hemerocallis* spp. (E)
Fendler's sundrops—*Calylophus hartwegii fendleri* (N)
Blue flax—*Linum perenne* (N)
Globemallow—*Sphaeralcea incana* (scarlet) (N)
Hollyhock—*Alcea rosea* (E, NZ)
Jimsonweed (datura, sacred datura)—*Datura
     meteloides* (N)
Lobelia—*Lobelia erinus* (E)
Maximilian's daisy—*Helianthus maximiliani* (NZ)
Paperflower—*Psilostrophe tagetina* (N)
Penstemon—*Penstemon* spp. (N)
Phlox—*Phlox* spp. (E)
Shasta daisy—*Chrysanthemum maximum* (E)
Violet—*Viola odorata* (N, E)
Wooly yarrow—*Achillea* spp. (N, E)

C. Bulbs

Canna—*Canna* spp. (E)
Daffodil—*Narcissus* 'King Alfred' (E)
Dutch crocus—*Crocus verus* (E)
Garden gladiolus—*Gladiolus hortulanus* (E)
Iris—*Iris* spp. (N, E)
Ranunculus—*Ranunculus asiaticus* (E)
Tulip—*Tulipa* spp. (E)

Big Ditch, Silver City

SILVER CITY

(founded in 1870), including Bayard, Central, Hanover, San Lorenzo, Mimbres, Cliff, Gila, and Glenwood

Silver City is located at 5300 feet (1620 m) in the picturesque, south-pitched foothills of the Los Pinos Range at the southwest edge of the Gila National Forest. The town has a remarkably pleasant, generally mild climate. The growing season is about 185 days. Annual rainfall is between 15 and 18 inches (375–450 mm). Most soils in the area are rocky and somewhat alkaline, but they can be productive.

Silver City lies just northeast of the Burro Mountains. This small range is home to an amazing collection of gray, Emory, and other oaks—an actual oak woodland. Beargrass, sotol, ocotillo, agave, yucca, desert willow, seepwillow, mountain mahogany, alligator juniper, singleseed juniper, and Arizona cypress are all found in the Silver City area as well. To the north and west, western soapberry, Arizona walnut, Arizona madrone, Arizona alder, Arizona ash, Fremont or Gila cottonwood, and mesquite are quite common. The towering and ghostly Arizona sycamore dominates many deep canyons and ravines. Box elder, cliff fendlerbush, serviceberry, snowberry, big sage, rabbitbrush, New Mexico locust, Apache plume, algerita, and common juniper are frequently found in the Gila National Forest to the north. Piñon and netleaf hackberry occur in stands in the foothills. Alkali sacaton, many grama species, buffalo grass, Indian ricegrass, and muhly are widespread grasses on the desert floor and in the nearby foothills.

Ponderosa, limber, Apache, and Chihuahua pines are common evergreens in the higher elevations. Douglas fir, Engelmann spruce, and white fir occur in good stands near the pines, as do aspens and narrowleaf cottonwoods. Most streams near Silver City support intensely green groves of box elders. Willows, bigtooth maples, Woods rose, currants, and thimbleberries (a delicious kind of raspberry) can be found thriving in the stony mountain soil.

The Gila National Forest is famous for its many open, grassy parks, or glades, scattered throughout the high country. Cattle and calves are by far the most important agricultural product in Grant County, and much livestock is grazed in the forest. Some hogs and chickens are also raised. A quantity of hay is produced, along with small amounts of corn, chile, and fruit. The primary croplands are located in narrow strips in the Gila and Mimbres river valleys.

Silver City itself is compact and quite hilly. A casual visitor would likely observe that the city's gardens and landscapes are generally modest, very colorful in season, and almost always laid out in a series of stony terraces and "pockets." The climate is quite similar to that of Albuquerque or Clovis, but the vertical topography creates unusual microclimates, and the town is more protected from temperature extremes than are its more northerly cousins.

Western red cedars grow very tall here, as do the native and Apache limber pines. Globe willow, Arizona walnut, ashes, Arizona cypress, deodar cedar, Atlas cedar, plum, apricot, pear, apple, and peach are all local favorites. Siberian elm, ailanthus, and Osage orange are widespread here, as in other old mining towns throughout the Gila country. White (silver) poplar, redbud, desert willow, and white fir flourish in Silver City. Snowball viburnum, many agave species, beargrass, spirea, very tall soaptree yucca, ocotillo, Spanish broom, staghorn and smooth sumac, New Mexico locust, magnolia, cotoneasters, bearberries, junipers, and Oregon grape are popular shrubs. Spring and summer color in many small, stone-walled planters is provided by tulips, daffodils, windflowers, cannas, marigolds, the incredible sacred datura or jimsonweed (with its enormous, poisonous flowers), petunias, pansies, daylilies, many irises, hollyhocks, penstemons, Indian paintbrush, Fendler's sundrops, lilacs, sand plums, hyacinths, and red hot pokers. For a city of moderate size, the plant list is rather astonishing —and, generally, most garden plants grow quite well indeed in Silver City.

The stateliest landscape of historic import in the county is the grounds of Fort Bayard, dating from New Mexico's territorial days. The fort's groves of cypresses are the tallest and finest in the state. St. Mary's Center on the northern edge of the city features wonderful brick buildings in a stone-walled compound with a well-developed (though aging) garden landscape. Elsewhere, the terrace and pocket landscapes of the city offer delightful "vignette" gardens for the visitor on foot. One of the best restored of these is found at the Silver City Museum, where a flourishing deodar cedar, flowering shrubs, and a tiny, emerald-colored lawn specked with flowers invite a closer look.

SELECTED BEST PLANTS FOR SILVER CITY

These plant species grow very well in Silver City. For the sake of convenience and quick reference, each plant is listed as native (N), naturalized (NZ), or exotic (E). Other plants also will perform well in landscape and garden situations in and around Silver City. Please see the New Mexico Plant File for these species.

TREES

A. Deciduous Shade, Street, and Specialty Trees

Arizona alder—*Alnus oblongifolia* (N)
Ash
    a.Modesto ash—*Fraxinus velutina* 'Modesto' (Arizona ash variety) (N)
    b.Raywood ash—*Fraxinus oxycarpa* 'Raywood' (E)
    c.White ash—*Fraxinus americana* and varieties (E)
Catalpa
    a.Umbrella catalpa—*Catalpa bignonioides* 'Nana' (E)
    b.Western catalpa—*Catalpa speciosa* (E)
Chinaberry—*Melia azedarach* (E)
Cottonwood, Aspen, and Poplar: Trees of the Genus *Populus*
    a.Carolina poplar—*Populus canadensis* (E)
    b.Fremont cottonwood—*Populus fremontii* (N)
    c.Lombardy poplar—*Populus nigra* 'Italica' (E)
    d.Narrowleaf cottonwood—*Populus angustifolia* (N)
    e.White (silver) poplar—*Populus alba* (E)
Chinese elm—*Ulmus parvifolia* (E)
Ginkgo (Maidenhair tree)—*Ginkgo biloba* (E)
Hackberry
    a.Common hackberry—*Celtis occidentalis* (E)
    b.Netleaf hackberry—*Celtis reticulata* (N)
Honey locust—*Gleditsia triacanthos inermis* varieties (E)
Horsechestnut
    a.Common horsechestnut—*Aesculus hippocastanum* (E)
    b.California buckeye—*Aesculus californica* (E)
Japanese pagoda—*Sophora japonica* (E)

Locust
    a.Black locust—*Robinia pseudoacacia* (NZ)
    b.Hybrid locusts—*Robinia ambigua* varieties (E)
    c.New Mexico locust—*Robinia neomexicana* (N)
Maple and Box elder
    a.Box elder—*Acer negundo* (N)
    b.Japanese maple—*Acer palmatum* (E)
    c.Silver maple—*Acer saccharinum* (E)
European mountain ash—*Sorbus aucuparia* (E)
Mulberry
    a.Fruitless mulberry—*Morus alba* (E)
    b.Weeping mulberry—*Morus alba* 'Pendula' (E)
Oak
    a.Gambel oak—*Quercus gambelii* (N)
    b.Southern live oak—*Quercus virginiana* (E)
    c.Texas oak—*Quercus texana* (E)
(Note: Emory oak, *Quercus emoryii*, is strongly recommended when available.)
Osage orange—*Maclura pomifera* (E)
Pecan—*Carya illinoiensis* (E)
Pistache—Pistachio
    a.Chinese pistache—*Pistacia chinensis* (E)
    b.Pistachio—*Pistacia vera* (E)
Russian olive—*Elaeagnus angustifolia* (NZ)
Sycamore (plane tree)
    a.Arizona sycamore—*Platanus wrightii* (N)
    b.London plane tree—*Platanus acerifolia* (E)
    c.Oriental plane tree—*Platanus orientalis* (E)
Walnut
    a.Arizona walnut—*Juglans major* (NZ)
    b.English (Carpathian) walnut—*Juglans regia* (E)
Willow
    a.Corkscrew willow—*Salix matsudana* 'Tortuosa' (E)
    b.Globe Navajo willow—*Salix matsudana* 'Navajo' (E)
    c.Peachleaf willow—*Salix amygdaloides* (N)
    d.Weeping willow—*Salix babylonica* (and other weeping willow species) (E)

B. Flowering Ornamental Trees

Flowering crab—*Malus* 'Hopa' et al (E)
Mexican elder—*Sambucus caerulea neomexicana* (N)
Desert willow—*Chilopsis linearis* (N)
Flowering peach—*Prunus persica* (E)
Bradford pear—*Pyrus calleryana* (E)
Purpleleaf plum—*Prunus cerasifera* (E)
Golden rain tree—*Koelreuteria paniculata* (E)
Smoke tree—*Cotinus coggygria* (E)
Vitex (chaste tree)—*Vitex agnus-castus* (E)

C. Evergreen Trees

Cedar
    a.Atlas cedar—*Cedrus atlantica* (E)
    b.Cedar of Lebanon—*Cedrus libani* (E)
    c.Deodar cedar—*Cedrus deodara* (E)
Cypress
    a.Arizona cypress—*Cupressus arizonica* (N)
    b .Italian cypress—*Cupressus sempervirens* (E)
Douglas fir—*Pseudotsuga menziesii* (N)
White fir—*Abies concolor* (N)
Juniper
    a.Alligator juniper—*Juniperus deppeana* (N)
    b.Rocky Mountain juniper—*Juniperus scopulorum* varieties (N)
Leyland false cypress—*Cupressocyparis leylandii* (E)
Madrone—*Arbutus texana* (N)
Southern magnolia—*Magnolia grandiflora* (E)
Chinese windmill palm—*Trachycarpus fortunei* (E)

Pine
- a.Afghan pine—*Pinus eldarica* (E)
- b.Austrian pine—*Pinus nigra* (E)
- c.Italian stone pine—*Pinus pinea* (E)
- d.Japanese black pine—*Pinus thunbergiana* (E)
- e.Limber pine—*Pinus flexilis* (N)
- f.Piñon pine—*Pinus edulis* (N)
- g.Ponderosa pine—*Pinus ponderosa* (N)

Spruce
- a.Blue spruce—*Picea pungens* (N)
- b.Engelmann spruce—*Picea engelmanni* (N)

Western red cedar—*Thuja plicata* (E)

Yucca
- a.Joshua tree—*Yucca brevifolia* (E)
- b.Palm yucca—*Yucca torreyi* (N)
- c.Soaptree yucca—*Yucca elata* (N)

SHRUBS

A. Deciduous

Glossy abelia—*Abelia grandiflora* (E)
Althea (Rose of Sharon)—*Hibiscus syriacus* (E)
Apache plume—*Fallugia paradoxa* (N)
Golden bamboo—*Phyllostachys aurea* (E)
Spanish broom—*Spartium junceum* (E)
Cotoneaster
- a.Cranberry cotoneaster—*Cotoneaster apiculatus* (E)
- b.Rock cotoneaster—*Cotoneaster horizontalis* (E)

Crape myrtle—*Lagerstroemia indica* (E)
Currant and gooseberry—*Ribes* spp. (N)
Cliff fendlerbush—*Fendlera rupicola* (N)
Fernbush—*Chamaebatiaria millefolium* (N)
Edible fig—*Ficus carica* (E)
Forsythia—*Forsythia* spp. (E)
Flowering jasmine—*Jasminum nudiflorum* (E)
Common lilac—*Syringa vulgaris* (E)
Mountain mahogany—*Cercocarpus montanus* (N)
Screwbean mesquite—*Prosopis pubescens* (N)
Sand plum—*Prunus americana* (N)
Pomegranate—*Punica granatum*
Flowering quince—*Chaenomeles speciosa* (E)
Raspberry—*Rubus* spp. (E, N)
Snakeweed—*Gutierrezia sarothrae* (N)
Snowball—*Viburnum opulus* 'Roseum' (E)
Spirea
- a.Bridal wreath—*Spiraea prunifolia* (E)
- b.Anthony Waterer—*Spiraea bumalda* 'Anthony Waterer' (E)

Sumac
- a.Littleleaf sumac—*Rhus microphylla* (N)
- b.Skunkbush—*Rhus trilobata* (N)
- c.Smooth sumac—*Rhus glabra* (N)
- d.Staghorn sumac—*Rhus typhina* (E)

Weigela—*Weigela florida* (E)

B. Evergreen

Agave (century plant, mescal)
- a.Century plant—*Agave americana* (N)
- b.Parry agave—*Agave parryi* (N)
- c.Lechugilla—*Agave lechugilla* (N)

Aucuba—*Aucuba japonica* (E)
Barberry
- a.Colorado barberry—*Berberis fendleri* (N)
- b.Japanese barberry—*Berberis thunbergii* (E)

Beargrass—*Nolina microcarpa* (N)
Cactus
- a.Claret cup—*Echinocereus triglochidiatus* (N)
- b.Common cholla—*Opuntia imbricata* (N)
- c.Prickly pear—*Opuntia chlorotica* or O.

engelmannii (N)
Chinese junipers
- a.Armstrong juniper—*Juniperus chinensis* 'Armstrong' (E)
- b.Pfitzer juniper—*Juniperus chinensis* 'Pfitzerana' (E)
- c.Sea Green juniper—*Juniperus chinensis* 'Sea Green' (E)

Common juniper—*Juniperus communis* (N)
Mahonia
- a.Algerita—*Mahonia haematocarpa* (N)
- b.Agritos—*Mahonia trifoliolata* (N)
- c.Oregon grape—*Mahonia aquifolium* (E, NZ)

Mormon tea—*Ephedra* spp. (N)
Ocotillo—*Fouquieria splendens* (N)
Photinia
- a.Chinese photinia—*Photinia serrulata* (E)
- b.Fraser's photinia—*Photinia fraseri* (E)

Mugo pine—*Pinus mugo* (E)
Rubber rabbitbrush—*Chrysothamnus nauseosus* (N)
Sage
- a.Big sage (sagebrush)—*Artemisia tridentata* (N)
- b.Sand sage—*Artemisia filifolia* (N)

Fourwing saltbush—*Atriplex canescens* (N)
Seepwillow -*Baccharis sarothroides* (N)
Silverberry—*Elaeagnus pungens* (E)
Sotol—*Dasylirion wheeleri* (N)
Alberta spruce—*Picea glauca* 'Conica' (*Picea albertiana*) (E)
Texas ranger—*Leucophyllum frutescens* (N)
Yucca
- a.Narrowleaf yucca—*Yucca glauca* (N)
- b.Softblade yucca—*Yucca recurvifolia* (*Yucca pendula*) (E)
- c.Spanish bayonet—*Yucca baccata* (N)
- d.Coral-flower yucca—*Hesperaloe parviflora* (E)

GROUND COVERS

A. Deciduous

Spring cinquefoil—*Potentilla tabernaemontani* (E)
Clover—*Trifolium* spp. (NZ, N)
Cranberry cotoneaster—*Cotoneaster apiculatus* (E)
Crown vetch—*Coronilla varia* (E, NZ)
Prairie sage—*Artemisia ludoviciana* (N)
Memorial rose (vine)—*Rosa wichuriana* (E)

B. Evergreen

Ajuga (bugleweed)—*Ajuga reptans* (E)
Bearberry cotoneaster—*Cotoneaster dammeri* (E)
Creeping euonymus—*Euonymus fortunei* (E)
Honeysuckle—*Lonicera japonica* varieties (E)
Horizontalis junipers
- a.Bar Harbor juniper—*Juniperus horizontalis* 'Bar Harbor' (E)
- b.Wilton carpet juniper—*Juniperus horizontalis* 'Wiltonii' (E)

Sabina junipers
- a.Broadmoor juniper—*Juniperus sabina* 'Broadmoor' (E)
- b.Buffalo juniper—*Juniperus sabina* 'Buffalo' (E)
- c.Tam (tammy) juniper—*Juniperus sabina* 'Tamariscifolia' (E)

Kinnickinnick (mountain bearberry)—*Arctostaphylos uva-ursi* (N)
Blue leadwort—*Ceratostigma plumbaginoides* (E)
Lilyturf (liriope)—*Liriope spicata* (E)
Creeping mahonia—*Mahonia repens* (N)
Periwinkle—*Vinca major* and *Vinca minor* (E)
Pussytoes—*Antennaria parviflora* (N)

Rosemary—*Rosmarinus officinalis* (E)
Santolina
    a.Green santolina—*Santolina virens* (E)
    b.Gray santolina—*Santolina chamaecyparissus* (E)
Sedum (stonecrop)—*Sedum* spp. (N, E)
Japanese spurge—*Pachysandra terminalis* (E)
Strawberry—*Fragaria* spp. (N, E)

GRASSES

A. Traditional Turf Species

Bentgrass—*Agrostis* spp. (E)
Bluegrass—*Poa pratensis* (E, NZ)
Fescue—*Festuca* spp. (E, N)
Ryegrass—*Lolium* spp. (E)

B. Native Turf and General-Use Species

Buffalo grass—*Buchlöe dactyloides* (N)
Galleta—*Hilaria jamesii* (N)
Grama
    a.Blue grama—*Bouteloua gracilis* (N)
    b.Sideoats grama—*Bouteloua curtipendula* (N)
Wheatgrass
    a.Western wheatgrass—*Agropyron smithii* (N)
    b.Crested wheatgrass—*Agropyron desertorum*
    (E, NZ)

C. Ornamental Species

Alkali sacaton—*Sporobolus airoides* (N)
Sand dropseed—*Sporobolus cryptandrus* (N)
Blue fescue—*Festuca caesia* (E)
Fountain grass—*Pennisetum* spp. (E)
Pampas grass—*Cortaderia selloana* (E)
Indian ricegrass—*Oryzopsis hymenoides* (N)
River cane—*Arundo donax* (NZ)
Purple threeawn—*Aristida longiseta* (N)

VINES

A. Deciduous

Canyon grape—*Vitis arizonica* (N, E)
Carolina jessamine—*Gelsemium sempervirens* (E)
Clematis—*Clematis jackmanni* (E)
Morning glory—*Ipomoea tricolor* (E)
Trumpet vine—*Campsis radicans* (E)
Virginia creeper (et al)—*Parthenocissus quinquefolia*
    (E, N)
Wisteria—*Wisteria sinensis* (E)

B. Evergreen

Algerian ivy—*Hedera canariensis* (E)
English ivy—*Hedera helix* (E)
Honeysuckle—*Lonicera* spp. (E)

FLOWERS

A. Annuals

Ageratum—*Ageratum houstonianum* (E)
Cosmos—*Cosmos* spp. (E)
Four o'clock—*Mirabilis jalapa* (E)
Gaillardia (blanketflower, firewheel)—*Gaillardia*
    pulchella (N)
Impatiens—*Impatiens wallerana* (E)
Lisianthus—*Eustoma grandiflorum* (E)
Marigold—*Tagetes* spp. (E)
Pansy—*Viola wittrockiana* (E)
Petunia—*Petunia* spp. (E)
Salvia—*Salvia* spp. (E)
Snapdragon—*Antirrhinum majus* (E)
Sunflower—*Helianthus annuus* (N)
Annual vinca (Madagascar periwinkle)—*Catharanthus*
    roseus (E)
Viola (Johnny jump-ups)—*Viola* spp. (E)
Wallflower—*Erysimum capitatum* (N)

B. Perennials

Desert baileya—*Baileya multiradiata* (N)
Bear's breech—*Acanthus mollis* (E)
Chrysanthemum—*Chrysanthemum morifolium* (E)
Colorado columbine—*Aquilegia* spp. (N)
Coneflower—*Ratibida columnifera* (N)
Daylily (asphodel)—*Hemerocallis* spp. (E)
Delphinium—*Delphinium belladonna* (E, N)
Dusty miller—*Senecio cineraria* (E)
Fendler's sundrops—*Calylophus hartwegii fendleri* (N)
Blue flax—*Linum perenne* (N)
Hollyhock—*Alcea rosea* (E, NZ)
Indian paintbrush—*Castilleja integra* (N)
Jimsonweed (datura, sacred datura)—*Datura*
    meteloides (N)
Lobelia—*Lobelia erinus* (E)
Maximilian's daisy—*Helianthus maximiliani* (NZ)
Paperflower—*Psilostrophe tagetina* (N)
Penstemon—*Penstemon* spp. (N)
Phlox—*Phlox* spp. (E)
California poppy—*Eschscholzia californica* (and *E.*
    mexicana) (E, N)
Primrose—*Primula vulgaris* (E)
Red rocket (scarlet gilia)—*Ipomopsis aggregata* (N)
Shasta daisy—*Chrysanthemum maximum* (E)
Violet—*Viola odorata* (N, E)
Wooly yarrow—*Achillea* spp. (N, E)

C. Bulbs

Common hyacinth—*Hyacinthus orientalis* (E)
Daffodil—*Narcissus* 'King Alfred' (E)
Garden gladiolus—*Gladiolus hortulanus* (E)
Grape hyacinth—*Muscari armeniacum* (E)
Iris—*Iris* spp. (E, N)
Tulip—*Tulipa* spp. (E)

Turtle Bay at New Mexico Tech

SOCORRO

(founded before 1628), including San Antonio, Lemitar, Polvadera, La Joya (Sevilleta), and Escondida

An ancient town, Socorro has a long and varied landscape history. Probably the earliest landscapes here were the plazas and patios of the Piro Indians, who displayed both Anasazi and Mogollón (Mimbres) influence in the landscape architecture of their pueblos scattered throughout Socorro County. After 1598, the Franciscan friars built *atrios* (courts) in front of their mission churches and constructed small, enclosed patios and kitchen gardens in their friaries. Grapes, peaches, and apples, as well as many vegetable crops, first became popular in Spanish colonial times.

At 4585 feet (1400 m), Socorro is nearly as high as Albuquerque, though it lies 75 miles south of the Duke City. Socorro is somewhat more exposed than Albuquerque to the elements. Its growing season is about 185 days —9 fewer than Albuquerque's—and annual rainfall ranges from a little less than 9 inches (225 mm) to 11 inches (275 mm). Most soils in the county are thin, alkaline, and stony, and many have a high caliche (lime) content. Riverside soils, by contrast, are fertile and frequently contain loamy mixtures of sand, silt, and clay.

Mesquite grows well in Socorro County but is generally shrubby. Desert willow, netleaf-hackberry, and singleseed juniper are common in foothills, along with creosote, fourwing salt-bush, Apache plume, dalea, and the enormous littleleaf sumac—perhaps the widest-spreading of all the sumacs. Mexican woodland oak species begin to appear in the draws south

and west of Socorro, often accompanied by threadleaf sage, ocotillo, yucca, and sotol. Rio Grande cottonwood and its accompanying willows are still plentiful in the Rio Grande bosque of Socorro County, but the native cottonwood is often infested with debilitating mistletoe, and the willows are hard-pressed in their range by the terribly invasive salt cedar —an unwelcome exotic. Naturalized Russian olive is also plentiful up and down the valley. Alkali sacaton grows in beautiful, wind-blown desert stands at the north edge of the Jornada del Muerto.

Piñon, alligator juniper, and Arizona walnut are common trees along the lower slopes of the Magdalena Range. At higher elevations, white fir, Douglas fir, Arizona alder, ponderosa and limber pine, Gambel oak, aspen, and narrowleaf cottonwood dominate the landscape. Snowberry, shrubby cinquefoil, currant, mountain mahogany, and spectacular agaves are found here in the midst of an abundance of mountain wildflowers.

Socorro County ranks twelfth in the state in agricultural production. Livestock raising is very important; cattle and calves, milk cows, and a few sheep and poultry species are grazed or kept. Hay, corn, chile, and vegetables are popular crops. A little sorghum and barley are also raised. Cotton was formerly important to the county's agriculture. Virtually all crops are irrigated.

Socorro itself has an abundance of ornamental landscape species. Arizona cypress is planted widely and grows happily. Other popular trees include chinaberry, fruitless mulberry, globe willow, sycamore, Afghan pine, Scotch pine, and New Mexico's ubiquitous Siberian elm. Western soapberry, Arizona ash, honey locust, and desert willow all grow exceptionally well here. Prickly pear and cholla cactus, Torrey and soaptree yucca, sotol, several agave species, Mexican elder, Spanish broom, althea, several cotoneasters, junipers, crape myrtle, and New Mexico olive thrive in the local microclimate. And petunias, cannas, marigolds, desert baileyas, salvia, red hot pokers, four o'clocks, lobelia, ageratum, gaillardia, and cosmos are widely planted as colorful accents in the city's gardens.

The campus of the New Mexico Institute of Mining and Technology (New Mexico Tech) is easily Socorro's most influential landscape. It is well maintained and intensely green, with numerous excellent specimen plantings. The edge of Tech's golf course even has a small stream and pond used for irrigation and frequented by much wildlife.

Several remnant, walled Victorian gardens are well cared for by their owners. Virtually all of these are found within a few blocks' walk of either the plaza or New Mexico Tech. The plaza itself, renovated in the late 1970s, is very attractive with its new bandstand, gazebo, and handsome tree plantings. The courtyard and streetscape of the Val Verde Hotel provide a pleasant glimpse into the late railroad era of the 1930s. However, the latest plantings at the Val Verde are strictly modern.

SELECTED BEST PLANTS FOR SOCORRO

These plant species grow very well in Socorro. For the sake of convenience and quick reference, each plant is listed as native (N), naturalized (NZ), or exotic (E). Other plants also will perform well in landscape and garden situations in and around Socorro. Please see the New Mexico Plant File for these species.

TREES

A. Deciduous Shade, Street, and Specialty Trees

Arizona alder—*Alnus oblongifolia* (N)
Ash
    a. Arizona ash—*Fraxinus velutina* (N)
    b. Modesto ash—*Fraxinus velutina* 'Modesto' (Arizona ash variety) (N)
    c. Green ash—*Fraxinus pennsylvanica* and varieties (E)
    d. Raywood ash—*Fraxinus oxycarpa* 'Raywood' (E)

Catalpa
    a. Umbrella catalpa—*Catalpa bignonioides* 'Nana' (E)
    b. Western catalpa—*Catalpa speciosa* (E)
Chinaberry—*Melia azedarach* (E)
Cottonwood, Aspen, and Poplar: Trees of the Genus *Populus*
    a. Carolina poplar—*Populus canadensis* (E)
    b. Lanceleaf cottonwood—*Populus acuminata* (N)
    c. Lombardy poplar—*Populus nigra* 'Italica' (E)
    d. Rio Grande cottonwood—*Populus fremontii* 'Wislizeni' (N)
    e. White poplar (silver) poplar—*Populus alba* (NZ)
Chinese elm—*Ulmus parvifolia* (E)
Hackberry
    a. Common hackberry—*Celtis occidentalis* (E)
    b. Netleaf hackberry—*Celtis reticulata* (N)
Honey locust—*Gleditsia triacanthos inermis* varieties (E)
Japanese pagoda—*Sophora japonica* (E)
Jujube—*Zizyphus jujuba* (E)
Locust
    a. Black locust—*Robinia pseudoacacia* (NZ)
    b. Hybrid locusts—*Robinia ambigua* varieties (E)
    c. New Mexico locust—*Robinia neomexicana* (N)
Maple and Box elder
    a. Box elder—*Acer negundo* (N)
    b. Japanese maple—*Acer palmatum* (E)
    c. Sycamore-leaf maple—*Acer pseudoplatanus* (E)
Mesquite—*Prosopis glandulosa* (N)
Mulberry (E)
    a. Fruitless mulberry—*Morus alba*
    b. Weeping mulberry—*Morus alba* 'Pendula'
    c. Paper mulberry—*Broussonetia papyrifera*
Pecan—*Carya illinoiensis* (E)
Pistache—Pistachio
    a. Chinese pistache—*Pistacia chinensis* (E)
    b. Pistachio—*Pistacia vera* (E)
Russian olive—*Elaeagnus angustifolia* (NZ)
Silk tree—*Albizia jilibrissin* (E)
Western soapberry—*Sapindus drummondii* (N)
Sycamore
    a. Arizona sycamore—*Platanus wrightii* (N)
    b. London plane tree—*Platanus acerifolia* (E)
    c. Oriental plane tree—*Platanus orientalis* (E)
Willow
    a. Corkscrew willow—*Salix matsudana* 'Tortuosa' (E)
    b. Globe Navajo willow—*Salix matsudana* 'Navajo' (E)
    c. Peachleaf willow—*Salix amygdaloides* (N)
    d. Weeping willow—*Salix babylonica* (and other weeping willow species) (E)

B. Flowering Ornamental Trees

Flowering apricot—*Prunus armeniaca* (E)
Flowering crab—*Malus* 'Hopa' et al (E)
Desert willow—*Chilopsis linearis* (N)
Flowering peach—*Prunus persica* (E)
Bradford pear—*Pyrus calleryana* (E)
Purpleleaf plum—*Prunus cerasifera* (E)
Eastern redbud—*Cercis canadensis* (E)
Golden rain tree—*Koelreuteria paniculata* (E)
Salt cedar—*Tamarix chinensis* (NZ)
Smoke tree—*Cotinus coggygria* (E)
Vitex (chaste tree)—*Vitex agnus-castus* (E)

C. Evergreen Trees

Cedar
    a. Atlas cedar—*Cedrus atlantica* (E)
    b. Cedar of Lebanon—*Cedrus libani* (E)
    c. Deodar cedar—*Cedrus deodara* (E)
Cypress
    a. Arizona cypress—*Cupressus arizonica* (N)
    b . Italian cypress—*Cupressus sempervirens* (E)

Juniper
  a. Alligator juniper—*Juniperus deppeana* (N)
  b. Chinese juniper—*Juniperus chinensis* varieties (E)
  c. Rocky Mountain juniper—*Juniperus scopulorum* varieties (N)
  d. Singleseed (one-seed) juniper—*Juniperus monosperma* (N)
Leyland false cypress—*Cupressocyparis leylandii* (E)
Chinese windmill palm—*Trachycarpus fortunei* (E)
Pine
  a. Afghan pine—*Pinus eldarica* (E)
  b. Austrian pine—*Pinus nigra* (E)
  c. Italian stone pine—*Pinus pinea* (E)
  d. Japanese black pine—*Pinus thunbergiana* (E)
  e. Limber pine—*Pinus flexilis* (N)
  f. Piñon pine—*Pinus edulis* (N)
  g. Ponderosa pine—*Pinus ponderosa* (N)
  h. Scotch pine—*Pinus sylvestris* (E)
Dawn redwood—*Metasequoia glyptostroboides* (E)
Spruce
  a. Blue spruce—*Picea pungens* (N)
  b. Engelmann spruce—*Picea engelmanni* (N)
Western red cedar—*Thuja plicata* (E)
Yucca
  a. Joshua tree—*Yucca brevifolia* (E)
  b. Palm yucca—*Yucca torreyi* (N)
  c. Soaptree yucca—*Yucca elata* (N)

SHRUBS

A. Deciduous

Althea (rose of Sharon)—*Hibiscus syriacus* (N, E)
Apache plume—*Fallugia paradoxa* (N)
Bird of paradise—*Caesalpinia gilliesii* (NZ)
Common butterfly bush—*Buddleia davidii* (E)
Shrubby cinquefoil—*Potentilla fruticosa* (N)
Cotoneaster
  a. Rock cotoneaster—*Cotoneaster horizontalis* (E)
  b. Rockspray cotoneaster—*Cotoneaster microphyllus* (E)
Crape myrtle—*Lagerstroemia indica* (E)
Currant and gooseberry—*Ribes* spp. (N, E)
Red osier dogwood—*Cornus stolonifera* (N)
Cliff fendlerbush—*Fendlera rupicola* (N)
Fernbush—*Chamaebatiaria millefolium* (N)
Forsythia—*Forsythia* spp. (E)
Shrub or Tatarian honeysuckle—*Lonicera tatarica* (E)
Flowering jasmine—*Jasminum nudiflorum* (E)
Common lilac—*Syringa vulgaris* (E)
Screwbean mesquite—*Prosopis pubescens* (N)
Mock orange
  a. Sweet mock orange—*Philadelphus coronarius* (E)
  b. Littleleaf mock orange—*Philadelphus microphyllus* (E, N)
Mountain mahogany—*Cercocarpus montanus* (N)
New Mexico olive—*Forestiera neomexicana* (N)
Privet—*Ligustrum* spp. (E)
Rose—*Rosa* spp. (E, N)
Snakeweed—*Gutierrezia sarothrae* (N)
Snowball—*Viburnum opulus* 'Roseum' (E)
Spirea
  a. Bridal wreath—*Spiraea prunifolia* (E)
  b. Van Houtte—*Spiraea vanhouttei* (E)
  c. Anthony Waterer—*Spiraea bumalda* 'Anthony Waterer' (E)
Sumac
  a. Littleleaf sumac—*Rhus microphylla* (N)
  b. Skunkbush—*Rhus trilobata* (N)
  c. Smooth sumac—*Rhus glabra* (N)
  d. Staghorn sumac—*Rhus typhina* (E)

Weigela—*Weigela florida* (E)
Willow
  a. Coyote willow—*Salix exigua* (N)
  b. Pussywillow—*Salix discolor* (N, E)
Winterfat—*Ceratoides lanata* (N)

B. Evergreen

Agave (century plant, mescal) (N)
Barberry
  a. Colorado barberry—*Berberis fendleri* (N)
  b. Japanese barberry—*Berberis thunbergii* (E)
  c. Three-spine barberry—*Berberis wisleyensis* (E)
  d. Wintergreen barberry—*Berberis julianae* (E)
Beargrass—*Nolina microcarpa* (N)
Cactus
  a. Claret cup—*Echinocereus triglochidiatus* (N)
  b. Common cholla—*Opuntia imbricata* (N)
  c. Prickly pear—*Opuntia chlorotica* or *O. engelmannii* (N)
Creosotebush—*Larrea tridentata* (N)
Holly
  a. Burford holly—*Ilex cornuta* 'Burfordii' (E)
  b. Wilson holly—*Ilex altaclarensis* 'Wilsonii' (E)
  c. Yaupon holly—*Ilex vomitoria* (E)
India hawthorn—*Rhaphiolepis indica* (E)
Chinese junipers
  a. Armstrong juniper—*Juniperus chinensis* 'Armstrong' (E)
  b. Pfitzer juniper—*Juniperus chinensis* 'Pfitzerana' (E)
  c. Sea Green juniper—*Juniperus chinensis* 'Sea Green' (E)
Common juniper—*Juniperus communis* (N)
Mahonia
  a. Algerita—*Mahonia haematocarpa* (N)
  b. Oregon grape—*Mahonia aquifolium* (E)
Mormon tea—*Ephedra* spp. (N)
Nandina (heavenly bamboo)—*Nandina domestica* (E)
Ocotillo—*Fouquieria splendens* (N)
Pittosporum (tobira)—*Pittosporum tobira* (E)
Pyracantha (firethorn)—*Pyracantha* spp. (E)
Rubber rabbitbrush—*Chrysothamnus nauseosus* (N)
Sage
  a. Big sage (sagebrush)—*Artemisia tridentata* (N)
  b. Sand sage—*Artemisia filifolia* (N)
Fourwing saltbush—*Atriplex canescens* (N)
Seepwillow -*Baccharis sarothroides* (N)
Sotol—*Dasylirion wheeleri* (N)
Yucca
  a. Softblade yucca—*Yucca recurvifolia* (*Yucca pendula*) (E)
  b. Spanish bayonet—*Yucca baccata* (N)
  c. Coral-flower yucca—*Hesperaloe parviflora* (E)

GROUND COVERS

A. Deciduous

Spring cinquefoil—*Potentilla tabernaemontani* (E)
Clover—*Trifolium* spp. (NZ, N)
Cranberry cotoneaster—*Cotoneaster apiculatus* (E)
Crown vetch—*Coronilla varia* (E, NZ)
Prairie sage—*Artemisia ludoviciana* (N)
Memorial rose (vine)—*Rosa wichuriana* (E)

B. Evergreen

Bearberry cotoneaster—*Cotoneaster dammeri* (E)
Creeping euonymus—*Euonymus fortunei* (E)

Germander—*Teucrium chamaedrys* 'Prostratum' (E)
Honeysuckle—*Lonicera japonica* varieties (E)
Horizontalis junipers
    a. Andorra juniper—*Juniperus horizontalis plumosa* (E)
    b. Bar Harbor juniper—*Juniperus horizontalis* 'Bar Harbor' (E)
    c. Wilton carpet juniper—*Juniperus horizontalis* 'Wiltonii' (E)
Sabina junipers
    a. Broadmoor juniper—*Juniperus sabina* 'Broadmoor' (E)
    b. Buffalo juniper—*Juniperus sabina* 'Buffalo' (E)
    c. Tam (tammy) juniper—*Juniperus sabina* 'Tamariscifolia' (E)
San Jose juniper—*Juniperus chinensis* 'San Jose' (E)
Kinnickinnick (mountain bearberry)—*Arctostaphylos uva-ursi* (N)
Blue leadwort—*Ceratostigma plumbaginoides* (E)
Creeping mahonia—*Mahonia repens* (N)
Compact nandina—*Nandina domestica* 'Harbor dwarf' (E)
Periwinkle—*Vinca major* and *Vinca minor* (E)
Pussytoes—*Antennaria parviflora* (N)
Rosemary—*Rosmarinus officinalis* (E)
Santolina
    a. Green santolina—*Santolina virens* (E)
    b. Gray santolina—*Santolina chamaecyparissus* (E)
Sedum (stonecrop)—*Sedum* spp. (N, E)
Strawberry—*Fragaria* spp. (N, E)

GRASSES

A. Traditional Turf Species

Bentgrass—*Agrostis* spp. (E)
Bluegrass—*Poa pratensis* (E, NZ)
Fescue—*Festuca* spp. (E, N)
Ryegrass—*Lolium* spp. (E)

B. Native Turf and General-Use Species

Buffalo grass—*Buchlöe dactyloides* (N)
Grama
    a. Black grama—*Bouteloua eriopoda* (N)
    b. Blue grama—*Bouteloua gracilis* (N)
    c. Sideoats grama—*Bouteloua curtipendula* (N)
Wheatgrass
    a. Western wheatgrass—*Agropyron smithii* (N)
    b. Pubescent wheatgrass—*Agropyron trichophorum* (N)

C. Ornamental Species

Alkali sacaton—*Sporobolus airoides* (N)
Sand dropseed—*Sporobolus cryptandrus* (N)
Fountain grass—*Pennisetum* spp. (E)
Pampas grass—*Cortaderia selloana* (E)
Indian ricegrass—*Oryzopsis hymenoides* (N)
River cane—*Arundo donax* (NZ)

VINES

A. Deciduous

Boston ivy—*Parthenocissus tricuspidata* (E)
Canyon grape—*Vitis arizonica* (N)
Carolina jessamine—*Gelsemium sempervirens* (E)
Clematis—*Clematis jackmanni* (E)
Morning glory—*Ipomoea tricolor* (E)
Silver lace vine—*Polygonum aubertii* (E)
Trumpet vine—*Campsis radicans* (E)
Virginia creeper (et al)—*Parthenocissus quinquefolia* (E)
Wisteria—*Wisteria sinensis* (E)

B. Evergreen

English ivy—*Hedera helix* (E)
Honeysuckle—*Lonicera* spp. (E)

FLOWERS

A. Annuals

Ageratum—*Ageratum houstonianum* (E)
Purple aster—*Aster bigelovii* (N)
Bedding begonia—*Begonia* spp. (E)
Cosmos—*Cosmos* spp. (E)
Four o'clock—*Mirabilis jalapa* (N, E)
Gaillardia (blanketflower, firewheel)—*Gaillardia pulchella* (N)
Geranium—*Pelargonium hortorum* (E)
Impatiens—*Impatiens wallerana* (E)
Marigold—*Tagetes* spp. (E)
Petunia—*Petunia* spp. (E)
Salvia—*Salvia* spp. (E)
Snapdragon—*Antirrhinum majus* (E)
Sunflower—*Helianthus annuus* (N)
Annual vinca (Madagascar periwinkle)—*Catharanthus roseus* (E)

B. Perennials

Desert baileya—*Baileya multiradiata* (N)
Carnation—*Dianthus caryophyllus* (E)
Chrysanthemum—*Chrysanthemum morifolium* (E)
Coneflower—*Ratibida columnifera* (N)
Daylily (asphodel)—*Hemerocallis* spp. (E)
Delphinium—*Delphinium belladonna* (E, N)
Dusty miller—*Senecio cineraria* (E)
Fendler's sundrops—*Calylophus hartwegii fendleri* (N)
Blue flax—*Linum perenne* (N)
Globemallow—*Sphaeralcea incana* (scarlet) (N)
Hollyhock—*Alcea rosea* (NZ)
Jimsonweed (datura, sacred datura)—*Datura meteloides* (N)
Lobelia—*Lobelia erinus* (E)
Maximilian's daisy—*Helianthus maximiliani* (NZ)
Paperflower—*Psilostrophe tagetina* (N)
Penstemon—*Penstemon* spp. (N)
Phlox—*Phlox* spp. (E)
Primrose—*Primula vulgaris* (N)
Shasta daisy—*Chrysanthemum maximum* (E)
Spectaclepod—*Dithyrea wislizenii* (N)
Wooly yarrow—*Achillea* spp. (N, E)

C. Bulbs

Canna—*Canna* spp. (E)
Daffodil—*Narcissus* 'King Alfred' (E)
Garden gladiolus—*Gladiolus hortulanus* (E)
Iris—*Iris* spp. (N, E)
Ranunculus—*Ranunculus asiaticus* (E)

Kit Carson State Park, Taos

TAOS

(settled about 1617), including Angel Fire, Eagle Nest, Questa, and Red River

There is nothing quite like Taos in May, with the last snowflakes falling and the white-pink sand plums in full flower and the gnarled apple trees finally swelling and budding next to the ancient Martinez hacienda, where the creek murmurs by on its springtime rush to the Rio Grande. This picturesque and legendary city is located at the chilly northern end of Spain's old empire.

Taos is really an ancient pair of towns—the Pre-Columbian Indian pueblo and the old Spanish settlement set next to each other in meadows alongside streams at the foot of the Rockies. It was the famous site of the spring rendezvous for the mountain men of the early nineteenth century and has been the setting for important writers' and artists' colonies for the past hundred years.

Taos is quite high at 7000 feet (2135 m), and its natural landscape is a study in contrasts. The nearby plains are nearly flat and covered in big sage (*Artemisia tridentata*); just beyond the town limits lie piñon and juniper-covered foothills with willow, cottonwood, and alder-lined streams running through them; and the jutting Rockies just east of town feature classic western forests of pine, Douglas fir, white fir, and aspen. The vistas are sometimes said to be unsurpassed in New Mexico.

Yet Taos itself only enjoys about 12 inches (300 mm) of rainfall a year, and it has a short

(127-day) growing season. The man-made landscape in Taos is primarily gardens, and these can be quite spectacular in spring and summer. Lilacs and willows set against towering firs and underplanted with daylilies, daisies, and other late-spring annuals are common sights in May and June. Flowering crabs against adobe walls or the blue sky are a wonderful sight in May.

Taos County produces good quality livestock, particularly sheep, chickens, and cattle, as part of its contribution to the state's agricultural economy. Hay and fruits are also grown in some quantity, but the county is, surprisingly, not heavily farm- and ranch-oriented.

Very imposing firs, peachleaf willows, and prairie cottonwoods may be found lining Taos's streets—particularly U.S. 64 as it runs east out of town. Kit Carson State Park and the old plaza, now redesigned into a series of outdoor "rooms," are two of the principal open spaces. Traces of the old Taos Territorial landscape may still be seen at the Manby house (now a gallery) and at Kit Carson's house near the plaza.

The fertile, spring-watered soil continues to provide excellent opportunities for small-scale gardening, for impressive streetside landscape plantings, and for charming but modest parks to serve a growing population.

SELECTED BEST PLANTS FOR TAOS

These plant species grow very well in Taos. For the sake of convenience and quick reference, each plant is listed as native (N), naturalized (NZ), or exotic (E). Other plants also will perform well in landscape and garden situations in and around Taos. Please see the New Mexico Plant File for these species.

TREES

A. Deciduous Shade, Street, and Specialty Trees

Arizona alder—*Alnus oblongifolia* (N)
Green ash—*Fraxinus pennsylvanica* and varieties (E)
Paper birch—*Betula papyrifera* (E)
Western chokecherry—*Prunus virginiana* (N)
Cottonwood, Aspen, and Poplar: Trees of the Genus *Populus*
    a. Aspen—*Populus tremuloides* (E)
    b. Lombardy poplar—*Populus nigra* 'Italica' (E)
    c. Narrowleaf cottonwood—*Populus angustifolia* (N)
    d. Plains cottonwood—*Populus sargenti* (N)
    e. Rio Grande cottonwood—*Populus fremontii* 'Wislizeni' (N)
    f. White (silver) poplar—*Populus alba* (NZ)
American elm—*Ulmus americana* (E)
Honey locust—*Gleditsia triacanthos inermis* varieties
    a. 'Moraine' (E)
    b. 'Shademaster' (E)
    c. 'Sunburst' (E)
Common horsechestnut—*Aesculus hippocastanum* (E)
Littleleaf linden—*Tilia cordata* (E)
Locust
    a. Black locust—*Robinia pseudoacacia* (NZ)
    b. New Mexico locust—*Robinia neomexicana* (N)
Maple and Box elder
    a. Box elder—*Acer negundo* (N)
    b. Rocky Mountain maple—*Acer glabrum* (N)
Gambel oak—*Quercus gambelii* (N)
Russian olive—*Elaeagnus angustifolia* (NZ)
Willow
    a. Globe Navajo willow—*Salix matsudana* 'Navajo' (E)
    b. Peachleaf willow—*Salix amygdaloides* (N)
    c. Weeping willow—*Salix babylonica* (and other weeping willow species) (E)

B. Flowering Ornamental Trees

Flowering crab—*Malus* 'Hopa' et al (E)
    (also bearing apple, *Malus sylvatica* varieties)
Hawthorn—*Crataegus* spp. (E, N)
Flowering peach—*Prunus persica* (N)
Bradford pear—*Pyrus calleryana* (E)
Purpleleaf plum—*Prunus cerasifera* (E)
Eastern redbud—*Cercis canadensis* (E)

C. Evergreen Trees

Douglas fir—*Pseudotsuga menziesii* (N)
White fir—*Abies concolor* (N)
Juniper
    a. Rocky Mountain juniper—*Juniperus scopulorum* varieties (N)
    b. Singleseed (one-seed) juniper—*Juniperus monosperma* (N)

Pine
    a. Austrian pine—*Pinus nigra* (E)
    b. Bristlecone pine—*Pinus aristata* (N)
    c. Limber pine—*Pinus flexilis* (E)
    d. Piñon pine—*Pinus edulis* (N)
    e. Ponderosa pine—*Pinus ponderosa* (N)
Spruce
    a. Blue spruce—*Picea pungens* (N)
    b. Engelmann spruce—*Picea engelmanni* (N)

SHRUBS

A. Deciduous

Apache plume—*Fallugia paradoxa* (N)
Common butterfly bush—*Buddleia davidii* (E)
Shrubby cinquefoil—*Potentilla fruticosa* (N)
Cotoneaster
    a. Cranberry cotoneaster—*Cotoneaster apiculatus* (E)
    b. Rock cotoneaster—*Cotoneaster horizontalis* (E)
    c. Rockspray cotoneaster—*Cotoneaster microphyllus* (E)
Currant and gooseberry—*Ribes* spp. (E)
Red osier dogwood—*Cornus stolonifera* (N)
Fernbush—*Chamaebatiaria millefolium* (N)
Forsythia—*Forsythia* spp. (E)
Shrub or Tatarian honeysuckle—*Lonicera tatarica* (E)
Hop tree—*Ptelea trifoliolata* (N)
Common lilac—*Syringa vulgaris* (E)
Mountain mahogany—*Cercocarpus montanus* (N)
Cistena plum—*Prunus cistena* (E)
Sand plum—*Prunus americana* (N)
Flowering quince—*Chaenomeles speciosa* (E)
Rose—*Rosa* spp. (N)
Snakeweed—*Gutierrezia sarothrae* (N)
Snowball—*Viburnum opulus* 'Roseum' (E)
Bridal wreath—*Spiraea prunifolia* (E)
Sumac
    a. Skunkbush—*Rhus trilobata* (N)
    b. Smooth sumac—*Rhus glabra* (N)
Weigela—*Weigela florida* (E)
Willow
    a. Coyote willow—*Salix exigua* (N)
    b. Pussywillow—*Salix discolor* (E)
Winterfat—*Ceratoides lanata* (N)

B. Evergreen

Barberry
    a. Colorado barberry—*Berberis fendleri* (N)
    b. Japanese barberry—*Berberis thunbergii* (E)
    c. Wintergreen barberry—*Berberis julianae* (E)
Parney cotoneaster—*Cotoneaster lacteus* (E)
Holly
    a. Burford holly—*Ilex cornuta* 'Burfordii' (E)
    b. English holly—*Ilex aquifolium* (E)
    c. Wilson holly—*Ilex altaclarensis* 'Wilsonii' (E)
Chinese junipers
    a. Armstrong juniper—*Juniperus chinensis* 'Armstrong' (E)
    b. Pfitzer juniper—*Juniperus chinensis* 'Pfitzerana' (E)
    c. Sea Green juniper—*Juniperus chinensis* 'Sea Green' (E)
Common juniper—*Juniperus communis* (N)
Mahonia
    a. Oregon grape—*Mahonia aquifolium* (E)
    b. Creeping mahonia—*Mahonia repens* (N)
Nandina (heavenly bamboo)—*Nandina domestica* (E)
Mugo pine—*Pinus mugo* (E)
Rubber rabbitbrush—*Chrysothamnus nauseosus* (N)
Big sage (sagebrush)—*Artemisia tridentata* (N)
Alberta spruce—*Picea glauca* 'Conica' (*Picea albertiana*) (E)

Taos street scene

GROUND COVERS

A. Deciduous

Spring cinquefoil—*Potentilla tabernaemontani* (E)
Clover—*Trifolium* spp. (NZ, N)
Cranberry cotoneaster—*Cotoneaster apiculatus* (E)
Mint—*Mentha* spp. (E, N, NZ)
Prairie sage—*Artemisia ludoviciana* (N)

B. Evergreen

Bearberry cotoneaster—*Cotoneaster dammeri* (N)
Creeping euonymus—*Euonymus fortunei* (E)
Honeysuckle—*Lonicera japonica* varieties (E)
Horizontalis junipers
    a. Bar Harbor juniper—*Juniperus horizontalis* 'Bar Harbor' (E) b. Wilton carpet juniper—*Juniperus horizontalis* 'Wiltonii' (E)
Sabina junipers
    a. Broadmoor juniper—*Juniperus sabina* 'Broadmoor' (E)
    b. Buffalo juniper—*Juniperus sabina* 'Buffalo' (E)
    c. Tam (tammy) juniper—*Juniperus sabina* 'Tamariscifolia' (E)
Kinnickinnick (mountain bearberry)—*Arctostaphylos uva-ursi* (N)
Creeping mahonia—*Mahonia repens* (N)
Periwinkle—*Vinca major* and *Vinca minor* (E)
Pussytoes—*Antennaria parviflora* (N)
Santolina
    a. Green santolina—*Santolina virens* (N)
    b. Gray santolina—*Santolina chamaecyparissus* (N)
Strawberry—*Fragaria* spp. (N)

GRASSES

A. Traditional Turf Species

Bluegrass—*Poa pratensis* (NZ)
Fescue—*Festuca* spp. (E)
Ryegrass—*Lolium* spp. (E)

B. Native Turf and General-Use Species

Buffalo grass—*Buchlöe dactyloides* (N)
Galleta—*Hilaria jamesii* (N)
Grama
    a. Blue grama—*Bouteloua gracilis* (N)
    b. Sideoats grama—*Bouteloua curtipendula* (N)
Wheatgrass
    a. Western wheatgrass—*Agropyron smithii* (N)
    b. Crested wheatgrass—*Agropyron desertorum* (E, NZ)
    c. Pubescent wheatgrass—*Agropyron trichophorum* (N)

C. Ornamental Species

Blue fescue—*Festuca caesia* (E)
Purple threeawn—*Aristida longiseta* (N)

VINES

A. Deciduous

Boston ivy—*Parthenocissus tricuspidata* (E)
Clematis—*Clematis jackmanni* (E)
Morning glory—*Ipomoea tricolor* (E)
Silver lace vine—*Polygonum aubertii* (E)
Trumpet vine—*Campsis radicans* (E)
Virginia creeper (et al)—*Parthenocissus quinquefolia* (N, E)
Wisteria—*Wisteria sinensis* (E)

B. Evergreen

English ivy—*Hedera helix* (E)
Honeysuckle—*Lonicera* spp. (E)

FLOWERS

A. Annuals

Ageratum—*Ageratum houstonianum* (E)
Purple aster—*Aster bigelovii* (N)
Bedding begonia—*Begonia* spp. (E)
Cosmos—*Cosmos* spp. (E)
Four o'clock—*Mirabilis jalapa* (E)
Gaillardia (blanketflower, firewheel)—*Gaillardia pulchella* (N)
Geranium—*Pelargonium hortorum* (E)
Impatiens—*Impatiens wallerana* (E)
Pansy—*Viola wittrockiana* (E)
Salvia—*Salvia* spp. (E)
Snapdragon—*Antirrhinum majus* (E)
Sunflower—*Helianthus annuus* (N)
Viola (Johnny jump-ups)—*Viola* spp. (E)
Wallflower—*Erysimum capitatum* (N)

B. Perennials

Chrysanthemum—*Chrysanthemum morifolium* (E)
Colorado columbine—*Aquilegia* spp. (N)
Coneflower—*Ratibida columnifera* (N)
Daylily (asphodel)—*Hemerocallis* spp. (E)
Delphinium—*Delphinium belladonna* (E, N)
Blue flax—*Linum perenne* (N)
Geranium (cranesbill)—*Geranium* spp. (N)
Hollyhock—*Alcea rosea* (E, NZ)
Indian paintbrush—*Castilleja integra* (N)
Lobelia—*Lobelia erinus* (E)
Maximilian's daisy—*Helianthus maximiliani* (NZ)
Penstemon—*Penstemon* spp. (N)
Phlox—*Phlox* spp. (E)
Primrose—*Primula vulgaris* (E)
Red rocket (scarlet gilia)—*Ipomopsis aggregata* (N)
Shasta daisy—*Chrysanthemum maximum* (E)
Violet—*Viola odorata* (N, E)
Wooly yarrow—*Achillea* spp. (N, E)

C. Bulbs

Daffodil—*Narcissus* 'King Alfred' (E)
Garden gladiolus—*Gladiolus hortulanus* (E)
Iris—*Iris* spp. (N)
Tulip—*Tulipa* spp. (E)

Native Rocky Mountain iris

Trinidad, Colorado, is an old mining and railroad town at the northern gateway to Raton Pass. Situated at an elevation of 6025 feet (1840 m), the city has vigorous winters and somewhat cooler summers than the nearby southeastern Colorado plains. Annual rainfall is about 14.5 inches/350 mm. Livestock raising is substantial in surrounding Las Animas County.

The Purgatoire ("Picket Wire") River rushes out of the Rockies through Trinidad and creates an unexpectedly beautiful, tree-spotted valley as it flows on toward its junction with the Arkansas. Keen observers aboard the transcontinental trains that pass through Trinidad to make their way over Raton Pass can easily spot narrowleaf cottonwood groves and thriving beaver dams along a tiny feeder of the Purgatoire only a mile or two outside town.

The city's modest home gardens are typical of settlements up and down the Rockies. Green ash, black locust, and silver poplar, always fortified with large quantities of Siberian elm, are among the most popular (and hardy) street and shade trees. Box elder, the native maple, is also common along streetsides and in nearby ravines. Lilac, chokecherry, and Spanish dagger yucca are widely planted shrubs. Iris and sunflower, good in thin soils and very rewarding to grow, add color to the hilly streets of the city. The grounds of Trinidad Junior College are perhaps the city's most extensive and attractive public landscape. In the mountainous nearby countryside, the spring-flowering New Mexico locust and Gambel oak are everywhere busy restoring slopes that have been damaged by roadcuts or intensive mining.

Successful plant species in Trinidad are either those that can adapt readily to rocky, alkaline soils or those that can survive in the small pockets of fertile ground found along streambeds or built up near houses at the cost of much labor by ambitious home gardeners. The city's landscape is quite similar to that of Raton, at the other end of the pass of the same name in northernmost New Mexico. (Please see Raton under its own listing.)

SELECTED BEST PLANTS FOR TRINIDAD

These plant species grow very well in Trinidad. For the sake of convenience and quick reference, each plant is listed as native (N), naturalized (NZ), or exotic (E). Other plants also will perform well in landscape and garden situations in and around Trinidad. Please see the New Mexico Plant File for these species.

TREES

A. Deciduous Shade, Street, and Specialty Trees

Green ash—*Fraxinus pennsylvanica* and varieties (E)
Paper birch—*Betula papyrifera* (E)
Western catalpa—*Catalpa speciosa* (E)
Western chokecherry—*Prunus virginiana* (N)
Cottonwood, Aspen, and Poplar: Trees of the Genus
    Populus
    a. Aspen—*Populus tremuloides* (N)
    b. Carolina poplar—*Populus canadensis* (E)
    c. Lombardy poplar—*Populus nigra* 'Italica' (E)
    d. Narrowleaf cottonwood—*Populus angustifolia* (N)
    e. Plains cottonwood—*Populus sargenti* (N)
    f. Rio Grande cottonwood—*Populus fremontii*
      'Wislizeni' (N)
    g. White (silver) poplar—*Populus alba* (NZ)
American elm—*Ulmus americana* (E)
Common hackberry—*Celtis occidentalis* (E)
Honey locust—*Gleditsia triacanthos inermis* varieties
    a. 'Moraine' (E)
    b. 'Shademaster' (E)
    c. 'Sunburst' (E)
Common horsechestnut—*Aesculus hippocastanum* (E)
Locust
    a. Black locust—*Robinia pseudoacacia* (NZ)
    b. Hybrid locusts—*Robinia ambigua* varieties (E)
    c. New Mexico locust—*Robinia neomexicana* (N)
Maple and Box elder
    a. Box elder—*Acer negundo* (N)
    b. Norway maple—*Acer platanoides* (E)
    c. Rocky Mountain maple—*Acer glabrum* (N)
    d. Silver maple—*Acer saccharinum* (E)
Gambel oak—*Quercus gambelii* (N)
Russian olive—*Elaeagnus angustifolia* (NZ)
Sycamore (plane tree)
    a. American sycamore—*Platanus occidentalis* (E)
    b. London plane tree—*Platanus acerifolia* (E)
    c. Oriental plane tree—*Platanus orientalis* (E)
English (Carpathian) walnut—*Juglans regia* (E), and
    black walnut, *Juglans nigra,* more commonly
    grown
Willow
    a. Corkscrew willow—*Salix matsudana*
      'Tortuosa' (E)
    b. Globe Navajo willow—*Salix matsudana*
      'Navajo' (E)
    c. Peachleaf willow—*Salix amygdaloides* (N)
    d. Weeping willow—*Salix babylonica* (and other
      weeping willow species) (E)

B. Flowering Ornamental Trees

Flowering crab—*Malus* 'Hopa' et al (E)
Hawthorn—*Crataegus* spp. (N, E)
Bradford pear—*Pyrus calleryana* (E)
Purpleleaf plum—*Prunus cerasifera* (E)
Eastern redbud—*Cercis canadensis* (E)
Golden rain tree—*Koelreuteria paniculata* (E)
Salt cedar—*Tamarix chinensis* (NZ)

C. Evergreen Trees

Douglas fir—*Pseudotsuga menziesii* (N)
White fir—*Abies concolor* (N)
Juniper
    a. Eastern red cedar—*Juniperus virginiana*
      varieties (E)
    b. Rocky Mountain juniper—*Juniperus scopulorum*
      varieties (N)

    c. Singleseed (one-seed) juniper—*Juniperus*
      monosperma (N)
Pine
    a. Austrian pine—*Pinus nigra* (E)
    b. Japanese black pine—*Pinus thunbergiana* (E)
    c. Bristlecone pine—*Pinus aristata* (N)
    d. Limber pine—*Pinus flexilis* (N)
    e. Piñon pine—*Pinus edulis* (N)
    f. Ponderosa pine—*Pinus ponderosa* (N)
    g. Scotch pine—*Pinus sylvestris* (E)
Spruce
    a. Blue spruce—*Picea pungens* (N)
    b. Engelmann spruce—*Picea engelmanni* (N)
Western red cedar—*Thuja plicata* (E)

SHRUBS

A. Deciduous

Apache plume—*Fallugia paradoxa* (N)
Common butterfly bush—*Buddleia davidii* (E)
Shrubby cinquefoil—*Potentilla fruticosa* (N)
Cotoneaster
    a. Cranberry cotoneaster—*Cotoneaster apiculatus* (E)
    b. Rock cotoneaster—*Cotoneaster horizontalis* (E)
    c. Rockspray cotoneaster—*Cotoneaster micro-*
      phyllus (E)
Currant and gooseberry—*Ribes* spp. (N)
Winged enonymus—*Euonymus alata* (E)
Cliff fendlerbush—*Fendlera rupicola* (N)
Shrub or Tatarian honeysuckle—*Lonicera tatarica* (E)
Hop tree—*Ptelea trifoliolata* (N)
Flowering jasmine—*Jasminum nudiflorum* (E)
Common lilac—*Syringa vulgaris* (E)
Mountain mahogany—*Cercocarpus montanus* (N)
New Mexico olive—*Forestiera neomexicana* (N)
Sand plum—*Prunus americana* (N)
Privet—*Ligustrum* spp. (E)
Rose—*Rosa* spp. (E, N)
Snowball—*Viburnum opulus* 'Roseum' (E)
Bridal wreath—*Spiraea prunifolia* (E)
Sumac
    a. Skunkbush—*Rhus trilobata* (N)
    b. Staghorn sumac—*Rhus typhina* (E)
Willow
    a. Coyote willow—*Salix exigua* (N)
    b. Pussywillow—*Salix discolor* (N)
Winterfat—*Ceratoides lanata* (N)

B. Evergreen

Barberry
    a. Colorado barberry—*Berberis fendleri* (N)
    b. Japanese barberry—*Berberis thunbergii* (E), includ-
      ing redleaf Japanese barberry, *B. japon.*
      'Atropurpurea'
Beargrass—*Nolina microcarpa* (N)
Common cholla—*Opuntia imbricata* (N)
Parney cotoneaster—*Cotoneaster lacteus* (E)
Chinese junipers
    a. Armstrong juniper—*Juniperus chinensis*
      'Armstrong' (E)
    b. Pfitzer juniper—*Juniperus chinensis* 'Pfitzerana' (E)
    c. Sea Green juniper—*Juniperus chinensis* 'Sea
      Green' (E)
Common juniper—*Juniperus communis* (N)
Oregon grape—*Mahonia aquifolium* (E)
Mugo pine—*Pinus mugo* (E)
Pyracantha (firethorn)—*Pyracantha* spp.(E)
Rubber rabbitbrush—*Chrysothamnus nauseosus* (N)
Big sage (sagebrush)—*Artemisia tridentata* (N)

Fourwing saltbush—*Atriplex canescens* (N)
Yucca
    a. Narrowleaf yucca—*Yucca glauca* (N)
    b. Spanish bayonet—*Yucca baccata* (N)

GROUND COVERS

A. Deciduous

Spring cinquefoil—*Potentilla tabernaemontani* (E)
Clover—*Trifolium* spp. (NZ, N)
Crown vetch—*Coronilla varia* (E, NZ)
Mint—*Mentha* spp. (E, N, NZ)
Prairie sage—*Artemisia ludoviciana* (N)
Snow-in summer—*Cerastium tomentosum* (E)

B. Evergreen

Bearberry cotoneaster—*Cotoneaster dammeri* (E)
Creeping euonymus—*Euonymus fortunei* (E)
Honeysuckle—*Lonicera japonica* varieties (E)
Horizontalis junipers
    a. Andorra juniper—*Juniperus horizontalis plumosa* (E)
    b. Bar Harbor juniper—*Juniperus horizontalis* 'Bar Harbor' (E) c. Wilton carpet juniper—*Juniperus horizontalis* 'Wiltonii' (E)
Sabina junipers
    a. Broadmoor juniper—*Juniperus sabina* 'Broadmoor' (E)
    b. Tam (tammy) juniper—*Juniperus sabina* 'Tamariscifolia' (E)
San Jose juniper—*Juniperus chinensis* 'San Jose' (E)
Kinnickinnick (mountain bearberry)—*Arctostaphylos uva-ursi* (N)
Blue leadwort—*Ceratostigma plumbaginoides* (E)
Creeping mahonia—*Mahonia repens* (N)
Periwinkle—*Vinca major* and *Vinca minor* (E)
Pussytoes—*Antennaria parviflora* (N)
Sedum (stonecrop)—*Sedum* spp. (N, E)
Japanese spurge—*Pachysandra terminalis* (E)
Strawberry—*Fragaria* spp. (N, E)

GRASSES

A. Traditional Turf Species

Bentgrass—*Agrostis* spp. (E)
Bluegrass—*Poa pratensis* (E, NZ)
Fescue—*Festuca* spp. (E, N)
Ryegrass—*Lolium* spp. (E)

B. Native Turf and General-Use Species

Buffalo grass—*Buchlöe dactyloides* (N)
Galleta—*Hilaria jamesii* (N)
Grama
    a. Black grama—*Bouteloua eriopoda* (N)
    b. Blue grama—*Bouteloua gracilis* (N)
    c. Sideoats grama—*Bouteloua curtipendula* (N)
Wheatgrass
    a. Western wheatgrass—*Agropyron smithii* (N)
    b. Crested wheatgrass—*Agropyron desertorum* (E, NZ)

C. Ornamental Species

Blue fescue—*Festuca caesia* (E)
Fountain grass—*Pennisetum* spp. (E)
Purple threeawn—*Aristida longiseta* (N)

VINES

A. Deciduous

Boston ivy—*Parthenocissus tricuspidata* (E)
Canyon grape—*Vitis arizonica* (N)
Clematis—*Clematis jackmanni* (E)
Morning glory—*Ipomoea tricolor* (E)
Virginia creeper (et al)—*Parthenocissus quinquefolia* (E, N)
Wisteria—*Wisteria sinensis* (E)

B. Evergreen

English ivy—*Hedera helix* (E)
Honeysuckle—*Lonicera* spp. (E)

FLOWERS

A. Annuals

Ageratum—*Ageratum houstonianum* (E)
Purple aster—*Aster bigelovii* (N)
Coleus—*Coleus x hybridus* (E)
Four o'clock—*Mirabilis jalapa* (E)
Gaillardia (blanketflower, firewheel)—*Gaillardia pulchella* (N)
Geranium—*Pelargonium hortorum* (E)
Impatiens—*Impatiens wallerana* (E)
Marigold—*Tagetes* spp. (E)
Petunia—*Petunia* spp. (E)
Salvia—*Salvia* spp. (E)
Snapdragon—*Antirrhinum majus* (E)
Sunflower—*Helianthus annuus* (N)
Viola (Johnny jump-ups)—*Viola* spp. (E)
Wallflower—*Erysimum capitatum* (N)

B. Perennials

Carnation—*Dianthus caryophyllus* (E)
Chrysanthemum—*Chrysanthemum morifolium* (E)
Colorado columbine—*Aquilegia* spp. (N)
Coneflower—*Ratibida columnifera* (N)
Daylily (asphodel)—*Hemerocallis* spp. (E)
Delphinium—*Delphinium belladonna* (E, N)
Blue flax—*Linum perenne* (N)
Geranium (cranesbill)—*Geranium* spp. (N)
Globemallow—*Sphaeralcea incana* (scarlet) (N)
Hollyhock—*Alcea rosea* (E, NZ)
Indian paintbrush—*Castilleja integra* (N)
Jimsonweed (datura, sacred datura)—*Datura meteloides* (N)
Lobelia—*Lobelia erinus* (E)
Maximilian's daisy—*Helianthus maximiliani* (NZ)
Penstemon—*Penstemon* spp. (N)
Phlox—*Phlox* spp. (E)
Primrose—*Primula vulgaris* (E)
Red rocket (scarlet gilia)—*Ipomopsis aggregata* (N)
Shasta daisy—*Chrysanthemum maximum* (E)
Violet—*Viola odorata* (N, E)
Wooly yarrow—*Achillea* spp. (N, E)

C. Bulbs

Daffodil—*Narcissus* 'King Alfred' (E)
Dutch crocus—*Crocus verus* (E)
Garden gladiolus—*Gladiolus hortulanus* (E)
Grape hyacinth—*Muscari armeniacum* (E)
Iris—*Iris* spp. (N, E)
Ranunculus—*Ranunculus asiaticus* (E)
Tulip—*Tulipa* spp. (E)

Butte Gardens

TRUTH OR CONSEQUENCES

(settled about 1876 as Hot Springs)

Modern Truth or Consequences is the child of Elephant Butte Dam, built before World War I a few miles northeast of the city. The Rio Grande, now controlled by the great sluice gates of the dam and a wonderful emerald green color, leaves bright and very barren desert uplands as it passes through the city and descends into the lush farmlands of the Hatch Valley.

At 4600 feet (1400 m), Truth or Consequences (T or C) feels the occasional bite of winter but is usually mild during the colder months. It is a very hilly place with thin, stony soil, and the hot springs that gave it its original name still flow out of the ground to supply a number of well-known spas and bathhouses downtown. The city is at the edge of New Mexico's greatest creosote desert. North and west of the town, this widespread shrub (*Larrea tridentata*) stretches as far as the eye can see into the distance, with a few scattered singleseed junipers, littleleaf sumacs, flat-leaved prickly pears, and the occasional waving bunch-grass (often alkali sacaton) scattered in for good measure. It is a spectacular, if harsh, landscape.

The nearby Rio Grande itself supports groves of mesquite, salt cedar, and screwbean. Catclaw acacia, desert willow, and netleaf hackberry are frequently found in local arroyos. Both south and east of the city there is a series of deep-cut east-west canyons that form the setting for some of the state's rarest and most remarkable native plant communities. Arizona sycamore, seepwillow, western soapberry, Arizona or velvet ash, Mexican elder, willows, cottonwoods, and other associated trees and shrubs make these watersheds delightful to visit.

Irrigated cropland in Sierra County has risen slowly in size since 1960 to more than 12,000 acres. Chile and lettuce are extensively grown, and hay, cotton, and pecans are also important crops in the southern reaches of the county. Truth or Consequences usually averages between almost 9 and 11.5 inches (about 280 mm) of rainfall per year, and its growing season is very long at about 227 days. Dairy farming and extensive beef cattle production round out the agricultural background in the surrounding county. As the thoughtful traveler might imagine, stock raising in the uplands around Truth or Consequences is often carried out under some of the most difficult conditions conceivable, with many areas of the range only supporting one head of cattle per 80–100 acres.

Truth or Consequences has modest gardens. Shade trees such as the fruitless mulberry, Rio Grande cottonwood, ailanthus, and Siberian elm are frequently found. Such local desert species as agave, ocotillo, prickly pear, and desert willow are also widely planted. Bermuda species are the commonest lawn grasses.

The grounds of the Old Carrie Tingley Children's Hospital and the finely terraced Butte Gardens, a CCC project on some 10 or 12 acres overlooking Elephant Butte Reservoir southeast of the dam, are the outstanding historic landscapes. The lack of thorough maintenance threatens the complete loss of the Butte Gardens, arguably southern New Mexico's greatest modern cultural landscape.

The spectacular and homey pair of old California fan palms in front of the Sierra Grande Lodge underlines the city's growing pride in itself as a resort community and introduces the visitor to the warm, almost subtropical quality of the Hatch and Mesilla valleys farther south. And the tantalizing small gardens and fountains of such nearby old mining towns as Kingston and Hillsboro round out the appealing landscape character of Sierra County's main settlements and byways.

SELECTED BEST PLANTS FOR TRUTH OR CONSEQUENCES

These plant species grow very well in Truth or Consequences. For the sake of convenience and quick reference, each plant is listed as native (N), naturalized (NZ), or exotic (E). Other plants also will perform well in landscape and garden situations in and around Truth or Consequences. Please see the New Mexico Plant File for these species.

TREES

A. Deciduous Shade, Street, and Specialty Trees

Arizona alder—*Alnus oblongifolia* (N)
Ash
  a. Arizona ash—*Fraxinus velutina* (N)
  b. Modesto ash—*Fraxinus velutina* 'Modesto' (Arizona ash variety) (N)
  c. Raywood ash—*Fraxinus oxycarpa* 'Raywood' (E)
Catalpa
  a. Umbrella catalpa—*Catalpa bignonioides* 'Nana' (E)
  b. Western catalpa—*Catalpa speciosa* (E)
Chinaberry—*Melia azedarach* (N)
Cottonwood, Aspen, and Poplar: Trees of the Genus *Populus*
  a. Bolleana poplar—*Populus alba* 'Pyramidalis' (E)
  b. Carolina poplar—*Populus canadensis* (E)
  c. Lombardy poplar—*Populus nigra* 'Italica' (E)
  d. Rio Grande cottonwood—*Populus fremontii* 'Wislizeni' (N)
Hackberry
  a. Common hackberry—*Celtis occidentalis* (E)
  b. Netleaf hackberry—*Celtis reticulata* (N)
Honey locust—*Gleditsia triacanthos inermis* varieties
  a. 'Moraine' (E)
  b. 'Shademaster' (E)
  c. 'Sunburst' (E)

Locust
  a. Black locust—*Robinia pseudoacacia* (NZ)
  b. New Mexico locust—*Robinia neomexicana* (N)
Mesquite—*Prosopis glandulosa* (N)
Mulberry
  a. Fruitless mulberry—*Morus alba* (E)
  b. Weeping mulberry—*Morus alba* 'Pendula' (E)
  c. Paper mulberry—*Broussonetia papyrifera* (E)
Oak
  a. Cork oak—*Quercus suber* (E)
  b. Southern live oak—*Quercus virginiana* (E)
  c. Texas oak—*Quercus texana* (E)
Osage orange—*Maclura pomifera* (E)
Pecan—*Carya illinoiensis* (E)
Pistache—Pistachio
  a. Chinese pistache—*Pistacia chinensis* (E)
  b. Pistachio—*Pistacia vera* (E)
Russian olive—*Elaeagnus angustifolia* (NZ)
Silk tree—*Albizia jilibrissin* (E)
Western soapberry—*Sapindus drummondii* (N)
Sycamore (plane tree)
  a. Arizona sycamore—*Platanus wrightii* (N)
  b. London plane tree—*Platanus acerifolia* (E)
  c. Oriental plane tree—*Platanus orientalis* (E)
Arizona walnut—*Juglans major* (N)
Willow
  a. Corkscrew willow—*Salix matsudana* 'Tortuosa' (E)
  b. Globe Navajo willow—*Salix matsudana* 'Navajo' (E)
  c. Peachleaf willow—*Salix amygdaloides* (N)
  d. Weeping willow—*Salix babylonica* (and other weeping willow species) (E)

B. Flowering Ornamental Trees

Flowering apricot—*Prunus armeniaca* (E)
Flowering crab—*Malus* 'Hopa' et al (E)
Desert willow—*Chilopsis linearis* (N)
Mexican elder—*Sambucus caerulea neomexicana* (N)
Flowering peach—*Prunus persica* (E)
Bradford pear—*Pyrus calleryana* (E)
Purpleleaf plum—*Prunus cerasifera* (E)
Golden rain tree—*Koelreuteria paniculata* (E)
Salt cedar—*Tamarix chinensis* (NZ)
Smoke tree—*Cotinus coggygria* (E)
Vitex (chaste tree)—*Vitex agnus-castus* (E)

C. Evergreen Trees

Cedar
  a. Atlas cedar—*Cedrus atlantica* (E)
  b. Deodar cedar—*Cedrus deodara* (E)
Cypress
  a. Arizona cypress—*Cupressus arizonica* (E)
  b. Italian cypress—*Cupressus sempervirens* (E)
Eucalyptus (cider gum)—*Eucalyptus gunnii* (E)
Juniper
  a. Alligator juniper—*Juniperus deppeana* (N)
  b. Eastern red cedar—*Juniperus virginiana* varieties (E)
  c. Singleseed (one-seed) juniper—*Juniperus monosperma* (N)
Leyland false cypress—*Cupressocyparis leylandii* (E)
Madrone—*Arbutus texana* (N)
Palm
  a. California fan palm—*Washingtonia filifera* (E)
  b. Chinese windmill palm—*Trachycarpus fortunei* (E)
  c. Mediterranean fan palm—*Chamaerops humilis* (E)
Pine
  a. Afghan pine—*Pinus eldarica* (E)
  b. Aleppo pine—*Pinus halepensis* (E)
  c. Italian stone pine—*Pinus pinea* (E)

d. Japanese black pine—*Pinus thunbergiana* (E)
e. Limber pine—*Pinus flexilis* (N)
f. Piñon pine—*Pinus edulis* (N)
g. Ponderosa pine—*Pinus ponderosa* (N)
h. Scotch pine—*Pinus sylvestris* (E)
Yucca
a. Joshua tree—*Yucca brevifolia* (E)
b. Palm yucca—*Yucca torreyi* (N)
c. Soaptree yucca—*Yucca elata* (N)

SHRUBS

A. Deciduous

Flowering almond—*Prunus glandulosa* (E)
Apache plume—*Fallugia paradoxa* (N)
Bird of paradise—*Caesalpinia gilliesii* (NZ)
Spanish broom—*Spartium junceum* (E)
Common butterfly bush—*Buddleia davidii* (E)
Cotoneaster
a. Cranberry cotoneaster—*Cotoneaster apiculatus* (E)
b. Rock cotoneaster—*Cotoneaster horizontalis* (E)
c. Rockspray cotoneaster—*Cotoneaster microphyllus* (E)
Crape myrtle—*Lagerstroemia indica* (E)
Currant and gooseberry—*Ribes* spp. (N, E)
Red osier dogwood—*Cornus stolonifera* (N)
Cliff fendlerbush—*Fendlera rupicola* (N)
Edible fig—*Ficus carica* (E)
Forsythia—*Forsythia* spp. (E)
Hop tree—*Ptelea trifoliolata* (N)
Flowering jasmine—*Jasminum nudiflorum* (E)
Common lilac—*Syringa vulgaris* (E, NZ)
Screwbean mesquite—*Prosopis pubescens* (N)
Mountain mahogany—*Cercocarpus montanus* (N)
New Mexico olive—*Forestiera neomexicana* (N)
Cistena plum—*Prunus cistena* (E)
Pomegranate—*Punica granatum* (E)
Rose—*Rosa* spp. (E, N)
Sumac
a. Littleleaf sumac—*Rhus microphylla* (N)
b. Skunkbush—*Rhus trilobata* (N)
c. Staghorn sumac—*Rhus typhina* (E)
Willow
a. Coyote willow—*Salix exigua* (N)
b. Pussywillow—*Salix discolor* (N, E)

B. Evergreen

Agave (century plant, mescal)
a. Century plant—*Agave americana* (N)
b. Parry agave—*Agave parryi* (N)
c. Lechugilla—*Agave lechugilla* (N)
Beargrass—*Nolina microcarpa* (N)
Cactus
a. Claret cup—*Echinocereus triglochidiatus* (N)
b. Common cholla—*Opuntia imbricata* (N)
c. Prickly pear—*Opuntia chlorotica* or *O. engelmannii* (E)
Creosotebush—*Larrea tridentata* (N)
India hawthorn—*Rhaphiolepis indica* (E)
Yaupon holly—*Ilex vomitoria* (E)
Chinese junipers
a. Armstrong juniper—*Juniperus chinensis* 'Armstrong' (E)
b. Pfitzer juniper—*Juniperus chinensis* 'Pfitzerana' (E)
c. Sea Green juniper—*Juniperus chinensis* 'Sea Green' (E)
Mahonia
a. Algerita—*Mahonia haematocarpa* (N)
b. Agritos—*Mahonia trifoliolata* (N)
Mormon tea—*Ephedra* spp. (N)

Ocotillo—*Fouquieria splendens* (N)
Oleander—*Nerium oleander* (E)
Fraser's photinia—*Photinia fraseri* (E)
Pittosporum (tobira)—*Pittosporum tobira* (E)
Pyracantha (firethorn)—*Pyracantha* spp. (E)
Sand sage—*Artemisia filifolia* (N)
Fourwing saltbush—*Atriplex canescens* (N)
Seepwillow -*Baccharis sarothroides* (N)
Sotol—*Dasylirion wheeleri* (N)
Texas ranger—*Leucophyllum frutescens* (E)
Yucca
a. Narrowleaf yucca—*Yucca glauca* (N)
b. Softblade yucca—*Yucca recurvifolia* (*Yucca pendula*) (E)
c. Spanish bayonet—*Yucca baccata* (N)

GROUND COVERS

A. Deciduous

Spring cinquefoil—*Potentilla tabernaemontani* (E)
Clover—*Trifolium* spp. (NZ, N)
Cranberry cotoneaster—*Cotoneaster apiculatus* (E)
Crown vetch—*Coronilla varia* (E, NZ)
Prairie sage—*Artemisia ludoviciana* (N)
Memorial rose (vine)—*Rosa wichuriana* (E)

B. Evergreen

Bearberry cotoneaster—*Cotoneaster dammeri* (E)
Dwarf coyotebrush—*Baccharis pilularis* (E)
Creeping euonymus—*Euonymus fortunei* (E)
Dichondra—*Dichondra micrantha* (E)
Germander—*Teucrium chamaedrys* 'Prostratum' (E)
Honeysuckle—*Lonicera japonica* varieties (E)
Horizontalis junipers
a. Andorra juniper—*Juniperus horizontalis plumosa* (E)
b. Bar Harbor juniper—*Juniperus horizontalis* 'Bar Harbor' (E)
c. Wilton carpet juniper—*Juniperus horizontalis* 'Wiltonii' (E)
Sabina junipers
a. Broadmoor juniper—*Juniperus sabina* 'Broadmoor' (E)
b. Buffalo juniper—*Juniperus sabina* 'Buffalo' (E)
c. Tam (tammy) juniper—*Juniperus sabina* 'Tamariscifolia' (E)
San Jose juniper—*Juniperus chinensis* 'San Jose' (E)
Blue leadwort—*Ceratostigma plumbaginoides* (E)
Lilyturf (liriope)—*Liriope spicata* (E)
Compact nandina—*Nandina domestica* 'Harbor dwarf' (E)
Pussytoes—*Antennaria parviflora* (N)
Rosemary—*Rosmarinus officinalis* (E)
Santolina
a. Green santolina—*Santolina virens* (E)
b. Gray santolina—*Santolina chamaecyparissus* (E)

GRASSES

A. Traditional Turf Species

Bermuda
a. African bermuda—*Cynodon transvaalensis* (E, NZ)
b. Common bermuda—*Cynodon dactylon* (E)
Ryegrass—*Lolium* spp. (E)

B. Native Turf and General-Use Species

Galleta—*Hilaria jamesii* (N)
Grama
    a. Blue grama—*Bouteloua gracilis* (N)
    b. Sideoats grama—*Bouteloua curtipendula* (N)

C. Ornamental Species

Alkali sacaton—*Sporobolus airoides* (N)
Sand dropseed—*Sporobolus cryptandrus* (N)
Pampas grass—*Cortaderia selloana* (E)
River cane—*Arundo donax* (NZ)
Purple threeawn—*Aristida longiseta* (N)

VINES

A. Deciduous

Canyon grape—*Vitis arizonica* (N)
Carolina jessamine—*Gelsemium sempervirens* (E)
Trumpet vine—*Campsis radicans* (E)
Virginia creeper (et al)—*Parthenocissus quinque-folia* (N, E)
Wisteria—*Wisteria sinensis* (E)

B. Evergreen

Algerian ivy—*Hedera canariensis* (E)
English ivy—*Hedera helix* (E)
Honeysuckle—*Lonicera* spp. (E)

FLOWERS

A. Annuals

Purple aster—*Aster bigelovii* (N)
Bedding begonia—*Begonia* spp. (E)
Cosmos—*Cosmos* spp. (E)
Four o'clock—*Mirabilis jalapa* (E)
Gaillardia (blanketflower, firewheel)—*Gaillardia pulchella* (N)

Marigold—*Tagetes* spp. (E)
Pansy—*Viola wittrockiana* (E)
Petunia—*Petunia* spp. (E)
Salvia—*Salvia* spp. (E)
Snapdragon—*Antirrhinum majus* (E)
Sunflower—*Helianthus annuus* (N)
Annual vinca (Madagascar periwinkle)—*Catharanthus roseus* (E)
Viola (Johnny jump-ups)—*Viola* spp. (E)
Wallflower—*Erysimum capitatum* (N)

B. Perennials

Desert baileya—*Baileya multiradiata* (N)
Chrysanthemum—*Chrysanthemum morifolium* (E)
Coneflower—*Ratibida columnifera* (N)
Daylily (asphodel)—*Hemerocallis* spp. (E)
Delphinium—*Delphinium belladonna* (E, N)
Dusty miller—*Senecio cineraria* (E)
Fendler's sundrops—*Calylophus hartwegii fendleri* (N)
Blue flax—*Linum perenne* (N)
Globemallow—*Sphaeralcea incana* (scarlet) (N)
Hollyhock—*Alcea rosea* (E, NZ)
Jimsonweed (datura, sacred datura)—*Datura meteloides* (N)
Lobelia—*Lobelia erinus* (E)
Maximilian's daisy—*Helianthus maximiliani* (NZ)
Paperflower—*Psilostrophe tagetina* (N)
Phlox—*Phlox* spp. (E)
California poppy—*Eschscholzia californica* (and *E. mexicana*) (E, N)
Shasta daisy—*Chrysanthemum maximum* (E)
Spectaclepod—*Dithyrea wislizenii* (N)
Wooly yarrow—*Achillea* spp. (N, E)

C. Bulbs

Canna—*Canna* spp. (E)
Daffodil—*Narcissus* 'King Alfred' (E)
Garden gladiolus—*Gladiolus hortulanus* (E)
Iris—*Iris* spp. (N, E)
Ranunculus—*Ranunculus asiaticus* (E)

Home garden in Kingston

Metro Park, Tucumcari

TUCUMCARI

(settled about 1902),
including Logan,
Mosquero, and Roy

Tucumcari has a large number of fine residential landscapes, particularly on First, Second, Third, and Fourth streets. The scale of the city's private gardens and yards is often quite generous. Tucumcari is blessed with relatively abundant rainfall for New Mexico (about 15–22 inches/375–550 mm per year), and the growing season on the average lasts 188 days. Gardeners take advantage of these conditions to produce uncommon quantities of cheerful sweet peas, daylilies, lobelias, and marigolds.

At roughly 4100 feet (1250 m) in elevation, Tucumcari is located on the eastern plains of the state amidst a series of scattered, rolling hills and mesas. Despite the northerly latitude, mesquite grows well here (especially east of the city near Cuervo), as do desert willow, salt cedar, the colorful and unusual shin oak (*Quercus havardii*), beargrass, evergreen scrub oaks, buffalo grass, several gramas, and the singleseed juniper so typical of the hilly New Mexico countryside.

Tucumcari has a number of well-maintained city parks. Popular street trees include the silk tree ("mimosa"), ailanthus (tree of heaven), pecan, and western catalpa. Afghan pine, blue spruce, Arizona cypress, and Japanese black pine are among the evergreen trees that are widely used as accents and for winter color.

Quay County ranks eleventh in the state in terms of its agricultural productivity. Cattle and calves are widely grazed for beef production, and wheat and sorghum are popular crops. The county grows a limited amount of cotton, corn, chile, and other crops. The soil of the plains here, which is sometimes thin, often overlies limestone. It is characteristically alkaline.

The Quay County Courthouse Square is the most notable extant historic landscape in Tucumcari. This central public garden was established in 1939. Ninemile Park on the western edge of town is a classic "Route 66" landscape constructed in the 1930s by the CCC. At Logan, New Mexico (elevation 3830 feet/1170 m), on the Canadian River just northeast of Tucumcari, the ruinous Casa Blanca Motel is a classic road court (or "Route 66") landscape from the early years of coast-to-coast automobile travel. The slogan of the Casa Blanca in its glory years was "Whata Spot."

SELECTED BEST PLANTS FOR TUCUMCARI

These plant species grow very well in Tucumcari. For the sake of convenience and quick reference, each plant is listed as native (N), naturalized (NZ), or exotic (E). Other plants also will perform well in landscape and garden situations in the Tucumcari area. Please see the New Mexico Plant File for these species.

TREES

A. Deciduous Shade, Street, and Specialty Trees

Ash
    a. Modesto ash—*Fraxinus velutina* 'Modesto' (Arizona ash variety) (N)
    b. Green ash—*Fraxinus pennsylvanica* and varieties (E)
Catalpa
    a. Umbrella catalpa—*Catalpa bignonioides* 'Nana' (E)
    b. Western catalpa—*Catalpa speciosa* (E)
Chinaberry—*Melia azedarach* (E)
Cottonwood, Aspen, and Poplar: Trees of the Genus *Populus*
    a. Bolleana poplar—*Populus alba* 'Pyramidalis' (E)
    b. Carolina poplar—*Populus canadensis* (E)
    c. Fremont cottonwood—*Populus fremontii* (N)
    d. Lombardy poplar—*Populus nigra* 'Italica' (E)
    e. Plains cottonwood—*Populus sargenti* (N)
    f. Rio Grande cottonwood—*Populus fremontii* 'Wislizeni' (N)
    g. White (silver) poplar—*Populus alba* (E, NZ)
American elm—*Ulmus americana* (E)
Common hackberry—*Celtis occidentalis* (E)
Honey locust—*Gleditsia triacanthos inermis* varieties
    a. 'Moraine' (E)
    b. 'Shademaster' (E)
    c. 'Sunburst' (E)
Locust
    a. Black locust—*Robinia pseudoacacia* (NZ)
    b. Hybrid locusts—*Robinia ambigua* varieties (E)
    c. New Mexico locust—*Robinia neomexicana* (N)
Maple and Box elder
    a. Box elder—*Acer negundo* (N)
    b. Norway maple—*Acer platanoides* (E)
    c. Silver maple—*Acer saccharinum* (E)
Mesquite—*Prosopis glandulosa* (N)
Texas oak—*Quercus texana* (E)
Osage orange—*Maclura pomifera* (E)
Pecan—*Carya illinoiensis* (E)
Russian olive—*Elaeagnus angustifolia* (NZ)
Silk tree—*Albizia jilibrissin* (E)
Western soapberry—*Sapindus drummondii* (N)
Sycamore (plane tree)
    a. American sycamore—*Platanus occidentalis* (E)
    b. London plane tree—*Platanus acerifolia* (E)
    c. Oriental plane tree—*Platanus orientalis* (E)
Walnut
    a. Arizona walnut—*Juglans major* (N)
    b. English (Carpathian) walnut—*Juglans regia* (E) (also black walnut, *Juglans nigra*)

Willow
    a. Corkscrew willow—*Salix matsudana* 'Tortuosa' (E)
    b. Globe Navajo willow—*Salix matsudana* 'Navajo' (E)
    c. Peachleaf willow—*Salix amygdaloides* (N)
    d. Weeping willow—*Salix babylonica* (and other weeping willow species) (E)

B. Flowering Ornamental Trees

Flowering crab—*Malus* 'Hopa' et al (E)
Desert willow—*Chilopsis linearis* (N)
Hawthorn—*Crataegus* spp. (E,N)
Flowering peach—*Prunus persica* (E)
Bradford pear—*Pyrus calleryana* (E)
Purpleleaf plum—*Prunus cerasifera* (E)
Eastern redbud—*Cercis canadensis* (E)
Golden rain tree—*Koelreuteria paniculata* (E)
Salt cedar—*Tamarix chinensis* (NZ)

C. Evergreen Trees

Cypress
    a. Arizona cypress—*Cupressus arizonica* (N)
b . Italian cypress—*Cupressus sempervirens* (E)
Juniper
    a. Eastern red cedar—*Juniperus virginiana* varieties (E)
    b. Rocky Mountain juniper—*Juniperus scopulorum* varieties (N)
    c. Singleseed (one-seed) juniper—*Juniperus monosperma* (N)
Leyland false cypress—*Cupressocyparis leylandii* (E)
Pine
    a. Afghan pine—*Pinus eldarica* (E)
    b. Austrian pine—*Pinus nigra* (E)
    c. Japanese black pine—*Pinus thunbergiana* (E)
    d. Piñon pine—*Pinus edulis* (N)
    e. Ponderosa pine—*Pinus ponderosa* (N)
    f. Scotch pine—*Pinus sylvestris* (E)
Spruce
    a. Blue spruce—*Picea pungens* (N)
    b. Engelmann spruce—*Picea engelmanni* (N)
Western red cedar—*Thuja plicata* (E)
Dawn redwood—*Metasequoia glyptostroboides* (E)
Yucca
    a. Palm yucca—*Yucca torreyi* (N)
    b. Soaptree yucca—*Yucca elata* (N)

SHRUBS

A. Deciduous

Glossy abelia—*Abelia grandiflora* (E)
Flowering almond—*Prunus glandulosa* (E)
Althea (rose of Sharon)—*Hibiscus syriacus* (E)
Apache plume—*Fallugia paradoxa* (N)
Bird of paradise—*Caesalpinia gilliesii* (NZ)
Common butterfly bush—*Buddleia davidii* (E)
Shrubby cinquefoil—*Potentilla fruticosa* (N)
Cotoneaster
    a. Cranberry cotoneaster—*Cotoneaster apiculatus* (E)
    b. Rock cotoneaster—*Cotoneaster horizontalis* (E)
    c. Rockspray cotoneaster—*Cotoneaster microphyllus* (E)
Crape myrtle—*Lagerstroemia indica* (E)
Currant and gooseberry—*Ribes* spp. (N, E)
Red osier dogwood—*Cornus stolonifera* (N)
Cliff fendlerbush—*Fendlera rupicola* (N)

Fernbush—*Chamaebatiaria millefolium* (N)
Flowering jasmine—*Jasminum nudiflorum* (E)
Common lilac—*Syringa vulgaris* (E, NZ)
Mock orange
    a. Sweet mock orange—*Philadelphus coronarius* (E)
    b. Littleleaf mock orange—*Philadelphus microphyllus*
       (E, N)
Mountain mahogany—*Cercocarpus montanus* (N)
New Mexico olive—*Forestiera neomexicana* (N)
Sand plum—*Prunus americana* (N)
Privet—*Ligustrum* spp. (E)
Rose—*Rosa* spp. (E, N)
Spirea
    a. Bridal wreath—*Spiraea prunifolia* (E)
    b. Van Houtte—*Spiraea vanhouttei* (E)
    c. Anthony Waterer—*Spiraea bumalda* 'Anthony
       Waterer' (E)
Sumac
    a. Skunkbush—*Rhus trilobata* (N)
    b. Staghorn sumac—*Rhus typhina* (E)
Willow
    a. Coyote willow—*Salix exigua* (N)
    b. Pussywillow—*Salix discolor* (N)
Winterfat—*Ceratoides lanata* (N)

B. Evergreen

Agave (century plant, mescal)
Century plant—*Agave americana* (N)
Barberry
    a. Colorado barberry—*Berberis fendleri* (N)
    b. Japanese barberry—*Berberis thunbergii* (E), includ-
      ing redleaf Japanese barberry, *B. japon.*
      'Atropurpurea'
    c. Wintergreen barberry—*Berberis julianae* (E)
Beargrass—*Nolina microcarpa* (N)
Cactus
    a. Common cholla—*Opuntia imbricata* (N)
    b. Prickly pear—*Opuntia chlorotica* or *O.*
      engelmannii (N)
Parney cotoneaster—*Cotoneaster lacteus* (E)
Creosotebush—*Larrea tridentata* (N)
Holly
    a. Burford holly—*Ilex cornuta* 'Burfordii' (E)
    b. Yaupon holly—*Ilex vomitoria* (E)
Chinese junipers
    a. Armstrong juniper—*Juniperus chinensis*
      'Armstrong' (E)
    b. Pfitzer juniper—*Juniperus chinensis* 'Pfitzerana' (E)
Common juniper—*Juniperus communis* (N)
Mahonia
    a. Algerita—*Mahonia haematocarpa* (N)
    b. Oregon grape—*Mahonia aquifolium* (E, NZ)
Mormon tea—*Ephedra* spp. (N)
Nandina (heavenly bamboo)—*Nandina domestica* (E)
Photinia
    a. Chinese photinia—*Photinia serrulata* (E)
    b. Fraser's photinia—*Photinia fraseri* (E)
Mugo pine—*Pinus mugo* (E)
Pyracantha (firethorn)—*Pyracantha* spp. (E)
Big sage (sagebrush)—*Artemisia tridentata* (N)
Fourwing saltbush—*Atriplex canescens* (N)
Silverberry—*Elaeagnus pungens* (E)
Sotol—*Dasylirion wheeleri* (N)
Yucca
    a. Softblade yucca—*Yucca recurvifolia* (*Yucca*
      pendula) (E)
    b. Spanish bayonet—*Yucca baccata* (N)
    c. Coral-flower yucca—*Hesperaloe parviflora* (E)

GROUND COVERS

A. Deciduous

Clover—*Trifolium* spp. (NZ, N)
Cranberry cotoneaster—*Cotoneaster apiculatus* (E)
Crown vetch—*Coronilla varia* (E, NZ)
Mint—*Mentha* spp. (E, N, NZ)
Prairie sage—*Artemisia ludoviciana* (N)
Memorial rose (vine)—*Rosa wichuriana* (E)
Snow-in summer—*Cerastium tomentosum* (E)

B. Evergreen

Bearberry cotoneaster—*Cotoneaster dammeri* (E)
Creeping euonymus—*Euonymus fortunei* (E)
Germander—*Teucrium chamaedrys* 'Prostratum' (E)
Honeysuckle—*Lonicera japonica* varieties (E)
Horizontalis junipers
    a. Andorra juniper—*Juniperus horizontalis*
      plumosa (E)
    b. Bar Harbor juniper—*Juniperus horizontalis* 'Bar
      Harbor' (E)
Sabina junipers
    a. Broadmoor juniper—*Juniperus sabina*
      'Broadmoor' (E)
    b. Buffalo juniper—*Juniperus sabina* 'Buffalo' (E)
    c. Tam (tammy) juniper—*Juniperus sabina*
      'Tamariscifolia' (E)
Kinnickinnick (mountain bearberry)—*Arctostaphylos*
    uva-ursi (N)
Blue leadwort—*Ceratostigma plumbaginoides* (E)
Periwinkle—*Vinca major* and *Vinca minor* (E)
Pussytoes—*Antennaria parviflora* (N)
Santolina
    a. Green santolina—*Santolina virens* (E)
    b. Gray santolina—*Santolina chamaecyparissus* (E)
Sedum (stonecrop)—*Sedum* spp. (N, E)
Strawberry—*Fragaria* spp. (N, E)

GRASSES

A. Traditional Turf Species

Bluegrass—*Poa pratensis* (E, NZ)
Fescue—*Festuca* spp. (E, N)
Ryegrass—*Lolium* spp. (E)

B. Native Turf And General-Use Species

Buffalo grass—*Buchlöe dactyloides* (N)
Grama
    a. Blue grama—*Bouteloua gracilis* (N)
    b. Sideoats grama—*Bouteloua curtipendula* (N)
Wheatgrass
    a. Western wheatgrass—*Agropyron smithii* (N)
    b. Pubescent wheatgrass—*Agropyron tricho-*
      phorum (N)

C. Ornamental Species

Alkali sacaton—*Sporobolus airoides* (N)
Sand dropseed—*Sporobolus cryptandrus* (N)
Blue fescue—*Festuca caesia* (E)
Fountain grass—*Pennisetum* spp. (E)
Pampas grass—*Cortaderia selloana* (E)
Indian ricegrass—*Oryzopsis hymenoides* (N)
River cane—*Arundo donax* (NZ)
Purple threeawn—*Aristida longiseta* (N)

VINES

A. Deciduous

Boston ivy—*Parthenocissus tricuspidata* (E)
Silver lace vine—*Polygonum aubertii* (E)
Wisteria—*Wisteria sinensis* (E)

B. Evergreen

English ivy—*Hedera helix* (E)
Honeysuckle—*Lonicera* spp. (E)

FLOWERS

A. Annuals

Purple aster—*Aster bigelovii* (N)
Bedding begonia—*Begonia* spp. (E)
Cosmos—*Cosmos* spp. (E)
Four o'clock—*Mirabilis jalapa* (E)
Gaillardia (blanketflower, firewheel)—*Gaillardia pulchella* (N)
Geranium—*Pelargonium hortorum* (E)
Impatiens—*Impatiens wallerana* (E)
Marigold—*Tagetes* spp. (E)
Petunia—*Petunia* spp. (E)
Snapdragon—*Antirrhinum majus* (E)
Sunflower—*Helianthus annuus* (N)

Annual vinca (Madagascar periwinkle)—*Catharanthus roseus* (E)

B. Perennials

Desert baileya—*Baileya multiradiata* (N)
Carnation—*Dianthus caryophyllus* (E)
Chrysanthemum—*Chrysanthemum morifolium* (E)
Colorado columbine—*Aquilegia* spp. (N)
Coneflower—*Ratibida columnifera* (N)
Daylily (asphodel)—*Hemerocallis* spp. (E)
Delphinium—*Delphinium belladonna* (E, N)
Dusty miller—*Senecio cineraria* (E)
Hollyhock—*Alcea rosea* (E)
Lobelia—*Lobelia erinus* (E)
Maximilian's daisy—*Helianthus maximiliani* (N)
Penstemon—*Penstemon* spp. (N)
Phlox—*Phlox* spp. (E)
California poppy—*Eschscholzia californica* (and *E. mexicana*) (E, N)
Shasta daisy—*Chrysanthemum maximum* (N)

C. Bulbs

Canna—*Canna* spp. (E)
Daffodil—*Narcissus* 'King Alfred' (E)
Dutch crocus—*Crocus verus* (E)
Garden gladiolus—*Gladiolus hortulanus* (E)
Iris—*Iris* spp. (N, E)
Tulip—*Tulipa* spp. (E)

Appendices

ADDITIONAL SOURCES OF PLANT AND DESIGN INFORMATION

1. COOPERATIVE EXTENSION SERVICE

An outreach program of New Mexico State University, the Cooperative Extension Service offers a tremendous wealth of information and assistance to homeowners, landscape contractors, landscape architects, farmers, and ranchers throughout the state.

The Cooperative Extension Service and its county agents are available for consultation regarding plants and plant selection on most weekdays during business hours.

County Offices:

Bernalillo County
County Program Director,
County Extension Agent
1510 Menaul NW
Albuquerque, NM 87107
(505) 243-1386

Catron County
County Program Director,
County Extension Agent
P.O. Box 378
Reserve, NM 87830
(505) 533-6430
(505) 533-6700 FAX

Chaves County
County Program Director,
County Extension Agent
200 E. Chisum, Door #4
Roswell, NM 88201
(505) 622-3210; (505) 622-3211
(505) 622-3882 FAX

Cibola County
County Program Director,
County Extension Agent

117 1/2 Silver Street
Grants, NM 87020
(505) 287-9266

Colfax County
County Program Director,
County Extension Agent
P.O. Box 370
Raton, NM 87740
(505) 445-8071
(505) 445-2615 FAX

Curry County
County Program Director,
County Extension Agent
County Courthouse - 7th and Main
Clovis, NM 88101
(505) 763-6505
(505) 762-0296

de Baca County
County Program Director,
County Extension Agent
County Courthouse
P.O. Drawer E
Fort Sumner, NM 88119
(505) 355-2831

Dona Ana County
County Program Director,
County Extension Agent
150 West Lohman
Las Cruces, NM 88005
(505) 525-6649

Eddy County
County Program Director,
County Extension 4-H Agent
1304 W. Stevens
Carlsbad, NM 88220
(505) 887-6595

Grant County
County Program Director,
County Extension Agent
County Courthouse
P.O. Box 151
Silver City, NM 88062
(505) 388-1559
(505) 388-1550

Guadalupe County
County Program Director,
County Extension Agent
County Court House
420 Parker Avenue
Santa Rosa, NM 88435
(505) 472-3652

Harding County
County Program Director,
County Extension Agent
County Courthouse
Mosquero, NM 87733
(505) 673-2341

Hidalgo County
County Program Director,
County Extension Agent
County Courthouse
Lordsburg, NM 88045
(505) 542-9291

Lea County
County Program Director,
County Extension Agent
County Courthouse, Drawer 10-C
Lovington, NM 88260
(505) 396-8521 Ext. 258

Lincoln County
County Program Director,
County Extension Agent
County Courthouse
P.O. Box 217
Carrizozo, NM 88301
(505) 648-2311
(505) 648-2312
(505) 648-2551 FAX

Los Alamos County
County Program Director,
County Extension Home Economist
Community Building, 475 20th Street
Los Alamos, NM 87544
(505) 662-2656

Luna County
County Program Director,
County Extension Agent
County Courthouse, Room 11
Deming, NM 88030
(505) 546-8806

McKinley County
County Program Director,
County Extension Agricultural 4-H Agent
McKinley County Courthouse, B9
201 W. Hill
Gallup, NM 87301
(505) 863-3432

Mora County
County Program Director,
County Extension Agent
County Courthouse
P.O. Box 390
Mora, NM 87732
(505) 387-2856

Otero County
County Program Director,
County Extension Agent
401 Fairgrounds Road
Alamogordo, NM 88310
(505) 427-0231

Quay County
County Program Director,
County Extension Agent
County Courthouse
P.O. Drawer B
Tucumcari, NM 88401
(505) 461-0562
(505) 461-0563

Rio Arriba County
County Program Director,
County Extension Agent
403 S. Paseo de Onate
Española, NM 87532
(505) 753-3405

Los Ojos (Rio Arriba County)
County Extension 4-H Agent
P.O. Box 135
Los Ojos, NM 87551
(505) 588-7423

Roosevelt County
County Program Director,
County Extension Home Economist
County Courthouse, B-6
Portales, NM 88130-0400
(505) 356-4417

Sandoval County
County Program Director,
County Extension 4-H Agent
P.O. Box 400
Bernalillo, NM 87004
(505) 867-2582
(505) 867-2951

San Juan County
County Program Director,
County Extension Home Economist, 4-H
213 S. Oliver Drive
Aztec, NM 87410
(505) 334-9496
(505) 334-9497

San Miguel County
County Program Director,
County Extension Agent
P.O. Box 2170, West Branch
Las Vegas, NM 87701
County Program Director,
County Extension Agent
(505) 454-1497

Santa Fe County
County Program Director,
County Extension Agent
County Fair Building
P.O. Box 1905
Santa Fe, NM 87504-1905
(505) 471-4711
(505) 471-4712
(505) 473-9516
(505) 471-6076

Sierra County
County Program Director,
County Extension Agent
100 Date Street, Suite 9
P.O. Box 631
Truth or Consequences, NM 87901
(505) 894-2375

Socorro County
County Program Director,
County Extension Agent
214 Neal Avenue NW
Socorro, NM 87801
(505) 835-0610

Taos County
County Program Director,
County Extension Agent
County Courthouse
P.O. Box 1266
Taos, NM 87571
(505) 758-3982

Torrance County
County Program Director,
County Extension Agent
P.O. Box 168
Estancia, NM 87016
(505) 384-2416
(505) 384-2372

Union County
County Program Director,
County Extension Agent
County Courthouse
P.O. Box 428
Clayton, NM 88415
(505) 374-9361

Valencia County
County Program Director,
County Extension Agent
P.O. Box 1059
Los Lunas, NM 87031
(505) 865-9561
(505) 865-9792

2. AVAILABLE PUBLICATIONS

For a list of publications available from the Cooperative Extension Service and the NMSU Agricultural Experimental Station, write:

Cooperative Extension Service
New Mexico State University
Las Cruces, NM 88003-0031

Plant Materials Center
NMSU Experimental Station
Los Lunas, NM 87031
(505) 865-4684

3. EDUCATION

Master Gardeners Program

This excellent program in practical horticulture and gardening is offered in late winter and early spring at the Albuquerque Garden Center. For information, contact:

Albuquerque Garden Center
10120 Lomas Blvd. NE
Albuquerque, NM 87112
(505) 292-7144

Landscape Design School

The landscape design school of the National Council of Garden Clubs is an intensive series of short courses sponsored locally by New Mexico Garden Clubs, Inc., and generally offered in both the spring and fall of the year in Albuquerque.

The Landscape Design School has a broad curriculum that deals with the history and theory of landscape architecture and many related horticultural and design issues.
For more information, write:

New Mexico Garden Clubs, Inc.
1708 East 21
Clovis, NM 88101

Education in horticulture

New Mexico State University (NMSU) offers an outstanding curriculum in horticulture. Both B.S. and M.S. degrees may be earned. For more information, write:

Department of Agronomy and Horticulture
College of Agriculture and Home Economics
Office of the Associate Dean/Director of
Resident Instruction
New Mexico State University
Box 30003, Department 3AG
Las Cruces, NM 88003-003

Education in landscape architecture

The University of New Mexico offers undergraduate and graduate education in landscape design and planning.

A B.A. degree in Environmental Design and an M.A. in Community and Regional Planning with an emphasis in landscape design are available. In addition, graduate architectural studies with an emphasis in landscape design have recently been added to the curriculum. The program is currently expanding and may soon be even more comprehensive. For more information, write:

Student Advisor
School of Architecture and Planning
University of New Mexico
2414 Central Avenue SE
Albuquerque, NM 87131

4. ARBORETUMS, BOTANICAL GARDENS, AND SPECIALTY GARDENS

Living Desert State Park, Carlsbad

This state institution features a series of botanical and zoological exhibits based on the flora and fauna of the Chihuahuan Desert.

For more information, write:
P.O. Box 100
Carlsbad, NM 88220
(505) 887-5516

Albuquerque Garden Center

A cooperative effort of the Albuquerque Council of Garden Clubs.

10120 Lomas Blvd., NE
Albuquerque, New Mexico 87112
(505) 296-6020

Prospect Park Rose Garden, Albuquerque

An excellent and wide-ranging selection of hybrid tea, polycantha, floribunda, and other rose varieties planted and maintained by the Albuquerque Rose Society at the Wyoming Regional (formerly Prospect Park) Library, 8205 Apache Avenue, NE, Albuquerque, NM 87110. Visit in spring and summer. The library is directly south of Hoffmantown Shopping Center. Plants are clearly identified.

Rio Grande Zoological Park, Albuquerque

The Southwest's best zoo. Hundreds of plant species, both native and exotic, are also grown and displayed here, and most are clearly identified. Well worth a day trip to observe both flora and fauna.

Rio Grande Zoological Park
903 10th Street SW
Albuquerque, NM 87103
(505) 843-7413

Rio Grande Botanical Garden, Albuquerque

Newly established after an exhaustive study performed in the late 1980s, this exciting facility promises to be a premier Southwestern institution for regional plant studies and horticulture. Part of the larger Albuquerque Biological Park, an ambitious City of Albuquerque project located at the Central Avenue bridge over the Rio Grande.

For more information contact:
Friends of Rio Grande Botanical Garden, Inc.
P.O. Box 27276
Albuquerque, NM 87125

University of New Mexico Arboretum

Newly established (1992), this exciting arboretum offers several hundred plants to the public in a series of three very pleasant walking tours. Self-guided. Pamphlets available.
For information, write or call:

Department of Facility Planning
University of New Mexico
Albuquerque, NM 87131
(505) 277-2236

University of New Mexico Herbarium

A dry or pressed plant "museum," the UNM Herbarium contains a vast collection of New Mexico's plants. There are literally thousands of selections that may be viewed, and the herbarium staff is quite helpful in identifying species brought in for examination. The herbarium is located in the lower level of the Biology Building on the main UNM campus.
For information, write or call:

Herbarium
Department of Biology
University of New Mexico
Albuquerque, NM 87131
(505) 277-3411
(Biology Department, for hours and information)

New Mexico State University Herbarium

The NMSU Herbarium offers many thousands of specimens of New Mexican plant species in a carefully catalogued collection to the public and researchers for basic identification and study. The herbarium staff is friendly, knowledgeable, and helpful. For information, write:

NMSU Herbarium
Box 3003 – Dept. 3A1
College of Agriculture and Home Economics
NMSU
Las Cruces, New Mexico 88003

5. LANDSCAPE ARCHITECTS

Landscape architects provide services such as site and planting design, irrigation design, land-use planning, and related kinds of consultation. They do not sell or install such items as plants or sprinkler heads; that is the job of the landscape contractor.

New Mexico requires landscape architects to be licensed to practice, and the state is a national leader in requiring stringent continuing education of its registered practitioners.

The State of Texas also requires its landscape architects to be licensed.

For a list of licensed landscape architects available for consultation or design, write or call:

New Mexico Board of Landscape Architects
P.O. Drawer 1388
Santa Fe, NM 87504-1388
(505) 827-7153

Texas State Board of Landscape Architects
8213 Shoal Creek Blvd., #107
Austin, TX 78758

6. LANDSCAPE CONTRACTORS

Reputable and qualified landscape contractors in New Mexico hold a GF-5 or MS-6 license, or both, from the State Construction Industries Commission. It is always wisest to use a licensed landscape contractor to install a commercial or private landscape. For information regarding licensed, experienced landscape contractors, write:

Construction Industries Commission
State of New Mexico
Bataan Memorial Building
Santa Fe, NM 87504
(505) 827-6251,

or check with a licensed landscape architect for a recommendation.

7. NURSERIES, IRRIGATION DEALERS, AND OTHER SUPPLIERS

New Mexico has a number of excellent retail nurseries that carry high-quality landscape plants. The number of wholesale or grower nurseries in the state is also increasing as the state's population and its urban areas expand. For information on nurseries, irrigation dealers and contractors, landscape materials suppliers, and related wholesale and retail businesses, write:

New Mexico Association of Nursery Industries (NMANI)
3820 Midway Place NE
Albuquerque, NM 87109
(505) 345-7799

8. NATIVE PLANT SOURCES

Although we may never reach a consensus on the precise definition of just what constitutes a native and what doesn't, there is no disputing the fast-rising popularity and usefulness of our local Southwestern species. Generally easy to care for and possessed of their own unique beauty and quality, native plants are now common in New Mexican landscapes of every kind.

Many species are still not available in mass commercial quantities, and the general quality of many cultivated native plants is not as high as it should be. Nevertheless, these problems will be solved as demand increases and buyers insist on consistency and prime stock in their purchases. For general information on native and regional species, contact:

Native Plant Society of New Mexico
P.O. Box 5917
Santa Fe, NM 87502

Commercial Sources

Several growers and sellers in New Mexico now offer excellent selections of regional plant species, both wholesale and retail.

Among the best sources are: Rowland Nurseries, Treeland Nursery, Curtis & Curtis, Bernardo Beach, Plants of the Southwest, H & H Wholesale Nursery, Albuquerque Chemical Company, Mountain States Chemical Company, Santa Fe Greenhouse, Trees That Please, Trees of Corrales, McClain Greenhouses, Gubbels Nursery, Agua Fria Nursery, Sunbelt Nursery, Plant World, Osuna Nursery, Santa Ana Tree Farm, Nature's Way Nursery, and others throughout the state.

An Additional Note on Native Plants

Native plants should never be removed from the wild for replanting in a domestic garden or landscape. Indiscriminate digging of trees and other plants inevitably results in a deterioration of forests, ranges, deserts, and river bottoms. It's very destructive and a poor conservation practice.

Always purchase native or regional plants that have been field-or nursery-grown, or plant from seed or cuttings and wait patiently. The goal of using native plants, after all, is to preserve water and soil and to upgrade the local environment. We need both a healthy townscape and a thriving wild landscape to maintain the wonderful sense of place that we all know and appreciate in the high Southwest.

**Cuttings, Seeds, and Plants in
Pots or Containers**
For information, write:
New Mexico Crop Improvement Association
Box 3C1
New Mexico State University
Las Cruces, NM 88003

Soil Testing

It is always a sound idea to test the local soil for alkalinity before undertaking a landscape or garden project.

Most New Mexican soils are somewhat basic or very basic, and many essential minerals may be tied up in existing chemical compounds and therefore unavailable for plant growth and development.

A good soils laboratory can provide advice on exact soil pH and on what to do to prepare the ground for a successful landscape planting. Most laboratory tests or analyses are quite inexpensive, especially when the typical 25- to 50-year lifespan of a designed landscape is considered. There is no excuse for a site to be poorly prepared and then misused for extensive plantings. And it is nearly impossible to genuinely improve the soil to any degree once large-scale ornamental planting is complete.

Test first, amend the soil carefully and only to the degree necessary for good plant health, and then plant. You'll be glad that you took the time to get to know your soil.

Among the best regional soils laboratories are:

IAS Labs
Inter Ag Services, Inc.
2643 University Drive - Suite 113
Phoenix, AZ 85034
(602) 273-7248

Assaigai Laboratories
7300 Jefferson NE
Albuquerque, NM 87109
(505) 345-8964

NMSU Soils Lab
Enviro Ag
P.O. Box 30003
Las Cruces, NM 88003
(505) 646-4422

SELECTED BIBLIOGRAPHICAL SOURCES:

MAGAZINES, MONOGRAPHS, BOOKLETS, CIRCULARS

Allison, Chris. "Seeding New Mexico Range-land." Circular 525, Cooperative Extension Service, New Mexico State University (September, 1988).

Allred, Kelly W. "New Mexico Grasses." Circular 509, Cooperative Extension Service, New Mexico State University (February, 1984).

_____. "A Field Guide to the Flora of the Jornada Plain." Bulletin 739, Agricultural Experiment Station, New Mexico State University (November, 1988).

Anonymous. "How to Buy Lawn Seed." Agricultural Marketing Service Home and Garden Bulletin No. 169, U. S. Department of Agriculture (1976).

Anonymous. "Pink Lady Winterberry Euonymus." Circular 464, Cooperative Extension Service, New Mexico State University (April, 1976).

Baltensperger, A. A., and R. Gaussoin. "'Fresa' Strawberry Clover: A New Ground Cover Variety." Bulletin 708, Agricultural Experiment Station, New Mexico State University (February, 1984).

Barbour, Charlotte A. and Earl Sinnamon. "What Tree is This?" Denver Botanic Gardens, Inc. (1965).

Beck, Reldon F. and Dwight A. Tober. "Vegetation Changes on Creosotebush Sites after Removal of Shrubs, Cattle, and Rabbits." Bulletin 717, Agricultural Experiment Station, New Mexico State University (June, 1985).

Cain, Robert et. al. "Conifer Pests in New Mexico." Cooperative Extension Service, New Mexico State University (April, 1990).

Cihacek, Larry J. "Humates as Commercial Soil Amendments." Cooperative Extension Service Circular 510, New Mexico State University (December, 1985).

Clevenger, Tom et. al. "The Wholesale and Processing Market in the Albuquerque/Santa Fe Area for Locally Grown, High-Value Crops." Research Report 572, Agricultural Experimental Station, New Mexico State University (July, 1985).

Clevenger, Tom and David G. Kraenzel. "Selected Market Alternatives for Fresh Market Strawberries Produced in Southern New Mexico." Research Report 558, Agricultural Experiment Station, New Mexico State University (January, 1985).

Duhigg, Pat et al. "Relationships Among Indices for Estimating Nitrogen Fixation in Alfalfa." Bulletin 669, Agricultural Experiment Station, New Mexico State University (November, 1979).

English, L. M. "The Peach Tree Borers." Circular 515, Cooperative Extension Service, New Mexico State University (May, 1984).

Environmental Protection Agency, U. S. Department of Agriculture. "Apply Pesticides Correctly." U.S. Government Printing Office, Washington, D.C. (no date).

Enzie, Joseph V. "Ground Covers for New Mexico." Circular 444, Cooperative Extension Service, New Mexico State University (Reprinted June, 1984).

_____. "Ornamental Shrubs for New Mexico." Circular 448, Cooperative Extension Service, New Mexico State University (Reprinted September, 1983).

_____. "Ornamental Vines for New Mexico." Circular 449, Cooperative Extension Service, New Mexico State University (Reprinted March, 1984).

Fancher, Gregory A. et al. "Planting and Handling Conifer Seedlings in New Mexico." Circular 526, Cooperative Extension Service, New Mexico State University (October, 1989).

Gay, Charles W. and Don D. Dwyer. "New Mexico Range Plants." Cooperative Extension Service Circular 374, New Mexico State University (June, 1984).

Glover, Charles R., R. D. Baker, and Larry Cihacek. "Fertilizer Guide for New Mexico." Circular 478, Cooperative Extension Service, New Mexico State University (January, 1984).

Glover, C. R., A. A. Baltensperger, and G. L. Horst, revisions. "Turfgrass in New Mexico." Circular 481, Cooperative Extension Service, New Mexico State University (July, 1983).

Gray, James R. "Kinds and Costs of Recreational Pollution in the Sandia Mountains." Bulletin 651, Agricultural Experiment Station, New Mexico State University (March, 1977).

Herbel, Carlton H. and Walter L. Gould. "Managing Semidesert Ranges of the Southwest." Circular 456, Cooperative Extension Service, New Mexico State University (October, 1980).

Herrera, Esteban. "Home Vegetable Gardening" (revised edition). Circular 457, Cooperative Extension Service, New Mexico State University (June, 1984).

_____. "Growing Grapes in New Mexico." Circular 483, Cooperative Extension Service, New Mexico State University (March, 1990).

Hooks, R. F., W. R. Oaks, and James Sais. "'Hope' Desertwillow." Circular 496, Cooperative Extension Service, New Mexico State University (June, 1982).

Hooks, R. F., L. C. Johnston, W. R. Oaks, J. M. Phillips, and J. R. Sais. "Native Plants for New Mexico Landscapes." Circular 513, Cooperative Extension Service, New Mexico State University (August, 1984).

Kinzer, H. G., B. J. Ridgill, and J. G. Watts. "Seed and Cone Insects of Ponderosa Pine." Bulletin 594, Agricultural Experiment Station, New Mexico State University (March, 1972).

Lansfort, Robert R., et. al. "Sources of Irrigation Water and Irrigated and Dry Cropland Acreages in New Mexico, by County, 1980-1984." Research Report 571, Agricultural Experiment Station, New Mexico State University (July, 1985).

Leedy, Clark. "Work Together for Community Beautification." Circular 394, Cooperative Extension Service, New Mexico State University (November, 1966).

Lymbery, Gordon A. and Rex D. Pieper. "Ecology of Pinyon-Juniper Vegetation in the Northern Sacramento Mountains." Bulletin 698, Agricultural Experiment Station, New Mexico State University (March, 1983).

Malm, Norman R., William S. Jackson, and Dick D. Davis. "New Acala 1517 Varieties for New Mexico." Circular 476, Cooperative Extension Service, New Mexico State University (June, 1977).

McDaniel, Kirk C., Rex D. Pieper, Lynn E. Loomis, and Abdelgader A. Osman. "Taxonomy and Ecology of Perennial Snakeweeds in New Mexico." Bulletin 711, Agricultural Experiment Station, New Mexico State University (August, 1984).

Moore, Michael. "Los Remedios de la Gente: A Compilation of Traditional New Mexican Herbal Medicines and Their Use." Published by the author, Santa Fe (1977).

Nash, Mohammad H. and LeRoy A. Daugherty. "Soil-Landscape Relationships in Alluvium Sediments in Southern New Mexico." Bulletin 746, Agricultural Experiment Station, New Mexico State University (October, 1990).

Native Plant Society of New Mexico. "Native Plants for Landscaping in Northern New Mexico," with supplement. Santa Fe (1978).
_____."Native Plants for Landscaping in Southern New Mexico." Las Cruces (1978).

New Mexico Crop and Livestock Reporting Service, USDA. "New Mexico Agricultural Statistics." New Mexico Department of Agriculture, Las Cruces (1984).

New Mexico Department of Agriculture. "New Mexico Agricultural Facts." (bulletin, 1987).

New Mexico Range Brush and Weed Control Technical Committee. "Mesquite Control in New Mexico." Circular 505, Cooperative Extension Service, New Mexico State University (May 1983).

O'Connor, G. A., et. al. "Solute Retention and Mobility in New Mexico Soils." Bulletin 701, Agricultural Experiment Station, New Mexico State University (April, 1983).

Pieper, Rex D. and Carlton H. Herbel. "Herbage Dynamics and Primary Productivity of a Desert Grassland Ecosystem." Bulletin 695, Agricultural Experiment Station, New Mexico State University (December, 1982).

Pieper, Rex D., Don D. Dwyer, and William W. Wile. "Burning and Fertilizing Blue Grama Range in South-Central New Mexico." Bulletin 611, Agricultural Experiment Station, New Mexico State University (November, 1973).

Pieper, Rex D., et al. "Ecological Characteristics of Walkingstick Cholla." Bulletin 623, Agricultural Experiment Station, New Mexico State University (July, 1974).

Quiñones, Ferdinand A. "Indian Ricegrass: Evaluation and Breeding." Bulletin 681, Agricultural Experiment Station, New Mexico State University (April, 1981).

Sullivan, Darrell T. et al. "'Mesa' Carpathian Walnut." Circular 504, Cooperative Extension Service, New Mexico State University (June, 1982).

Sullivan, Darrell T., et. al. "'Mesa' Carpathian Walnut." Circular 504, Cooperative Extension Service, New Mexico State University (June, 1982).

Sullivan, D. T., F. B. Widmoyer, and James R. Sais. "'Goldmint' Lantana." Circular 498, Cooperative Extension Service, New Mexico State University (June, 1982).

Wolfe, Helen, et. al. "'Bandera' Rocky Mountain Penstemon." Circular 472, Cooperative Extension Service, New Mexico State University (June, 1982).

Wolfe, Helen E., Wendall R. Oaks, and Ronald F. Hooks. "'Viva' Galleta." Circular 503, Cooperative Extension Service, New Mexico State University (June, 1982).

Wolfe, Helen G., et. al. "'Ganada' Yellow Bluestem." Circular 502, Cooperative Extension Service, New Mexico State University (June, 1982).

Woodward, Guy O., et. al. "Irrigation Water Measurement." Circular 497, Cooperative Extension Service, New Mexico State University (March, 1983).

SELECTED BIBLIOGRAPHY

American Horticultural Society. *Encyclopedia of Garden Plants.* New York: Macmillan Publishing Company, 1989.

Arizona–New Mexico Handbook Committee. *Tree and Shrub Planting Handbook for Arizona and New Mexico.* Las Cruces: New Mexico State University Cooperative Extension Service (c. 1983).

Arnberger, Leslie P. *Flowers of the Southwest Mountains.* Globe: Southwest Parks and Monuments Association, 1982.

Austin, Richard W. *Designing the Interior Landscape.* New York: Van Nostrand Reinhold, 1985.

_____. *Designing with Plants.* New York: Van Nostrand Reinhold, 1982.

Barnett, Jonathan. *An Introduction to Urban Design.* New York: Harper and Row, 1982.

Beck, Warren A., and Ynez D. Haase. *Historical Atlas of New Mexico.* Norman: University of Oklahoma Press, 1976.

Beckett, Kenneth A. *The Complete Book of Evergreens.* New York: Van Nostrand Reinhold, 1981.

Blackmore, Stephen, ed. *The Penguin Dictionary of Botany.* New York: Penguin Books, 1984.

Blake, J. Warner. *Don Caliche's Gardening Book,* second edition. El Paso: Don Caliche Press, 1977.

Borland, Hal. *A Countryman's Woods.* New York: Alfred A. Knopf, 1983.

Brookes, John. *Gardens of Paradise.* New York: New Amsterdam Books/The Meredith Press, 1987.

Burba, Nora, and Paula Panich. *The Desert Southwest.* New York: Bantam Books, 1987.

Carpenter, Philip L., Theodore D. Walker, and Frederick O. Lanphear. *Plants in the Landscape.* San Francisco: W. H. Freeman and Company, 1975.

Carter, Jack L. *Trees and Shrubs of Colorado.* Boulder: Johnson Books, 1988.

Carter, Vernon Gill, and Tom Dale. *Topsoil and Civilization.* Norman: University of Oklahoma Press, 1976.

Chilton, Lance, et al. *New Mexico: A New Guide to the Colorful State.* Albuquerque: University of New Mexico Press, 1984.

Courtright, Gordon. *Trees and Shrubs for Western Gardens.* 3rd rev. ed. Portland, Oregon: Timber Press, 1979.

Crawley, Michael J., ed. *Plant Ecology.* Oxford: Blackwell Scientific Publications, 1986.

Crocker, Cedric, ed. *Gardening in Dry Climates.* San Ramon (California): Ortho Books, 1989.

Crockett, James Underwood. *Landscape Gardening.* New York: Time-Life Books, 1971.

Diekelmann, John, and Robert Schuster. *Natural Landscaping.* New York: McGraw-Hill Book Company, 1982.

Doolittle, Rosalie. *Southwest Gardening.* Albuquerque: University of New Mexico Press, 1982.

Duffield, Mary Rose, and Warren D. Jones. *Plants for Dry Climates.* Tucson: HP Books, 1981.

Earle, W. Hubert. *Cacti of the Southwest.* Phoenix: Desert Botanical Garden, 1980.

Eckbo, Garrett. *The Art of Home Landscaping.* New York: F. W. Dodge, 1956.

Editors, A. B. Morse Company. *Home Landscaping.* Clearwater: Countryside Books, 1984.

Editors, *Sunset* Magazine and Sunset Books. *Desert Gardening.* Menlo Park: Lane Publishing Company, 1967.

_____. *Western Garden Book.* Menlo Park: Lane Publishing Company, 1988.

Editors, Time-Life Gardener's Guide. *Trees.* Alexandria: Time-Life Books, 1988.

Eyre, S. R. *World Vegetation Types.* New York: Columbia University Press, 1971.

Ferguson, Barbara, ed. *Ortho's Complete Guide to Successful Gardening.* San Francisco: Ortho Books, 1983.

Feucht, James R., and Jack D. Butler. *Landscape Management.* New York: Van Nostrand Reinhold, 1988.

Foth, Henry D. *Fundamentals of Soil Science.* New York: John Wiley and Sons, 1978.

Fox, Eugene J., and Mary Sublette. *Roadside Flowers of New Mexico.* Portales: Natural Sciences Research Institute, 1978.

Furuta, Tok. *Interior Landscaping.* Reston: Reston Publishing Company, 1983.

Garland, Sarah. *The Herb Garden.* New York: Viking Penguin, Inc., 1984.

Garrett, Howard F. *Landscape Design—Texas Style.* Dallas: Taylor Publishing Company, 1986.

Gehlbach, Frederick R. *Mountain Islands and Desert Seas.* College Station: Texas A. & A. University Press, 1981.

Hacker, Leroy W. *Soil Survey of Bernalillo County and Parts of Sandoval and Valencia Counties, New Mexico.* Albuquerque: Soil Conservation Service, 1973.

Hardin, Garrett. *Nature and Man's Fate.* New York: New American Library, 1961.

Harrington, H. D. *How to Identify Grasses and Grasslike Plants.* Chicago: The Swallow Press, Inc., 1977.

_____. *Western Edible Wild Plants*. Albuquerque: University of New Mexico Press, 1972.

Haughton, Claire Shaver. *Green Immigrants*. New York: Harcourt Brace Jovanovich, Inc., 1978.

Hay, Roy, and Patrick M. Synge. *The Color Dictionary of Flowers and Plants*. New York: Crown Publishers, 1976.

Heriteau, Jacqueline, with H. Marc Cathey. *The National Arboretum Book of Outstanding Garden Plants*. New York: Simon and Schuster, 1990.

Holmes, Sandra. *Flowers of the World*. New York: Bantam Books, 1974.

_____. *Trees of the World*. New York: Bantam Books, 1974.

Hora, Bayard, ed. *The Oxford Encyclopedia of Trees of the World*. Oxford: Oxford University Press, 1981.

Howard, Robert West. *The Vanishing Land*. New York: Ballantine Books, 1986.

Huddleston, Sam, and M. Hussey. *Grow Native: Landscaping with Native and Apt plants of the Rocky Mountains*. Fort Collins: Apple Tree Image Publishers, Inc., 1975.

Humphrey, Robert R. *Arizona Range Grasses*. Tucson: University of Arizona Press, 1977.

Huxley, Anthony. *Plant and Planet*. New York: Penguin Books, 1978.

Jackson, J. B. *Discovering the Vernacular Landscape*. New Haven: Yale University Press, 1984.

Johnson, Carl M. *Common Native Trees of Utah*. Logan: Agricultural Experiment Station, Utah State University, 1970.

Kelly, George. *Ground Covers for the Rocky Mountains*. Cortez: Rocky Mountain Horticultural Publishing Co., Inc., 1980.

_____. *Rocky Mountain Horticulture*. Boulder: Pruitt Press, 1967.

_____. *Trees for the Rocky Mountains*. Cortez: Rocky Mountain Horticultural Publishing Co., 1976.

Lamb, Samuel L. *Woody Plants of the Southwest*. Santa Fe: Sunstone Press, 1975.

Li, Hui-Lin. *The Origin and Cultivation of Shade and Ornamental Trees*. Philadelphia: University of Pennsylvania Press, 1974.

Little, Elbert L. *The Audubon Society Field Guide to North American Trees* (Western Region). New York: Alfred A. Knopf, 1980.

Littlewood, Michael. *Tree Detailing*. New York: Van Nostrand Reinhold, 1988. Los Alamos Garden Club. *High Altitude Gardening*. Santa Fe: Rydal Press, 1967.

Martin, E. C., Jr. *Landscape Plants in Design*. Westport: AVI Publishing Company, 1983.

Martin, William C., and Charles R. Hutchins. *Fall Wildflowers of New Mexico*. Albuquerque: University of New Mexico Press, 1988.

_____. *A Flora of New Mexico (two vols.)*. Vaduz (West Germany): J. Cramer, 1980.

_____. *Spring Wildflowers of New Mexico*.

Albuquerque: University of New Mexico Press, 1984.

_____. *Summer Wildflowers of New Mexico*. Albuquerque: University of New Mexico Press, 1986.

McHarg, Ian L. *Design with Nature*. Garden City: Doubleday/Natural History Press, 1971.

McPherson, Alan and Sue. *Edible and Useful Wild Plants of the Urban West*. Boulder: Pruett Publishing Company, 1979.

Miller, George O. *Landscaping with Native Plants of Texas and the Southwest*. Stillwater, MN: Voyageur Press, Inc., 1991.

Miller, James D. *Design and the Desert Environment*. Tucson: University of Arizona Arid Lands Resource Information Paper No. 13, 1978.

Mollison, Bill. *Permaculture Two*. Stanley: Tangari Books, 1979.

Moore, Michael. *Medicinal Plants of the American West*. Santa Fe: Museum of New Mexico Press, 1979.

Morrow, Baker H. *A Dictionary of Landscape Architecture*. Albuquerque: University of New Mexico Press, 1987.

Natural Vegetation Committee, Arizona Chapter, Soil Conservation Society of America. *Landscaping with Native Arizona Plants*. Tucson: University of Arizona Press, 1978.

Panich, Paula, and Nora Burba Trulsson. *Desert Southwest Gardens*. New York: Bantam Books, 1990.

Patraw, Pauline M. *Flowers of the Southwest Mesas*. Globe: Southwest Parks and Monuments Association, 1977.

Pearce, T. M., ed. *New Mexico Place Names: A Geographical Dictionary*. Albuquerque: University of New Mexico Press, 1965.

Perry, Frances, ed. *Simon and Schuster's Complete Guide to Plants and Flowers*. New York: Simon and Schuster, 1974.

Phillips, Judith. *Southwestern Gardening with Native Plants*. Santa Fe: Museum of New Mexico Press, 1987.

Phillips, Roger. *Trees of North America and Europe*. New York: Random House, 1978.

Pirone, P. P. *Tree Maintenance* (Fifth Edition). New York: Oxford University Press, 1978.

Roach, Dr. Archibald W. *Field Guide: Outdoor Plants of the Southwest*. Dallas: Taylor Publishing Company, 1982.

Robinette, Gary O. *Plants/People/and Environmental Quality*. Washington: U.S. Department of the Interior and the Landscape Architects Foundation, 1972.

Rondon, Joanne. *Landscaping for Water Conservation in a Dry Environment*. Aurora: City of Aurora, Colorado, 1980.

Rutledge, Albert J. *Anatomy of a Park*. New York: McGraw-Hill, 1971.

Schenk, George. *Rock Gardens*. Menlo Park: Lane Publishing Company, 1970.

Schiechtl, Hugo. *Bioengineering for Land Recla-*

mation and Conservation. Edmonton: University of Alberta Press, 1980.

Schuler, Stanley, ed. *Simon and Schuster's Guide to Garden Flowers*. New York: Simon and Schuster, 1983.

_____. *Simon and Schuster's Guide to Trees*. New York: Simon and Schuster, 1978.

Smith, Ken. *Western Home Landscaping*. Los Angeles: HP Books, 1978.

Staff of the L. H. Bailey Hortorium, Cornell University. *Hortus Third*. New York: Macmillan Publishing Co., Inc., 1978.

Stone, Christopher D. *Should Trees Have Standing?* New York: Avon Books, 1975.

Struever, Stuart, ed. *Prehistoric Agriculture*. Garden City: The Natural History Press, 1971.

Stubbendich, J., Stephan L. Hatch, and Kathie J. Hirsch. *North American Range Plants*. Lincoln: University of Nebraska Press, 1986.

Taylor, Norman, ed. *Taylor's Encyclopedia of Gardening*. Boston: Houghton Mifflin Company, 1976.

Thoreau, Henry David. *Walden and Other Writings*. New York: Bantam Books, 1982.

Vines, Robert A. *Trees, Shrubs and Woody Vines of the Southwest*. Austin: University of Texas Press, 1960 (reprinted 1974).

Wasowski, Sally, and Julie Ryan. *Landscaping with Native Texas Plants*. Austin: Texas Monthly Press, 1985.

Watkins, James A. *Turf Irrigation Manual*. Dallas: Telsco Industries, 1977.

Whitford, W. G., ed. *Pattern and Process in Desert Ecosystems*. Albuquerque: University of New Mexico Press, 1986.

Williams, Jerry L., ed. *New Mexico in Maps*. Albuquerque: University of New Mexico Press, 1986.

Winegar, David. *Desert Wildflowers*. Beaverton: Beautiful America Publishing Company, 1982.

Wooton, E. O., and Paul C. Standley. *Flora of New Mexico* (reprint). New York: Wheldon and Wesley, Ltd., 1972.

Zim, Herbert S. *Trees: A Guide to Familiar American Trees*. New York: Golden Press, 1956.

Zion, Robert L. *Trees for Architecture and the Landscape*. New York: Van Nostrand Reinhold, 1968.

Index

Plants are indexed by their common names, scientific names, and Spanish names. Boldface page numbers indicate the primary description of plants listed in the New Mexico Plant File (Section Three of the book). Cross references direct the reader to mentions of a particular plant by other names. In general, the largest number of page citations is listed under the common name.

purple aster, 31, **104**, 124
purple robe locust, 25, 42
purple threeawn, 30, **100**
purpleleaf plum (flowering plum), 23, 55, 125,
    138, 140
purshia (antelope bitterbrush), 143, 160, 186
pussytoes, 30, **93**
pussywillow, **74**
pyracantha (firethorn), 25, 85, 125, 138, 143, 199
pyracantha spp., **85**; *P. coccinea,* and *P. coccinea*
    'Lalandei' and 'Government Red,' 85. *See*
    also pyracantha (firethorn)
Pyramid Mountains, 182
Pyrus calleryana 'Bradford,' **54** (*see also*
    Bradford pear); 'Aristocrat,' 'Chanticleer,'
    and 'Redspire,' 54

Q

Quarai, 13; Salinas mission at, 157
Quay County, 232; Courthouse Square, 232
Quercus emoryii. See Emory oak
Quercus gambelii, **46**. *See also* Gambel oak
Quercus havardii (shin oak), 132, 171, 193,
    199, 232
Quercus palustris, **46**
Quercus shumardii, **47**
Quercus suber, **46**
Quercus texana, **47**. *See also* Texas oak
Quercus virginiana, **47**. *See also* southern live oak
Questa, 222

R

Rabbit Ears Mountain, 137
rabbitbrush, 74, 143, 214.
    See also rubber rabbitbrush
Radium Springs, 175
ranúnculo, **116**
ranunculus, **116**
Ranunculus asiaticus, **116**
raspberry, 74, 190
ratíbida, **109**. *See also* coneflower
Ratibida columnifera, **109**. *See also* coneflower
Raton, 196–98, 225; Pass, 196, 225
Rayado, 13
Raywood ash, 23, **35**
recycling, 6
red horsechestnut, **41**. *See also* horsechestnut
red hot poker, 187, 214, 219
red osier dogwood, 26, 30, **70**, 135, 157, 179,
    196, 206
Red River, 222
red rocket (scarlet gilia), **113**
redbud, 153, 172, 193, 199, 214.
    See also eastern redbud
redleaf barberry, 79, 203
redwood, 64, 206; coast, 64
Registry of Historic Landscapes, 12
resacas, 132
retama española, **68**. *See also* Spanish broom
Rhaphiolepis indica, **81**. *See also* India hawthorn
Rhus glabra, **76**. *See also* smooth sumac
Rhus microphylla, **76**. *See also* littleleaf sumac
Rhus trilobata, **76**. *See also* skunkbush

Rhus typhina, **76**. *See also* staghorn sumac
Ribes spp. **70** (*see also* currant; gooseberry);
    R. aureum, R. inerme, R. odoratum, R.
    pinetorum, and *R. sanguineum,* 70
ricegrass, 12, **182**. *See also* Indian ricegrass
Rio Arriba County, 135
Rio Grande, 125, 146, 153, 222, 228;
    floodplain, 124; tributary valleys of, 12;
    valley, 124, 132
Rio Grande Botanical Garden, Albuquerque, 241
Rio Grande cottonwood (valley cottonwood), 29,
    38, 124, 153, 157, 161, 167, 175, 218, 228
Rio Grande palm, 61
Rio Grande Zoological park, Albuquerque, 125,
    241
Rio Rancho, 124
riparian vegetation, 5
river cane, 25, **100**, 129, 182
Robinia ambigua and varieties, **42**;
    'Decaisneana,' 'Idahoensis,' and 'Purple
    Robe' (purple robe locust), 25, 42
Robinia neomexicana, **42**. *See also* New Mexico
    locust
Robinia pseudoacacia, **42**. *See also* black locust
roble, **46**, **47**. *See also* Gambel oak; Texas oak
Robledos, 175
rock cotoneaster, **69**
rockspray cotoneaster, 24, **69**
Rocky Mountain iris (blue flag;
    Iris missouriensis), 31, 116, 186
Rocky Mountain juniper, 25, 30, **59**; localities
    found in, 137, 143, 157, 167, 175, 179, 196,
    199, 203
Rocky Mountain maple, 28, 29, **44**
Rocky Mountain penstemon, 112, 150, 207
Rocky Mountain woodbine, 102
Rocky Mountains, 2, 160, 222; southern, 125;
    trees of, 3
Rodey, 175
romero, **93**. *See also* rosemary
Roosevelt, Teddy, Rough Riders of, 14
Roosevelt County, 193
rosa, **75** (*see also* rose[s]); *de Siria,* **67**
    (*see also* althea)
Rosa spp., **75** (*see also* rose[s]); *R. alba,* 75;
    R. foetida, 75 (*see also* Austrian copper rose);
    R. rugosa, 167, 186; *R. wichuriana,* 75; *R.*
    woodsii, 74 (*see also* Woods rose)
rose(s), **75**, 150, 161, 186, 187, 193, 196;
    old and modern, 75
rose crown sedum, 94
rose of Sharon. *See* althea
rosemary, **93**, 175
roseroot sedum, 94
Rosmarinus officinalis, **93** (*see also* rosemary);
    'Prostratus,' dwarf rosemary, 93
Roswell, 182, 199–202
Roy, 232
rubber rabbitbrush (chamisa), 24, 30, **85**;
    localities found in, 124, 125, 179, 187, 196,
    206–7. *See also* rabbitbrush
Rubus spp., **74** (*see also* raspberry);
    R. deliciosus, 74
rudbeckias, 179
Ruidoso, 186, 203–5

U

V